GOLD RUSH

About This Book

Gold Rush: A Literary Exploration was produced in conjunction with the California Council for the Humanities, a pioneer in public programming that explores the history, literature, ideas, and cultures of California. The Council and the Publisher are grateful to the California State Library for providing the major support that made this publication possible.

This anthology is the centerpiece of the Council's California Sesquicentennial Project. From 1998 to the year 2000, the Council and its partners are leading a statewide effort to present the stories of the people and events that shaped the founding of the state of California 150 years ago and to explore the impact those events continue to have on the lives of Californians today.

The California Council for the Humanities is an independent state affiliate of the National Endowment for the Humanities. The Council has been creating and supporting cultural projects and programs for the California public since 1975.

To learn more about the California Council for the Humanities, please contact us at:

California Council for the Humanities
312 Sutter Street, Suite 601
San Francisco, CA 94108

Telephone: 415/391-1474
Email: cch@netcom.com
Web site: http://www.calhum.org

G O L D

R U S H

A Literary Exploration

Edited by Michael Kowalewski

HEYDAY BOOKS
Berkeley, California
In conjunction with the
California Council for the Humanities

Library of Congress Cataloging-in-Publication Data
  Gold rush: a literary exploration / edited by Michael Kowalewski.
    p.cm.
  Includes bibliographical references and index.
  ISBN 0-930588-99-1

    1. California—Gold discoveries—Miscellanea.2. California—History—1846—1850—Miscellanea.I. Kowalewski, Michael.II. California Council for the Humanities.

    F865.G669 1997
    979.4'03—dc21   97-33324 CIP

Research: Josh Paddison, chief researcher; Peter Johnstone;
    Andrew Nystrom; Tom Lombardo
Photo Editor: Jane Levy
Cover Design: Jack Myers, DesignSite, Berkeley, California
Interior Design/Typesetting: Dolores Jalbert, Josh Paddison, Rebecca
    LeGates
Printing and Binding: Publishers Press, Salt Lake City, Utah

Orders, inquiries, and correspondence should be addressed to:
    Heyday Books
    P. O. Box 9145
    Berkeley, CA 94709
    510/549-3564, Fax 510/549-1889
    heyday@heydaybooks.com

Printed in the United States of America

10 9 8 7 6 5 4 3 2

CONTENTS

ACKNOWLEDGMENTS

THIS ANTHOLOGY was a collaborative effort, combining the talents and hard work of many individuals. The following people deserve hearty thanks: Josh Paddison, who as chief researcher compiled much of the material for this book, wrote most of the introductions to the pieces, and helped shape this anthology in innumerable ways; Jane Levy, who as photo editor spent hours visiting museums and sifting through archives; Peter Johnstone, whose tireless research and intellectual curiosity did much to improve this book; Tom Lombardo for research, production, and graphics help; Kirsten Janene-Nelson and David Peattie for copyediting and proofreading; Andrew Nystrom for intelligent research and a hasty trip into gold country; Beth Reisberg and Angela Balcita for research assistance; David Peattie, Jeannine Gendar, and Rebecca LeGates for help with design; and Dolores Jalbert and Emelie Gunnison for tackling permissions and production.

Grateful appreciation to the following people who helped gather literary and photographic materials: The entire staff of the Bancroft Library; Herbert Garcia, Susan Haas, and Bill McMorris at the Society of California Pioneers; Diane Curry, Cherie Newell, and Drew Johnson at the Oakland Museum of California; Betty Smart and Sandy Taugher at the California State Museum Resource Center; John Hutchinson and Matt Sugarman at the Marshall Gold Discovery Historic State Park; Georgia Barnhill at the American Antiquarian Society; Linda Cooper at the Shasta State Historic Park; Lynn Downey at the Levi Strauss Archives; Dan Holmes at the Museum of the Sierra Nevada; Kirk A. Myers at the Pasadena Historical Museum; Kaari Groscup at the Placer County Visitor Information Center; Susan Morris at the Judah L. Magnes Museum; and John Kuss at the New York Historical Society.

Michael Kowalewski would especially like to thank the California State Library and State Librarian, Kevin Starr, for recognizing the need for this anthology and providing major support to make it possible; James D. Houston for thinking of him when he heard of this project; Malcolm Margolin for his warm friendship, good humor, guidance, and insight on every aspect of this anthology; Ralph Lewin and Jim Quay at the California Council for the Humanities for their encouragement; Nicolas Witschi at the University of Oregon for helpful suggestions; Cathy Kowalewski for love, support, and a sharp editorial eye; and Nicholas, Sarah, and Kevin Kowalewski, who embody some of the fun—and chaos—of the gold rush.

INTRODUCTION

THE EVENT HAS LONG since become glittering folklore. In the spring of 1848, talk of gold had reached the hamlet of San Francisco (which until a year earlier had been called Yerba Buena, Spanish for "good herb," in honor of the wild mint that grew nearby). Rumors of gold seemed at least poetically appropriate, as the town lay just inside the entrance to the bay that the explorer John C. Frémont, with a touch of grandeur, had recently named *Chrysopylae,* or the Golden Gate, on the same principle, he later explained, that "the harbor of *Byzantium* (Constantinople afterward) was called *Chrysoceras* (golden horn)."[1] But in May of 1848, the residents of the ramshackle collection of plank buildings and cotton-sheet tents clustered on the leeward side of the sand hills (the better to avoid drifting fogs and chilling breezes from the Pacific) were thinking less of geographical nomenclature to the west than they were of reports trickling in from the east, from Sacramento and the Sierra foothills.

The two weekly newspapers in town had mentioned the discovery of gold in March and April, but the news was met with considerable skepticism. Reports of gold were not uncommon in frontier California. Gold had been discovered six years earlier in the mountains north of Los Angeles, but it had proven to be of limited supply and had made people dubious about such findings. Edward Kemble, the young editor of one of San Francisco's newspapers, the *California Star,* decided to "ruralize among the rustics" at the reputed gold discovery sites for a few weeks and he returned with his skepticism confirmed. In large letters across the top of his notes from camp he emblazoned the word HUMBUG. Still, bits of gold continued to be shown in San Francisco, and rumors were rampant in the first days of May that workers at Sutter's Fort in Sacramento were decamping en masse and heading for the hills. Expectation and interest continued to escalate.

Even as Kemble was jotting down his impressions, a storekeeper at Sutter's Fort noted that some of the Mormon workers were paying for their purchases with gold they had washed out of a sandbar called Mormon Island in the south fork of the American River using tightly meshed Indian baskets. Word reached the Mormon elder Sam Brannan, one of the owners of the store/ cantina at Sutter's Fort, and he quickly traveled from San Francisco to Sacramento to collect tithes from the Mormon prospectors for Brigham Young's new settlement in Utah (money he conveniently neglected to forward to Salt Lake City). A shrewd businessman with an exquisite sense of timing, Brannan expeditiously laid out plans for a new store and a new warehouse in the gold-fields and then returned to San Francisco to recruit a flood of customers. With an act of showmanship that would warm the heart of a Hollywood publicist, Brannan stepped off the boat on May 12th and paraded down Montgomery Street waving a quinine bottle full of gold in one hand (the gold dust he had received as tithes) and flapping his hat with the other, crying "Gold! Gold! Gold from the American River!" It was, as historian Richard Dillon puts it, "the shout heard 'round the world."[2]

The effect was electric. The male population of San Francisco on May 12, 1848, was roughly 600. In three days it was perhaps 200. Everyone else—doctors, lawyers, teachers, sailors, shopkeepers—was feverishly attempting to get up the Carquinez Straits or to the east side of the bay in order to head for Sutter's Fort and the American River. On May 19th John Sutter noted the onslaught in his diary: "The great rush from San Francisco arrived at the fort .... All was in a confusion."[3] On May 25th Sutter was so overwhelmed by customers that he had to abandon his diary altogether. On May 29th San Francisco's other newspaper, the *Californian,* shut down operations, breathlessly proclaiming, "The whole country ... from the seashore to the base of the Sierra Nevada resounds to the sordid cry of gold, gold!, GOLD! while the field is left half-planted, the house half-built, and everything neglected but the manufacture of shovels and pickaxes."[4] Finally, in the middle of June even Edward "Humbug" Kemble could resist the siren call of the mines no longer. "We have done," he wrote as the *Star* ceased publication. "Let our word of parting be, *Hasta Luego*."[5]

Within weeks, settlements from Sonoma to San Diego became veritable ghost towns as other forty-eighters (not a term to inspire the name of a professional football team) poured in pell-mell from around the state. When confirmation of the gold discovery reached Monterey in June, the consular agent Walter Colton reported that "the excitement produced was intense.... The blacksmith dropped his hammer, the carpenter his plane, the mason his trowel, the farmer his sickle, the baker his loaf, and the tapster his bottle. All were off for the mines, some on horses, some on carts, and some on crutches, and one went in a litter."[6] At a time when a good day's wages in the thirty eastern states would garner a dollar or a dollar and a half, the prospect of making hundreds, perhaps thousands of dollars a week (in the height of the rush, Brannan's store at Sutter's Fort grossed as much as $5,000 a *day*) was simply too much for people to resist. Like the sudden queues of thousands today who will line up overnight to purchase lottery tickets when the jackpot gets large enough, people were bedazzled by the thought of fabulous instant riches. Sergeant

James H. Carson, who was on garrison duty in Monterey when the news of the discovery arrived, found himself suffering a singular affliction:

"A frenzy seized my soul; unbidden my legs performed some entirely new movements of Polka steps—I took several—houses were too small for me to stay in; I was soon in the street in search of the necessary outfits; piles of gold rose up before me at every step; castles of marble, ... thousands of slaves, bowing to my beck and call; myriads of fair virgins contending with each other for my love, were among the fancies of my fevered imagination. The Rothschilds, Girard, and Astors appeared to me but poor people: in short, I had a very violent attack of the *Gold Fever.*" One hour after being thus affected, Carson was "armed with a wash hand basin, fire shovel, ... a rifle, [and] a few yards of jerked beef" and going at "high pressure mule speed for the diggins."[7]

Traders carried the news to the Sandwich Islands (Hawaii), attracting native-born "Kanakas," as they were known, along with whalers and merchant sailors. By the end of the summer news had spread to the Pacific Northwest, Mexico, and the Pacific nations of South America. In early December a dispatch from California's military governor Richard B. Mason arrived in Washington D.C. along with more than 200 ounces of pure gold in an oyster can. President James K. Polk had already finished preparing his State of the Union speech, but he quickly appended Mason's document to his annual message, thereby officially verifying for the nation that there was an "abundance of gold" of "an extraordinary character" in California.[8] By the end of 1848 news of the discovery was confirmed in Europe and in China, and the international, polyglot stampede that would bring miners from Japan, France, Sweden, Chile, Germany, Australia, and a famine-stricken Ireland was on. Tens of thousands of miners were soon boarding ships to sail across the Pacific or around Cape Horn, riding dugout canoes across the Isthmus of Panama, or goading oxen across the Great Basin. The news of the discovery spread like wildfire and, in J. S. Holliday's words, "the world rushed in."

Once news of the gold discovery was nationally known, easterners were full of inventive ideas about how to propel people to California quickly. Rufus Porter, a New England inventor who founded *Scientific American,* proposed what he called an "Aerial Locomotive" to the West Coast. He offered to take 300 passengers at $50 a head for a three-day trip from New York to San Francisco, "wines included." Porter's thousand-foot long balloon was to be powered by two steam engines, and he was so confident of its success that he predicted the whole trip to San Francisco might take only twenty-four hours, certainly no more than five days in the case of massive headwinds. The artist

Nathaniel Currier quickly used such goofy schemes as the basis for a set of satirical cartoons entitled "How They Go to California." One of them suggested that the miners might most efficiently be *launched* to the West Coast by means of a giant rubber band that would, by the jerk of a colossal sling-shot, send the migrants flying from Brooklyn to Sacramento.

Whimsy aside, where were these self-styled "argonauts" in search of the Golden Fleece rushing *to?* What was waiting to meet these greenhorns pouring in from around the world? Before the discovery of gold, California was a remote, sparsely settled, maritime province casually ruled by the Republic of Mexico. Upon arriving in the region, American migrants like John Bidwell, who led the first wagon train into California in 1841, had to obtain passports from Mexican officials. Separated by a 1500-mile land moat from "the states" back East, California was closer, travel-wise, to Tokyo and Guangdong province than it was to Boston or New York. At the conclusion of the Mexican war, on February 2, 1848, in the treaty of Guadalupe Hidalgo, the "Department of California" was a conquered province ceded to the United States (along with present-day Nevada, Utah, New Mexico, Arizona, and parts of Wyoming and Colorado) .

By the end of the war, American soldiers and Mexican residents had raised the non-Indian population of California to about 13,000, with roughly equal numbers of North Americans and "Californios," as the California-born Mexican natives were known. A handful of wealthy Californios presided over huge land-grant ranchos along the coast and in nearby valleys from San Diego to Sonoma. The vast 800-mile interior of the state was home to dozens of Indian tribes. As Malcolm Margolin reminds us, California had the densest pre-Columbian population anywhere north of Mexico. The region was a rich palimpsest of tribal customs, technologies, beliefs, and local ecologies, all reflected in the more than one hundred Indian languages, "seventy percent of them as mutually unintelligible as English and Chinese," spoken in California when the first white explorers arrived.[9] The fertility and biological diversity of the landscapes that supported these cultures is difficult to imagine. The abundance of life in the Great Central Valley before the arrival of Anglo-European settlers has prompted some to call it the American Serenghetti. Early writers noted free-ranging herds of antelope, deer, and elk. Grizzly bears roamed along the coast as well as in the valleys and foothills. Clouds of waterfowl and wild pigeons filled the skies over sloughs and swamplands; vast flocks of quail filled the manzanita scrublands and hillside forests. Trout and white sturgeon abounded in the Sacramento River, along with the salmon that choked mountain spawning grounds on their fall runs. Rolling oak woodland gave way to dry chapparal and alkali desert in the south and to mountain streams and tangled riparian forest in the north. Vast marshes and tule wetlands were rich with aquatic life and dense with insects. Wild berries and herbs grew in abundance.

The aspects of the land that had been absorbed by the indigenous cultures for centuries also quickly influenced the character of the mining that took place there. The gold most readily available in California was *placer* gold, that is, loose gold which had been extracted, transported, and deposited in foothills and streambeds by the ancient actions of water and erosion. Although gold was also discovered on the Trinity River and in other areas of California, the central portion of the gold country was located in the foothills of the Sierra Nevada. This region was thought of as divided into northern and southern halves, with Sacramento as the supply depot for the north and Stockton the point of embarkation for the south. The southern "mines," often only a few hundred feet above sea level, were known as "dry diggings." They were gulleys and gulches, sometimes no more than a few feet across, full of rainwater in the winter but often dry and dusty in the summer heat of the valley. The northern mines were located at higher elevations (rising to more than 6,500 feet at Yuba Pass) and featured steep-sided ravines along fast-flowing rivers such as the Yuba, the Feather, and the American.

California was the first region of the United States to undertake precious metal mining on a large scale, and between 1849 and 1855 some 400 million dollars in gold was harvested by miners. But it was not simply a new extractive industry that made the gold rush a historical phenomenon. It was the carnivalesque atmosphere of swagger and possibility, heightened expectation, and boomtown hokum that sent fortune-seekers from around the world to "see the elephant" in California. The gold rush radically accelerated and compressed California history. It precipitated the largest mass migration in American history. In 1848 there were roughly 13,000 white residents of the state. By 1854 there were 300,000. In the single year of 1849, when more than 65,000 new migrants arrived, the growth rate was 600 percent. The state's first constitutional convention chose well in placing the goddess Minerva (who sprang full grown from the brain of Jupiter) on the state seal. It signaled the way the state had bypassed the typical waiting period as a territory, vaulting directly into statehood two years after gold was discovered. As Malcolm Rohrbough says, the gold rush was "a shared national experience," one that had profound effects not only on California but on all the families and communities "back home." All told, Rohrbough says, the gold rush was "the most significant event in the first half of the nineteenth century, from Thomas Jefferson's purchase of Louisiana in the autumn of 1803 to South Carolina's secession from the Union in the winter of 1860."[10] Many of the argonauts understood that they were involved in a momentous, once-in-a-lifetime undertaking that was much larger than themselves. "It is impossible for me to give you an account of the interesting incidents that occur on this route," a doctor from Michigan on the overland trail wrote to his wife in July of 1849. "Neither the Crusades nor Alexander's expedition to India (all things considered) can equal this emigration to California."[11]

The miners were typically young (in their twenties, on average) and they were predominantly male. It was as unusual to see a woman, one remarked, as it was to see an old man. They were also people who had to have a fairly substantial amount of money—often up to two years worth of salary back home—to pay for equipment and the cost of transportation to the goldfields. They tended to be adventurous, restless, and curious by nature. They went heavily armed by day and night, but would weep openly over the picture of a wife or a child. Many—perhaps most—of them did not intend to stay long; they wished to "make their pile" and return home, whether to Connecticut, China, or the Oregon territory. They also tended to be enthusiastic and optimistic, at least at first. Take Stephen J. Field, for instance. Field would eventually be elected to the first California legislature, write the state's first civil and criminal codes, serve as chief justice of the state supreme court, and be appointed to the U.S. Supreme Court. But when he arrived in San Francisco in 1849 he was just another greenhorn with great expectations. "There was something exhilarating and exciting in the atmosphere which made everyone cheerful and buoyant," he wrote. "Everyone in greeting me said, 'It's a glorious country,' or 'Isn't it a glorious country?'... or something to that effect. In every case the word 'glorious' was sure to come out.... I had not been out many hours before I caught the infection, and though I had but a single dollar in my pocket and no business whatever and did not know where I should get my next meal, I found myself saying to everybody I met, 'It's a glorious country.' "[12]

As many of the excerpts in this collection suggest, however, initial exuberance about one's golden prospects in California was often quickly tempered by the sobering realities of cholera, sickness, and bad weather, by exorbitant prices, blisters, muscle aches, sunburn, fleas, and the boredom of hard, repetitive labor. Like Edward Kemble's first skepticism about the discovery of gold, every glowing report of wonder and riches in the Golden State was matched by dispirited letters home from impoverished or homesick miners. "The greatness of California! Faugh!" Alonzo Delano harrumphed in 1850. "When the sufferings of the emigrants both on the plains and after their arrival is known at home, our people will begin to see California stripped of her gaudy robes, ... and they will be content to stay at home and reap their own grain."[13]

The gold rush was assessed in radically divergent and contradictory terms from the start, both by the argonauts themselves and by outside observers speculating about what it all meant. At first, for instance, Ralph Waldo Emerson, one of the most widely known and respected American intellectuals, saw only "a rush and a scramble of needy adventurers, and, in the western country, a general jail delivery of all the rowdies of the rivers."[14] Two years later, however, he felt a witness to an emerging pattern of history: "Nature watches over all, and turns this malfeasance to good. California gets peopled and subdued, civilized in this immoral way, and on this fiction a real prosperity is rooted and grown.... Out of Sabine rapes, and out of robbers' forays, real Romes and their heroisms come in fullness of time."[6] Emerson's prickly friend Henry David Thoreau, on the other hand, was appalled by the gigantic spectacle of what he considered simple whoring after quick money: "The hog that roots his own living, and so makes manure, would be ashamed of such company. If I could command the wealth of all the worlds by lifting my finger, I would not pay such a price for it.... Going to California. It is only three thousand miles nearer to hell."[15] Either a triumph of American enterprise and determination, or the final proof of an American insanity of greed and restlessness only seventy-five years after the Declaration of Independence—the gold rush was open to either interpretation.

The multiple perspectives engendered by the gold rush are usefully dramatized by one of its central figures, the Swiss entrepreneur, John Augustus Sutter. Gold had been discovered on the morning of January 24, 1848, in the tailrace of a sawmill being built by James Marshall, a carpenter from New Jersey working for Sutter. Sutter initially attempted to convince the millworkers to tell no one about the gold until the sawmill had been completed, but that, as Donald Dale Jackson aptly puts it, "was like trying to contain a sunrise in a bottle."[16] Sutter had carefully assembled a 50,000 acre agrarian barony he named Nueva Helvetia, or New Switzerland, that centered around an adobe fort at the junction of the Sacramento and the American rivers. Sutter had abandoned his wife and five children in poverty in Europe, but he had become a respected figure in Mexican California and was known for his generosity in helping early American settlers as they struggled over the Sierras. He hoped that the discovery of gold would augment his good fortune. It had exactly the opposite effect. Although Sutter was a member of the Monterey convention that drew up the California state convention in 1849, unscrupulous miners and squatters soon swindled him out of his holdings, and he became an increasingly besieged and marginalized figure in a land where he had, but a few years before, been known for his princely hospitality (while his Indian workers ate out of feeding troughs).

In his novel *Gold* (1925), the Swiss writer Blaise Cendrars painted an unforgettable portrait of an elderly and destitute Sutter in Washington D.C., a loner, down-at-the-heel, flecked with dandruff, and petitioning Congress to be reimbursed for his losses. His final petitions were ignored in the summer of 1880 as Congress hurried to an early adjournment for an election year. Two days after the adjournment, Sutter died alone and despairing in a Pennsylvania hotel. (James Marshall died five years later, a drunkard with $218 to his name.) As the Polish poet Czeslaw Milosz points out, Cendrars' imagination was "struck less by Sutter's scaling of the heights than by his sudden downfall, resembling that, as he puts it, of Shakespeare's kings." But where Cendrars injected dramatic clarity, Milosz says, the moral of the story is actually unclear. Sutter's biography could have been presented ten different ways "each with equal right to claim verisimilitude. Sutter was a cutthroat, a slave trader, an example of the highest courage and the energy able to realize dreams, an exploiter of Polynesians and Indians, their patriarchal protector, a farmer, a civilizer, ... a braggart, a madman—whatever you like." The truth of that bygone California, Milosz reminds us, "is elusive, [and] ambiguous, and it would be pointless to seek it in myths devised to keep us from being overly troubled by the disorder of the world."[17]

The California mines were a truly international frontier. Nearly a quarter of the miners were born outside the United States. Yet the vast majority of those arriving were Yankees from New England or New York with little previous contact with Native Americans, Asians, or Latin Americans. Like everyone else emigrating to the goldfields, they carried their customs, attitudes, and prejudices with them. But unlike others, their sheer force of numbers, their connection to governmental power, and their ability to appeal for laws that could institutionalize their prejudices granted them a prominence and influence other cultural groups did not have. More effectively than the Mexican War, the thousands of migrants flooding into the region allowed for the American conquest of California.

The chances for intercultural communication between indigenous peoples and Anglo-European and Asian immigrants were, from the start, attenuated at best. They were far less promising than the Spanish and then Mexican interactions with native Californians—which had been, in their turn, beset with mutual incomprehension and tragic consequences. As so often in the history of the American West, the conflict in California was that between an extremely rooted culture and an extremely restless one. Most miners could not comprehend native peoples' sense of deep history and spirituality in connection with the land, nor did many wish to, except in special circumstances. Many miners contemptuously referred to all California Indians as "diggers" and assumed that they had a crude, primitive culture based exclusively on gathering roots, eating insects, and trapping rodents. Even those with some curiosity about Native American culture tended to see native Californians in culturally distorted ways. In 1850 a miner in northern California named J. Goldsborough Bruff drew sketches of Indian petroglyphs he had seen and excitedly dubbed them "Ancient Hieroglyphics," thinking they might be related to Egyptian hieroglyphics. That exotic (and mistaken) possibility simply underscores the fact that even those settlers intrigued by some aspect of indigenous culture in California could place it only in the context of what might be called familiar forms of exoticism. To most American newcomers there was no "there" in California to understand in a cultural sense, only a physical landscape to possess and reshape. The land to their eyes was, in the words of Robert Frost, "still unstoried, artless, unenhanced."[18] They saw only a mute, ahistorical landscape, physically rich but devoid of previous cultural accretions of meaning.

Though eighty years of previous contact with Spanish and Mexican settlers had already begun to decimate native Californians, Indians still outnumbered whites by nearly ten to one before the gold discovery.[19] Many of the richest mining regions, however, were in places of densest Indian population, so confrontation and conflict were inevitable. By the early 1850s, California Indians had been reduced to minority status in their own homeland, outnumbered by whites two to one. Communicable disease, malnutrition, and starvation caused by the degradation of the natural resources all disrupted and in some cases exterminated California tribes. The rape of Indian women and forced concubinage were frequently reported in newspapers. County governments actually paid bounty hunters five dollars for each severed Indian head, and fifty cents a scalp. In 1854 alone the federal government reimbursed the state over a million dollars in expense claims from those who hunted Indians. The killing was done by a relatively small number and some settlers sympathized with the Indians' plight, but the majority of whites passively accepted the destruction. The Indians, increasingly desperate, turned to raids and small retaliations, which increased tensions on the frontier.

Mexican, Chinese, South American, and African-American miners all suffered various forms of discrimination, as did Mormons, who were reviled for their polygamy and their clannishness. The intolerance and violence in California, as throughout the American West, were real and undeniable. They are what a Wallace Stegner character calls "some history that I want not to have happened." After decades of overly heroic or "triumphal" historical accounts of the settlement of the West, many recent historians have insisted that the darker aspects of the gold rush be illuminated. Their insights into the everyday lives and sufferings of minority groups on the frontier, and their new understanding of the environmental havoc wreaked on the landscapes of the West, have been invaluable. Yet as with any complex phenomenon, the composite truth of the gold rush cannot be found in any single story, new or old. *Any* perspective that oversimplifies or devitalizes the complexity and nuance of gold rush life does an historical disservice. It is important to remember that there was an undeniable harshness to life in frontier California for the vast majority of *every* cultural group. Life expectancy was short (within six months of arriving, one in every five forty-niners was dead), medicine was often primitive, and there was a grim ethos of survival of the fittest that often contrasted with a sense of compassion, fair play, and equal opportunity. High rates of suicide and alcoholism (or opium use among the Chinese) testified to this grim side of gold rush life. So did the miners' recourse to prostitution and a mania for gambling (compulsive gambler's syndrome, we might call it today).

In addition, it was not merely white Protestant Americans who were judging and interacting with other racial, ethnic, or religious groups: *everyone* was watching everyone else and confiding their opinions to friends, to barroom or campfire acquaintances who spoke their language, or in their private journals and letters home. The selections in this volume reveal a crisscrossing field of social observation and moral orientation: a Jewish merchant tells of translating Chinese newspapers, a Mexican general records his views of French and Australian miners, a Japanese migrant describes his first view of a black man in San Francisco, a Canadian describes the clothes worn by Lascar and South American miners, a German relates the encounter between a lascivious Bombay-man and a local Indian tribe, a French physician comments on the dental hygiene of the Spanish. The eclecticism of cross-cultural encounters in gold-rush writing can be dizzying. And like all engaging history and literature, the gold rush continues to surprise us out of our own responses.

Despite the cultural, political, and social importance of the gold rush, however, it remains in many respects an ill-understood historical phenomenon. It seems oddly estranged, in the popular imagination, from a real time and place, populated by faceless miners hunched over gold pans. Hollywood cannot be blamed for this, as it has been unable to exploit the dramatic possibilities of the gold rush in the way, say, the Civil War provides the backdrop for innumerable movies. There has been no *Gone with the Wind*, no *Glory*, about the California gold rush. Charlie Chaplin's wonderfully inventive comedy *The Gold Rush* (1925) was set in the Yukon gold rush of fifty years later. The one recent film that deals centrally with the California gold rush—the musical *Paint Your Wagon*, which nearly bankrupted Paramount Studios when it was released in 1969 but which has since become something of a cult classic—is merely the exception that proves the rule. Why should this be the case? Is it because the gold rush does not have a familiar dramatic structure (a discernible beginning, but no clear finish)? Is it because it lacked focal points of interest such as climactic battles or dramatic confrontations between homesteaders and ranchers? Is it because the rush to California was motivated by a seemingly base motive, the desire to get rich quick? Is it that mining is an unglamorous occupation incapable of capturing the imagination? Yet the lumber industry, which certainly has its share of unromantic hard work, spawned the legend of Paul Bunyan and his big ox, Babe. When a character like Joaquín Murieta springs into the popular mind during the 1850s in California, it is as an outlaw, as someone who has *abandoned* mining and ridden off in a cloud of dust, that he gains his mythic dimensions.

Whatever the reasons for the low status of the miner in the popular imagination, the fact remains that the gold rush encompassed far more than miners alone. It involved everyone—doctors, preachers, shoe salesmen, cooks, dance-hall girls, wheelwrights, impresarios—who was a part of the human avalanche that roared into the Golden State. The boom-and-bust mentality of the gold rush helped sponsor an art and literature that tended to stress the novel and the picturesque. Franklin Walker has pointed out that the emphasis was on lawlessness rather than law; gambling rather than the slow accrual of a fortune; the prostitute with a heart of gold rather than the pioneer mother; the abandoned orphan rather than the extended family with solicitous relatives in China, Mexico, or New Jersey.[20] The trials of the patiently grubbing, homesick "honest miner" did not captivate writers' imaginations. As Joseph Henry Jackson puts it, "a hero hip deep in an icy mountain torrent is a chilly hero at best; there is ... little greatness in subsisting on moldy pork and soggy biscuit in order to get rich. A dyspeptic shaking with ague is not the stuff of which legends are built."[21]

The jostle of competitive publishing venues open to writers on the California frontier also undoubtedly contributed to the sensationalistic or melodramatic cast of much gold rush writing. As early as 1850, some fifty printers worked in San Francisco, and the city boasted that by the mid-fifties it published more newspapers than London (many in languages other than English). Writers could see print quickly in reputable journals like the *Pioneer*, the *Golden*

Era, and, after 1868, the *Overland Monthly,* as well as in ephemeral local publications with names like *Hombre, Satan's Bassoon,* or the *Wine, Women, and Song Journal.*

Poetry tended to be an undistinguished genre in early California, characterized by either belabored dialect poems or overly lush and self-consciously literary celebrations of the landscape by California "songsters." In fiction, the one notable work that was inspired by the mining camps was John Rollin Ridge's sensationalist romance, *The Life and Adventures of Joaquín Murieta, the Celebrated California Bandit* (1854), the first novel published by an American Indian. Ridge played an important part in suggesting the generally uneasy, often violent interracial relations of miners on a polyglot frontier. The tensions were not only between whites and nonwhites but among various minority groups as well. The California Indians are treated as subhuman by Murieta's gang and Chinese miners are repeatedly brutalized by the Mexican desperadoes: 150 Chinese at one point are left scattered "along the highways like so many sheep with their throats cut by the wolves."[22] Ridge portrayed the gold mines as rough but bustling communities where a romantic landscape of secluded arroyos and dusty, campfire canyons matched the larger-than-life human spectacle of the camps.

Gold rush drama embodied the love of action-packed melodrama displayed in *Joaquín Murieta.* One of the first eyewitness dramas about the gold rush was David G. ("Doc") Robinson's *Seeing the Elephant* in the early 1850s. The manuscript of this and other plays by Robinson have been lost, but contemporary accounts of the play indicate that it dealt with gullible miners who head west with overblown hopes of striking it rich, only to encounter bad weather, hunger, and bandits. Among the popular melodramas and farces of the day like *Bombastes Furioso* (many given unisex performances in the predominantly male camps), a number of plays dealt with mining life in California: Warren Baer's musical satire *The Duke of California* (1856), Alonzo Delano's sentimental melodrama *A Live Woman in the Mines; or, Pike County Ahead!* (1857), and Joseph Nunes' *Fast Folks; or the Early Days of California* (1858). Often more historical curiosities than fully realized plays, many of these works nevertheless have a kind of rough-and-ready impudence that can still beguile. Delano's *A Live Woman in the Mines,* for instance, features characters with names like Sluice Box and High Betty Martin and includes fresh portraits of the miners yearning for feminine company or news from home. When the food in camp runs out, the men dine on rats and boots and then hit upon an innovative expedient. They tie the last piece of pork to a string; each man swallows the pork, then pulls it out and passes it on.

Whatever attention is due gold rush poetry, fiction, and drama, however, the true imaginative wealth of the gold rush resides in its nonfictional prose. No other aspect of the American frontier witnessed such an outpouring of letters, journals, diaries, and personal narratives: much of it, until Gary Kurutz's magisterial bibliography, still uncataloged, let alone read and interpreted. There are more written documents about the California gold rush than about any other nineteenth-century historical event except the Civil War. As linguistic historians have noted, the gold rush migrants were "the first—and the last—frontiersmen to have the education and the inclination to describe what they saw and heard."[23] Although this nonfictional writing has primarily been read by historians emphasizing its documentary value, its imaginative and aesthetic complexity also deserve to be celebrated.

Gold rush letters and diary entries often consisted of simple, unrefined, sometimes ungrammatical prose ("the schoolmaster certainly was abroad," John Banks wryly commented about notes he saw along the California trail).[24] The writing frequently addressed practical matters such as the price of meals or hardware, mining techniques, and claim disputes. Many of the diary jottings and letters were inscribed with cramped fingers after an exhausting day of work or travel. "I write by candlelight and think by starlight," wrote Israel Lord while on the overland trail in 1849.[25] Yet in the best works, this very emphasis on the demands of everyday life—on the mud, heat, and fleas in the camps—contributes to the roughhewn piquancy of these memoirs. Gold rush chronicles mix pedestrian detail with a sudden sense of wonder or fresh curiosity. In *The Shirley Letters* (1854–55), arguably the finest firsthand account of the gold rush, Louise Clappe (using the nom de plume "Dame Shirley") wrote a series of twenty-three letters from two high-country camps in the upper reaches of the Feather River to her stay-at-home sister in Massachusettes. The primitive living conditions startled her eastern notions of decorum: "How would you like to winter in such an abode? in a place where there are no newspapers, no churches, lectures, concerts, or theaters; no fresh books, no shopping, calling, nor gossiping little tea-drinkings; no parties, no balls, no picnics, no *tableaux*, no charades, no latest fashions, no daily mail (we have an express once a month), no promenades, no rides nor drives; no vegetables but potatoes and onions, no milk, no eggs, no nothing?" Yet just when conditions seem most crude and unredeemable, Clappe adds a characteristic sparkle of candor and mischief. "I expect to be very happy here," she tells her sister. "This strange, odd life fascinates me."[26]

Realistic prose accounts of the gold rush were often less wellknown in California than the work of frontier humorists like Alonzo Delano and George

Horatio Derby. Delano published works under his legal name in the East, but presented himself as the long-nosed character Old Block in San Francisco. He wrote popular whimsical sketches, or "whittlings from his penknife," of western types such as the miner and the gambler for San Francisco's *Pacific News.* George Horatio Derby was a caricaturist and U.S. Army topographical engineer assigned to California in the early 1850s after service in the Mexican War. Like many nineteenth-century writers, he loved pseudonyms, writing under the penname John Phoenix and John P. Squibob, and his letters, squibs, and burlesques appeared in various California papers. Striking a pose of boisterous urbanity, Derby's writing is full of a racy, irresponsible humor and comic earnestness that reads like a cross between Mrs. Malaprop and Groucho Marx.

Full of raillery, literate satire, and vivid social portraiture, the writing of Derby, along with that of Delano, Ridge, Clappe, and others, helped lodge the California gold rush in the American imagination. Their writing was followed by a second generation of authors in the 1860s and 1870s, including Twain, Harte, Joaquin Miller, Ambrose Bierce, and Prentice Mulford, who transformed the event into mythic history. Bret Harte in particular, as Kevin Starr says, "depicted the gold rush as quaint comedy and sentimental melodrama, already possessing the charm of antiquity. As pseudo-history, as an uproarious and Dickensian saga, Harte's gold rush gave Californians a stabilizing sense of time past."[27] Harte's stout-hearted, red-shirted forty-niner went through further permutations until, drained of his melancholy and unruliness, he was made into an entrepreneuring pioneer by California boosters in the late 1870s.

Naturalist writers at the turn of the century like Frank Norris and Ambrose Bierce used mining camps (often in deserted towns with dank mine shafts) to create a spooky, surreal atmosphere for dark parables about violence and psychic collapse. Their legacy can be seen in a contemporary writer like Roy Parvin, whose stories in *The Loneliest Road in America* (1997) use the hardscrabble mines of the Trinity Alps as the backdrop for haunting tales of violent misfits and solitary dope growers. Contemporary writers concerned with nature and ecology like David Rains Wallace and Gary Snyder have followed the lead of earlier writers such as John Muir and Mary Austin in studying both the human and natural history of California mining. The paucity of firsthand accounts of the gold rush (at least translated into English) by Native Americans, Asians, and Latinos have also inspired rich revisionist imaginings by contemporary writers of color of what it must have been like for marginalized groups to participate in the gold rush. Their attempts to resurrect the lost lives of, say, a widowed Maidu mother surrounded by her dying children or a young Chinese woman unexpectedly forced into prostitution have added a fresh, challenging complexity to our understanding of the California frontier.

The gold rush has been interpreted by each generation; the process began with the original gold seekers themselves. Just a few years after Marshall's discovery, placer gold had become increasingly scarce. The extraction of what gold remained (buried in subterranean strata) required large capital and elaborate hydraulic equipment and explosives. The individual miner and the image of competitive democracy he exemplified was increasingly eclipsed by "big ditch" companies that employed day laborers and undertook large-scale operations. For this and for other reasons, like the way the familiar routines of life back home seemed a little anticlimactic for many of the returning argonauts, the rough fraternity of the "early days" began to take on a golden glow. Having lived out the greatest adventure of their lives, what before had been simply boredom or hard work was now regarded by the miners as an heroic example of perseverance and obstacles overcome. Frontier hardship was viewed through the lens of a later and easier life, and many citizens—like those who founded the Society of California Pioneers, dedicated to remembering "those whose sagacity, enterprise, and love of independence induced them to settle in the wilderness"—felt such experiences deserved to be honored and preserved. The public memory of the gold rush has continued to be reshaped through the years, and the two previous fifty-year celebrations afford a glimpse of how Californians viewed themselves and their future as they commemorated this event.

By 1898, the surviving forty-niners were in their seventies and eighties and scores of them had published or dictated memoirs of their experiences for preservation. Many of the most valuable accounts of life during the gold rush—based on contemporary diaries, journals, and letters, along with later interviews and oral histories—were written during the 1870s, 1880s, and 1890s. In addition, the bookseller Hubert Howe Bancroft had assembled a self-proclaimed "history factory" that produced, among other projects, a seven-volume *History of California,* published between 1886 and 1890. Bancroft's history of the gold rush was a self-consciously epic, celebratory, and often inaccurate attempt to confer an historical authority and grandeur on the state's ad hoc and often violent beginnings. Writers such as Josiah Royce (in his important revisionist history, *California: ...A Study of American Character* [1886]), Clarence King, and John Muir all variously expressed reservations about the refashioning of the argonauts as Pioneer Entrepreneurs basking in the glow of civic rectitude. Yet even a critic such as King felt a "tenderly blent" pathos and comedy in the deserted mining districts. True, King took Californians to task for ignoring the violence and racial intolerance of their history. But he himself used a mining analogy to counter those who focused only on California's present and ignored its future prospects: "Show these gloomy critics a bare stretch of vulgar Sierra earth, and they will tell you how barren, how valueless it is, ignorant that the art of any Californian can banish every grain of sand into the Pacific's bottom, and gather a residuum of solid gold. Out of the race of men whom they have in the same shallow way called common, I believe Time shall separate a noble race."[28]

Like similar celebrations for the Civil War and World War II, the fiftieth anniversary of the gold rush, or Golden Jubilee as it was officially known, commemorated a living history, an event that had not yet faded into archival memory and featured living survivors. It also coincided with the new rush to the Klondike the same year. The governor proclaimed Monday, January 24th, a legal holiday, and there was a Grand Parade in San Francisco featuring veterans of the Mexican War, a float of Sutter's Mill, a carriage full of James Marshall's companions at the gold discovery site, and a "Chinese Battalion, in Oriental costume, bearing the decorative emblems peculiar to their nation." For five weeks following the Jubilee Week there was an exposition of California's mining resources, showcasing "rare and precious specimens and ores" and mining equipment.[29] The festivities highlighted state pride by celebrating the gold rush as a picturesque bas-relief of antebellum pioneer industry.

The centennial celebration in 1948 occurred just after the end of World War II. The trauma of that recent upheaval colored the way the gold rush was viewed, particularly the mismatch between the argonauts' initial expectations and the reality of what they actually encountered. Historian Joseph Henry Jackson's words in the foreword to a celebratory volume in 1949 might as aptly have characterized the war experiences of returning GIs: "Mining turned out not to be quite the simple affair the high-hearted, cocksure boys and young men thought."[30] Still, the colossal relief of the war's end had put the country in a confident, expansive mood. Defense industry jobs connected with the war had helped swell the population of California to ten million people. The emphasis of the centennial celebration was not only on the gold rush itself, but on its legacy of growth and prosperity. Wallace Stegner's remarkable study of minority groups in America, *One Nation,* published in 1945, suggested that all was not right on the home front. "A wall of suspicion, distrust, snobbery, hatred, and guilt" ran down the middle of America, Stegner said a decade and a half before the Civil Rights movement: a wall separating a WASP majority from "people who because of color, religion, or cultural background are not allowed to be full citizens of the U.S." But the country was not yet ready for such pronouncements. John Caughey struck a more characteristic note when he admitted that yes, there had been a reckless, often exploitative and violent cast to the gold rush. But the golden boost the rush had provided the state overshadowed all that. "Today's Californians," Caughey said, "like relay racers handed a tremendous lead by their first teamsman, have a confidence that sometimes alarms strangers. They are in the habit of having great expectations, of entertaining roseate hopes and seeing them all come true."[31]

Stegner's remarks seem more penetrating today because they foretell the concerns of contemporary life, concerns that prompt a more troubled and morally ambiguous appraisal of the California frontier. Modern readers have become more acutely attuned to particular themes that arise in the gold rush: the special hardships of frontier life on women, the extent of the environmental damage caused by mining, and the legacy of frontier violence and vigilantism that stretches into our own time in ghetto druglords and domestic terrorism. Today our tone of nostalgia or yearning may be reserved less for the roughneck life of muddy tent cities and saloons than for the animal life, wild ecosystems, and indigenous cultures disrupted or annihilated by the influx of forty-niners. But whatever our response to the gold rush—and surely many readers will have multiple, perhaps contradictory responses—its impress upon contemporary life should not be underestimated.

Anyone who has spent time on the Trinity, Yuba or Feather rivers knows that individual miners continue to look for gold from makeshift campsites and brightly colored pontoon floats. The majority of gold mining in the state is now a large industrial venture, however; one whose cyanide leach ponds, metallurgical processing, and environmental monitoring seem unlikely to fire the imagination in a way that sheds light on the events of 1848 and 1849. The impact of the gold rush seems both more subtle and more longstanding. "Subtle" because the vocabulary and slang of the mining frontier have been so easily absorbed into our everyday language that many do not recognize their origins. Terms like prospector, lucky strike, bonanza (originally a Spanish word for "fair weather"), panning out (as in, "that didn't pan out for me"), staking a claim, diggings (or "digs"), paydirt, nuggets, following a vein, coyoting, the mother lode—all pay homage, in their linguistic roots, to the freewheeling ebullience of gold rush life and speech.

The impact of the gold rush seems more longstanding because as a collective experience it called into question values about wealth, family, independence, gender, cultural diversity, and our relation to the land. It embodied

America's new sense of itself as mirrored in California, whether the image reflected back was seen as a cautionary tale about monetary greed and xenophobia or a triumphal exemplification of American know-how and self-government. As Stephen Birmingham says, the gold rush created a new version of California *élan,* "a special doughtiness, a certain daring, a refusal to be fazed or put off by bad luck or circumstances, an unwillingness to give up."[32] Of course, it is sometimes a fine line between daring and derangement, open-spiritedness and short-sightedness, risk-taking and irresponsibility. But the gold rush ensured that Californians would henceforth be willing to walk that line. The gold rush permanently altered the cultural adrenaline of the state, creating an electric sense of possibility, a new scale of ambition and a new standard for life in the fast lane, life on the edge. Anything might happen in California, the feeling went, and *very* quickly.

However one feels about such an ethos, the legacy of this quality in California life can be seen in everything from the success of microbreweries and Silicon Valley to the state's mammoth water projects, its booming biotech industries, and billion-dollar agricultural empires. The writer Richard Rodriguez felt the gravitational pull of this feeling growing up in Sacramento.

> I was not a boy preoccupied with tragedy. I was a boy in love with cinemascope, and all-you-can-eat, and S & H Green Stamps and cool inside. I wanted possibility.... I remember telling my Mexican father—I was about twelve or thirteen, we were polishing our second-hand but very beautiful blue DeSoto—I remember telling my Mexican father one day that I was going to be somebody someday Papa.... And I remember my father saying to me: "you'll see." And I said "what do you mean, 'you'll see?' " Everybody in America, everybody in California, everybody in the West had encouraged my ambitions: "you can be anything you want, dye your hair, marry Vanna White, become President." "You'll see." "You'll see what, Papa?" "Life is harder than you think." It came at me like this wind....What did that promise of tragedy mean? I was polishing the second-hand blue DeSoto, I saw myself in that ocean of blue in the hood watching myself polishing the blue DeSoto. "You'll see. Life is harder than you think."[33]

If all this seems a little remote from the rude tree-stump camps where sunburned miners worked, surrounded by poison oak and the sound of summer grasshoppers, think again. For it is precisely from such unlikely beginnings that the lure and magnetism that continue to attract millions of people from around the globe to the Golden State has arisen. The gold rush was the central formative event in California history, and anyone interested in understanding the state's special place in the American imagination will need to grapple with that fact. Debated and pondered at the time, the precise significance of the gold rush still remains open to question. The variety of opinions about its meaning and desirability has been rich and contradictory since the moment it began. *Gold Rush* aims to sample that panoply of anecdote, observation, and artistic expression as a way of deepening our understanding of this complex historical phenomenon. It seeks to illuminate our sense of how and why the gold rush opened a magic casement in the middle of the nineteenth-century. For a few brief years when all the world was California (or so it seemed), America got a new glimpse of its future. It was not a future the country could have foreseen or perhaps even wanted, but it was the one California was already busy inventing.

Michael Kowalewski
Northfield, Minnesota
August, 1997

NOTES

1. Frémont, John C., *Geographical Memoir* (San Francisco: Book Club of California) 1970, 54.

2. Dillon, Richard, *Captain John Sutter: Sacramento Valley's Sainted Sinner* (Santa Cruz, CA: Western Tanager Press) 1981, 284.

3. Quoted in Dillon, 289.

4. Quoted in Holliday, J. S., *The World Rushed In: The California Gold Rush Experience* (New York: Simon & Schuster) 1981, 35.

5. Quoted in Jackson, Donald Dale, *Gold Dust* (New York: Alfred A. Knopf) 1980, 27.

6. Colton, Walter, *Three Years in California* (New York: A. S. Barnes & Co.) 1850, 247.

7. Carson, James H., "Early Recollections of the Mines" in *Bright Gem of the Western Seas,* edited by Peter Browning (Lafayette, CA: Great West Books) 1991, 3.

8. Quoted in Browning, Peter, ed., *To the Golden Shore* (Lafayette, CA: Great West Books, 1995, 36.

9. Margolin, Malcolm, *The Way We Lived: California Indian Reminiscences, Stories, and Songs* (Berkeley: Heyday Books) 1993, 2.

10. Rohrbough, Malcolm, *Days of Gold: The California Gold Rush and the American Nation* (Berkeley: University of California Press) 1997, 2.

11. Quoted in Holliday, 59.

12. Quoted in Rice, Richard B., et al., *The Elusive Eden: A New History of California* (New York: Alfred A. Knopf) 1988, 181.

13. Delano, Alonzo, *Alonzo Delano's California Correspondence* (Sacramento: Sacramento Book Collectors Club) 1952, 95.

14. Emerson, Ralph Waldo, *The Conduct of Life* (Boston: Ticknor and Fields) 1860, 255–256.

15. Thoreau, Henry David, *The Journal of Henry D. Thoreau.* Vol. 1. (New York: Dover Publications, Inc.) 1962, 210–211.

16. Jackson, 13.

17. Milosz, Czeslaw, "On the Western" in *Visions from San Francisco Bay* (New York: Farrar, Straus, & Giroux) 1986, 59–60.

18. Frost, Robert, "The Gift Outright" in *The Poetry of Robert Frost* (New York: Henry Holt) 1979, 348.

19. Hurtado, Albert L, *Indian Survival on the California Frontier* (New Haven: Yale University Press) 1988, 100-124.

20. Walker, Franklin, *San Francisco's Literary Frontier* (New York: Alfred A. Knopf) 1939, 1–27.

21. Jackson, Joseph Henry, "Introduction" in *Joaquín Murieta* (Norman, OK: University of Oklahoma Press) 1986, xix–xx.

22. Ridge, John Rollin, *Joaquín Murieta* (Norman, OK: University of Oklahoma Press) 1986, 252.

23. McCrum, Robert, et al., *The Story of English* (New York: Penguin) 1987, 252.

24. Banks, John, *The Buckeye Rovers in the Gold Rush,* edited by H. Lee Scamehorn, Edwin P. Banks, and Jamie Lytle-Webb (Athens: Ohio University Press) 1989, 72.

25. Lord, Israel, *At the Extremity of Civilization,* edited by Necia Dixon Liles (Jefferson, NC: McFarland and Co.) 1995.

26. Clappe, Louise Amelia Knapp Smith, *The Shirley Letters* (Salt Lake City: Peregrine Smith) 1970, 54.

27. Starr, Kevin, *Americans and the California Dream, 1850–1915* (New York: Oxford University Press) 1973, 49.

28. King, Clarence, *Mountaineering in the Sierra Nevada* (New York: Penguin) 1989, 259, 262.

29. *California's Golden Jubilee: Official Souvenir and Program* (San Francisco: Golden Jubilee Committee) 1898.

30. Jackson, Joseph Henry, "Foreword" in *Gold Rush Album* (New York: Charles Scribner's Sons) 1949, vi.

31. Caughey, John Walton, *Gold Is the Cornerstone* (Berkeley: University of California Press) 1948, 299.

32. Birmingham, Stephen, *California Rich* (New York: Simon and Schuster) 1980, 29.

33. Rodriguez, Richard, "Gone West: The Exhaustion of an American Metaphor" in *Western Voices,* vol. 1, no. 2 (Winter 1996), 13.

Note: Many of the selections in this anthology have been abridged from their original forms. Missing text within paragraphs has been noted with an ellipse; missing text between paragraphs has not. Spelling and punctuation have been silently standardized only in cases of possible confusion. Readers should refer to the original works for scholarly use.

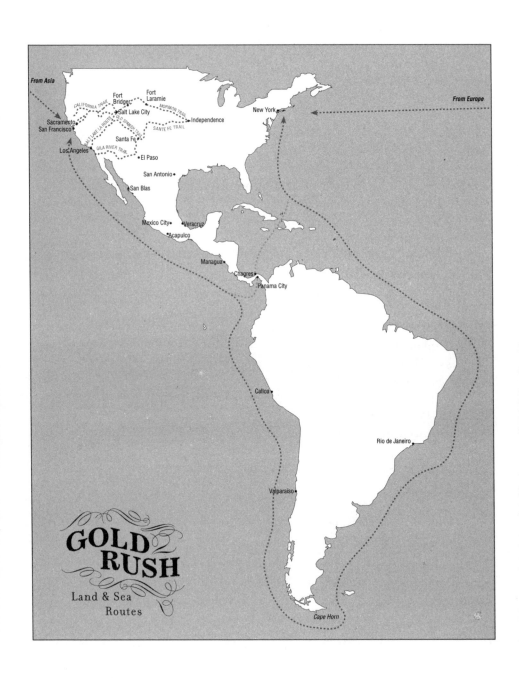

From Asia

From Europe

CALIFORNIA TRAIL

Fort
Bridger

Fort
Laramie

MORMON TRAIL

New York

Sacramento
San Francisco

SALT LAKE LA ROUTE

Salt Lake City

OLD SPANISH TRAIL

Independence

Los Angeles

GILA RIVER TRAIL

Santa Fe

SANTE FE TRAIL

El Paso

San Antonio

San Blas

Mexico City

Veracruz

Acapulco

Managua

Chagres

Panama City

Calloa

Rio de Janeiro

Valparaiso

GOLD
RUSH

Land & Sea
Routes

Cape Horn

BEFORE THE RUSH

I remember as a child living in the cedar bark house with my grandparents. How wonderful it was, lying awake at night sometimes, to hear the coyotes bark, and the hoot owls uttering their calls among the trees. Sometimes there would be the running clatter of squirrels on the bark slabs above us; and in spring and summer, just as it grew light before the sun rose, there came the enchantment of the bird chorus, the orchestra of the Great Spirit all around us.

—Marie Potts, Maidu

In the hands of an enterprising people, what a country this might be!

—Richard Henry Dana, Jr.

"Maidu Village" c. 1853, by Henry Brown

The Presidio of Monterey, c. 1793, by J. Sykes

from THE NORTHERN MAIDU

MARIE POTTS

For 12,000 years before the gold rush, hundreds of thousands of Native Americans lived in the land later known as California—in fact, California was more densely populated than any other region north of Mexico. They were a diverse people, belonging to more than five hundred independent tribal groups and speaking widely disparate languages. The Northern Maidu Indians lived in present-day Lassen, Butte, and Plumas counties, near what would become gold country. Marie Potts, a Northern Maidu tribe member born in 1895, gave this account in 1977 of her ancestors' life.

OUR COUNTRY WAS BEAUTIFUL, with vast open valleys or meadows—Mountain Meadow, Hebe Meadow, Big Meadow (now covered by Lake Almanor), and others. The surrounding mountains, their flanks mantled with forests, were covered with snow most of the year, such as Barter Mountain, and, looming above all, Mount Lassen, where the snow never completely melted. Among the mountains were many fine lakes where there was good fishing, and plenty of deer roamed from valley to valley across ridges covered with sugar and ponderosa pine, fir, cedar, spruce, and tamaracks. Among these grew brush—manzanita, buck bushes, and squaw carpet, a shrub that grew close to the ground, with leaves like holly.

There were all kinds of berry bushes on both meadows and hillsides: raspberries, strawberries, elderberries, gooseberries, sometimes thimbleberries, and, of course, there were huckleberries. The chokecherries we ate after mashing—then spit the seeds out. Our country was rich in nature's food, there for the taking.

We had a good climate of the kind that makes mountain people energetic and strong, and not enervating, as in the hot summers in the Great Valley. The winter snow cover was often six to eight feet deep. "Big Meadow" might give to people now a picture of a vast hayfield, but this meadow and others was more like a swamp, with mounds and hillocks in places. It had many springs around the borders; they ran along in pools rich with fish, mostly trout. It is easy to see why we did not live down in the meadows, but on higher ground along the borders.

Mono bark house, 1902

I also remember as a child living in the cedar bark house with my grand-parents. How wonderful it was, lying awake at night sometimes, to hear the coyotes bark, and the hoot owls uttering their calls among the trees. Some-times there would be the running clatter of squirrels on the bark slabs above us; and in spring and summer, just as it grew light before the sun rose, there came the enchantment of the bird chorus, the orchestra of the Great Spirit all around us. That clean pine smell on the morning wind—where can we find it now?

from Las Sergas de Esplandián

GARCI RODRÍGUEZ ORDÓÑEZ DE MONTALVO

The picaresque romance Las Sergas de Esplandián *was one of the most popular books in Spain in the early 1500s. It described a mythical island called California, rich with gold and ruled by queen Calafía. The notion of California as an island persisted in European imaginations until 1747, when Ferdinand VI put an end to the myth by decreeing, "California is not an island."*

KNOW YE that on the right hand of the Indies there is an island called California, very near the Terrestrial Paradise and inhabited by black women without a single man among them and living in the manner of Amazons. They are robust of body, strong and passionate in heart, and of great valor. Their island is one of the most rugged in the world with bold rocks and crags. Their arms are all of gold, as is the harness of the wild beasts which, after taming, they ride. In all the island there is no other metal.

In this island called California, with the great roughness of the land and the multitude of wild animals, are many griffins the like of which are not found in any other part of the world. In the season when the griffins give birth to their young, these women cover themselves with thick hides and go out to snare the little griffins, taking them to their caves where they raise them. And being quite a match for these griffins, they feed them the men taken as prisoners and the males to which they have given birth. All this is done with such skill that the griffins become thoroughly accustomed to them and do them no harm. Any male who comes to the island is killed and eaten by the griffins.

Over this island of California rules a queen, Calafía, statuesque in proportions, more beautiful than all the rest, in the flower of her womanhood, eager to perform great deeds, valiant and spirited, and ambitious to excel all those who have ruled before her.

from TWO YEARS BEFORE THE MAST

RICHARD HENRY DANA, JR.

Even before the gold discovery, Americans from the Eastern seaboard perceived Califor-nia as a remote land of adventure, freedom, and romance. Richard Henry Dana, Jr. (1815–1882) escaped a life of ill health and oppressive social constraints at Harvard by joining a hide ship bound for California in 1834. He worked as a sailor on the long journey around Cape Horn, reveling in the camaraderie, danger, and breathtaking natural beauty of the ocean voyage. Safely back at Harvard, he recorded his memories of rural, pre-gold rush California in Two Years Before the Mast, *an immediate and enduring bestseller first published in 1840.*

WE RETURNED BY SUNDOWN, and found the *Loriotte* at anchor within a cable's length of the *Pilgrim.* The next day we were "turned-to" early, and began taking off the hatches, overhauling the cargo, and getting everything ready for inspection. At eight, the officers of the [Monterey] customs, five in number, came on board, and began overhauling the cargo, manifest, etc. The Mexican revenue laws are very strict, and require the whole cargo to be landed, exam-ined, and taken on board again; but our agent, Mr. R——, had succeeded in compounding with them for the last two vessels, and saving the trouble of taking the cargo ashore. The officers were dressed in the costume which we found prevailed through the country—a broad-brimmed hat, usually of a black or dark brown color, with a gilt or figured band round the crown, and lined inside with silk; a short jacket of silk or figured calico (the European skirted body-coat is never worn); the shirt open in the neck; rich waistcoat, if any; pantaloons wide, straight, and long, usually of velvet, velveteen, or broadcloth; or else short breeches and white stockings. They wear the deer-skin shoe, which is of a dark brown color, and (being made by Indians) usually a good deal ornamented. They have no suspenders, but always wear a sash round the waist, which is generally red, and varying in quality with the means of the wearer. Add to this the never-failing cloak, and you have the dress of the Californian. This last garment, the cloak, is always a mark of the rank and wealth of the owner. The *gente de razon*, or aristocracy, wear cloaks of black or dark blue broadcloth, with as much velvet and trimmings as may be; and from this they go down to the blanket of the Indian, the middle classes wearing something like a large table-cloth, with a hole in the middle for the head to go through. This is often as coarse as a blanket, but being beautifully woven with various colors, is quite showy at a distance. Among the Spaniards there is no working class (the Indians being slaves and doing all the hard work) and every rich man looks like a grandee, and every poor scamp like a broken-down gentleman.

For a week or ten days all was life on board. The people came off to look and to buy—men, women, and children; and we were continually going in the boats, carrying goods and passengers—for they have no boats of their own. Everything must dress itself and come aboard and see the new vessel, if it were only to buy a paper of pins. The agent and his clerk managed the sales, while we were busy in the hold or in the boats. Our cargo was an assorted one; that is, it consisted of everything under the sun. We had spirits of all kinds (sold by the cask), teas, coffee, sugar, spices, raisins, molasses, hardware, crockery ware, tin-ware, cutlery, clothing of all kinds, boots and shoes from Lynn, calicoes and cottons from Lowell, crapes, silks; also, shawls, scarfs, necklaces, jewelry, and combs for the ladies; furniture; and in fact, everything that can be imagined, from Chinese fire-works to English cart-wheels—of which we had a dozen pairs with their iron rims on.

The Californians are an idle, thriftless people, and can make nothing for themselves. The country abounds in grapes, yet they buy bad wine made in Boston and brought round by us, at an immense price, and retail it among themselves at a *real* (twelve and a half cents) by the small wineglass. Their hides too, which they value at two dollars in money, they give for something which costs seventy-five cents in Boston; and buy shoes (as like as not, made of their own hides, which have been carried twice round Cape Horn) at three and four dollars, and "chicken-skin boots" at fifteen dollars apiece. Things sell on an average at an advance of nearly three hundred per cent upon the Boston prices.

By being thus continually engaged in transporting passengers with their goods, to and fro, we gained considerable knowledge of the character, dress, and language of the people. The dress of the men was as I have before described it. The women wore gowns of various texture—silks, crape, calicoes, etc.—made after the European style, except that the sleeves were short, leaving the arm bare, and that they were loose about the waist, having no corsets. They wore shoes of kid, or satin, sashes or belts of bright colors, and almost always a necklace and ear-rings. Bonnets they had none.... They wear their hair (which is almost invariably black, or a very dark brown) long in their necks, sometimes loose, and sometimes in long braids; though the married women often do it up on a high comb. Their only protection against the sun and weather is a large mantle, which they put over their heads, drawing it close round their faces, when they go out of doors, which is generally only in pleasant weather.

Their complexions are various, depending—as well as their dress and manner—upon their rank; or, in other words, upon the amount of Spanish blood they can lay claim to. Those who are of pure Spanish blood, having never intermarried with the aborigines, have clear brunette complexions, and sometimes even as fair as those of English women. There are but few of these families in California, being mostly those in official stations, or who, on the expiration of their offices, have settled here upon property which they have acquired; and others who have been banished for state offenses. These form the aristocracy; intermarrying, and keeping up an exclusive system in every respect. They can be told by their complexions, dress, manner, and also by their speech; for, calling themselves Castilians, they are very ambitious of speaking the pure Castilian language, which is spoken in a somewhat corrupted dialect by the lower classes. From this upper class they go down by regular shades, growing more and more dark and muddy, until you come to the pure Indian, who runs about with nothing upon him but a small piece of cloth, kept up by a wide leather strap drawn round his waist.... Yet the least drop of Spanish blood, if it be only of quatroon or octoon, is sufficient to raise them from the rank of slaves, and entitle them to wear a suit of clothes—boots, hat, cloak, spurs, long knife, and all complete, though coarse and dirty as may be—and to call themselves Españolos, and to hold property, if they can get any.

The fondness for dress among the women is excessive, and is often the ruin of many of them. A present of a fine mantle, or of a necklace or pair of ear-rings gains the favor of the greater part of them. Nothing is more common than to see a woman living in a house of only two rooms, and the ground for a floor, dressed in spangled satin shoes, silk gown, high comb, and gilt, if not gold, ear-rings and necklace. If their husbands do not dress them well enough, they will soon receive presents from others. They used to spend whole days on board our vessel, examining the fine clothes and ornaments, and frequently made purchases at a rate which would have made a seamstress or waiting-maid in Boston open her eyes.

Next to the love of dress, I was most struck with the fineness of the voices and beauty of the intonations of both sexes. Every common ruffian-looking fellow, with a slouched hat, blanket cloak, dirty underdress, and soiled leather leggings, appeared to me to be speaking elegant Spanish. It was a pleasure simply to listen to the sound of the language.... A common bullock-driver, on horseback, delivering a message, seemed to speak like an ambassador at an audience. In fact, they sometimes appeared to me to be people on whom a curse had fallen, and stripped them of everything but their pride, their manners, and their voices.

Another thing that surprised me was the quantity of silver that was in circulation. I certainly never saw so much silver at one time in my life, as during the week that we were at Monterey. The truth is, they have no credit system, no banks, and no way of investing money but in cattle. They have no circulating medium but silver and hides—which the sailors call "California bank notes." Everything that they buy they must pay for in one or the other of these things. The hides they bring down dried and doubled, in clumsy ox-carts, or upon mules' backs, and the money they carry tied up in a handkerchief—fifty, eighty, or an hundred dollars and half dollars.

from ECHOES OF THE PAST

JOHN BIDWELL

As glowing reports of California's fertile soil and abundant resources trickled eastward, restless entrepreneurs organized emigration companies to help finance the journey out. John Bidwell (1819–1900) formed the Western Emigration Society and led the first wagon train into California in 1841. After a grueling six-month overland journey— many miles of which had not been previously mapped—Bidwell arrived in California, working for Swiss rancher John Sutter for several years before establishing his own ranch in the Sacramento Valley. For Bidwell, dreams of wealth in California came true; he eventually built an opulent mansion in Chico and owned his own steamboat on the Sacramento River. He was one of the state's first prominent statesmen, serving as a member of California's first state senate and later as a U.S. congressman. He ran three times unsuccessfully for California governor and once for president as a Prohibitionist in 1892. In 1891, fifty years after arriving, Bidwell described his first impressions of pre-gold rush California in Century Magazine.

THE PARTY WHOSE FORTUNES I have followed across the plains was not only the first that went direct to California from the East; we were probably the first white people, except Bonneville's party of 1833, that ever crossed the Sierra Nevada. Dr. Marsh's ranch, the first settlement reached by us in California, was located in the eastern foothills of the Coast Range Mountains, near the northwestern extremity of the great San Joaquin Valley and about six miles east of Monte Diablo....There were no other settlements in the valley; it was, apparently, still just as new as when Columbus discovered America, and roaming over it were countless thousands of wild horses, of elk, and of antelope. It had been one of the driest years ever known in California. The country was brown and parched; throughout the State wheat, beans, everything had failed. Cattle were almost starving for grass, and the people, except perhaps a few of the best families, were without bread, and were eating chiefly meat, and that often of a very poor quality.

Dr. Marsh had come into California four or five years before by way of New Mexico....With the exception of Dr. Marsh there was then no physician of any kind anywhere in California. We were overjoyed to find an American, and yet when we became acquainted with him we found him one of the most selfish of mortals. The night of our arrival he killed two pigs for us. We felt very grateful; for we had by no means recovered from starving on poor mule meat, and when he set his Indian cook to making tortillas (little cakes) for us, giving one to each—there were thirty-two in our party—we felt even more grateful; and especially when we learned that he had had to use some of his seed wheat, for he had no other.... The next morning I rose early, among the first, in order to learn from our host something about California—what we could do and where we could go—and, strange as it may seem, he would scarcely answer a question. He seemed to be in an ill humor, and among other things he said, "The company has already been over a hundred dollars' expense to me, and God knows whether I will ever get a *real* of it or not." I was at a loss to account for this and went out and told some of the party, and found that others had been snubbed in a similar manner. We held a consultation and resolved to leave as soon as convenient. Half our party concluded to go back to the San Joaquin River, where there was much game, and spend the winter hunting, chiefly for otter, the skins being worth three dollars apiece. The rest—about fourteen—succeeded in gaining information from Dr. Marsh by which they started to find the town of San José, about forty miles to the south, then known by the name of Pueblo de San José, now the city of San José. More or less of our effects had to be left at Marsh's, and I decided to remain and look out for them, and meantime to make short excursions about the country on my own account.

After the others had left I started off traveling south, and came to what is now called Livermore Valley, then known as Livermore's Ranch, belonging to Robert Livermore, a native of England. He had left a vessel when a mere boy, and had married and lived like the native Californians, and, like them, was very expert with the lasso. Livermore's was the frontier ranch, and more exposed than any other to the ravages of the horse-thief Indians of the Sierra Nevada (before mentioned). That valley was full of wild cattle—thousands of them—and they were more dangerous to one on foot, as I was, than grizzly bears.

On the way [back to Marsh's ranch], as I came to where two roads, or rather paths, converged, I fell in with one of the fourteen men, M. C. Nye, who had started for San José. He seemed considerably agitated, and reported that at the Mission of San José, some fifteen miles this side of the town of San José, all the men had been arrested and put in prison by General Vallejo, Mexican commander-in-chief of the military under Governor Alvarado, he alone having been sent back to tell Marsh and to have him come forthwith to explain why this armed force had invaded the country.

The next morning before day found me starting for the Mission of San José to get a passport for myself. Mike Nye, the man who had brought the news of the arrest, went with me. A friend had lent me a poor old horse, fit only to carry my blankets. I arrived in a heavy rain-storm, and was marched into the calaboose and kept there three days with nothing to eat, and the fleas were so numerous as to cover and darken anything of a light color. There were four or five Indians in the prison. They were ironed, and they kept tolling a bell, as a punishment, I suppose, for they were said to have stolen horses; possibly they belonged to the horse-thief tribes east of the San Joaquin Valley. Sentries were stationed at the door. Through a grated window I made a motion to an Indian boy outside and he brought me a handful of beans and a handful of manteca, which is used by Mexicans instead of lard. It seemed as if they were going to starve me to death. After having been there three days I saw through the door a man whom, from his light hair, I took to be an American, although he was clad in the wild picturesque garb of a native Californian, including *serape* and the huge spurs used by the vaquero. I had the sentry at the door hail him. He proved to be an American, a resident of the Pueblo of San José, named Thomas Bowen, and he kindly went to Vallejo, who was right across the way in the big Mission building, and procured for me the passport.

We had already heard that a man by the name of Sutter was starting a colony a hundred miles away to the north in the Sacramento Valley. No other civilized settlements had been attempted anywhere east of the Coast Range—before Sutter came the Indians had reigned supreme. As the best thing to be done I now determined to go to Sutter's, afterward called "Sutter's Fort," or New Helvetia. Dr. Marsh said we could make the journey in two days, but it took us eight. Winter had come in earnest, and winter in California then, as now, meant rain. I had three companions. It was wet when we started, and much of the time we traveled through a pouring rain. Streams were out of their banks; gulches were swimming; plains were inundated; indeed, most of the country was overflowed. There were no roads, merely paths, trodden only by Indians and wild game. We got out of provisions and were about three days without food. Game was plentiful, but hard to shoot in the rain. Besides, it was impossible to keep our old flint-lock guns dry, and especially the powder dry in the pans. On the eighth day we came to Sutter's settlement; the fort had not then been begun. Sutter received us with open arms and in a princely fashion, for he was a man of the most polite address and the most courteous manners, a man who could shine in any society.

John A. Sutter was born in Baden in 1803 of Swiss parents, and was proud of his connection with the only republic of consequence in Europe. He was a warm admirer of the United States, and some of his friends had persuaded him to come across the Atlantic.... He took a vessel that went to the Sandwich Islands [Hawaii], and there communicated his plans to people who assisted him. But as there was no vessel going direct from the Sandwich Islands to California, he had to take a Russian vessel by way of Sitka. He got such credit and help as he could in the Sandwich Islands and induced five or six natives to accompany him to start the contemplated colony. He expected to send to Europe and the United States for his colonists. When he came to the coast of California, in 1840, he had an interview with the governor, Alvarado, and obtained permission to explore the country and find a place for his colony.

A short time before we arrived Sutter had bought out the Russian-American Fur Company at Fort Ross and Bodega on the Pacific. That company had a charter from Spain to take furs, but had no right to the land. The charter had about expired. Against the protest of the California authorities they had extended their settlement southward some twenty miles farther than they had any right to, and had occupied the country to, and even beyond, the bay of Bodega. The time came when the taking of furs was no longer profitable; the Russians were ordered to vacate and return to Sitka. They wished to sell out all their personal property and whatever remaining right they had to the land. So Sutter bought them out—cattle and horses; a little vessel of about twenty-five tons burden, called a launch; and other property, including forty-odd pieces of old rusty cannon and one or two small brass pieces, with a quantity of old French flint-lock muskets pronounced by Sutter to be of those lost by Bonaparte in 1812 in his disastrous retreat from Moscow. This ordnance Sutter conveyed up the Sacramento River on the launch to his colony.

As soon as the native Californians heard that he had bought out the Russians and was beginning to fortify himself by taking up the cannon they began to fear him. They were doubtless jealous because Americans and other foreigners had already commenced to make the place their headquarters, and they foresaw that Sutter's fort would be for them, especially for Americans, what it naturally did become in fact, a place of protection and general rendezvous; and so they threatened to break it up. Sutter had not yet actually received his grant; he had simply taken preliminary steps and had obtained permission to settle and proceed to colonize. These threats were made before he had begun the fort, much less built it, and Sutter felt insecure. He had a good many Indians whom he had collected about him, and a few white men (perhaps fifteen or twenty), and some Sandwich Islanders. When he heard of the coming of our thirty men he inferred at once that we would soon reach him and be an additional protection.

With this feeling of security, even before the arrival of our party Sutter was so indiscreet as to write a letter to the governor or to some one in authority, saying that he wanted to hear no more threats of dispossession, for he was now able not only to defend himself but to go and chastise them. That letter having been despatched to the city of Mexico, the authorities there sent a new governor in 1842 with about six hundred troops to subdue Sutter. But the new governor, Manuel Micheltorena, was an intelligent man. He knew the history of California and was aware that nearly all of his predecessors had been expelled by insurrections of the native Californians. Sutter sent a courier to meet the governor before his arrival at Los Angeles, with a letter in French, conveying his greetings to the governor, expressing a most cordial welcome, and submitting cheerfully and entirely to his authority. In this way the governor and Sutter became fast friends, and through Sutter the Americans had a friend in Governor Micheltorena.

Nearly everybody who came to California made it a point to reach Sutter's Fort. Sutter was one of the most liberal and hospitable of men. Everybody was welcome—one man or a hundred, it was all the same. He had peculiar traits; his necessities compelled him to take all he could buy, and he paid all he could pay; but he failed to keep up with his payments. And so he soon found himself immensely—almost hopelessly—involved in debt. His debt to the Russians amounted at first to something near one hundred thousand dollars. Interest increased apace. He had agreed to pay in wheat, but his crops failed. He struggled in every way, sowing large areas to wheat, increasing his cattle and horses, and trying to build a flouring mill.... Every year found him worse and worse off; but it was partly his own fault. He employed men—not because he always needed and could profitably employ them, but because in the kindness of his heart it simply became a habit to employ everybody who wanted employment.

Most of the labor was done by Indians, chiefly wild ones, except a few from the Missions who spoke Spanish. The wild ones learned Spanish so far as they learned anything, that being the language of the country, and everybody had to learn something of it. The number of men employed by Sutter may be stated at from 100 to 500—the latter number at harvest time. Among them were blacksmiths, carpenters, tanners, gunsmiths, vaqueros, farmers, gardeners, weavers (to weave coarse woolen blankets), hunters, sawyers (to saw lumber by hand, a custom known in England), sheep-herders, trappers, and, later, millwrights and a distiller. In a word, Sutter started every business and enterprise possible. He tried to maintain a sort of military discipline. Cannon were mounted and pointed in every direction through embrasures in the walls and bastions. The soldiers were Indians, and every evening after coming from work they were drilled under a white officer, generally a German, marching to the music of fife and drum. A sentry was always at the gate, and regular bells called men to and from work.

Harvesting, with the rude implements, was a scene. Imagine three or four hundred wild Indians in a grain field, armed, some with sickles, some with butcher-knives, some with pieces of hoop iron roughly fashioned into shapes like sickles, but many having only their hands with which to gather by small handfuls the dry and brittle grain; and as their hands would soon become sore, they resorted to dry willow sticks, which were split to afford a sharper edge with which to sever the straw. But the wildest part was the threshing. The harvest of weeks, sometimes of a month, was piled up in the straw in the form of a huge mound in the middle of a high, strong, round corral; then three or four hundred wild horses were turned in to thresh it, the Indians whooping to make them run faster. Suddenly they would dash in before the band at full speed, when the motion became reversed, with the effect of plowing up the trampled straw to the very bottom. In an hour the grain would be thoroughly threshed and the dry straw broken almost into chaff. In this manner I have seen two thousand bushels of wheat threshed in a single hour. Next came the winnowing, which would often take another month. It could only be done when the wind was blowing, by throwing high into the air shovelfuls of grain, straw, and chaff, the lighter materials being wafted to one side, while the grain, comparatively clean, would descend and form a heap by itself. In this manner all the grain in California was cleaned.

The kindness and hospitality of the native Californians have not been overstated. Up to the time the Mexican regime ceased in California they had a custom of never charging for anything; that is to say, for entertainment—food, use of horses, etc. You were supposed, even if invited to visit a friend, to bring your blankets with you, and [you] would be thoughtless if [you] traveled and did not take a knife with [you] to cut [your] meat. When you had eaten, the invariable custom was to rise, deliver to the woman or hostess the plate on which you had eaten the meat and beans—for that was about all they had—and say, "*Muchas gracias, Señora*" ("Many thanks, madame"); and the hostess as invariably replied, "*Buen provecho*" ("May it do you much good").

It is not generally known that in 1841—the year I reached California—gold was discovered in what is now a part of Los Angeles County. The yield was not rich; indeed, it was so small that it made no stir. The discoverer was an old Canadian Frenchman by the name of Baptiste Ruelle, who had been a trapper with the Hudson Bay Company, and, as was not an infrequent case with those trappers, had drifted down into New Mexico, where he had worked in placer mines. The mines discovered by Ruelle in California attracted a few New Mexicans, by whom they were worked for several years. But as they proved too poor, Ruelle himself came up into the Sacramento Valley, five hundred miles away, and engaged to work for Sutter when I was in Sutter's service.

Early in the spring of 1844, a Mexican working under me at the Hock Farm for Sutter came to me and told me there was gold in the Sierra Nevada. His name was Pablo Gutierrez. The discovery by [James] Marshall, it will be remembered, was in January, 1848. Pablo told me this at a time when I was calling him to account because he had absented himself the day before without permission. I was giving him a lecture in Spanish, which I could speak quite well in those days. After my lecture he said, "*Señor*, I have made an important discovery; there surely is gold on Bear River in the mountains." This was in March, 1844. A few days afterwards I arranged to go with him up the Bear River. We went five or six miles into the mountains when he showed me the signs and the place where he thought the gold was. "Well," I said, "can you not find some?" No, he said, because he must have a *batea*.

He talked so much about the "batea" that I concluded it must be a complicated machine. "Can't Mr. Keiser, our saddle-tree maker, make the batea?" I asked. "Oh, no." I did not then know that a batea is nothing more nor less than a wooden bowl which the Mexicans use for washing gold. I said, "Pablo, where can you get it?" He said, "Down in Mexico." I said, "I will help pay your expenses if you will go down and get one," which he promised to do. I said, "Pablo, say nothing to anybody else about this gold discovery, and we will get the batea and find the gold."

In the autumn of that year, 1844, a revolt took place. The native chiefs of California, José Castro and ex-Governor Alvarado, succeeded in raising an insurrection against the Mexican governor, Micheltorena, to expel him from the country. They accused him of being friendly to Americans and of giving them too much land. The truth was, he had simply shown impartiality. When Americans had been here long enough, had conducted themselves properly, and had complied with the colonization laws of Mexico, he had given them lands as readily as to native-born citizens. He was a fair-minded man and an intelligent and a good governor, and wished to develop the country. His friendship for Americans was a mere pretext; for his predecessor, Alvarado, and his successor, Pio Pico, also granted lands freely to foreigners, and among them to Americans. The real cause of the insurrection against Micheltorena, however, was that the native chiefs had become hungry to get hold again of the revenues. The feeling against Americans was easily aroused and became their main excuse. The English and French influence, so far as felt, evidently leaned towards the side of the Californians. It was not open but it was felt, and not a few expressed the hope that England or France would some day seize and hold California.

In a few days the first blow was struck, the insurgents taking all the horses belonging to the government at Monterey, setting the governor and all his troops on foot. He raised a few horses as best he could and pursued them, but could not overtake them on foot. However, I understood that a sort of parley took place at or near San José, but no battle, surrender, or settlement. Meanwhile, having started to return by land to Sutter's Fort, two hundred miles distant, I met the governor returning to Monterey. He stopped his forces and talked with me half an hour and confided to me his plans. He desired me to beg the Americans to be loyal to Mexico; to assure them that he was their friend, and in due time would give them all the lands to which they were entitled. He sent particularly friendly word to Sutter. Then I went on to the Mission of San José and there fell in with the insurgents, who had made that place their headquarters: I staid all night, and the leaders, Castro and Alvarado, treated me like a prince. The two insurgents protested their friendship for the Americans, and sent a request to Sutter to support them.

On my arrival at the fort the situation was fully considered, and all, with a single exception, concluded to support Micheltorena. He had been our friend; he had granted us land; he promised, and we felt that we could rely upon, his continued friendship; and we felt, indeed we knew, we could not repose the same confidence in the native Californians. This man Pablo Gutierrez, who had told me about the gold in the Sierra Nevada, was a native of Sinaloa in Mexico, and sympathized with the Mexican governor and with us. Sutter sent him with despatches to the governor stating that we were organizing and preparing to join him. Pablo returned, and was sent again to tell the governor that we were on the march to join him at Monterey. This time he was taken prisoner with our despatches and was hanged to a tree, somewhere near the present town of Gilroy. That of course put an end to our gold discovery; otherwise Pablo Gutierrez might have been the discoverer instead of Marshall.

from ON LAND AND SEA
IN 1843, '44, AND '45

WILLIAM H. THOMES

William H. Thomes (1824–1899) was a Boston publisher and author who, as a teenager, like Richard Henry Dana, Jr. before him, hitched a ride on a hide-and-tallow ship in 1842 and explored the California coast. Thomes, unlike most easterners, thought highly of the Californios he encountered and returned to the state several times during his life. Published in 1883, his On Land and Sea in 1843, '44 and '45 *offered a firsthand account of the Hispanic residents of pre-gold rush California through the eyes of an earnest sympathizer.*

TOWARD NIGHT THE WIND DIED AWAY, but left just enough air to keep the ship on her course, and at daybreak we got a few fresh puffs from the south, and, with studding sails alow and aloft, we worked our way toward the entrance of the Golden Gate.... At three o'clock on the afternoon of the 25th of April, 1843, we saw right ahead of us Alcatraz Island, looking like variegated marble, with the deposits of sea birds, and the air full of shrieking and quarreling gulls, while on the rocks were a hundred or more old sea lions, whose roars, as they fought or struggled for good places, were enough to chill the blood of those who did not know that the animals were harmless, unless attacked and brought to bay. Off our larboard bow was a beautiful island, wooded and green, even to the water's edge. This was Angel Island, in those days as lovely a spot as the eye needed to rest on. Off the starboard beam was the presidio, or fort, to guard the entrance of the Golden Gate, and containing two brass pieces, but, as neither was mounted on a carriage that was capable of sustaining a discharge, it was evident that they were intended more for ornament than use.

As we drew near the presidio a Mexican flag was run up, in answer to our signal, and then the solitary soldier, who seemed to have charge, thinking that he had done his duty, pulled it down, put it away, lighted a cigarette, and went to sleep for the afternoon.

In the evening the fresh breeze died away, and it was calm all night. During my anchor watch I could hear the huge sea lions on the rocks, roaring and grumbling, and all over the town, what little there was, the barking of numerous dogs. There were no lights in the houses, as every one seemed to have gone to sleep early, to prepare for the onerous duties of the morrow. Without sleep, and plenty of it, the Mexican's life would not be a pleasant one. He can sleep easier and oftener than any people I know of, except his ancestors, the Spaniards.

The next morning the old man ordered his boat manned to go on shore. We landed on a little piece of beach, at the side of Telegraph Hill, where there was a small ravine, or water course, and where we used to dry our hides in sunny weather, if any came on board wet from the various ranches.

The first building we came to was the poop-cabin of some condemned ship, hauled up on the shore, and made into a comfortable, though rather contracted, abode. A kanaka whom we met—and there was a colony of them living on the beach, near the cabin—said that it was occupied by a Captain Spear and his Mexican wife, and he intimated, by a gesture, that the captain was fond of a glass of wine, and, if it was native wine, I pitied his wife. The owner and his lady had not arisen, so Lewey and I could not call and pay our respects, which must have hurt their feelings very much when they awoke, and learned what distinguished company had been near them.

The kanakas, or Sandwich Islanders, were all seated in front of a rough shanty, which they had erected from pieces of boards, bits of sail-cloth, tarpaulins, beach-grass, and boughs of trees, and seemed to be taking life easy, having eaten breakfast, and were now passing around a huge clay pipe, with a stem not over an inch long. Each person took a pull, inflated his cheeks to their fullest extent, and, when strangulation seemed quite evident, slowly allowed the smoke to escape from his mouth, with a grunt of satisfaction, and a look of regret that his chance for another puff did not come again for ten minutes. Those whose cheeks were not distended were chatting in their musical tongue, like so many magpies, but they found time to bid us welcome, and to offer us a piece of smoked salmon, there being many large fish lying on the ground near the hut, which they had purchased for a hand of tobacco from some Sacramento River Indians, who had been to the bay to trade furs and salmon, and get a stock of auguardiente, which they valued more than anything else in the world.

We found the smoked salmon very nice. I asked the price of one that weighed nearly twenty pounds, and the leader of the gang said that I could have it for two *reales*, or a plug of tobacco. I had a hand of the weed in my pocket, and willingly made the exchange, and then, having no more tobacco, paid a quarter for a second salmon, nearly as large as the first, which I intended

"Monterey, California Rancho Scene," 1849, by Alfred Sully

to present to the crew, but when the old man saw it, he admired it so much, that I generously made him a present of it, for the use of the cabin, and he gave me four large hands of tobacco in return, so that my first visit to San Francisco resulted in a speculation that gave me several hundred per cent profit, for the next day I bought a third fish for a plug of mighty poor cavendish, and there was feasting fore and aft.

We ... wandered on, across lots, for there were no roads, or sidewalks, and came to the plaza, but the only building near it was a wooden, one-story structure, containing a dilapidated billiard table, the cloth torn and greasy, and the proprietor, an American, looking as though it would not take much to tempt him to commit suicide, as the Mexicans did not play billiards, and there was no vessel in port, except the *Admittance*. If living had not been cheap the fellow would have starved to death in a week's time. He asked us if we had money enough to buy a glass of auguardiente, and we said that we had, but were not drinking much that morning, and the man groaned, as he exclaimed— "Just my blanked luck," and went into his saloon, and fell asleep at once, for he had nothing else to do to pass away the time, when there were no vessels in port. I suppose the fellow committed suicide before the gold discoveries. I think that I could, even at this late day, pick out the very spot where the billiard saloon was located.

Away to the southern of the sand-hills, on the border of a small creek, were the adobe walls of the Mission Dolores, once a power in the northern part of the State, and with thousands of cattle and Indians at its disposal, but now stripped of all influence by the government. The fathers had nothing to do but hear confessions, and administer absolution to the sick and dying. Part of the mission roof had fallen in, the walls were crumbling, and no signs of life could be seen near the place.

Across the bay was the green and fertile district of Saint Leandy, with one solitary ranche, close to the head of a shallow creek, and near where now stands the prosperous city of Oakland, and the terminus of the Pacific Rail-road. How little did I think, as I stood there, that morning in April, 1843, what wonderful changes would occur within the next thirty years; that at my feet would spring up a great and flourishing city and that the now solitary bay would harbor thousands of vessels, from all parts of the world; that noble piers would take the place of shallow water and mud in front of the town, and spacious hotels and warehouses the lonely billiard saloon and deserted store-house, and elegant residences the miserable adobe huts, with naked children playing in front of the places where it is customary to hang doors, in civilized countries.

We pulled back to our ship in time for dinner, and then hoisted out the launch, and the next morning four of us were sent in her, with the second mate, to fill some gang-casks at Saucelito, on the other side of the bay, as the water at Yerba Buena was bad, and very scarce, the Mexicans having no use for the beverage, except in the form of coffee, so but few wells were dug, and those were not over clean, in our estimation.

We drifted out with the tide, and then took a slight breeze, and ran close to Alcatraz Island, where the sea fowl had built thousands of nests, and the guano was over a foot thick in some places. The sea lions raised their ponderous heads, and roared at us, but did not otherwise move, so tame were they, although we could have touched them with our oars, had we been so disposed, which we were not, as we were rather fearful of them, and did not know but that they would stave our boat, if disturbed.

When we got over to Saucelito, the watering place, we found the spring was so obstructed by rubbish and filth, that it required a long time to cleanse it, and, as one man could do all that was needed, Mr. Davidson told Lewey and me that we might wander off for an hour or more, and we took advantage of the permission, and climbed a small hill near the beach and spring, and found the ground covered with wild strawberries, of delicious flavor. We laid down on the grass at full length, and ate and ate, until we could consume no more, then picked a hatful, and carried [it] to the second mate, and the rest of the men. As the spring was too roily to fill the casks, we again wandered off, and this time in an opposite direction, and came to a ranche, where we saw two handsome young ladies, who looked at us in wondering surprise, for they had no idea we were a portion of a watering party, supposing for a moment that we were deserters from some vessel.

They spoke to us in Spanish, and asked us who we were, and where we belonged, and, while we were talking, a man came out of the adobe house, and addressed us in English, and said that his name was Richardson, that he was an early pioneer in California, and had married a Mexican wife, and was quite comfortably settled, owning thousands of acres of land, and many head of cattle.

But his daughters had many attractions for our eyes, for they were very handsome, and Lewey and I fell in love with them immediately, and deliberated whether we had not better run away, and ask them to marry us off hand, and then lead the life of a California ranchero. The ladies little suspected the impression they created on two young and susceptible hearts, and, if they had, would have laughed, for they flew at higher game than common sailor boys, as they had a right to, from position and beauty. We saw them many times afterward, when they visited the ship with their father, and they always had a pleasant smile for the French lad and myself and we were glad when we had them in our boat. They were rather diffident about conversation, and knew their stations in life, and were well aware of ours, so we seldom ventured on familiar topics unless they led up to them by asking questions about our life and standing at home.

Captain Richardson, as he was called, gave us some frijoles for dinner, and we bid the host and ladies a polite farewell, and returned to the spring, and passed water to the gang-casks until near sundown, before they were filled, and then we started for the ship, and were nearly swamped before we got under the lee of Telegraph Hill, the sea was so rough in the channel. The casks were hoisted out, and the next day the launch was despatched for more water, but I did not go, although I did want to have one more look at the dark eyes and faces of the Señoritas Richardson.

One day a flatboat came alongside, manned by ten naked Indians, and in the stern was a white man. He brought us two hundred hides, and a large lot of beaver and other skins. When he came on deck Mr. Prentice told me the visitor was the celebrated Captain Sutter, that he lived a long way off, up the Sacramento River somewhere, and had ten thousand wild Indians under his command, a strong fort, and employed all the white men who came in his way, but that the banks of the river were infested with a cruel and blood-thirsty race of cannibals, who preferred white men's flesh to that of bullocks, and so murdered and ate all who attempted to join forces with the captain. I believed all that was told me and circulated the report among the crew. The story was started for the purpose of preventing the men from deserting, as it was feared they might do, after learning that Captain Sutter harbored every one who had a good trade, like that of blacksmith, carpenter, or mason.

The captain was a short, stout man, with broad shoulders, large, full face, short, stubby mustache, a quiet, reserved manner, and a cold blue eye, that seemed to look you through and through, and to read your thoughts, no matter how much you tried to conceal them. He was a person who would have been noted anywhere as something above the ordinary rank of humanity. He must have had courage and coolness to live as many years as he did surrounded by wild Indians, yet keep them in perfect subjection, and ready to follow him to any part of the State, and fight as he dictated, when there was a revolution worthy of his attention, as the captain did not often mingle with the little affairs of the country.... In many respects he was the most remarkable man that ever settled in California, and the only one who laughed at all attempts to control his movements, and the men he had in his employ. What a dreary life the man must have led for so many years, in his fort near the Sacramento and American Rivers, with no companions but wild Indians.

Captain Sutter remained all night on board. He was reported to be a Swiss by birth, and formerly an officer of the Great Napoleon's army. When Lewey learned this he wanted to fall down and worship him, and he did succeed in exchanging a few words with the gentleman, but the discipline of the ship prevented a long conversation. This was the man on whose land gold was first discovered in California, and it was the means of reducing him from affluence to poverty, for hordes of vandals ran off his stock, killed his cattle, and took possession of his farm, and mocked him when he remonstrated, for his wild Indians were scattered, ... and [they] shunned the white man as though he was an evil spirit, and good reasons they had for keeping out of his company, as it was not considered a crime to shoot at a buck, or squaw, to see how near a bullet could go and not hit or kill outright. On Feather River, in 1849, I saw a young, beardless boy shoot an inoffensive native, and there were but few expressions of regret for the crime. I am sorry to state that the murderer was

23

native of my own State, and born within ten miles of Boston.

After the hides and skins were discharged the Indians rowed the flatboat ashore, near the kanakas, built a rousing fire, cooked the hind quarter of a bullock, had a great feast, smoked, and drank auguardiente, until they were in a fit state for howling, and yell they did, and danced around their fire, until near daylight, and then they went to sleep, while the people of the town felt of the hair of their heads to see that it was safe, and unanimously turned to, and thanked Captain Sutter and his aids in no measured terms; even the inoffensive kanakas returned from the sand-hills where they had taken refuge during the night, and sat down to a breakfast of smoked salmon, and looked with wonder and dread at the naked savages, who were sleeping off their debauch, with many bows and arrows by their sides, all ready for use. Half a dozen resolute men, well armed, could have driven the whole crowd of barbarians into the bay, had they been so disposed.

That same day a wooding party was sent off, near the Mission Dolores, where there was a grove of oak-trees. Four men were detailed, and they took a week's provisions, and one of the ship's old muskets, to kill a bear or two, in case they came along toward the camp, and in the afternoon I was ordered to prepare for a week's excursion in a large sloop-launch, called the *Paul Jones*.... in 1843, The second mate was to go in command, and I was detailed to act as clerk, to give receipts; and deliver such goods as were demanded by the Mexicans who called for them.

We hauled the *Paul Jones* alongside, loaded her, and took on such stores as we would need for a week's absence. The old man went on shore, and shipped two kanakas, one called Kanaka Charlie, and the other Kanaka Jack, both natives of the Sandwich Islands, but quite different in style and actions. Charley was a silent, reserved fellow, a good pilot all over the bay, and a very fair sailor, using but few words, yet attentive and obliging. His cheeks were tattooed in red and blue India ink, and his hair was long, black, and coarse, but well oiled with cocoanut butter. He was also a good cook, and could fry steaks, and make gravies. I liked him on the latter account, for a boy can never get all the gravy he wants, when camping out, and has a vigorous appetite, and good digestion.

Kanaka Charley did not utter more than a dozen words during our passage across the bay. When we asked him where San José was located, he would wave his hand, say "Dar," and that was all. We had a spanking breeze, and passed over flats and shoals where the water was not more than three feet deep, and still we could not see the entrance to the San José creek, but just as we thought we should plump into a mud bank, we saw a narrow opening, and into it we run, and found ourselves surrounded by high tules, and large flocks of wild ducks, which hardly took the trouble to fly or dive at our approach, so tame were they in that vast solitude.

The wind died out, and left us becalmed, and then the tide commenced ebbing, and we found that we could not stem it. Just as we were about to tie up to the bank of the stream, a ranchero, mounted on a splendid-looking horse, galloped up, looked over the rushes, and said that he would tow us to the landing if we desired. We did desire it, so he threw us the end of his reata, which we made fast to the mast, and then the horseman secured the other end to the iron pommel of his saddle, started his steed very gently, and up the stream we went, at the rate of two knots an hour, and in a short time the Mexican signified to us that we had reached our destination. We found a nice clear space, where he could moor the sloop, discharge cargo, and look all over the country. The ranchero told us that he had been expecting us for the last forty-eight hours, and that the next day he would send down an ox team with some hides, and take away the goods we had on board. He stated that his name was Don Jesus, rather a funny cognomen, but there was a greaser at San Francisco who sported the full title of Don Jesus Christ, or Don Jesus Christo. The fathers and mothers who give such singular names to their children think that it is a mark of deep piety to thus honor their offspring, and there is no suggestion of profanity in the act.

As we had goods marked for the don we supposed he was what he represented himself to be, made him welcome, and invited him to dinner. He lived at a ranche about a mile from the landing, the only house in sight, and requested us to call and see him, and said that he would supply us with all the beef and milk we needed while there.

He was as good as his word, but the milk tasted so strong of wild onions that we could not use it, although the Mexicans did not seem to mind it in the least. The meat was good, however, and we had all that we wanted, but did not require much, as near the landing was a small, brackish lake, and every night thousands of geese and ducks used to alight there to feed and rest, and the noise they made was something to be remembered for many a day.... Leaving Charley to get supper we crawled toward the pond, but there was no need of caution. The ducks and geese merely looked at us in simple surprise, quacked a little, honked at each other, and continued to feed. When we were within ten fathoms or less the second mate discharged the musket at a flock of geese, and killed seven, and wounded many more. I waded in, and secured the dead, but had to let the fluttering, injured ones escape. In all that vast mob of fowl not one took to its wings, and sought to escape to safer quarters.

There was no pleasure in shooting such tame game, and when we wanted to carry ducks and geese to the ship, being all ready to leave, we simply threw clubs at them, and knocked them over, and thus saved our powder and shot. I never saw so many wild fowl at one time before or since, and all we secured were just bursting with fat, in such good condition that the efforts to fly were a little fatiguing, we judged, by their refusing to take wing at our approach. A steady diet of goose flesh is not so desirable as one might think, and we soon tired of it, and returned to beefsteaks and gravy.

I am told that San José is now a beautiful and prosperous place, and I suppose the creek is filled up, the adobe house gone, and the pond drained, and covered with houses, but I should like to see it as I saw it in April, 1843, when the country was wild, and the mission an important one for cattle, and the plain covered with them.

The next day Don Jesus was on hand, and brought us two hundred hides, for which I gave him a receipt. We loaded his goods on the cart, for the Indians would not do the work, they were so lazy. We offered the Mexican Don two of our geese, but he laughed, and declined the tempting prizes, saying that his peons could load our sloop down in a single night with game, if he wanted them to do so, but he did not relish geese. He had tired of them, and wished the ducks and the geese to a region that sounded very hot, although people do dispute on the subject, and say there is no such place.

Don Jesus had come down to visit us, and see to our wants, leaving his horse, a powerful, spirited animal, standing near the *Paul Jones,* fastened to a peg driven in the ground. While I was admiring the steed the Mexican invited me to "*lomo de caballo,*" or to take a ride, and I was only too glad to accept of the kind invitation.

Even to this late day I can vividly remember that morning ride. It had rained a little the night before, and the air was filled with the scent of wild flowers, and the rich green grasses. The warm, bright sun, with not a cloud in the heavens, seemed to render the whole place a paradise for those who loved solitude, and retirement from the world.

As I galloped along I saw half a dozen sneaking coyotes in the tall grass, and gave chase to them, but they suddenly disappeared in some hole in the ground. Near the ranche I met a black bear, at which the horse shied, and did not seem to care to come to close quarters, so I checked him, and watched the brute for a long time, and shouted to him just as he was inclined to turn tail. Then he would halt, sniff at me with a look of contempt, and sit up on his haunches, and stretch out his arms, as though longing for an embrace, and daring me to come near him. At last the bear, with a final angry growl, waddled off, stopping every few minutes to watch if I was following him. The horse seemed to be much relieved to see the savage brute disappear, and to find that I was not disposed to follow.

Then I saw two or three thousand wild geese feeding near the pond, or lake, and making much noise with their complaints and honks. I thought it would be fun to dash into their midst, and see them take to flight. But to my surprise, they did not seem to care for me, or the horse, being accustomed to seeing the latter in immense runs, feeding on the plains. When I was close upon them they parted to the right and left, and waddled out of the way, aided by their wings, and simply hissed at me for disturbing them in feeding, and would not move except for a rod or two. They could not have acted more stupid if they had been hatched in a barn-yard, in Rhode Island, and waiting for their daily supply of corn.

We remained at San José six days, and very pleasant ones they were to me. Mr. Davidson permitted me to do as I pleased. Sometimes I was at the ranche, or watching the ducks and geese in their endless flights overhead, or splashing in the creek, close to the sloop. The hides came down very slowly, and I was always on hand to give receipts, so that there was nothing to do but dream away the day, the weather being just perfect, with only an occasional shower in the night time, and from those we were well protected by tarpaulins. Kanaka Charley did the cooking, and smoked his black, short-stemmed pipe all day long, while the second mate took siestas, and an occasional pull at a bottle of wine.

from THE EMIGRANTS' GUIDE TO OREGON AND CALIFORNIA

LANSFORD HASTINGS

Lansford Hastings (1819–1870) was one of the most enthusiastic supporters of California expansion. Born in Ohio, he took the Oregon Trail to the Pacific Ocean in 1842 and explored California the following year. He hoped to see the United States annex California and attempted to direct emigrants there instead of Oregon in The Emigrant's Guide to Oregon and California, *published in 1845. The popular overland guide directed travelers south toward a supposed "Hastings's Cut-off" he had heard reports of but had never seen. The Donner Party, in 1846, took his advice with disastrous results. Hastings was later a California judge and a delegate to the first Constitutional Convention. In closing his 1845 guidebook, he offered a prophetic vision of what the future held for his beloved California.*

BY THE CAREFUL OBSERVANCE of the foregoing directions and suggestions, as well as a close adherence to their own experience, emigrants will avoid all those hardships and dangers which they would, otherwise, necessarily experience. It is true that emigrants in traveling, through these wild regions, are cut off in a measure from society, deprived of many of the luxuries of civilized life; and it is also true, that their way is not studded with magnificent churches, and spacious houses of public entertainment; but they have enough of the enjoyments of society for their present purposes, and as many of the luxuries of life, as are conducive to health and happiness.

It is hoped that [this guide] will afford some valuable and practical information, in reference to both those highly important countries. Nothing, however, has been attempted but an extremely brief, though practical, description of those countries, which was designed to enable the reader to draw tolerably correct conclusions, in reference to their extent, mountains, rivers, lakes, islands, harbors, soil, climate, health, productions, governments, society, trade, and commerce; and to give the emigrant such practical information, relative to the routes, the equipment, supplies, and the method of traveling, as is thought to be essential, to his success and safety: all of which I have now done.

In view of their increasing population, accumulating wealth, and growing prosperity, I can not but believe that the time is not distant when those wild forests, trackless plains, untrodden valleys, and the unbounded ocean will present one grand scene of continuous improvements, universal enterprise, and unparalleled commerce: when those vast forests shall have disappeared before the hardy pioneer; those extensive plains shall abound with innumerable herds of domestic animals; those fertile valleys shall groan under the immense weight of their abundant products: when those numerous rivers, shall teem with countless steam-boats, steam-ships, ships, barques, and brigs; when the entire country will be everywhere intersected, with turnpike roads, rail-roads, and canals; and when all the vastly numerous and rich resources, of that now almost unknown region, will be fully advantageously developed.

To complete this picture, we may fancy to ourselves a Boston, a New York, a Philadelphia and a Baltimore, growing up in a day, as it were, both in Oregon and California; crowded with a vast population, and affording all the enjoyments and luxuries of civilized life. And to this we may add numerous churches, magnificent edifices, spacious colleges, and stupendous monuments and observatories, all of Grecian architecture, rearing their majestic heads, high in the aerial region, amid those towering pyramids of perpetual snow, looking down upon all the busy, bustling scenes of tumultuous civilization, amid the eternal verdure of perennial spring. And in fine, we are also led to contemplate the time, as fast approaching, when the supreme darkness of ignorance, superstition, and despotism, which now so entirely pervade many portions of those remote regions, will have fled forever, before the march of civilization, and the blazing light of civil and religious liberty; when genuine *republicanism,* and unsophisticated *democracy,* shall be reared up, and tower aloft, even upon the now wild shores of the great Pacific; where they shall forever stand forth, as enduring monuments to the increasing wisdom of *man,* and the infinite kindness and protection of an all-wise and overruling *Providence.*

from RECUERDOS HISTÓRICOS Y PERSONALES
TOCANTE A
LA ALTA CALIFORNIA

MARIANO GUADALUPE VALLEJO

The Bear Flag Revolt was a series of attacks against the ruling Mexican government in June of 1846 by Americans living in Alta (or Upper) California. Led by Captain John C. Frémont and William B. Ide, the Americans seized Mexican strongholds and established the independent Republic of California, which lasted for one month before the U.S. government officially declared war with Mexico.

Mariano Guadalupe Vallejo (1808–1890), perhaps the most powerful man in Mexican California, was born in Monterey and, as a teenager, became a cadet at the Monterey Garrison. Favored by Governor José Figueroa, Vallejo was put in charge of the northern California frontier, where he constructed a vast barony with vineyards, sweeping estates, and a large adobe mansion in present Sonoma County. During the Bear Flag Revolt he was imprisoned in Sutter's Fort for two months, but he actually supported annexation and was later elected to the new state's first senate. He gave this account in 1875.

ALL DURING THE FIRST WEEK of the month of June various interviews took place between Captain Frémont and his compatriots. What passed between them is not public knowledge, but if the antecedents may be drawn from what followed, it is easy to presume that they were perfecting the plans they thought most appropriate for seizing Alta California and devising the means to come off victorious in their undertaking.

The gentlemen under Captain Frémont's command took the road leading through the Napa Hills to Sonoma and at dawn on the 14th of June they surrounded my house located on the *plaza* at Sonoma. At daybreak they raised the shout of alarm and when I heard it, I looked out of my bedroom window. To my great surprise, I made out groups of armed men scattered to the right and left of my residence. The recent arrivals were not in uniform, but were all armed and presented a fierce aspect. Some of them wore on their heads a visorless cap of coyote skin, some a low-crowned plush hat, [and] some a red cotton handkerchief. As for the balance of the clothing of the assaulters of my

Mariano Guadalupe Vallejo with daughters and granddaughters

residence, I shall not attempt to describe it, for I acknowledge that I am incapable of doing the task justice. I suspected that the intruders had intentions harmful not to my [property] interests alone, but to my life and that of the members of my family. I realized that my situation was desperate. My wife advised me to try and flee by the rear door, but I told her that such a step was unworthy and that under no circumstances could I decide to desert my young family at such a critical time. I had my uniform brought, dressed quickly, and then ordered the large vestibule door thrown open. The house was immediately filled with armed men. I went with them into the parlor of my residence. I asked them what the trouble was and who was heading the party, but had

31

to repeat that question a second time, because almost all of those who were in the parlor replied at once, "Here we are all heads." When I again asked with whom I should take the matter up, they pointed out William B. Ide, who was the eldest of all. I then addressed that gentleman and informed him that I wanted to know to what happy circumstance I owed the visit of so many individuals.

In reply he stated that both Captain Merritt and the other gentlemen who were in his company had decided not to continue living any longer under the Mexican government, whose representatives, Castro and Pío Pico, did not respect the rights of American citizens living in the *Departamento*; that Castro was every once in a while issuing proclamations treating them all as bandits and, in a desire to put a stop to all these insults, they had decided to declare California independent; that while he held none but sentiments of regard for me, he would be forced to take me prisoner along with all my family.

We were at this point when there appeared in the room *don* Salvador Vallejo, *don* Pepe de la Rosa, Jacob P. Leese, and *don* Victor Prudon, all friends of mine for whom an order of arrest was suggested until it was decided what should be my fate. I thought for a moment that through some sacrifice on my part I might get rid of so many and such little desired guests, but my hopes were frustrated by the unworthy action of the Canadian, Olivier Beaulieu, who, knowing from his own experiences that liquor is an incentive for all kinds of villainous acts, had gone to his house and procured there a barrel full of brandy, which he distributed among the companions of Merritt and Ide. Once under the influence of the liquor, they forgot the chief object of their mission and broke into shouts of "Get the loot, get the loot!"

Fortunately, these seditious cries emitted by Scott, Beaulieu, Sears, and others attracted the attention of Doctor Semple, who stepped very angrily to the door of the entrance vestibule and by means of a speech of much feeling, in which there were not a few threats, gave them to understand that he would kill the first man who by committing robbery would cast a blot upon the expedition he had helped organize to advance a political end and that, so long as he was alive, he would not allow it to be turned into a looting expedition.

It seems that a hidden but powerful hand has taken great pains to garble all the facts relative to the capture of the Sonoma *plaza* by the group of adventurers to whom history has given the name of "The Bear Flag Party." I, who was made the chief victim those *patriotic gentlemen* sacrificed upon the altar of their well-laid plans, have no interest whatsoever in bespattering them with mud, nor do I aspire to ennoble myself at the expense of their reputation. All I desire is that the impartial public may know what took place at Sonoma on fateful

June 14th, 1846, and that it may, after learning all there is to know in regard to this scandalous violation of law that deprived of liberty those who for years had been making countless sacrifices to redeem from the hands of the barbarous heathen the territory known as the Sonoma Frontier, decide in favor of one or the other of the participants in the events I have just related. All I demand is that the decision arrived at may be upon a basis of fact.

On the fourth day that Mr. Ide was in command at the Sonoma *plaza* ... he issued a document in which he set forth the reasons that had impelled him to refuse to recognize the authority of the Mexican government. The original proclamation, which was very brief, merely stated that, since the lives of foreigners were in imminent danger, he had felt it his duty to declare Alta California independent and that, counting as he did upon the definite support and cooperation of the "fighting men" who had rallied around him, he aimed to do all he could to prevent the Californians or the Mexicans from recovering the military post and arms which the valor of his men had seized from them. This is approximately what "Captain" Ide read aloud before the flagpole in the Sonoma *plaza*.

After the reading of the Commander-in-chief's proclamation, they proceeded with great ceremony to hoist the flag by virtue of which those who had assaulted my home and who had by that time appropriated to themselves two hundred fifty muskets and nine cannon proposed to carry on their campaign.

This flag was nothing more nor less than a strip of white cotton stuff with a red edge and upon the white part, almost in the center, were written the words "California Republic." Also on the white part, almost in the center, there was painted a bear with lowered head. The bear was so badly painted, however, that it looked more like a pig than a bear.... Of course, both the bear and the star were very badly drawn, but that should not be wondered at, if one takes into consideration the fact that they lacked brushes and suitable colors.

The running up of this queer flag caused much fear to the families of the Californians established in the neighborhood of Sonoma, Petaluma, and San Rafael, for they realized that the instigators of the uprising that had disturbed the tranquility of the frontier had made up their minds to rule, come what might, and, as the rumor had been spread far and wide that Ide and his associates had raised the bear flag in order to enjoy complete liberty and not be obliged to render any account of their activities to any civilized governments, the ranchers, who would have remained unperturbed should the American flag have been run up in Sonoma and who would have considered it as the harbinger of a period of progress and enlightenment, seized their *machetes* and guns and fled to the woods, determined to await a propitious moment for getting rid of the disturbers of the peace. Strange to relate, the first victim that the ranchers sacrificed was the painter of the "Bear Flag," young Thomas Cowie who, along with P. Fowler, was on his way to Fitch's ranch to get one-eyed Moses Carson (brother of the famous explorer Colonel Kit Carson), who was employed as an overseer by Captain Henry Fitch, to give them a half barrel of powder he had locked up in one of the storage closets of his farmhouse.

Fowler and Cowie were taken by surprise at the Yulupa Rancho by the party operating under the command of Captains Padilla and Ramón Carrillo.... Neither of the two extemporaneous commanders thought it right to take the lives of their young captives, upon whom there had been found letters that proved beyond any doubt that Moses Carson and certain others of the Americans employed at the Fitch Ranch were in accord with Ide, Merritt, and others of those who had made up their minds to put an end to Mexican domination in California; so they decided to tie them up to a couple of trees while they deliberated as to what should be done with the captives, whose fate was to be decided at the meeting that night to which had been summoned all the ranchers who by their votes had shared in entrusting command of the Californian forces to those wealthy citizens, Padilla and Carrillo. I am of the opinion that the lives of Cowie and Fowler would have been spared, had it not been that a certain Bernardo García, better known under the name of "Three-fingered Jack," taken advantage of the darkness of the night, approached the trees to which the captives were tied and put an end to their existence with his well-sharpened dagger.

After committing the two murders I have just told about, Bernardo García entered the lonely hut in which Padilla, Carrillo, and others had met and were discussing as to what disposition should be made of the prisoners. Without waiting for them to ask him any questions, he said to his compatriots, "I thought you here were going to decide to free the prisoners and, as that is not for the good of my country, I got ahead of you and took the lives of the Americans who were tied to the trees."

Those few words, spoken with the greatest of sang-froid by the wickedest man that California had produced up to that time, caused all who heard him to shudder. No one dared to object to what had been done, however, for they knew that such a step would have exposed them to falling under the knife of the dreaded Bernardo García, who for years past had been the terror of the Sonoma Frontier.

Equally with the relatives of the unfortunate youths, Cowie and Fowler, I regretted their premature death, for, in spite of the fact that they belonged to a group of audacious men who had torn me from the bosom of my family and done as they pleased with my horses, saddles, and arms, I did not consider that the simple fact that they were the bearers of a few letters made them deserving of the supreme penalty. Until that fatal June 21st, neither they nor their companions had shed any Mexican blood and it was not right for the Mexicans to begin a war *á outrance*, that could not help but bring very grievous consequences upon them and their families.

When we reached New Helvetia, the Canadian, Alexis, who was heading our escort, gave three knocks upon the main gate with his lance and it was immediately thrown open by Captain Sutter, who, feigning surprise at seeing us as prisoners, led us into his living quarters. He then promised to comply with the orders that Captain Frémont had delivered to him by the mouth of his lieutenant, Alexis, who had said in our presence, "Captain Frémont is turning these gentlemen over to you for you to keep as prisoners behind these walls and upon your own responsibility."

"All right," said Sutter, and without any further ceremony he turned to us and suggested that we accompany him to a large room situated on the second floor where the only furniture [was a kind of rude bench.] When we were all inside this room, Sutter locked the door and thought no more about us that night.

I leave my readers to imagine how we cursed at finding ourselves locked up in a narrow room and forced to sleep upon the floor, without a mattress and without a blanket, even without water with which to quench our burning thirst.

After a sleepless night, I greeted the dawn of the new day with enthusiasm, for we were by then beginning to experience the urge of a voracious appetite. Our jailer, however, who had doubtless made up his mind to make us drain the last drop of gall which a perverse fate had meted out to us, sent us no food until eleven o'clock in the morning, at which time he came and opened the door to permit the entrance of an Indian carrying a jar filled with broth and pieces of meat. He did not send us spoons, knives, and forks, for Captain Sutter no doubt thought that since we had lost our liberty we had also ceased to retain our dignity. Such behavior on the part of a companion in arms (at that time Captain Sutter was still an official of the Mexican Government) could not help but inspire our disgust, for we all recognized the insult that he was inflicting upon us by taking advantage of the circumstances. There are times in life, however, when man should resign himself to suffering every kind of adversity. Doubtless, God had decreed that the month of June, 1846, should be the blackest month of my life.

from WHAT I SAW IN CALIFORNIA

EDWIN BRYANT

The United States declared war on the Republic of Mexico on May 13, 1846. Many American emigrants in California volunteered as soldiers or as members of the upstart Bear Flag Revolt. Edwin Bryant (1805–1869), a Kentucky newspaper editor, was in California only a few short weeks before joining Captain John C. Frémont in southern California. The fighting proved to be short lived, although the American conquest was not formally sealed until the drafting of the Treaty of Guadalupe Hidalgo in 1848. Bryant's account of his 1846 overland journey from Louisville, Kentucky, to San Francisco, What I Saw in California, *had the good fortune to be published in 1848—just as the gold discovery made such trail guides essential reading for the thousands now attempting the arduous trip. Bryant's was the most popular and well-written of the dozens of guides that emerged seemingly overnight.*

IN THE COURSE OF THE MORNING, I noticed the phenomenon of *mirage* in great perfection. A wide cascade or cataract of glittering, foaming, and tumbling waters was represented and perfectly well defined on the slope of the mountain to our left, at an apparent distance of five or six miles. Below this was a limpid lake, so calm and mirror-like that it reflected with all the distinctness of reality the tall, inverted shapes of the mountains and all the scenery beyond its tempting but illusory surface. Nature, in this desert region, if she does not furnish the reality, frequently presents the ghosts of beautiful objects and scenery.

At half-past twelve o'clock we saw at the distance of about two miles the course of Truckee River, indicated by a line of willows, grass, and other green herbage, and a number of *tall* trees—the last a sight that has not saluted us for five hundred miles. Our animals, as if reinvigorated by the prospect of grass and the scent of water, rushed forward with great speed, and we were soon in the middle of the stream, from the clear current of which all drank copious draughts. We immediately crossed to the bottom on the opposite side and encamped, much fatigued, as the reader may imagine.

Truckee River at this point is about fifty feet in breadth, with a rapid current of clear water about two feet in depth and a gravelly bed. The bottom, or fertile land, is here about a mile in width, with a growth of small willows, hawthorns, and a few tall cotton-wood trees. In the openings, wild peas and a variety of grasses and other herbage, grow with luxuriance. The shade of the trees is most agreeable, and adds greatly to the pleasantness of our encampment, when contrasting our cool shelter from the sun, with its scorching fervor upon the surrounding desolation.

August 21.—I was wakened from a profound slumber, this morning, by piercing shrieks and wailings. I was not quite certain when I woke whether it was a dream or reality. Satisfying myself that I was not asleep, I listened attentively for a repetition of the strange and mournful sounds which had disturbed my repose. They were soon renewed with greater distinctness than before, and appeared to proceed from some animal, or person in distress or danger, on the opposite side of the river. They soon, however, ceased altogether, and it being quite dark, exhausted as I was, I concluded that I would lie down again, and when daylight dawned, ascertain the cause of these singular vocal performances in this desert region. I soon fell asleep again, however, and did not wake until after sunrise.

When I rose, Messrs. Craig and Stanley were riding towards our camp, and they informed us that their wagons had reached the opposite bank of the river just before daylight, having travelled all night, and that they were now crossing the stream for the purpose of encamping for the day. I was much gratified that these, our good friends, had crossed the desert in safety, and had reached a point where they could recruit their animals. I inquired of them, if they had heard the shrieks and wailings which had disturbed my slumbers early in the morning?

Mr. Craig informed me that one of their party, soon after leaving the boiling springs, from some cause had become quite frantic, with, as he hoped, temporary insanity, brought on by the fatigues and hardships of the march, or from drinking the impure water of the desert. They had been compelled to place him inside of one of the wagons and confine him to it, in order to get him along. When, early this morning, they commenced the descent of the bluffs to the river, he leaped from the wagon, under the influence of a paroxysm of insanity, with loud cries and shrieks, and after describing several times by his movements, a circle, he declared that the destiny of Providence, so far as regarded himself, was accomplished; that nothing more was expected of him or could be demanded from him, and he was willing to submit to his fate and die on that spot, and be buried within that circle. It was some time, and the united strength of two or three men was required before he could be got back again into the wagon.

By the request of Mr. Craig, after his camp was made, I visited the man so strangely attacked. His paroxysms had considerably abated in their strength, and he seemed to be returning to a more rational state of mind. He was continually endeavoring to vomit. Being a stout, vigorous young man, with an abundance of hard muscular flesh upon him, and having an excited pulse, but not one indicating physical disease, I inquired of him why he so frequently endeavored to vomit? He answered that soon after he left the boiling springs, strange sensations of pain and apprehension came over him, and he demanded some remedy for them;—that a large vial containing camphor partially dissolved in alcohol was the only medicine they possessed, which was given to him;—that he had first drank the liquid solution, and then, as he supposed, in an unconscious state, had swallowed a quantity of the undissolved gum, for he had already thrown up several pieces of the size of the end of his thumb, and still he believed there was a large quantity inside of him. I told him that I would prepare an emetic for him, by which he would be entirely relieved and restored to perfect health—that nothing was the matter with him but over-excitement.

AUGUST 22.—We resumed our journey at seven o'clock. Our mules are considerably recruited by the rest we have allowed them, and by the nutritious grass and refreshing water at our last encampment.

The river flows down, with a lively current of limpid water, over a rocky bed; and the green vegetation along its banks contrasts finely with the brown sterility of the adjacent mountains. My sensations while travelling along its banks and in sight of its sparkling waters are something like those experienced in a stormy and wintry day, when comfortably seated in a warm library or parlor, with a view from the window of the violent strife and bitter frigidity of the elements without. The water and grass are our comfort, and our security for the realization of our hopes, in regard to our destination.

I experimented with the hook and line in the river again, but without success. Not even a nibble compensated my patient perseverance. Along the banks of the river there are myriads of diminutive toads, or frogs, about an inch in length, which, when disturbed, leap into the water, furnishing abundant food for all the fish in the stream. The bait on the hook, therefore, has no temptations for these well-fed gentry of the clear mountain torrent. Distance twenty-five miles.

AUGUST 23.—When I rose this morning, just after the dawn of day, I discovered that the dew-drops condensed upon an India-rubber cloth lying by my side were congealed, and that my buffalo-skins were hoary with frost. Ice as thick as window-glass had also formed upon the water left in our buckets. The dawn was glorious, and the sun, when it rose above the mountain peaks, shone with unusual splendor through the clear atmosphere.

AUGUST 24.—Soon after we crossed Truckee River this morning, and just as we were commencing the ascent of the mountain, several Indians made their appearance, about fifty yards from the trail. The leader and chief was an old man, with a deeply-furrowed face. I rode towards him, holding out my hand in token of friendship. He motioned me not to advance further, but to pass on and leave him, as he desired to have no communication with us. I insisted upon the reason of this unfriendly demonstration; assuring him, as well as I could by signs, that we desired to be at peace, and to do them no harm. His response was, if I understood it, that we, the whites, had slaughtered his men, taken his women and children into captivity, and driven him out of his country. I endeavored to assure him that we were not of those who had done him and his tribe these wrongs, and held out my hand a second time, and moved to approach him. With great energy of gesticulation, and the strongest signs of excited aversion and dread, he again motioned us not to come nearer to him, but to pass on and leave him. The other Indians, some six or eight in number, took no part in the dialogue, but were standing in a line, several yards from their chief, with their bows and arrows in their hands. Finding that it would be useless, perhaps dangerous, to press our friendship further, we continued our march. I have but little doubt that these Indians are the remnant of some tribe that has been wantonly destroyed in some of the bloody Indian slaughters which have occurred in California. Distance twenty miles.

AUGUST 26.—We did not leave our encampment until the sun, rising above the lofty mountains to the east, dispensed its warm and cheerful rays through the openings of the magnificent forest, by which we had been sheltered for the night. It is quite impossible to convey by language an adequate conception of the symmetrical beauty and stateliness of the forest trees surrounding the lake, and covering the sides of the adjacent mountains. A skilful artist with his pencil and his brush alone can do justice to this contrast of Alpine and Elysian scenery. The sublime altitude of the mountains, their granite and barren heads piercing the sky; the umbrageous foliage of the tall pines and cedars, deepening in verdure and density as the forest approaches the more gentle and grassy slopes along the banks of the lake, the limpid and tranquil surface of which *daguerreotypes* distinctly [capture] every object, from the moss-covered rocks laved by its waves to the bald and inaccessible summits of the Sierra—these scenic objects, with the fresh incense of the forest, and the fragrant odor of the wild rose, constituted a landscape that, from associations, melted the sensibilities, blunted as they were by long exposure and privation, and brought back to our memories the endearments of home and the pleasures of civilization.

Our progress during the entire day, owing to the obstructions in our route, has been slow. A little before 5:00 pm, after having labored up to the summit of the mountain, we commenced its descent again. I left our party here, riding on as rapidly as I could, or rather plunging down the steep side of the mountain, in order to find and select an encampment for the night. About a mile after I had reached the foot of the mountain, I found a small opening in the timber, with an easy access to the stream, but deficient in grass, and here, there being no better spot in view, I concluded to encamp for the night.

I had not remained long in this place before two or three of the pack-mules came rushing towards me, with their packs much disarranged, snorting with excitement, and smoking with perspiration. Others soon came following after them, in the same condition. Not being able to account for this singular excitement of the mules, after waiting a few moments, I started back to meet the party, and ascertain what had occurred since I left them to produce so much irregularity in our usual order of march. I met one of them near the foot of the mountain. In response to my inquiries, he said that in descending the mountain they had been attacked by a numerous swarm of yellow hornets. [The mules] became frantic with pain and uncontrollable; and with their rushing down the mountain and through timber and brush, in order to force their venomous assailants to leave them, some of their riders had been thrown, and the baggage had been so much scattered that considerable time had been required to recover it.

Returning to camp, and assisted by McClary, (no other member of the party volunteering,) we drove the mules across the stream, and after picketing them in the tall grass, and kindling a good fire from some dead logs of fallen timber for their protection, we bivouacked among them in the opening for the night. The timber surrounding the circular space which we occupied is very tall. The bright blaze of our fire defined indistinctly the columnar shapes of the pines and their overarching branches. Fancy soon pictured our residence for the night a spacious gothic temple, whose walls had mouldered away, leaving the pillars and the skeleton roof, through which the bright stars were twinkling, standing in defiance of the assaults of time and the fury of the elements. The temperature of the evening is delightful, and the sky serene and cloudless.

One of our party this morning picked up a human skull near the trail. Some unfortunate emigrant, probably, had been interred near the spot, and, being exhumed by the Indians or wolves, this was a portion of his skeleton. I saw large numbers of pheasants during our march to-day, and shot one with my pistol while riding along. Raspberries, and a small, bitter cherry, have been quite abundant in places. Distance twenty-five miles.

AUGUST 29.—The morning was clear and severely cold. The keen atmosphere, as soon as I threw off my blankets, just before daylight, produced an aguish sensation that I have not previously felt on the journey. The depth and consequent dampness of our encampment, probably, was one cause of this affection. Our physical exhaustion from incessant labor, and the want of adequate nourishment, was another.

Nuttall, a young gentleman of our mess, of fine intelligence and many interesting and amiable qualities of mind and heart, feeling, as we all did, the faintness, if not the pangs of hunger, insisted that if we would delay the commencement of our day's march a short time, he would prepare a soup from the rancid bacon-skins remaining in our provision-sack. In compliance with his request, the camp-kettle was placed on the fire, and the scraps placed in it, and in about fifteen minutes the soup was declared to be made. We gathered around it, with high expectations of a repast, under the circumstances, of great richness, and a high, if not a delicate flavor. But a single spoonful to each seemed to satisfy the desires of the whole party for this kind of food, if it did not their appetites. It produced a nausea that neither hunger nor philosophy could curb or resist.

We crossed, near the close of our day's march, one or two small valleys or bottoms timbered with evergreen oaks (*Quercus Ilex,*) giving them the appearance of old apple-orchards. The shape and foliage of this oak, previous to minute examination, presents an exact resemblance of the apple-tree. The channels of the water-courses running through these valleys were dry, and the grass parched and dead....We saw in a number of places ladders erected by the Indians, for climbing the pine-trees to gather the nuts, and the poles used for the same purpose. An Indian was seen, but he ran from us with great speed, disappearing behind the forest-trees. Some hares and a fox were started, and a hare was killed by one of the party.

AUGUST 30.— After traveling some three or four miles rising and descending a number of hills, from the summit of one more elevated than the others surrounding it, the spacious valley of the Sacramento suddenly burst upon my view, at an apparent distance of fifteen miles. A broad line of timber running through the centre of the valley indicated the course of the main river, and smaller and fainter lines on either side of this, winding through the brown and flat plain, marked the channels of its tributaries. I contemplated this most welcome scene with such emotions of pleasure as may be imagined by those who have ever crossed the desert plains and mountains of western America, until Jacob, who was in advance of the remainder of the party, came within the reach of my voice. I shouted to him that we were "out of the woods"—to pull off his hat and give three cheers, so loud that those in the rear could hear them. Very soon the huzzas of those behind were ringing and echoing through the hills, valleys, and forests, and the whole party came up with an exuberance of joy in their motions and depicted upon their countenances. It was a moment of cordial and heartfelt congratulations.

About one o'clock we discovered at the distance of half a mile a number of men, apparent twenty or thirty. Some of them were dressed in white shirts and pantaloons, with the Mexican sombrero, or broad-brim hat, others were nearly naked and resembled the Indians we had frequently seen on the eastern side of the Sierra. They had evidently discovered us before we saw them, for they seemed to be in great commotion, shouting and running in various directions.... We moved forward to the point (a small grove of oaks on a gentle elevation) where the most numerous body of the strange men were concentrated. We rode up to them, at the same time holding out our hands in token of friendship, a signal which they reciprocated immediately.

They were evidently very much rejoiced to find that we had no hostile designs upon them. With the exception of two half-breed Spaniards, they were Indians, and several of them conversed in Spanish, and were or had been the servants of settlers in the valley. One of the half-breeds, of a pleasing and intelligent countenance and good address, introduced us to their chief (*El Capitan*) and wished to know if we had not some tobacco to give him. I had a small quantity of tobacco, about half of which I gave to the chief, and distributed the residue among the party as far as it would go. I saw, however, that the chief divided his portion among those who received none. *El Capitan* was a man of about forty-five, of large frame and great apparent muscular power, but his countenance was heavy, dull, and melancholy, manifesting neither good humor nor intelligence. His long, coarse, and matted hair fell down upon his shoulders in a most neglected condition. A faded cotton handkerchief was tied around his head. I could see none of the ornaments of royalty upon him, but his clothing was much inferior to that of many of his party, who I presume had obtained theirs by laboring for the white settlers. Many of them were in a state of nudity.

We soon learned from them that they were a party engaged in gathering acorns, which to these poor Indians are what wheat and maize are to us. They showed us large quantities in their baskets under the trees. When dried and pulverized, the flour of the acorn is made into bread or mush, and is their "staff of life." It is their chief article of subsistence in this section of California. Their luxuries, such as bull-beef and horse-meat, they obtain by theft, or pay for in labor at exorbitant rates. The acorn of California, from the evergreen oak ... is much larger, more oily, and less bitter than on the Atlantic side of the continent. In fruitful seasons the ground beneath the trees is covered with the nuts, and the Indians have the providence, when the produce of the oak is thus plentiful, to provide against a short crop ... by laying up a supply greater than they will consume in one year.

We inquired the distance to the residence of Mr. Johnson. They made signs indicating that it was but a short distance.... Mr. Johnson was not at home, add the house was shut up. This we learned from a little Indian, the only human object we could find about the premises; he intimated by signs, however, that Mr. Johnson would return when the sun set.

We encamped under some trees in front of the house, resolved to do as well as we could, in our half-famished condition, until Mr. J. returned.

In the mean time we performed our ablutions in the creek, and having shed our much-worn clothing, we presented most of it to the naked Indian who acted as our guide. He was soon clad in a complete suit from head to feet, and strutted about with a most dandified and self-satisfied air. A small pocket looking-glass completed his happiness. He left us with a bundle of rags under his arms, nearly overjoyed at his good luck.

At sunset the dogs about the house began to bark most vociferously, and ran off over a gentle rise of ground to the north. Two men on horseback soon made their appearance on the rising ground, and, seeing us, rode to our camp. They were two Franco-Americans, originally from Canada or St. Louis, who had wandered to California in some trapping expedition, and had remained in the country.... From them we learned the gratifying intelligence that the whole of Upper California was in possession of the United States. Intelligence, they further stated, had been received that General Taylor, after having met and defeated the Mexican forces in four pitched battles, killing an incredible number, some forty or fifty thousand, had triumphantly marched into the city of Mexico. The last part of this news, of course, judging from the situation of General Taylor when we left the United States, (war not having then been declared,) was impossible; but sifting the news and comparing one statement with another, the result to our minds was that General T. had been eminently successful, defeating the Mexicans, whenever he had met them, with considerable slaughter. This, of course, produced much exultation and enthusiasm among us.

Mr. Johnson returned home about nine o'clock. He was originally a New

England sailor, and cast upon this remote coast by some of the vicissitudes common to those of his calling, had finally turned farmer or ranchero. He is a bachelor, with Indian servants, and stated that he had no food prepared for us, but such as was in the house was at our service. A pile of small cheeses, and numerous pans of milk with thick cream upon them, were exhibited on the table, and they disappeared with a rapidity dangerous to the health of those who consumed them.

On the 30th of January, after passing two or three deserted houses, we reached an inhabited rancho, situated at the extremity of a valley and near a narrow gorge in the hills, about four o'clock, and our jaded animals performing duty with reluctance, we determined to halt for the night, if the prospect of obtaining any thing to eat (of which we stood in much need) was flattering. Riding up to the house, a small adobe, with one room, and a shed for a kitchen, the *ranchero* and the *ranchera* came out and greeted us with a hearty "*Buenos tardes Señores, paisanos, amigos,*" shaking hands, and inviting us at the same time to alight and remain for the night, which invitation we accepted. The kind-hearted *ranchera* immediately set about preparing supper for us.... The meal consisted of *tortillas*, stewed jerked-beef, with *chile* seasoning, milk, and *quesadillas*, or cheesecakes, green and tough as leather. However, our appetites were excellent, and we enjoyed the repast with a high relish.

Our host and hostess were very inquisitive in regard to the news from below, and as to what would be the effects of the conquest of the country by the Americans. The man stated that he and all his family had refused to join in the late insurrection. We told them that all was peaceable now; that there would be no more wars in California; that we were all Americans, all Californians—*hermanos, hermanas, amigos*. They expressed their delight at this information by numerous exclamations.

We asked the woman how much the dress which she wore, a miserable calico, cost her? She answered, "*Seis pesos,*" (six dollars). When we told her that in a short time, under the American government, she could purchase as good a one "*por un peso,*" she threw up her hands in astonishment, expressing by her features at the same time the most unbounded delight. Her entire wardrobe was soon brought forth, and the price paid for every article named. She then inquired what would be the cost of similar clothing under the American government, which we told her. As we replied, exclamation followed upon exclamation, expressive of her surprise and pleasure, and the whole was concluded with "*Viva los Americanos—viva los*

Americanos!" I wore a large coarse woollen pea-jacket, which the man was very desirous to obtain, offering for it a fine horse. I declined the trade.

In the evening several of the brothers, sisters, and brothers and sisters-in-law of the family collected, and the guitar and violin, which were suspended from a beam in the house, were taken down, and we were entertained by a concert of instrumental and vocal music. Most of the tunes were such as are performed at fandangos. Some plaintive airs were played and sung with much pathos and expression, the whole party joining in the choruses. Although invited to occupy the only room in the house, we declined it, and spread our blankets on the outside.

The next morning (January 31st) when we woke the sun was shining bright and warm, and the birds were singing gayly in the grove of evergreen oaks near the house. Having made ready to resume our journey, as delicately as possible we offered our kind hostess compensation for the trouble we had given her, which she declined, saying that although they were not rich, they nevertheless had enough and to spare. We however insisted, and she finally accepted, with the condition that we would also accept of some of her *quesadillas* and *tortillas* to carry along with us. The *ranchero* mounted his horse and rode with us three or four miles, to place us on the right trail, when, after inviting us very earnestly to call and see him again, and bidding us an affectionate *adios*, he galloped away.

Wherever the Anglo-Saxon race plant themselves, progress is certain to be displayed in some form or other. Such is their "go-ahead" energy, that things cannot stand still where they are, whatever may be the circumstances surrounding them. Notwithstanding the wars and insurrections, I found the town of San Francisco, on my arrival here, visibly improved. An American population had flowed into it; lots, which heretofore have been considered almost valueless, were selling at high prices; new houses had been built, and were in progress; new commercial houses had been established; hotels had been opened for the accommodation of the traveling and business public; and the publication of a newspaper had been commenced. The little village of two hundred souls, when I arrived here in September last, is fast becoming a town of importance. Ships freighted with full cargoes are entering the port, and landing their merchandise to be disposed of at wholesale and retail on shore, instead of the former mode of vending them afloat in the harbor. There is a prevailing air of activity, enterprise, and energy; and men, in view of the advantageous position of the town for commerce, are making large calculations upon the future; calculations which I believe will be fully realized.

45

Marshall's Own Account of the Gold Discovery

James W. Marshall

James W. Marshall (1810–1885), born in New Jersey, traversed the Oregon Trail by wagon train in 1844. After serving in the Bear Flag Revolt, Marshall agreed to build a small sawmill at Coloma for Swiss rancher John Sutter. On January 24, 1848, Marshall found a few small nuggets of gold in a river bed—a discovery that had momentous effects on Marshall and indeed the world. During the gold rush, he was hounded by miners as a celebrity and a good luck charm; in later years he drank heavily, perhaps to escape his fame. He died bitter and impoverished in Coloma in 1885, not far from his famous discovery site. This account of the gold discovery, one of several given by Marshall, was allegedly the first.

In May, 1847, with my rifle, blanket, and a few crackers to eat with the venison (for the deer then were awful plenty), I ascended the American River, according to Mr. Sutter's wish, as he wanted to find a good site for a saw-mill, where we could have plenty of timber, and where wagons would be able to ascend and descend the river hills. Many fellows had been out before me, but they could not find any place to suit; so when I left I told Mr. Sutter I would go along the river to its very head and find the place, if such a place existed anywhere upon the river or any of its forks. I traveled along the river the whole way. Many places would suit very well for the erection of the mill, with plenty of timber everywhere, but then nothing but a mule could climb the hills; and when I would find a spot where the hills were not steep, there was no timber to be had; and so it was until I had been out several days and reached this place, which, after first sight, looked like the exact spot we were hunting.

You may be sure Mr. Sutter was pleased when I reported my success. We entered into partnership; I was to build the mill, and he was to find provisions, teams, tools, and to pay a portion of the men's wages. I believe I was at that time the only millwright in the whole country. In August, everything being ready, we freighted two wagons with tools and provisions, and accompanied by six men I left the fort, and after a good deal of difficulty reached this place

Sutter's Mill, after being converted into living quarters, c. 1850

one beautiful afternoon and formed our camp on yon little rise of ground right above the town.

Our first business was to put up log houses, as we intended remaining here all winter. This was done in less than no time, for my men were great with the ax. We then cut timber, and fell to work hewing it for the framework of the mill. The Indians gathered about us in great numbers. I employed about forty of them to assist us with the dam, which we put up in a kind of way in about four weeks.... I left for the fort [after] giving orders to Mr. Weimar to have a ditch cut through the bar in the rear of the mill, and after quitting work in the evening to raise the gate and let the water run all night, as it would assist us very much in deepening and widening the tail-race.

I returned in a few days, and found everything favorable, all the men being at work in the ditch. When the channel was opened it was my custom every evening to raise the gate and let the water wash out as much sand and gravel through the night as possible; and in the morning, while the men were getting breakfast, I would walk down, and, shutting off the water, look along the race and see what was to be done, so that I might tell Mr. Weimar, who had charge of the Indians, at what particular point to set them to work for the day. As I was the only millwright present, all of my time was employed upon the framework and machinery.

One morning in January—it was a clear, cold morning; I shall never forget that morning—as I was taking my usual walk along the race after shutting off the water, my eye was caught with the glimpse of something shining in the bottom of the ditch. There was about a foot of water running then. I reached my hand down and picked it up; it made my heart thump, for I was certain it was gold. The piece was about half the size and of the shape of a pea. Then I saw another piece in the water. After taking it out I sat down and began to think right hard. I thought it was gold, and yet it did not seem to be of the right color: all the gold coin I had seen was of a reddish tinge; this looked more like brass. I recalled to mind all the metals I had ever seen or heard of, but I could find none that resembled this.

Suddenly the idea flashed across my mind that it might be iron pyrites. I trembled to think of it! This question could soon be determined. Putting one of the pieces on a hard river stone, I took another and commenced hammering it. It was soft, and didn't break: it therefore must be gold, but largely mixed with some other metal, very likely silver; for pure gold, I thought, would certainly have a brighter color.

When I returned to our cabin for breakfast I showed the two pieces to my men. They were all a good deal excited, and had they not thought that the gold only existed in small quantities they would have abandoned everything and left me to finish my job alone. However, to satisfy them, I told them that as soon as we had the mill finished we would devote a week or two to gold hunting and see what we could make out of it.

While we were working in the race after this discovery we always kept a sharp lookout, and in the course of three or four days we had picked up about three ounces—our work still progressing as lively as ever, for none of us imagined at that time that the whole country was sowed with gold.

In about a week's time after the discovery I had to take another trip to the fort; and, to gain what information I could respecting the real value of the metal, took all that we had collected with me and showed it to Mr. Sutter, who at once declared it was gold, but thought with me that it was greatly mixed with some other metal. It puzzled us a good deal to hit upon the means of telling the exact quantity of gold contained in the alloy; however, we at last stumbled on an old American encyclopedia, where we saw the specific gravity of all the metals, and rules given to find the quantity of each in a given bulk.

After hunting over the whole fort and borrowing from some of the men, we got three dollars and a half in silver, and with a small pair of scales we soon ciphered it out that there was no silver nor copper in the gold, but that it was entirely pure.

This fact being ascertained, we thought it our best policy to keep it as quiet as possible till we should have finished our mill. But there was a great number of disbanded Mormon soldiers in and about the fort, and when they came to hear of it, why it just spread like wildfire, and soon the whole country was in a bustle. I had scarcely arrived at the mill again till several persons appeared with pans, shovels, and hoes, and those that had not iron picks had wooden ones, all anxious to fall to work and dig up our mill; but this we would not permit. As fast as one party disappeared another would arrive, and sometimes I had the greatest kind of trouble to get rid of them. I sent them all off in different directions, telling them about such and such places, where I was certain there was plenty of gold if they would only take the trouble of looking for it. At that time I never imagined that the gold was so abundant. I told them to go to such and such places, because it appeared that they would dig nowhere but in such places as I pointed out, and I believe such was their confidence in me that they would have dug on the very top of yon mountain if I had told them to do so.

The second place where gold was discovered was in a gulch near the Mountaineer House, on the road to Sacramento. The third place was on a bar on the South Fork of the American River a little above the junction of the Middle and South forks. The diggings at Hangtown [now Placerville] were discovered next by myself, for we all went out for a while as soon as our job was finished. The Indians next discovered the diggings at Kelsey's and thus in a very short time we discovered that the whole country was but one bed of gold. So there, stranger, is the entire history of the gold discovery in California—a discovery that hasn't as yet been of much benefit to me.

THE DISCOVERY OF GOLD
IN CALIFORNIA

JOHN SUTTER

John Augustus Sutter (1803–1880), the "Father of California," was born Johann August Sutter in Germany and was raised in Switzerland. In 1834 he left behind mounting debts and a young family and moved to New York. From there he spent time in St. Louis, Santa Fe, Oregon, and Hawaii before arriving in San Francisco in 1839. He acquired an enormous land grant at the junction of the Sacramento and American rivers from Governor Alvarado. There Sutter built a fort with wheat fields, cattle and sheep ranches, orchards, and vineyards worked by Native American, Hawaiian, and Mexican servants. Sutter was famously hospitable to American emigrant parties, frequently helping them cross the Sierra, giving them work, and selling them cheap land.

The gold found at Sutter's sawmill ultimately destroyed him. His workers deserted their posts and squatters overran his properties. Alcohol abuse and bankruptcy followed. The man who, more than any other person, developed and promoted California's agricultural and mineral wealth died destitute in a Pennsylvania hotel room after repeated failures to convince Congress to redress his losses. His version of the gold discovery appeared in Hutchings' California Magazine *in 1857.*

IT WAS A RAINY AFTERNOON when Mr. Marshall arrived at my office in the Fort, very wet. I was somewhat surprised to see him, as he was down a few days previous; and when I sent up to Coloma a number of teams with provisions, mill irons, etc., etc. He told me then that he had some important and interesting news which he wished to communicate secretly to me, and wished me to go with him to a place where we should not be disturbed, and where no listeners could come and hear what we had to say. I went with him to my private rooms; he requested me to lock the door; I complied, but I told him at the same time that nobody was in the house except the clerk, who was in his office in a different part of the house; after requesting of me something which he wanted, which my servants brought and then left the room, I forgot to lock the door, and it happened that the door was opened by the clerk just at the moment when Marshall took a rag from his pocket, showing me the yellow metal: he had about two ounces of it; but how quick Mr. M. put the yellow metal in his pocket again can hardly be described. The clerk came to see me on business, and excused himself for interrupting me and as soon as he had left I was told, "now lock the doors; didn't I tell you that we might have listeners?" I told him that he need fear nothing about that, as it was not the habit of this gentleman; but I could hardly convince him that he need not to be suspicious. Then Mr. M. began to show me this metal, which consisted of small pieces and specimens, some of them worth a few dollars; he told me that he had expressed his opinion to the laborers at the mill that this might be gold; but some of them were laughing at him and called him a crazy man, and could not believe such a thing.

After having proved the metal with aqua fortis, which I found in my apothecary shop, likewise with other experiments, and read the long article "gold" in the *Encyclopedia Americana*, I declared this to be gold of the finest quality, of at least twenty-three carats. After this Mr. M. had no more rest nor patience, and wanted me to start with him immediately for Coloma; but I told him I could not leave, as it was late in the evening and nearly supper time, and that it would be better for him to remain with me till the next morning, and I would travel with him, but this would not do: he asked me only "will you come to-morrow morning?" I told him yes, and off he started for Coloma in the heaviest rain, although already very wet, taking nothing to eat. I took this news very easy, like all other occurrences good or bad, but thought a great deal during the night about the consequences which might follow such a discovery. I gave all my necessary orders to my numerous laborers, and left the next morning at seven o'clock, accompanied by an Indian soldier, and vaquero, in a heavy rain, for Coloma.

The next day I went with Mr. M. on a prospecting tour in the vicinity of Coloma, and the following morning I left for Sacramento. Before my departure I had a conversation with all hands: I told them that I would consider it as a great favor if they would keep this discovery secret only for six weeks, so that I could finish my large flour mill at Brighton, (with four run of stones,) which had cost me already about from 24,000–25,000 dollars—the people up there promised to keep it secret so long. On my way home, instead of feeling happy and contented, I was very unhappy, and could not see that it would benefit me much, and I was perfectly right in thinking so; as it came just precisely as I expected. I thought at the same time that it could hardly be kept secret for six weeks; and in this I was not mistaken, for about two weeks later, after my return, I sent up several teams in charge of a white man, as the teamsters were Indian boys. This man was acquainted with all hands up there, and Mrs. Wimmer told him the whole secret; likewise the young sons of Mr. Wimmer told him that they had gold, and that they would let him have some too; and so he obtained a few dollars' worth of it as a present. As soon as this man arrived at the fort he went to a small store in one of my outside buildings, kept by Mr. Smith, a partner of Samuel Brannan, and asked for a bottle of brandy, for which he would pay the cash; after having the bottle he paid with these small pieces of gold. Smith was astonished and asked him if he intended to insult him; the teamster told him to go and ask me about it; Smith came in, in great haste, to see me, and I told him at once the truth—what could I do? I had to tell him about it.

So soon as the secret was out my laborers began to leave me, in small parties first, but then all left, from the clerk to the cook, and I was in great distress; only a few mechanics remained to finish some very necessary work which they had commenced, and about eight invalids, who continued slowly to work a few teams, to scrape out the mill race at Brighton. The Mormons did not like to leave my mill unfinished, but they got the gold fever like everybody else.

Then the people commenced rushing up from San Francisco and other parts of California, in May, 1848: in the former village only five men were left to take care of the women and children. The single men locked their doors and left for "Sutter's Fort," and from there to the Eldorado. For some time the people in Monterey and farther south would not believe the news of the gold discovery, and said that it was only a *"Ruse de Guerre"* of Sutter's, because he wanted to have neighbors in his wilderness. From this time on I got only too many neighbors, and some very bad ones among them.

It is very singular that the Indians never found a piece of gold and brought it to me, as they very often did other specimens found in the ravines. I requested them continually to bring me some curiosities from the mountains, for which I always recompensed them. I have received animals, birds, plants, young trees, wild fruits, pipe clay, stones, red ochre, etc., etc., but never a piece of gold.

By this sudden discovery of the gold, all my great plans were destroyed. Had I succeeded with my mills and manufactories for a few years before the gold was discovered, I should have been the richest citizen on the Pacific shore; but it had to be different. Instead of being rich, I am ruined.

GETTING THERE

Ho for California was the rallying cry throughout the civilized world.... Not since the days of
the Crusades has such an uprising taken place.
—George D. Dornin

The farmer left his plough in the furrow, the
schoolmaster abandoned his books and blackboards, the sailor deserted his ship, the barber flung
down his razor, and the tailor his shears. Even the
lover relinquished the hand of his sweetheart to
clutch the pick and shovel and rush forth in search
of the longed-after metal.
—Mariano Guadalupe Vallejo

"The Way They Go to California" 1849, by Nathaniel Currier

"The Way They Come from California," 1849, by Nathaniel Currier

from To the Golden Shore

PETER BROWNING, EDITOR

News of Marshall's gold discovery did not appear in an eastern newspaper until August 19, 1848—more than six months after the fact. Early reports were wildly exaggerated, and the public was understandably skeptical. It wasn't until December, that President Polk, in an annual message to the American people, officially confirmed that Californian gold was very real. The following articles and advertisements appeared in the New York Herald in early 1849 and were republished by Peter Browning in 1995.

The Rush to California
Incidents on the Increase—Scenes in New York

JANUARY 22, 1849. We will endeavor to give some idea of the revolution that is going on in our midst, caused by the thirst after gold. It is an epidemic, and now rages with a violence that threatens to depopulate New York.

In January, 1849, the city is divided into three great divisions: First, Those who are decided to go to California. Second, Those who have not decided to go, but will leave as soon as they can raise the wind. Third, Those who cannot leave under any circumstances.

In order to give a faithful and correct history of the events connected with this extraordinary state of things, and to impress the community with the magnitude and importance of the epoch, it will be necessary to preface it with an account of the great outpourings of a people from one land to another— from one section to another section of country. The first on record is related by Moses, who gave a very faithful account of the original sort of a California movement among the ancestors of our Chatham street people. They made a move "from Egypt into a land—good land and large—unto a land flowing with milk and honey; unto the place of the Hittites, the Amonites, and the Perizites, and the Hivites, and the Jebusites." The first exodus resembled in many respects the present California exodus. God commended the original emigrators, "Ye shall not go empty; but every one shall borrow of his neighbor," &c. Judging from the proceedings in the courts of law here, to arrest absconding debtors, &c., our goers have been doing it without any command.

"California News," 1850, by William S. Mount

Moses gives a very graphic account of the trouble he and his party had before they got out of Egypt, and tells the whole story with great simplicity, and no doubt truthfulness, about the water, the frogs, the flies, the cattle, the biles, and every man borrowing of his neighbor—"the battened unleavened cakes," and victuals and provisions in general, which they took along with them, as also Joseph's bones, which they dug up, and the general confusion and mixed up mess before they all got off; or, to use the words of Moses, before the Lord "led the people about through the way of the wilderness and the Red Sea, and they went up harnessed out of the land Egypt." There are equally interesting details which can be minutely described in this modern exodus to California—the chartering of ships and brigs, the squads about the corners down in Wall Street, at the Custom House; the financial arrangements, the renting of houses, sales of real estate, duping and victimizing, right and left, borrowing money, overcoats, pantaloons, old boots, cast off stockings, coal scuttles, sifters, and shovels, and iron utensils of all kinds. The burning bush, the serpent and rod, could not have astonished Moses and his friends more than the official documents of President Polk astonished this entire community.

Preparations were at once commenced to cross the sea, go to California, and upset and drive out the modern "Hittites, Amonites, and Hivites"—the Mexicans, Mormons, and Indians. There was a general ignorance in the community as to the whereabouts of this new region. Geography has never been a favorite study with the democracy. They know where the democratic headquarters are held in every ward, and there was a general rush to those places to compare notes and get information.

Previous to this, large parties, amounting, it has been supposed, to several hundreds, from the number found suddenly missed, had started off of the sly, to be first in the gold field. Some put across Jersey, others followed the Harlem Railroad track; and letters have been received from various parts of the eastern and middle States, from individuals wandering about the country inquiring at every farm house on the road "the distance to California?" The counting rooms of all our shipping merchants were crowded with new faces, anxious to get a passage somewhere. They rushed down town from the upper wards, hopping and jumping over cotton bales and sugar boxes, worse than ever the frogs in Egypt did.

ADVERTISEMENTS (MARCH 2, 1849)

PISTOL BELTS FOR CALIFORNIA, AT REDUCED PRICES. The subscriber has on hand, and is constantly manufacturing, all kinds of Pistol Belts, Holsters, Knapsacks, Knife Sheaths, Gun Slings, Bullet Pouches, &c. &c., which he is selling at reduced prices. Companies and dealers in the above articles supplied on the most liberal terms. Also for sale, all kinds of military goods. Joseph T. Bell, 185 Fulton Street, opposite Church.

CALIFORNIA. SINGER'S PATENT DRILLING MACHINE for mining purposes. Houses of iron or wood, galvanized iron and copper Boats, Gold Washers of various patterns, deep-water shovels, Cooking Apparatus, Quicksilver Retorts, &c. Manufactured and for sale by Shepard & Co., 242 Water Street.

FOR SAN FRANCISCO—RARE OPPORTUNITY. The *Rising Sun* is nearly full, and will sail in a day or two. This is a new and very fast sailing clipper built bark, and is likely to overhaul and pass most of the heavy freighted ships which have preceded her. The Rising Sun Company consists of sixty members. Five shares may yet be had if applied for immediately. Three airy and commodious staterooms, for families and single passengers, may also be secured. Competent geologists and mineralogists, under the instructions and advice of Prof. Silliman and of Prof. J. D. Dana, of the United States Exploring Expedition, are connected with the company, and will precede it overland. For further particulars apply to Isaac T. Smith, 101 Wall Street, corner of Front street.

"Mr. Golightly Bound for California," 1849

"Moze, Lize, and Little Moze Going to California," c. 1849

from THIRTY YEARS AGO

GEORGE D. DORNIN

George D. Dornin (1830–1907) arrived in California in 1849 intending to seek his fortune in the burgeoning metropolis of San Francisco rather than the mines. A list of his occupations over the next six decades illustrates the diversity of California's growing economy: he found work as a launderer, sign painter, baker, wallpaper hanger, restaurateur, jewelry store owner, merchant, daguerreotype artist, express agent, telegraph operator, bookkeeper, stage line owner, politician, and insurance agent. In 1879, Dornin recreated his 186-day sea voyage around Cape Horn for his children in Thirty Years Ago.

THE FIRST REPORTS concerning the discovery of Gold, which I can remember, reached me in October or November, 1848. I was then a lad, approaching my eighteenth year, having been born in the City of New York on the 30th day of December, 1830.... The rumors of the gold discoveries received confirmation in the official report of the Acting and Military Governor, General Mason, to the Secretary of War, and the Gold Fever immediately became epidemic.

"Ho, for California!" was the rallying cry throughout the civilized world, inviting the enterprising, the adventurer, whatever might be his condition; the uprising was as if by magic; wherever, and as rapidly as, the news spread, men turned and joined the Great Migration toward the Golden State. Not since the days of the Crusades has such an uprising taken place, and like the Crusaders, the pilgrims were (with rare exceptions) men—young men, or under the middle age.

The newspapers were crowded with advertisements of California Outfits, California Hats, and California Pistols. Companies for mining and trading were formed, with elaborate laws and rules, and equipped with tents, provisions, and machinery for extracting the gold; these, I may here say, by way of parenthesis, were generally disbanded on or before their arrival in California, and the gold-washing machinery, which was rarely of practical use, was strewn along the beach in San Francisco Bay.

My impatience to be off grew as winter approached, every day's delay seeming precious time wasted. Of the several routes, that by way of Cape

Horn was finally settled upon, and through the kind of offices of my uncle, the means were advanced to pay for my passage and outfit.

My "outfit" consisted of several suits of heavy and coarse clothing, including three pairs of "stogy" boots, which, in consideration of that fact that I was yet a "growing" boy, were of graduated sizes; these, with sundry tarpaulin hats, salt-water soap, and many knick-knacks and conveniences which kind friends provided, were packed in a seamen's chest, which during the long voyage also served as my seat at the table.

It was thought prudent to provide [for] the possibilities of famine, and several barrels of mess-beef, pork, and ship biscuit were purchased and shipped on a vessel to follow the *Panama*.

For protection against the wild Indians and wilder Spaniards, with which imagination peopled the land, I provided myself with an "Arsenal" consisting of a double-barreled gun (cost $8) with rifled and smooth bore; an Allen's revolver of pepper-box pattern, and a bowie knife of formidable dimensions.

The former weapons served a useful purpose by employing my time on board ship—cleaning and oiling. The revolver was thrown away, soon after my arrival in California, as being more dangerous to the shooter than to the shot-at; the gun, which, through lack of taste for firearms, I had discharged a few times only, provided me with some ready money, when hard-up a few days after I landed, finding sale at $35. The bowie knife, alas, was reduced to the ignoble service of carving my meat.

I must not omit to mention as among my outfit a small library of selected books for reading on the voyage; a stoutly bound blank book for my "Log" or Journal, in which, by special understanding with my good cousin Avis, who entered enthusiastically into all my plans and aspirations, every day's events, whether trivial or otherwise, was carefully and faithfully written down; plenty of paper and pens, for I promised to be and was for several years a faithful correspondent; a Bible, presented to me by my grand-mother on my thirteenth birthday, on the fly-leaf of which I now read: "Ship *Panama* at sea, Sunday, Feb. 11, 1849; commenced with the intention of reading regularly until I read it through," but which the ear-marks make evident that the resolution did not carry me beyond "Exodus"; and my mother's daguerreotype, over which I cried often and bitterly, when suffering from that most distressing of all heart-diseases, "home-sickness."

At nine o'clock of that day [February 3rd] ... passengers and their friends crowded the decks and the wharf; and, as the lines were cast off and the ship moved slowly from the wharf, the former gathered in the rigging, and lustily joined in the then popular refrain, to the tune of "Oh, Susannah!"

"Off for California," c. 1849

Ho, for California! that's the land for me,
I'm bound for the Sacramento
With my wash-bowl on my knee.

As the ship passed rapidly toward Sandy Hook, I sat upon the taffrail watching the receding city until, with the setting sun glistening the cross of Trinity Church, as it sank below the horizon, I saw the last of my boyhood's home, and thought how long in the future seemed then *three years* which must intervene before I should return to it; that the time would be longer, did not then seem possible.

If I remember rightly, there were, all told, including officers and crew, 220 souls on board. Of these, four were women; the Captain and First Mate had each their wives, and there were two lady passengers, a Mrs. Leavett, accompanying her husband, and a Mrs. M. E. Longley, a widow of thirty-eight or forty years. All these occupied state-rooms in the house on deck, eating at the Captain's table. The rest of the passengers were young men, with very few exceptions, under thirty years of age; for their accommodation, the space "between decks" from stem to stern was fitted up, through the entire length on each side, with wide bunks one above the other, each capable of holding

61

two persons with tolerable comfort....Whale oil lamps (these were days before petroleum and coal oil were discovered) here and there suspended from the ceiling shed a dim, uncertain light during the night, or when the hatches were closed and battened down off the stormy Cape.

One of the rules of the Association made it necessary to select our berths by lot, so it happened that a Mr. Martin became my berth-mate; this gentleman was about ten years my elder; an Artist and a Bohemian, a *bon-vivant,* whose sea-chest was filled with choice cigars and liquors, which rendered the neighborhood of his berth a favorite resort for the "good fellows" on board. I remember well a small keg, which occupied a central portion of the chest, with a flexible rubber syphon attachment to draw out the contents; my firm temperance principles prevented me from participating in it, nor was I ever fully in sympathy with the games of cards, which seemed of interminable length, during the days and nights when stormy weather kept all hands below deck.

By Monday (third day out) we ran into the gulf stream, where the uneasy cross-seas brought the landsmen to a full realization of the nature of sea-sickness. I will not attempt a description of it, but I remember well the utter disregard of life or care for the future, as I lay upon the deck or reached limply over the side "paying tribute to Neptune." Remembering the advice of good, old Captain Coffin, I had, as soon as the first qualmish feeling manifested itself, obtained some warm water from the ocean, and drinking copiously of this, not only aggravated the retching but hastened the reaction and cure.

Two days after, I had materially recovered, and could enjoy my meals with tolerable comfort; many, however, were for several days afterward still under its influence, and one elderly gentleman did not fully recover as long as we were at sea.

We soon ran into warmer latitudes, and as we neared and passed the Equator, the constellations of the Southern Hemisphere, new to Northern eyes, came into view; conspicuous among them, being the Southern Cross, the mysterious Clouds of Magellan, etc.

Reading, writing, the inevitable card playing, lounging about the decks in fair weather, cleaning and repairing guns and pistols, occupied the time.

Early in April we began to get a foretaste of Cape Horn by much rough weather, and when the sailors sent down the topmasts, and otherwise put the ship in condition to encounter the storms which continually hold high carnival around the Icy Cape, there was a very decided longing for terra-firma in the minds of many who were making their first sea voyage.

At length we cleared Cape Victory at the entrance of the Straits of Magellan, on the Pacific, and had thus actually "doubled the Cape." Among the amuse-

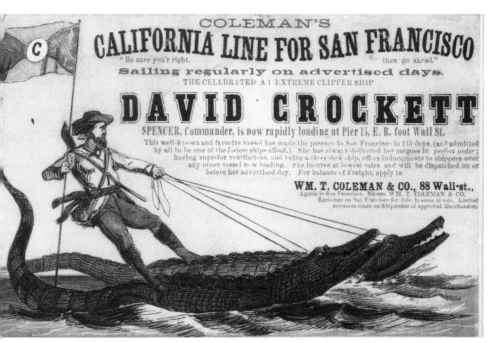

Clipper ship advertisement, 1849

ments, during the weather which permitted us to remain on deck, was "fishing" for Albatross; this was done by baiting a shark hook with a piece of pork, and this being fastened to a bit of wood, was towed astern by a strong rope; the bird seeing it, was caught in his hooked bill, which his efforts to escape only caused to cling tighter to the hook, and he was drawn on board. They are of beautiful plumage, perfectly white, and exceedingly graceful as they rest upon the water, but awkward and unsteady when placed on deck, from which they cannot arise without assistance. One that I caught in this manner measured ten feet six inches from tip to tip of his wings when spread.

With warmer weather came renewed spirits; we were now on the "home stretch," and every day's sailing took us nearer our goal, and we should speedily know for ourselves, if these things were so; if our long voyage was to end in disappointment, or if the news which had impelled us was indeed true. Plans for future guidance in California were discussed, partnerships formed—all based upon actual mining operations; the deck in fair weather was transformed into a workshop, where gold-rockers, tents, etc., were made.

On the fifteenth day of May (our 101st day out) we heard the cheering sound of "Land Ho!" which brought every one on deck. Far away on the horizon appeared what to me seemed a low bank of clouds, but which the Captain said was the Island of Mocha; we kept along the coast [of Chili] until the eighteenth day of May, when we made the Island of Santa Maria. At this juncture an accident occurred, which came near ending me and my aspirations altogether.

I have already mentioned that every Californian had furnished himself with an outfit of guns and pistols, and that cleaning these furnished much relief from the monotony of the voyage; in preparation for use on shore, these were now brought out, cleaned, and discharged, the seagulls and other aquatic birds furnishing fair targets; a friend had prepared to discharge his gun at a distant gull, and I was seated near by watching intently to see the effect of the shot; suddenly a blinding discharge and a stinging blow toppled me from my seat, and for a few hours I was unconscious. When I recovered, I found myself in the cabin, with the surgeon probing a wound in my left temple; the gun had bursted at the breech, and the nipple had struck me sufficiently near the temple to leave a most uncomfortable wound, with no permanent effects, however, except to leave a scar.

And now we began to look anxiously for the end of our voyage. Over five months had passed since we set sail, and we began to make calculations as to the probable day when we should set our feet in California. The long confinement and indifferent food had become irksome, and great efforts were required to prevent petty bickerings and quarreling; old arrangements were broken up; new partnerships were formed, and new plans for mining and trading enterprises were entered into. As for myself, the future, and my own plans in connection with it, were very indefinite. The "mines" were, of course, the objective point, but where they were, or how mining was prosecuted, I do not think I had formed an idea. I can only recall now a determination to do my best with whatever came to hand. In this spirit we approached the latitude of San Francisco and began to get indications of the land, a principal one being the prevalence of heavy fogs, which then, as now, hung along the coast during July and August.

For a few days before we reached the entrance to the harbor, a sharp look-out had to be kept up, not only for the breakers, but for other vessels. I remember that early in the evening of the seventh of August, as I sat on the taffrail at the stern of the vessel, peering out into the fog, there suddenly loomed up a dark and shadowy object of immense size, magnified, perhaps, by the fog and indistinctness. She passed quickly across our stern and disappeared almost as suddenly as she had appeared; neither ship hailed the other, but from the glimpse we got of her build, we thought it was the British ship which the next day hailed us for information as to our reckoning, and for which we acted as pilot, as she followed closely in our wake into the harbor.

Creeping slowly along through the fog, which occasionally lifted or became thin, we first made land, as I now remember it, at Helmet Rock, so called from its shape. Thus getting our bearings we passed rapidly eastward through the Golden Gate; as we entered, the fog entirely lifted and the sun shone out brightly, giving us a cheering welcome. On our left the brown hills back of Saucelito were dotted with cattle; on our right we noticed an earthwork fortification, with dismantled guns pointing towards the channel. Followed closely by the British ship referred to, with flags flying and the band playing, we passed up the channel, rounded Clark's Point, and at about six o'clock on the afternoon of the *eighth day of August,* 1849, cast anchor opposite the cove, on the slopes of which were located the tents and shanties then constituting the infant City of San Francisco.

Every man was on deck and straining his eyes to gather in the strange scenes before him. Nearly every man was in his "uniform" of red shirt, and this, with our Band, making us conspicuous among the many vessels which daily dropped anchor from all parts of the world, attracting a number of small boats; in the leading one some of our passengers recognized an old acquaintance—"Commodore" Robert Martin—and this colloquy ensued, which, being the first interchange of salutations between ship and shore, became fixed in my memory:

"Hallo, Bob! What's the news?"

"Plenty of gold, but hard to get!"

And thus were the reports confirmed to us. The men from the boats soon came on board, and speedily formed the nuclei of eager passengers, hungry for information concerning the city, the mines, and the news from "the States," for it will be remembered that one hundred and eighty-six days had passed since we had heard a word of what had transpired in the world at large.... Of California news, I can only remember how I drank in, open-mouthed, all that they said, so much of which sounded like romance; my head whirled and my brain tired in the effort to grasp it all; there was no sleep for me, but I sat on the taffrail, watching the glimmer of the lights as they shone through the many tents of which the city was then largely made up. Toward midnight, those of our passengers who had gone ashore returned in the ship's boats, and these were obliged to tell again and again of the strange scenes they had encountered in their visit.

from EL DORADO

BAYARD TAYLOR

Bayard Taylor (1825–1878), a young editor for Horace Greeley's New York Tribune *who already had a travel guidebook to Europe under his belt, was sent to California in 1849 to appraise the situation for Greeley's east coast readers. Taylor, perhaps the most accomplished writer to experience the gold rush firsthand, sent back frequent letters describing everything from the boredom of his grueling sea voyages to details of the latest mining techniques. Later in life, Taylor went on to write travel guides to Africa, India, China, Russia, and Egypt, but his gold rush sketches, published as* El Dorado *in 1850, remain his best-known work. This excerpt recounts his trek across the Isthmus of Panama in 1849.*

I LEFT THE FALCON at daybreak in the ship's boat. We rounded the high bluff on which the castle stands and found beyond it a shallow little bay, on the eastern side of which, on low ground, stand the cane huts of Chagres. Piling up our luggage on the shore, each one set about searching for the canoes which had been engaged the night previous, but, without a single exception, the natives were not to be found, or when found, had broken their bargains. Everybody ran hither and thither in great excitement, anxious to be off before everybody else, and hurrying the naked boatmen, all to no purpose. The canoes were beached on the mud, and their owners engaged in re-thatching their covers with split leaves of the palm. The doors of the huts were filled with men and women, each in a single cotton garment, composedly smoking their cigars, while numbers of children, in Nature's own clothing, tumbled about in the sun. Having started without breakfast, I went to the "Crescent City" Hotel, a hut with a floor to it, but could get nothing. Some of my friends had fared better at one of the native huts, and I sat down to the remains of their meal, which was spread on a hen-coop beside the door. The pigs of the vicinity and several lean dogs surrounded me to offer their services, but maintained a respectful silence, which is more than could be said of pigs at home. Some pieces of pork fat, with fresh bread and a draught of sweet spring water from a coco shell, made me a delicious repast.

A returning Californian had just reached the place, with a box containing

$22,000 in gold dust, and a four-pound lump in one hand. The impatience and excitement of the passengers, already at a high pitch, was greatly increased by his appearance. Life and death were small matters compared with immediate departure from Chagres. Men ran up and down the beach, shouting, gesticulating, and getting feverishly impatient at the deliberate habits of the natives; as if their arrival in California would thereby be at all hastened. The boatmen, knowing very well that two more steamers were due the next day, remained provokingly cool and unconcerned. They had not seen six months of emigration without learning something of the American habit of going at full speed. The word of starting in use on the Chagres River is "go ahead!" Captain C—— and Mr. M——, of Baltimore, and myself were obliged to pay fifteen dollars each, for a canoe to Cruces. We chose a broad, trimly-cut craft, which the boatmen were covering with fresh thatch. We stayed with them until all was ready, and they had pushed it through the mud and shoal water to the bank before Ramos's house. Our luggage was stowed away, we took our seats and raised our umbrellas, but the men had gone off for provisions and were not to be found. All the other canoes were equally in limbo. The sun blazed down on the swampy shores, and visions of yellow fever came into the minds of the more timid travelers. The native boys brought to us bottles of fresh water, biscuits, and fruit, presenting them with the words: "bit!" "picayune!" "Your bread is not good," I said to one of the shirtless traders. "Si, señor!" was his decided answer, while he tossed back his childish head with a look of offended dignity which charmed me.

Our chief boatman, named Ambrosio Mendez, was of the mixed Indian and Spanish race. The second, Juan Crispin Bega, belonged to the lowest class, almost entirely of Negro blood. He was a strong, jovial fellow, and took such good care of some of our small articles as to relieve us from all further trouble about them. This propensity is common to all of his caste on the Isthmus. In addition to these, a third man was given to us, with the assurance that he would work his passage; but just as we were leaving, we learned that he was a runaway soldier, who had been taken up for theft and was released on paying some sub-alcalde three bottles of liquor, promising to quit the place at once. We were scarcely out of sight of the town before he demanded five dollars a day for his labor. We refused, and he stopped working. Upon our threatening to set him ashore in the jungle, he took up the paddle, but used it so awkwardly and perversely that our other men lost all patience. We were obliged, however, to wait until we could reach Gatun, ten miles distant, before settling matters. Juan struck up "Oh, Susanna!" which he sang to a most ludicrous imitation of the words, and I lay back under the palm leaves, looking out of

67

"Incident on the Chagres River," 1867, by Charles Nahl

the stern of the canoe on the forests of the Chagres River.

There is nothing in the world comparable to these forests. No description that I have ever read conveys an idea of the splendid overplus of vegetable life within the tropics. The river, broad, and with a swift current of the sweetest water I ever drank, winds between walls of foliage that rise from its very surface. All the gorgeous growths of an eternal summer are so mingled in one impenetrable mass that the eye is bewildered. From the rank jungle of canes and gigantic lilies, and the thickets of strange shrubs that line the water, rise the trunks of the mango, the ceiba, the coco, the sycamore, and the superb palm. Plantains take root in the banks, hiding the soil with their leaves, shaken and split into immense plumes by the wind and rain. The zapote, with a fruit the size of a man's head, the gourd tree, and other vegetable wonders, attract the eye on all sides. Blossoms of crimson, purple, and yellow, of a form and magnitude unknown in the north, are mingled with the leaves, and flocks of paroquets and brilliant butterflies circle through the air like blossoms blown away.

All outline of the landscape is lost under this deluge of vegetation. No trace of the soil is to be seen; lowland and highland are the same; a mountain is but a higher swell of the mass of verdure. As on the ocean, you have a sense rather than a perception of beauty. The sharp, clear lines of our scenery at home are here wanting. What shape the land would be if cleared, you cannot tell. You gaze upon the scene before you with a never-sated delight, till your brain aches with the sensation, and you close your eyes, overwhelmed with the thought that all these wonders have been from the beginning—that year after year takes away no leaf or blossom that is not replaced, but the sublime mystery of growth and decay is renewed forever.

In the afternoon we reached Gatun, small village of bamboo huts thatched with palm leaves, on the right bank of the river. Two wooden drums, beaten by boys in another part of the village, gave signs of a coming fandango, and, as it was Sunday night, all the natives were out in their best dresses. They are a very cleanly people, bathing daily, and changing their dresses as often as they are soiled. The children have their heads shaved from the crown to the neck, and, as they go about naked with abdomens unnaturally distended from an exclusive vegetable diet, are odd figures enough. They have bright black eyes, and are quick and intelligent in their speech and motions.

The inside of our hut was but a single room, in which all the household operations were carried on. A notched pole, serving as a ladder, led to a sleeping-loft, under the pyramidal roof of thatch. Here a number of the emigrants who arrived late were stowed away on a rattling floor of cane, covered with hides. After a supper of pork and coffee, I made my day's notes by the light of a miserable starveling candle, stuck in an empty bottle, but had not written far before my paper was covered with fleas. The owner of the hut swung my hammock meanwhile, and I turned in, to secure it for the night. To lie there was one thing, to sleep another. A dozen natives crowded round the table, drinking their *auguardiente* and disputing vehemently; the cooking fire was on one side of me, and everyone that passed to and fro was sure to give me a thump, while my weight swung the hammock so low that all the dogs on the premises were constantly rubbing their backs under me. I was just sinking into a doze when my head was so violently agitated that I started up in some alarm. It was but a quarrel about payment between the Señora and a boatman, one standing on either side. From their angry gestures, my own head and not the reckoning seemed the subject of contention.

Our men were to have started at midnight, but it was two hours later before we could rouse and muster them together. We went silently and rapidly up the river till sunrise, when we reached a cluster of huts called *Dos Hermanos* (Two Brothers). Here we overtook two canoes, which, in their anxiety to get ahead, had been all night on the river. There had been only a slight shower since we started; but the clouds began to gather heavily, and by the time we had gained the ranch of Palo Matida a sudden cold wind came over the forests, and the air was at once darkened. We sprang ashore and barely reached the hut, a few paces off, when the rain broke over us, as if the sky had caved in. A dozen lines of white electric heat ran down from the zenith, followed by crashes of thunder, which I could feel throbbing in the earth under my feet. The rain drove into one side of the cabin and out the other, but we wrapped ourselves in India-rubber cloth and kept out the wet and chilling air. During the whole day the river rose rapidly and we were obliged to hug the bank closely, running under the boughs of trees and drawing ourselves up the rapids by those that hung low.

I crept out of the snug nest where we were all stowed as closely as three unfledged sparrows, and took my seat between Juan and Ambrosio, protected from the rain by an India-rubber poncho. The clothing of our men was likewise waterproof, but without seam or fold. It gave no hindrance to the free play of their muscles, as they deftly and rapidly plied the broad paddles. Juan kept time to the Ethiopian melodies he had picked up from the emigrants, looking round from time to time with a grin of satisfaction at his skill. I preferred, however, hearing the native songs, which the boatmen sing with a melancholy drawl on the final syllable of every line, giving the music a peculiar but not unpleasant effect, when heard at a little distance.

We stopped four hours short of Gorgona, at the hacienda of San Pablo, the residence of Padre Dutaris, curé of all the interior. Ambrosio took us to his house by a path across a rolling, open savanna, dotted by palms and acacias of immense size. Herds of cattle and horses were grazing on the short, thick-leaved grass, and appeared to be in excellent condition. The padre owns a large tract of land, with a thousand head of stock, and his ranch commands a beautiful view up and down the river. Ambrosio was acquainted with his wife, and by recommending us as *buenos caballeros,* procured us a splendid supper of fowls, eggs, rice boiled in coco milk, and chocolate, with baked plantains for bread. Those who came after us had difficulty in getting anything. The padre had been frequently cheated by Americans and was therefore cautious. He was absent at the time, but his son Felipe, a boy of twelve years old, assisted in doing the honors with wonderful grace and self-possession. His tawny skin was as soft as velvet, and his black eyes sparkled like jewels. He is almost the only living model of the Apollino that I ever saw. He sat in the hammock with me, leaning over my shoulder as I noted down the day's doings, and when I had done, wrote his name in my book, in an elegant hand. I slept soundly in the midst of an uproar, and only awoke at four o'clock next morning, to hurry our men in leaving for Gorgona.

Next morning at daybreak our horses—tough little mustangs, which I could almost step over—were at the door. We started off with a guide, trusting our baggage to the honesty of our host, who promised to send it the same day. A servant of the alcalde escorted us out of the village, cut us each a good stick, pocketed a *real*, and then left us to plunge into the forests. The path at the outset was bad enough, but as the wood grew deeper and darker and the tough clay soil held the rains which had fallen, it became finally a narrow gully, filled with mud nearly to our horses' bellies.... So strong is their mutual confidence that they invariably step in each other's tracks, and a great part of the road is thus worn into holes three feet deep and filled with water and soft mud, which spurts upward as they go, coating the rider from head to foot.

The mountain range in the interior is broken and irregular. The road passes over the lower ridges and projecting spurs of the main chain, covered nearly the whole distance to Panama by dense forests. Above us spread a roof of transparent green, through which few rays of the sunlight fell. The only sounds in that leafy wilderness were the chattering of monkeys as they cracked the palm nuts, and the scream of parrots, flying from tree to tree. In the deepest ravines spent mules frequently lay dead, and high above them, on the large boughs, the bald vultures waited silently for us to pass. We overtook many trains of luggage, packed on the backs of bulls and horses, tied head-to-tail in long files. At intervals on the road we saw a solitary ranch, with a cleared space about it, but all the natives could furnish us was a cup of thick, black coffee.

As we were leaving Gorgona, our party was joined by a long Mississippian, whose face struck me at the first glance as being peculiarly cadaverous. He attached himself to us without the least ceremony, leaving his own party behind. We had not ridden far before he told us he had felt symptoms of cholera during the night, and was growing worse. We insisted on his returning to Gorgona at once, but he refused, saying he was "bound to go through." At the first ranch on the road we found another traveler, lying on the ground in a state of entire prostration. He was attended by a friend, who seemed on the point of taking the epidemic, from his very fears. The sight of this case no doubt operated on the Mississippian, for he soon became so racked with pain as to keep his seat with great difficulty. We were alarmed; it was impossible to stop in the swampy forest, and equally impossible to leave him, now that all his dependence was on us. The only thing resembling medicine in our possession was a bottle of claret. It was an unusual remedy for cholera, but he insisted on drinking it.

71

After urging forward our weary beasts till late in the afternoon, we were told that Panama was four hours further. We pitied the poor horses, but ourselves more, and determined to push ahead. After a repetition of all our worst experience, we finally struck the remains of the paved road constructed by the buccaneers when they held Panama. I now looked eagerly forward for the Pacific, but every ridge showed another in advance, and it grew dark with a rain coming up. Our horses avoided the hard pavement and took bypaths through thickets higher than our heads. The cholera-stricken emigrant, nothing helped by the claret he drank, implored us, amid his groans, to hasten forward. Leaning over the horse's neck, he writhed on his saddle in an agony of pain, and seemed on the point of falling at every step. We were far in advance of our Indian guide and lost the way more than once in the darkness. At last he overtook us, washed his feet in a mudhole, and put on a pair of pantaloons. This was a welcome sign to us, and in fact we soon after smelt the salt air of the Pacific.

Thus terminated my five days' journey across the Isthmus—decidedly more novel, grotesque, and adventurous than any trip of similar length in the world. It was rough enough, but had nothing that I could exactly call hardship, so much was the fatigue balanced by the enjoyment of unsurpassed scenery and a continual sensation of novelty. In spite of the many dolorous accounts which have been sent from the Isthmus, there is nothing, at the worst season, to deter anyone from the journey.

from DIARY OF A PHYSICIAN IN CALIFORNIA

JAMES L. TYSON

James L. Tyson was one of the many physicians who headed for the California goldfields in 1849. The gold rush's widespread disease and violence provided these doctors— licensed and self-appointed alike—with plenty of patients. Tyson sailed from Baltimore on January 16, 1849, landed at Chagres, Panama, thirteen days later, and arrived in San Francisco on May 18. He gave his first impressions of San Francisco in Diary of a Physician in California, *published in New York in 1850.*

THE TOWN [SAN FRANCISCO] in front of us consisted of tents and scattered frame-tenements, a few presenting quite a neat and cottage-like aspect, either resting in the amphitheatre made by the surrounding barren-looking hills, or picturesquely perched on their sides. The question which was very forcibly suggested to the mind at first view was, what commercial inducements could such a mean and insignificant-looking place as this present, to bring together such a forest of masts as the harbor disclosed? We soon learned that every vessel which had arrived since the first discovery of gold in the country, was quickly deserted by its crew, and left to idly swing at its cable's length; however anxious the captains or owners might be to depart, it was impossible to man a ship with a sufficient number to work her to the nearest port. The wages for even a common laborer in the town were higher per day than a sailor was accustomed to receive monthly.

Desirous to see a place offering so many attractions, and to again step foot on *terra firma*, some half a dozen of us engaged one of the boats that were quickly along side, and were at once indoctrinated with California prices, a trip of a quarter of a mile costing us twelve dollars. Arrived at the shore, each seemed anxious to be the first to step foot on the soil, and in the eagerness and haste which followed, some measured their length on the sand, and others were knocked sprawling into the bottom of the boat; and amid many merry peals of laughter, we climbed the steep and rugged hill, proceeded to the post-office, and sought a cookshop. Long abstinence had sharpened the appe-

San Francisco, 1851, by R. E. Collison and W. Boosey

tite, for we were almost famished, and did full justice to the beefsteak, bread, butter, and coffee that were set before us.

The state of affairs here we found to be on the high-pressure principle, and truly anomalous. Without going into lengthened details, it will suffice to state that unoccupied ground, thought to be in an eligible location, met with ready sale and at higher rates than the same amount would bring in the most business parts of any of the great cities of the union. Pistols were fired in rapid succession in every direction. Horses with their drunken riders were dashing through the town, the gay *serapa* and other gaudy trappings flying in the wind. Blasphemous oaths were heard on all sides. The vice of gambling prevailed to an enormous extent. Immense piles of gold, in its natural state and in coin, could be seen heaped upon the numerous monte and roulette tables. Owing to the high rents which the proprietors of these places are able and willing to pay, it has contributed to give a fictitious value to property. Most of the titles to land sold or leased being of the same character, I have known as many as six claimants for one lot. A revulsion will come, and much litigation must ensue.

The climate of San Francisco we found anything but agreeable. In the forepart of the day, the sun was intensely hot, but from eleven or twelve o'clock, a cold raw northwest wind would set in from the ocean, which by night would nearly amount to a gale, scattering the fine particles of dust and sand in every direction. This would often be attended with a thick heavy fog, which made the nights most disagreeable. By sundown all would be calm, but the atmosphere was chilly and unpleasant. The transition from the heat of the morning to the cool of the evening was frequently so sudden and unexpected that those not familiar to the climate were often in situations where they could not make the change of clothing that was requisite; and severe colds, not infrequently settling upon the lungs, were apt to be the result of these exposures. I noticed that all who had any tendency to disease of the chest suffered during their stay in San Francisco.... The wretched, brackish water from the wells at San Francisco is another objection to the place, as it is very liable to cause senior and fatal mischief. The mortality from dysenteric complaints during the past summer and fall was truly frightful, and almost every one, even among the older residents, during those months suffer from this cause.

Upon the whole, in a medical point of view, I would not regard San Francisco as the most desirable locality for a large commercial city, which the requirements of our great western continent will so soon demand, and the emigration there will so soon call into existence. The positions of Benicia or Sancolito [Sausalito] would be far preferable in this respect, while their other advantages would be equal if not superior to those of San Francisco. The latter of the two certainly presents many inducements to the enterprising capitalist, while the former, from its being the point of our naval station, must always hold a prominent place. Sancolito, situated on a beautiful little bay of that name, within the northern termination of the entrance from the sea, is admirably shielded from the northwest winds which prevail at San Francisco, and the harbor itself is even superior to the latter, vessels of the largest class being able to anchor close to the shore, in a position of the most perfect security, while here is their main reliance for obtaining supplies of good water. These advantages must in time tell on its prosperity, and though a powerful impulse has been given to San Francisco, I should greatly prefer the position of Sancolito for a residence, and doubt not but it will eventually become, if not *the city*, one of the great cities of the Pacific.

LETTER TO
FREDERICK DOUGLASS

JAMES R. STARKEY

In 1849 the eastern abolitionist press trumpeted the opportunities available to African-Americans in California, where the hard work of mining supposedly tempered racial hatred. California entered the Union as a free state in 1850, following a long tradition of Mexican antislavery sentiment in the region. But enforcement was weak and southern slaveholders found regions where slavery openly flourished. The California Fugitive Slave Law, passed in 1852, made fleeing from masters illegal within the state's supposedly free borders. Free blacks from the east, along with the few slaves who managed to buy their own freedom, lived under a constant threat of arrest.

James R. Starkey, a former slave who bought his freedom in North Carolina, came to San Francisco via Nicaragua in 1852. He hoped to raise enough money to buy the freedom of his son and daughter in the east, but never succeeded. He stayed in California and founded the San Francisco Athenaeum Institute (a library and debating society for working-class African-Americans) with Mifflin Wistar Gibbs and other prominent African-American leaders. During his sea voyage to California via Nicaragua, he wrote occasional letters to Frederick Douglass that were printed in Frederick Douglass' Paper.

SAN JUAN DE NICARAGUA, GRAY TOWN, FEB. 26, 1852

Mr. Editor—Sir:— I left New York on the 3d of Jan., in the Bark Pocahontas, in company with another gentleman and his wife, from Buffalo, to this place. We took passage in this vessel, because we thought (and being assured by the owners) that accommodations would be much better for us than on one of the Steamers, which are generally so crowded.

But how mistaken were we, after leaving New York; for the Captain, whom I understand, is a Virginian, would not admit us to the cabin of the vessel with the other passengers, who were of the very lowest class, although we *paid the same fare.* The sailors were made to leave their berths, and take our previous secured births in the cabin, and we to take theirs. He would not admit us to table until the other passengers and even the sailors had taken their meals. It is needless for me to say that this most unjust distinction was made simply on account of the tincture of the skin.

But at last, we arrived in the port of San Juan, the famous port of Promethean notoriety: and when he learned that we intended to stop at this place, I at once discovered quite a change in his manners toward us.—I suppose he thought as I did, that I should be able to meet him on equal grounds here. But even in this, I was mistaken: for this place, a town containing five hundred inhabitants, of which one hundred are white Americans, and the other four hundred, which are composed of Indians and colored persons from the American States, suffer themselves to be ruled at the will and pleasure of the few pale faces who come among them only to benefit their pockets. Out of the eight hotels in this place, five are kept by colored persons from the States: and among them, are some of the best houses in town.

And imagine my surprise, when I saw, a few days ago, a colored young man on his way home from California, in the company with a number of white companions; they had seen many a hard day together, in the Mountains of California; he was well-dressed, and the best looking man, not only in the company but in the house; when the dinner bell rang, he, of course, seated himself at the table, having previously bought his ticket at the bar, and paid as much for it as anybody. I say, imagine my surprise, when I saw the landlord (colored) walk up to him and take him by the collar, and say to him, in a loud and insulting tone, "I thought, by your appearance, that you had sense enough to know the American character better than to seat yourself at my first table." For this, he (the landlord) received quite a merited rebuke, not only from the colored young man, but also the "American characters" who were at the table manifested their disapprobation at his course. The young man, and those in company with him, left the house, and went to a hotel kept by a white man, and were entertained alike, without distinction.

It is very strange that our people will suffer themselves to be carried away by this "American character," even here, in a country like this, whose king is a colored man, and the police officers, colored men.... And with this colored government, colored persons from the States seek to enforce what they call the "American character," but more justly the slaveholding character, on their own color who come among them. Is it not time we had begun to open our eyes, and see the folly of our own doings? Is it not time that we had begun to appreciate freedom and real liberty, particularly in a country like this?

Yours respectfully,
James R. Starkey

LETTER FROM CALIFORNIA

HANNCHEN HIRSCHFELDER

The rush to California was an international one—nearly a quarter of the miners were born outside of the United States. Hannchen Mayer Hirschfelder (1831–1869) was a German Jewish woman who came to California via Panama in 1856. She wrote to her family in New York of the trip from her new home in Downieville. Her letter, published here for the first time, has been translated from German.

DEAR MOTHER, BROTHERS, AND SISTERS—

In accordance with my promise and your wishes I am sending you the notes I took during our trip from New York to here. Our trip was, with God's help, one of the best and most beautiful that has been made in a long time. On Sept. 20th at two in the afternoon we left New York on the *George Law,* a big steamer, while a great crowd waved good-bye to us, among whom were my brother, brother-in-law, and sister-in-law, and while the cannons fired off a shot which announced the mailboat. The exit from the harbor was as lovely as the entrance which I recently described to you in detail. We still had 700 passengers on board, several of whom my husband introduced to me immediately as friends from San Francisco. They were very friendly and even offered me an armchair, sour pickles, apples, etc. the first few days when I was somewhat seasick. The gentlemen had made the trip several times and knew what was prudent to take as precaution. The first few days passed fairly quietly, just ocean....After four or five days it got so warm in the cabins that many people preferred to spend the nights up on deck, which we also tried.

We traveled first class and the price in the upper saloon was $270 per person—in the lower saloon $200. We had to take the latter because first class was already filled. Very few Germans like the American food, and it takes a long time until one gets used to it. All the waiters and servants were Negroes and sometimes, despite my seasickness, I had to laugh....As you know, I don't speak English, but managed to get everything anyway. For example I got ice water and other things very readily from the Negroes.... On the 24th we saw a lovely rainbow and on the 25th many birds, which means that land is near.

78

Toward noon we saw islands which I thought to be Cuba, but when I looked at the map I saw that they were West Indies, that is, a part of them. In the afternoon I saw land on the other side, Haita, and the weather was very humid but toward evening it got nicer. The passengers are full of gaiety, many groups sing, play guitar, and so on. On the 26th we passed Cuba, and it is a very large island.

Every day we cover about 206 miles; one must calculate 3 1/2 miles per hour. I believe we also passed Havana and in the evening we saw the island San Domingo at sunset. Very picturesque. On the 27th, beautiful blue sea, reflection of the sky, many islands in sight. About 10 AM a Negro ship's pilot came on board and we had a lovely view of Jamaica. At 11 AM we saw the capital, Kingsdon, the fort jutting out into the sea. One cannot see much more beautiful sights than that. The fort in the ocean, the ship near the shore, pastel-colored small houses smiling at you, and between and around them palm and coconut trees. One should look at paintings and pictures of this area to see how beautiful it is. Many people on the shore, mostly Negroes.

About ten Negro boys come swimming to the boat. The passengers throw small silver coins to them and they dive for them ... and bring them back up, show them quickly, put them in their mouths, and the game starts all over again. To a lover of beautiful scenery today would be worth the trip. Around twelve o'clock we stopped and took on water and coals. Many Negro women came in the most outrageous outfits and with vessels on their heads, dancing and singing, to do this job, since the men are too lazy to do this kind of work. After three o'clock we and many other passengers went on land.

Here it is very hot and the fruit that grow here wild are very tempting—but one must beware of eating them. Maybe oranges are okay. But pineapple, for a few cents, are not good for your health. Kingsdon is an old town. The women come to market on mules, laden with fruit, like wild ones, similar to gypsy, pipe or cigar in mouth, often wearing ballgowns, checked scarves on their heads, and usually without shoes.... But you also meet English and German business people....A Negro Jew showed us the very beautiful synagogue. We returned early to our ship, where I received from a gentleman a pretty shell basket. At ten o'clock in the evening we left. I forgot: there were many policemen in the street, black men with shiny white trousers and jackets, cloth caps with a big P in the middle. We left at ten o'clock. The moon made the sea shine like so many lights.

This morning we see land and immediately afterward fog and rain, which indicates that we are near the Isthmus. We passed several small islands and land finally, about 3 PM in Aspinwale.... October 2, in the morning at nine o'clock we left on the Panama Railroad via the Isthmus from the Gulf of Darien, where it was awfully hot and my arm which held the umbrella got blisters. Then we traveled through rain forests, past swamps, and straw huts of the natives, who sat on the floor, practically naked....We saw immense trees, palm trees, etc. but I did not see monkeys or the like. The train often crosses canyons that make you shudder. A few narrow oaken planks serve as bridge. But inside the car we had wine and other drinks to pass the time, and good company made us forget the scary sights. But this is "gold" compared to earlier days, when you had to make the crossing by mule.... About 3 PM we arrived in Panama, a Spanish fortress, or rather ruin. Here it is quite nice and we saw Spanish troops exercise. Meat is being sold in strips, about two finger-wide bands, and sold by length. We stayed here about [ ] hours and then were taken by small steamboats two miles out to the *Golden Age,* a big beautiful steamer that was lying between the mountains.

It is nice on this ship and we got one of the best rooms, next to the captain's quarters. Although we were now on the Pacific, several passengers got seasick. The first few days passed uneventfully.... At night, the men make music on the accordion, and so I had to, despite my protestations, dance a polka with the purser on the foredeck. My husband wanted to take along a young Negro from Panama as a servant. I however did not want to take on a burden to make it easier on myself, and so another man took him along for the price of the passage. On the ship we cover 280 miles per day, and we have very good travel companions. Also several Jewish families. I am very popular on board; so are my husband and Emma.

OCTOBER 7TH. This morning huge rocks and islands. We are approaching the Am. fortress Acapulco. Here, it is very hot and one has to watch out for sunstroke. A lot of small boats arrive, partly to take passengers to land, since the ship stays at sea because of low tide, partly to sell fruit and shells. I prefer to stay on board. The scenery is very romantic.... The Mexican men are good looking and muscular with colored appearance. The waves are gently caressing the rocks. After a few hours we left. Water has to be freshened up with ice which costs twenty-five cents per portion. The following days we saw islands every day. I got so used to travel by sea, since the pleasant company made the time pass quickly, that it all seemed like a beautiful dream. Our "Day of Atonement" [Yom Kippur], which was on the 9th, we spent very well. However, the next day I felt somewhat weak.

OCTOBER 11TH. From Acapulco, we went north, and during the night it was rather cold. We saw land again.... The closer we come to the coast, the colder and foggier the weather.... October 14th the ship swayed a lot, a sign of

approaching land. About [?] o'clock we came between two high mountains to the Golden Gate, and then we saw from a distance San Francisco,
which offered a beautiful sight. This, after NY, is the most beautiful approach
in the world. The city lay on the mountain like in a sea of fog. About eight
o'clock we arrived in San Francisco where we were met by a cousin
Hirschfelder....We stayed ten days, I liked it very much, and I will, dear mother,
describe in detail the Inner of California with its gold mines at the next opportunity. For this time it should be enough for you, for my arm is really very
tired from writing.

With cordial greetings to you and the whole family I remain your loving

Hannchen Hirschfelder

FOR
CALIFORNIA!
Mutual Protection
Trading & Mining Co.

Having purchased the splendid, Coppered and very fast Sailing

Barque EMMA ISIDORA,

Will leave about the 15th of February. This vessel will be fitted in the very best manner and is one of the fastest sailing vessels that goes from this port.

Each member pays 300 dollars and is entitled to an equal proportion of all profits made by the company either at mining or trading, and holds an equal share of all the property belonging to the company. Experienced men well acquainted with the coast and climate are already engaged as officers of the Company. A rare chance is offered to any wishing a safe investment, good home and Large profits.

This Company is limited to 60 and any wishing to improve this opportunity must make immediate application.

An Experienced Physician will go with the company.

For Freight or Passage apply to 23 State Street, corner of Devonshire, where the list of Passengers may be seen.

JAMES H. PRINCE, Agent,
23 State Street, corner of Devonshire St., Boston.

For further Particulars, see the Constitution.

Propeller Power Presses,
142 Washington St., Boston.

Advertisement, c. 1849

from TO CALIFORNIA IN 1849
THROUGH MEXICO

A. C. FERRIS

Other less commonly traveled routes were available to forty-niners courageous enough to risk them. A. C. Ferris, from Hackensack, New Jersey, sailed from New York to Vera Cruz and crossed Mexico on horseback, passing battlefields from the recently concluded Mexican War. He sailed north at San Blas, arriving in San Francisco eighty-four days later. He recreated his tumultuous journey for Century Magazine *in 1891.*

CALIFORNIA, WITH ITS MINES of gold, and how soonest to get there was the ruling excitement of the hour, in the fall of 1848. The "gold fever" was at its height. Many desired to go gold-hunting that could not for want of money, and many that had the wherewithal could not abandon families, homes, and business with any degree of self-approval. So in many instances the matter was compromised, and he who could spare the cash (and sometimes he that could not) entered into agreement with the impecunious but enterprising adventurer who desired to go, to furnish him the means, the proceeds to be shared between them on his return.

These arrangements enabled thousands of energetic and fearless men to start on the pilgrimage for gold in many ways. One of these, which I am about to narrate, was the formation of a company of two hundred adventurous spirits fitted out in New York. The plan was to go by sea to Vera Cruz, Mexico, thence overland to the Pacific coast at San Blas or Mazatlan, and in the absence of vessels at these ports to continue the journey of two thousand miles by land through Mexico and Lower and Upper California to the mines. A part of the company embarked from San Blas, a part from Mazatlan, and a part made the entire journey overland from Vera Cruz.

This company, mostly composed of picked young men, was organized under the comprehensive title of the "Manhattan-California Overland Association," and numbered about two hundred members. We were full of a sanguine spirit of adventure and eager to dig our fortunes from the mines in the shortest possible time. We were fitted out with very wide-brimmed soft hats, boots of rubber or leather reaching above the knee, woolen and rubber blankets, red flannel shirts, a liberal supply of tin pans for washing out the gold, shovels, picks, spades, crowbars, camp-kettles, frying-pans, tin plates, tin cups, daguerreotypes, locks of hair, Spanish books, a few patent gold-washers, musical instruments, etc., the most of which assortment was early scattered along the Mexican trails or in the chaparral, or perhaps sold to the natives for a few small coins. To these were added rifles, carbines, shot-guns, revolvers, and bowie-knives, to which we clung closely all the way. We chartered the bark *Mara,* Captain Parks, in ballast, of some two hundred tons.

We presented a remarkable appearance as we boarded the bark at the foot of Burling Slip on the last day of January, 1849, every man in full California costume, his armament in his belt—boots and buckskin-gauntleted gloves, a roll of blankets strapped *á la militaire* on his shoulders, a carbine or rifle slung upon his back, and frying-pans, coffee-pots, camp-kettles, and assorted tinware in his hands. The bark had a poop-deck on her quarter in which were a few small rooms for which lots were drawn, and I was fortunate in drawing one, which freed me from the confinement of the packed and darkened bunks of the vessel's hold, with its foul atmosphere of bilge-water and heated humanity.

Captain Parks enlisted but a small crew, depending on volunteers, but he was wisely provided with his own cook and caboose. His cook had a remarkable personality: a light copper-colored negro over six feet in height, exceedingly slim, gaunt and gray, wrinkled and crippled, with but one eye, three fingers on one hand and none on the other, and with a vocabulary in English which consisted entirely of the most emphatic oaths, which he freely bestowed upon us.

Among our number, gathered on the vessel's deck at the wharf, was one young man of striking physique, very tall, wearing a broad sombrero and boots reaching to his hips and already fitted with spurs for the Mexican mustang he expected to ride, and with buckskin gauntlets reaching to his elbows, and two revolvers and a bowie-knife in his broad belt.... [A] pretty, fair-haired girl, her rosy cheeks wet with tears, put up her lips that our booted hero might impart his farewell kiss. His heart was tender if his boots were large, and, just as we were casting loose from the wharf, he sprang upon the deck, threw his baggage ashore, and followed it with agility, renouncing for love all his golden visions of California.

We arrived off the coast of Mexico just as the evening sun was descending amid the golden clouds over the mountain peaks, flanked by dark and somber masses, the snow-crowned Orizaba, or star mountain, set high in the blue heavens, flashing as with a coronal of diamonds. Two snow-white birds of flowing plumage came off from the yet distant land, and with an easy and graceful movement of their wings circled around our mastheads, and then flew straight landward again. They were the mariners' pilot-birds of the tropics come to guide us ashore.

As Vera Cruz is in a section of sand, cactus, and lizards, surrounded by a large tract of chaparral, messengers were sent to the nearest ranches and haciendas to announce that an arrival of "Los Yankees" was in want of horses, mules, and "burros." We were constrained to remain for the night in the yellow-fever-producing city among its so-called "greasers" (as our soldiers had termed them). This we passed in a caravansary, the first floor of which was packed with two hundred head of pack-mules and "burros." We spread our blankets on the boards of the second floor, disturbing large colonies of fleas who held preemption rights, and who resisted our encroachment by furious onslaughts on every part of our bodies. There were openings in the wall of our room but no windows, and from below, the whole night through, there was one continual braying and uproar from the two hundred hungry mules. Nothing could parallel this first night in Mexico but a page of Dante's *Inferno*.

As our war with Mexico had just closed, and the ignorant masses yet held us in the same enmity with which they had regarded their conquerors, matters did not look favorable for a peaceful passage over the whole extent of Mexico, as we expected to follow the route taken by [U.S. General Winfield] Scott's army, and to pass over battle-fields where, as we learned, bleached skeletons lay still unburied. The government, in fact, the whole country, was yet in a state of demoralization, and guerrillas and robbers infested almost every mile of the way. Besides this, merchants of intelligence in Vera Cruz warned us that we were almost sure to be robbed and murdered, that if we should escape this fate we could not find provisions on our journey for men or beasts, and that we would most surely break down our animals, and be glad to resort to horse or mule meat to sustain life. Impressed by these tales ... about fifty of the most pronounced and boastful among our company took a return passage on the vessel for New York.

On Monday Mexican horse-traders presented themselves, in comparison with whom the sharpest Yankee horse-jockey sunk into utter insignificance. They drove in before them, with a "whoop la" and a Comanche yell, caravans of horses and mules that included not only the halt and the maimed, the lame and the blind, but also some of the most vicious and worthless brutes that were ever collected together—galled and chafed, sore-backed, buckers, jumpers, and balky. Yet with wonderful skill the owners of these gothic animals covered up and disguised their defects and their vicious tricks, so that in most cases the deception and trickery were not discovered till the vendors were well on their way to their ranches again. From twenty-five to forty dollars or *pesos* each was paid by anxious buyers for animals which the owners would have been glad to sell for one-quarter the money.

We made our first start for a day's march on the morning of the 28th day of February. The first camp-fires, the cooking, the saddling-up, the loading of baggage and equipments on the vicious, kicking, biting mustangs and donkeys, and the final mount and start were altogether beyond description. Besides the rider, they had to carry two blankets, his mining tools, coffee-pot, camp-kettle, and frying-pan laid on or hanging from his saddle, and his bag of tin cups, spoons, and tin plates, and his gun, rifle, or carbine slung on his back, and a variety of other articles supposed to be essential. Don Quixote and Sancho Panza joined to Falstaff's regiment would not have presented half so motley a group. The rattle of tinware and the orders and the shouting in an unknown tongue excited the wild and half-broken mustangs to madness. I soon had to organize a rear-guard under Captain Pierce to pick up stragglers, help reload broken cargoes, and lift stubborn and refractory mules to their feet. It was also necessary constantly to halt the column, knowing well that a man who should be left out of sight in the rear would be speedily gobbled up by the watchful robbers trailing after us.

Along the day's route, as all the way across the whole of Mexico, we found wooden crosses, indicating that a murder had been committed there. This first day's ride of ten miles brought us to a stream known as Murderer's Den. Here, before starting from camp in the morning, a detail of organization was made, and by adopting a rigid military discipline, and discarding worthless encumbrances in the way of mining tools, gold-washers, etc., I was able to train my troop so that when the trail was not very rough or mountainous over twenty Mexican leagues a day was made between camps. As we left the low-lying, malarious sea-coast, our road and climate both improved, and on the first Saturday we camped for rest over Sunday in the suburbs of the beautiful city of Jalapa, a city of fruits and flowers, of which the Mexican proverb says: "See Jalapa and die."

On the plaza of Jalapa the hostile feeling against the Yankees had its first outbreak. A great crowd gathered about the red-shirted horsemen as we rode into the plaza on Sunday, and a rush was made by the mob to dismount us and drive us from our saddles. But a vigorous charge promptly made against the mob with threatening revolvers drove them back and gave safe escape to the hard-pressed horsemen. Through the villages of the country parts we were received by the *señoras* and *señoritas* with kindness, but by the males with frowns and threats, and with the significant gesture of a finger drawn across the throat. In no place were we safe from attack except in groups which commanded safety and respect. To them in their ignorance we were still Yankees and *soldados*.

Camp was aroused usually at three o'clock in the morning; fires were kindled, pots of coffee were boiled, and, when possible, eggs (*wavos*) also. Then came a march in military order of about twenty miles, when halt was ordered for dinner, provided water and corn were to be had for the horses. Supplies of whatever could be purchased were foraged for along the route, bananas and sweet potatoes being the staple; occasionally pork could be had, and in the larger places very poor beef, cut into long strips and sold always by the yard. This tough beef was eaten by the Mexicans cut first in small pieces and then stewed in a quantity of red peppers resembling stewed tomatoes (called *carne de Chili*). If our halt was made at a hacienda, the universal national dish of "tortillas" and "frijoles" was to be obtained, served with coffee, at three cents a meal. But our hungry and robust riders could dispose of many meals at a sitting, and when camping and with a sufficient supply of yards of meat to satisfy their hungry stomachs, the quantity they fed themselves from their frying-pans was not only an astonishment but almost a horror to the natives, who crowded our camp to see the show.

Upon one occasion, after a hard day's ride of over forty miles along a route where supplies were not to be had, we camped by a clear stream, where but a few native huts of poles and branches sheltered the population. Two priests, with a large, mule-drawn carriage, were just in advance of us, and in receiving the monthly tithes for the church had carried away all the wealth of the place, and there was but one answer to our calls for food: "*Nada, Señor, nada. No hai tortillas. No hai frijoles.*" Lieutenant Gray, a stray soldier, who had been left adrift in Mexico, volunteered to bring me some supper from among the villagers. In utter fatigue, I threw myself upon the ground in one of the huts, and was soon in a deep slumber. At about eleven o'clock Gray returned and awakened me. The hut was crowded full of men and women gazing at me with great interest, but they were careful to keep at a safe distance from me. Gray explained his stratagem thus: He had told them the *capitan* was a great warrior, and had eaten the prisoners he took in battle; that I was hungry and would also eat corn and hay, but liked eggs and onions better. He brought eggs, onions, and salt, leaving outside a supply of corn and hay for me to eat, an operation which the ignorant but curious natives had come to witness. So far as the boiled eggs and onions were concerned, being my first meal of the day, I was glad to be able to gratify them. In camping for the night, sentries were stationed, and pickets were posted, and the animals were secured with lariats inside the picket line, but sometimes, when guerrillas abounded, in the center of the camp. Once only did these *ladrones* make an open demonstration.

We were in a section of country covered with low bushes, in which jack-rabbits, wild turkeys, and other game were present. No towns were near, and, feeling secure, a large part of the company was scattered in pursuit of the game, hoping to secure enough to fill our camp-kettles on our next halt, for we had been some days on short rations. The Mexican women were always friendly, and presently some were met on the trail, calling out to us: "*Ladrones! ladrones!*" and pointing forward on our path. At this our stragglers were called in. The robbers were a large band of well-mounted and well-armed men, and had filed across our road in the bed of an *arroya* or dry stream. To fight as a troop of cavalry with camp equipage and cooking-utensils dangling from our saddles, or to wait a charge from them, would have been sure defeat. So I dismounted a part of my troop, and in platoons at double quick charged towards the guerrillas. Evidently a fight with the hated Yankees in red shirts was not what they desired, for as we came within short range, their leader gave the word "*Vamos,*" and away they galloped down the ravine helter-skelter, and we saw them no more. We certainly were not a handsome crowd at this time.

Upon the heights of Cerro Gordo we camped for our noonday meal. Upon its central battlefield, where [Mexican President Antonio López de] Santa Anna made his most stubborn fight, we kindled our camp-fires, and, dipping water from its sunken pools covered with slimy green vegetation, we drank our coffee under the shade of the same trees where the desperately wounded lay to die, glad of the luxury of that stagnant pool to quench their thirst. It was the best those heights afforded amid that deathly struggle. All around us lay scattered uncoffined bones, and ghastly skulls looked down upon us where in mockery they had been secured among the branches of the trees, and everywhere earth and trees and broken armament gave silent witness of the awful struggles of our little army. All the way up the heights for miles the pine trees from the roadside yet obstructed the national road as they had been felled to hinder the onward march of our soldiers, while from point to point the Mexican troops and batteries were rallied for another stand. We left the historic spot with a triumphant three-times-three and with uncovered heads in honor both of our dead and our living heroes.

We were soon well up the Rio Frio mountains, and were received near the summit by a terrible war of the elements in the pine forest—thunder, lightning, rain, hail, snow, intense cold, and a howling hurricane. We were drenched through and through, and shook as with an ague, and our poor animals, used to the warm plains below, chilled with cold and in terror from fright, trembled in every limb and crouched helplessly upon the ground, dazed by the lightning and shocked by the thunder which seemed to discharge at our very sides; they seemed almost to cling to us for safety. It was Saturday afternoon, and we found welcome shelter in the hacienda BuenaVista near the mountain summit, a spot made historic afterward as a place of refuge for the unfortunate Emperor Maximilian.

We stopped for our lunch at noon, and were entertained by a company of Mexican rangers or lancers, handsomely uniformed and armed with a long spear with a red pennant and the indispensable lasso of raw-hide, and mounted on superior, hardy Mexican horses.... With their gay trappings of silver-ornamented riding outfit, their swarthy faces, black hair, fierce mustaches, and fiery eyes, the lancers were well calculated to affright the souls of fearful adversaries. Their favorite method of attack was to throw the lasso over their victim, then with their well-trained horses to jerk him from the saddle, drag him to death over the ground, or in mercy lance him. By their invitation I stood at a considerable distance from them to test their skill with the lasso. By the utmost agility I was utterly unable to escape its folds.

Across the valley of Mexico, picturesque with parallel rows of the century plant, which furnishes the national drink of *pulque,* we entered through open gates, the ancient city of Montezuma [Mexico City] not long before conquered and evacuated by the small army of the United States. We found quarters in a comfortable hacienda.... *Pulque* is the lager beer of Mexico. It is everywhere transported on the backs of mules in skins of hogs stripped from them in some mysterious way by which legs and all are utilized for a great bottle.

On the following day the antipathy to Americans was shown on the public plaza near the great cathedral, during the passage of a religious procession of the Host preceded by the ringing of a bell. Every one within hearing indoors or on the street reverently knelt where he was, removed his hat, and made the sign of the cross. This was not regarded by the gold-hunters, who stood erect, curiously gazing at the scene. At once they were set upon by those nearest them, dragged to their knees, and their hats knocked off their heads. A mob quickly gathered. The men resisted with desperation, and had it not been for the prompt interference of others, lives would undoubtedly have been lost and our travels would have ended inside prison walls. This made our longer stay in the city both uncomfortable and hazardous, and once again we mounted our now rested steeds for the trip to the Pacific.

Dissatisfied with my purpose to halt on Sundays for rest and to recruit the horses, some thirty of the company now detached themselves from my command. They were in haste to reach California before the gold was all "dug out," and considered such halting a waste of time. So they bade us good-by and started at a rapid gait in advance.

On this part of the journey we had an illustration of justice in an alcalde's court. Two of our men, who differed about the ownership of a mule, agreed to arbitrate before the alcalde of the village where they chanced to be. One claimant slipped a $2.50 gold piece in the alcalde's hand, and a speedy decision was rendered in his favor. After leaving the town a short distance the other claimant rode back, put a $5 gold piece in the alcalde's hand, and speedily came back with a decision written out in his favor and reversing the other.

Our journeying led us, on Saturday night, to a small walled town not far from the large city of Guadalajara. It had abundant orange as well as banana groves, and a clear stream swept along part of the town. Three hundred miles, in part of rough mountainous travel, had been made during the week; and men and horses were alike worn and weary and glad of so enticing a place of rest. While sipping a cup of coffee in the fonda on Sunday morning I heard the report of a gun in our quarters and a messenger entered hurriedly to say that young W—— (from New Jersey) had shot himself dead. Our quarters were at once crowded by the excited natives, who desired to administer summary punishment on us for what they considered a murder. We held them off till nightfall. As best we could we extemporized a coffin from some rude boards, prepared his body for burial, and I read over him the burial service, and waiting till the town was silent, in midnight darkness, we silently stole out of the town and buried him in a secluded spot, placing at the head of his grave a rude wooden cross to preserve it from desecration.

We arrived at San Blas in excellent health and condition, having lost but one of our number. In port we providentially found the brig *Cayuga,* Captain Savage, of some two hundred tons, belonging to the firm of Pacific traders, Howland & Aspinwall. Captain Savage, an Austrian, had sailed her down the coast in ballast, on the chance that some party of gold-hunters might cross Mexico and require a vessel to transport them to San Francisco.... In the absence of water-casks, red-wood or dug-out canoes filled with supplies of water were stowed below the floor.

As before, we furnished our own sea-stores. They consisted of old whalers' sea-bread, condemned after one voyage of three years to the Arctic seas, well-filled with vermin, which, however, were rendered innocuous by being baked over in a well-heated oven; a supply of well-salted Mexican jerked beef as sold by the yard, sun-dried till it would have answered as well for harness-leather as for food, with coffee and sugar for luxuries. These provisions were placed in sacks and stowed under the flooring, where they were always accessible through an open hatch.

As water was an important factor for so large a number at sea, in addition to the supply in canoes in the hold, a very large canoe was secured on the brig's deck and filled with water, but for economy of stowage a deck of rough boards covered it. In addition to our party Captain Savage had taken on board a full complement of cabin passengers in the little rooms on the after part of the brig. As these few aristocrats of the voyage had paid fabulous prices the captain had contracted to supply them with fresh provisions, and for this purpose a number of goats were taken on board, which were duly served on the cabin table. Added to these Captain Savage, as a perquisite, had embarked a Mexican saddle-horse on deck, so that on this small brig we had about one hundred and fifty men including our gold-diggers, besides the crew, the horse, and a dozen goats. We had no tables, but ate our hardtack and jerked beef and drank our tin mugs of coffee wherever and whenever we found it convenient.

On the eighty-fourth day from New York, anchor was weighed and we set sail for San Francisco. By this time all hardships were accepted as a matter of course, and each man made himself especially jolly over every new danger or deprivation that was encountered. But the old whalers' bread had to be well soaked before it could be eaten, and the writer as well as others lost teeth in the effort to masticate it. On account of the saltness and toughness of the jerked beef, it was found necessary to attach it to ropes and tow it in the sea for forty-eight hours before any attempt could be made either to cook it or eat it without cooking. Sea-bathing may accomplish much good, but it never yet made tender Mexican jerked beef. Our supply certainly never tempted the most hungry shark in our course. The roll of the sea and the tacking of our ship so far emptied our canoes of water that ... we were promptly put on an allowance of something over a pint of water a day each, with which to make our coffee, dampen our whalers' bread, and gratify our thirst. Water of a red color and impregnated with the peculiar odor and taste of the canoes was served daily in this proportion to each mess. But there was no grumbling. Did we not already see the enticing glitter of the yellow gold in the mines of California?

After thirty days on the *Cayuga*, we entered the Golden Gate on the 14th day of May, 1849, and I claim that we were the first organized body to reach that port both by sea and land, although at that date a hundred sail of vessels were at anchor in the harbor.

The time of the journey of the main company was:

From New York by bark *Mara* to Vera Cruz	24 days
From Vera Cruz to embarkation on brig *Cayuga*	60 days
Voyage on the Pacific to San Francisco	30 days
Total	114 days

The thirty seceders who left us at Mexico City arrived at San Blas two weeks after our party, most of them too late to be included in the benefits of the *Cayuga* charter. Both men and horses had broken down on the seven-days-a-week system. They straggled into San Blas, and continued their journey by land to Mazatlan, 200 miles north.... The writer met the first one to arrive in San Francisco in the month of November, ten months after the departure of the buoyant party on the deck of the *Mara*.

from LIFE ON THE PLAINS AND AMONG THE DIGGINGS

ALONZO DELANO

Born in New York, Alonzo Delano (c. 1802–1874) came to California overland in 1849. A merchant and banker by trade, he put to use his good-natured sense of humor and his eye for detail in a series of popular articles for California journals under the pseudonym Old Block. Old Block, as portrayed by Delano and his long-time collaborator artist Charles Nahl, was a long-nosed, cheerful fellow who poked gentle fun at the eccentricities of California's tumultuous new society. His first and most serious work, Life on the Plains and among the Diggings, *was one of the hundreds of overland diaries to emerge from the gold rush.*

NINETY DAYS PREVIOUS to the 5th of April, 1849, had any one told me that I should be a traveler upon the wild wastes between the Missouri River and the Pacific Ocean, I should have looked upon it as an idle jest; but circumstances, which frequently govern the course of men in the journey of life, were brought to bear upon me.

My constitution had suffered sad inroads by disease incident to western climate, and my physician frankly told me that a change of residence and more bodily exertion was absolutely necessary to effect a radical change in my system—in fact, that my life depended upon such a change, and I finally concluded to adopt his advice. About this time, the astonishing accounts of the vast deposits of gold in California reached us, and besides the fever of the body, I was suddenly seized with the fever of mind for gold; and in hopes of receiving a speedy cure for the ills both of body and mind. I turned my attention "westward ho!" and immediately commenced making arrangements for my departure.

I bid adieu to my family and ... proceeded to St. Louis on the steamer *Revolution,* and there took passage for St. Joseph on the *Embassy.*

There was a great crowd of adventurers on the *Embassy.* Nearly every State in the Union was represented. Every berth was full, and not only every settee and table occupied at night, but the cabin floor was covered by the sleeping emigrants. The decks were covered with wagons, mules, oxen, and mining implements, and the hold was filled with supplies. But this was the condition of every boat—for since the invasion of Rome by the Goths, such a deluge of mortals had not been witnessed, as was now pouring from the States to the various points of departure for the golden shores of California. Visions of sudden and immense wealth were dancing in the imaginations of these anxious seekers of fortunes, and I must confess that I was not entirely free from such dreams; and ... I wondered what I should do with all the money which must necessarily come into my pocket! Our first day out was spent in these pleasing reflections, and the song and the jest went round with glee—while the toil, the dangers, and the hardships, yet to come, were not thought of, for they were not yet understood.

A tedious passage of ten days brought us, on the 19th, to St. Joseph, where we learned that the Dayton company, which had preceded us, had left that day, with the intention of moving up the river to some other point for crossing into the Indian Territory, where they would halt until the grass was sufficiently advanced to afford forage for our cattle, and which would give us ample time to overtake them before setting out from the land of civilization, on our arduous journey across the plains.... Our goods and wagon were soon landed, and as every public house in town was crowded by emigrants to overflowing, (having a portable cooking stove,) we slept and messed in our wagon, in one of the back streets; and up to Sunday night, all were enjoying our usual health.

About four o'clock on Monday morning, we were awakened by groans, and cries of distress, from the outside of our wagon. "Who is that?—what is the matter?" I exclaimed, starting from a sound sleep. "Who is sick?"

"It must be Mr. Harris," said Brown, "for he is not in here." We sprang out, and indeed found poor Harris, writhing and agonized, under an attack of cholera. I immediately gave him a large dose of laudanum, the only palliative we had at hand, and dispatched a messenger for a physician. He was violently taken with the worst symptoms, but within an hour was undergoing regular treatment from a skillful physician. For about three hours he suffered intense pain, with vomiting, purging, cramps, and cold extremities, while a clammy sweat started from every pore. During the day we moved him to a more quiet and secluded spot, and his symptoms became more favorable. The evacuations and vomitings ceased, his limbs became warm, his eye brightened, and he thought, as we did, that he better. He remained in this state about three hours, during which we continued our exertions in rubbing him, and making the applications advised by the physician, when all looked upon him out of danger. Suddenly, and without any warning, he began to gasp for breath, and in five minutes lay a corpse before us. We could scarcely credit our senses. He, who but the night before bid as fair to live as any one of us—he, who passed the good natured jest with us, in the fullness of health and strength, now lay extended, an inanimate mass of clay, "one of the things that were." Alas! it was too true, and our friend had "gone to that bourn, from which no traveler returns."

We laid him out on the ground decently, and as well as our slender means would allow, and Brown and myself lay near him that night, keeping a melancholy watch by the light of our camp fire, over the remains of our companion and friend. If an honest, well-meaning man ever lived, poor Harris was one and his simple habits, and virtuous inclinations, had endeared him to us all. We dug his grave ourselves, in the morning, and with no tolling bell to mark the sad requiem, we buried him in a cluster of trees, by the side of a beautiful rivulet.

While I was at work repairing my wagon, the day was very warm, and being unaccustomed to labor, when night came, I went early to bed, at a house where I had obtained lodgings, exhausted by the fatigues of the last few days. Before I got to sleep, I felt strangely. Was there a change in the weather? I could not get warm. I piled on more clothes. I felt as if I was in an ice-house. Ugh! the cold chills were creeping along my back. I involuntarily drew up my knees, and put my head under the bed clothes, but to no purpose—I was shivering, freezing, and then so thirsty!—I wanted a stream of ice-water running down my throat. At length I began to grow warm, warmer; then hot, hotter, hottest. I felt like a mass of living fire—a perfect engine, without the steam and smoke. There seemed to be wood enough from some source, but I poured in water till I thought my boiler would burst, without allaying the raging thirst which consumed me. At last the fever ceased, and then, indeed, the steam burst in a condensed form through the pores of my burning skin, and my body was bathed in a copious perspiration, that left me as weak as any "sucking dove." I had had a visit from my old friends, chill and fever.

Thursday came, and I felt too ill to ride. I lay up to dry; but on Friday morning I went through another baptism of fire and water, the ceremony of which closed about noon. Determined to be with my friends if I was doomed to be sick, and as our medicines were in the wagon, I mounted the pony, Old Shabanay, which had been left for me, and although so weak that I could hardly keep my seat, I started. I soon found my strength increase in the fine air, and when I reached Savannah, a pretty town fourteen miles above St. Joseph, I felt quite well, though weak.

The camp of the company had been about a mile and a half below the ferry, on the bottom, but I found it vacated when I reached it, though the trail of their wagons was plainly to be seen, leading up the high bluff, which runs parallel with the river, and I turned my pony's head towards the Platte. Ascending a long hill, I found the land sparsely covered with timber, and much broken, as far as the eye could see among the trees; but the road marked by our train was on an easy ridge, which led beyond the broken ground into the interior.

The timber [had] continued four or five miles when it ceased, and the eye rested on a broad expanse of rolling prairie, till the heavens and earth seemed to meet on one vast carpet of green. In vain did the eye endeavor to catch a glimpse of some farmhouse, some cultivated field, some herd of cattle cropping the luxuriant grass in the distance; yet no sign of civilization met the eye. All was still and lonely, and I had an overwhelming feeling of wonder and surprise at the vastness and silence of the panorama. It seemed as if the sight of an Indian would have given relief, but not one appeared, and on, on I rode, without seeing a sign of life, and with none but my own thoughts to commune with.

A little before night-fall, on rising a hill, I came suddenly in sight of the encampment of our company, consisting of seventeen wagons and fifty men.... Putting Old Shab to his best gait, in three minutes I stood among my friends, with a glorious appetite to partake of their savory supper of bacon, bread, and coffee.... Soon after my arrival, all hands were summoned, by the blast of the bugle, for the purpose of adopting general rules for mutual safety in traveling and also to detail a guard for the night.

from A FRONTIER LADY

SARAH ROYCE

Sarah Royce (1819–1891) came as an infant from England to the United States and grew up in New York. In the spring of 1849, she and her husband embarked for California, bringing along their two-year-old daughter and an unshakable faith in God. Armed with a pitiful map and a dwindling water supply, Royce endured hostile Indians, battles with cholera, and gnawing hunger during her long overland journey, made longer because (like many emigrants) she refused to travel on Sundays. Thirty years later, Royce recreated her memories of that trip for her son Josiah, a Harvard historian who had his mother's memoirs published in 1932 under the title A Frontier Lady.

Our only guide from Salt Lake City consisted of two small sheets of note paper, sewed together, and bearing on the outside in writing the title "Best Guide to the Gold Mines, 816 miles, by Ira J. Willes, GSL City." This little pamphlet was wholly in writing, there being at that time no printing press at Salt Lake. It was gotten up by a man who had been to California and back the preceding year. The directions, and the descriptions of camping places, together with the distances, seemed pretty definite and satisfactory until they reached the lower part of the Mary's or Humboldt River; when poor camping and scarcity of water were mentioned with discouraging frequency. From the sink of the Humboldt, all seemed confusion.

The only man who now accompanied my husband was considerably advanced in years, and not in perfect health. He was extremely anxious to reach California, but had no means in the world save one solitary ox, a little clothing, and sufficient food to sustain him till he reached El Dorado, if he could go straight through. He offered to put his ox into the team, to help drive and take care of the cattle and assist otherwise, so far as able, for the privilege of traveling in company and having his few things carried. Thus we set forth on the last, and by far the most perilous, stage of our great journey.

We had traveled but a few days when, after camping one evening, we saw approaching a couple of young men, scarcely beyond boyhood, having with them a horse and a mule. They stopped not far from us, turned out their animals to feed, made a fire and took their evening meal, as we were doing;

and, after awhile, came over to our camp to talk. They also had launched out alone, and would be very glad to keep in company with us. As they appeared civil, and one of them rather gentlemanly, we of course did not object. This seemed like a little more protection; but it had its drawbacks; for we soon found out they had very little to eat; and in a few days they began to plead for some of our flour; promising they would hunt, away from the road, every day and bring in game to keep up the supply of provisions. But game was scarce, and very few were the times along the whole way that they caught any. We had allowed a very small margin of provisions for contingencies, because the necessity for the fastest possible traveling was so great.

Still we kept on, sharing, and hoping for the best. Their efforts at hunting, fruitless as they usually were, kept the young men away from the road most of the time, so that we were nearly as much alone as ever. On the morning of the 11th of September they had been away from us for some hours. We were moving quietly along our way, no living creature, save our plodding team and our own feeble company, within sight, when suddenly there appeared from between the hills a party of Indians. As they came nearer we saw they were all armed; and presently several arranged themselves in a sort of a semi-circle closing the road, and one of them laid his rifle across the foreheads of our leaders, and stopped the team.

From my seat in the wagon I had from their first appearance observed every movement. I saw we were completely in their power. Their numbers and their arms were enough to destroy us in a few moments.

At first every appearance was hostile. They were importunate in demanding various things, acted with the air of victors, some of the younger ones pressed close to the wagon, and looked in, with boisterous exclamations and impertinent gestures. But I was enabled to keep a firm unblenching front, taking care that my little Mary did not stir from my side. She was too young to realize any danger, and thought the whole rather amusing. My husband met them from the first with a calm, business-like air, as if he thought they wanted to hold a consultation with him; and when they became overbearing, he still kept on making speeches to them, though we could not perceive that they understood what he said. Their behavior changed several times quite strangely. They would draw nearer together and consult with puzzled looks, some of them still guarding the team. Then they would scowl and seem to differ among themselves. Thus they kept us for perhaps an hour, when, all at once, my husband raised the big ox-whip, shouted to the cattle, and rushed them forward so suddenly that those nearest Indians instinctively stepped aside, then pompously exclaiming "I'm going to move on" he called the old man to follow, and we were once more in motion. But would they let us keep on? I looked through a small gap in the wagon. They were evidently puzzled by such unusual behavior, and as evidently divided in their counsels. Some were vociferating—with their guns in threatening positions—others plainly differed from them, but it was certain they had not quite decided what to do when a turn of the road took us out of sight.

We expected they would way-lay us again; for we were passing through several narrow defiles that day—but the hours went by and night came, without another sight of the enemy. My husband kept guard that night, and I slept very little. The others of our little company disappeared among the bushes and seemed to sleep as well as usual.

Two days after this we met a band of Mormons who had been gold-hunting in California for the summer, and were on their return to Salt Lake. This was the company whose leader was to tell us how we might get from the Sink of the Humboldt ... to Carson River; for that was a part of our journey which yet lay shrouded in grim mystery. The directions given us seemed very plain. He traced out the road in the sand with a stick—I think it was his whip handle. It was taken for granted that we knew our way to the "Sink of the Mary's [Humboldt] River" so he took *that* for his starting point in giving us directions, and showed us that, soon after passing there, we would see a plain wagon track leading to the left, which we were to follow, and it would bring us to grassy meadows, lying two or three miles from the main road, and so, still abounding in feed. Here also, he said, we would find several shallow wells, dug but recently—in the last part of the season—by Mormons, who had gone to spend the winter in California, and on their way there had found these meadows.... The wells, he said had good water in them when he was there a few days before. None of them were deep, but the water was near the surface all about there, and we could, if we found it desirable, scoop out one or two of the holes deeper, let them settle all night, and in the morning have plenty of fresh water.

He was evidently an old and experienced traveler of deserts, plains, and mountains. He advised us to camp in the meadows he described for at least two or three days, let the cattle rest and feed freely, while the men made it their first business to cut as much hay as there was room for in the wagon. This would partly dry while the cattle were recruiting; then load it up, fill every available vessel with water, and set out on the desert about noon of the day, if the weather were cool—otherwise toward evening. When once out on the desert we were to stop at intervals of a few hours, feed some of the hay to the cattle, give them a moderate drink, let them breathe a short time, and then go on. In this way, he said, we would be able to reach Carson River in about twenty-four hours from the time of starting on the desert.

After hearing his instructions, and having the road made thus plain to us, we went on with renewed cheerfulness and energy.

It was now getting late in the season, and we could not help feeling it rather ominous that a thunder-storm overtook us one evening followed by cold nights; and on the evening and night of the 1st of October a terrific wind blew, threatening for hours to strangle us with thick clouds of sand, and to blow our wagon, with all our means of living, over the steep bluff. But a good Providence preserved us, and with the morning calm returned. We had now nearly reached the head of Humboldt Lake, which, at this late period in the dry season, was utterly destitute of water, the river having sunk gradually in the sand, until hereabout it entirely disappeared.

Our director had told us that within about two or three miles beyond the Sink we might look for the road to the left, and we did look, and kept looking, and going on, drearily, till the sun got lower and lower, and night was fast approaching. Then the conviction, which had long been gaining ground in my mind, took possession of the whole party. We had passed the forks of the road before daylight, that morning, and were now miles out on the desert without a mouthful of food for the cattle and only two or three quarts of water in a little cask.

What could be done? Halt we must, for the oxen were nearly worn out and night was coming on. The animals must at least rest, if they could not be fed; and, that they might rest, they were chained securely to the wagon, for, hungry and thirsty as they were they would, if loose, start off frantically in search of water and food, and soon drop down exhausted. Having fastened them in such a way that they could lie down, we took a few mouthfuls of food, and then, we in our wagon and the men not far off upon the sand, fell wearily to sleep; a forlorn little company wrecked upon the desert.

The first question in the morning was, "How can the oxen be kept from starving?" A happy thought occurred. We had, thus far on our journey, managed to keep something in the shape of a bed to sleep on. It was a mattress-tick, and, just before leaving Salt Lake, we had put into it some fresh hay—not very much, for our load must be as light as possible; but the old gentleman traveling with us had also a small straw mattress; the two together might keep the poor things from starving for a few hours. At once a small portion was dealt out to them and for the present they were saved. For ourselves we had food which we believed would about last us till we reached the Gold Mines if we could go right on: if we were much delayed anywhere, it was doubtful. The two or

"Crossing the Plains," 1856, by Charles Nahl

three quarts of water in our little cask would last only a few hours, to give moderate drinks to each of the party. For myself I inwardly determined I should scarcely take any of it as, I had found, throughout the journey, that I could do with less drink than most land travelers. Some of the men, however, easily suffered with thirst, and, as to my little girl, it is well known, a child cannot do long without either water or milk. Everything looked rather dark, and dubious.... All the human aid we had could do but little now; and if, in trying to do that little, one more mistake were made, it must be fatal.

Whence then this calm strength which girded me round so surely, while I and all surrounding me were so weak? I had known what it was to *believe* in God, and to pray that He would never leave us. Was it thus then, that when all other helpers failed, He came so near that I no longer simply *believed* in Him, but *knew* His presence there, giving strength for whatever might come?...That calm strength, that certainty of One near and all sufficient hushed and cheered me. Only a woman who has been alone upon a desert with her helpless child can have any adequate idea of my experience for the next hour or two. But that consciousness of an unseen Presence still sustained me.

When the explorers returned from their walk to the ridge, it was only to report no discovery: nothing to be seen on all sides but sand and scattered sagebrush interspersed with the carcasses of dead cattle. So there was nothing to be done but to turn back and try to find the meadows. Turn back! What a chill the words sent through one. *Turn back* on a journey like that; in which every mile had been gained by most earliest labor, growing more and more intense, until, of late, it had seemed that the certainty of *advance* with every step, was all that made the next step possible. And now for miles we were to go *back*. In all that long journey no steps ever seemed so heavy, so hard to take, as those with which I turned my back to the sun that afternoon of October 4th, 1849.

The next morning we resumed our backward march after feeding out the last mouthful of fodder. The water in the little cask was nearly used up in making coffee for supper and breakfast; but, if only each one would be moderate in taking a share when thirst impelled him, we might yet reach the wells before any one suffered seriously. We had lately had but few chances for cooking; and only a little boiled rice with dried fruit, and a few bits of biscuit remained after we had done breakfast.

If we could only reach the meadows by noon. But that we could hardly hope for, the animals were so weak and tired. There was no alternative, however, the only thing to be done was to go steadily on, determined to do and endure to the utmost.

I found no difficulty this morning in keeping up with the team. They went so slowly, and I was so preternaturally stimulated by anxiety to get forward, that before I was aware of it I would be some rods ahead of the cattle, straining my gaze as if expecting to see a land of promise, long before I had any rational hope of the kind. My imagination acted intensely. I seemed to see Hagar in the wilderness walking wearily away from her fainting child among the dried up bushes, and seating herself in the hot sand. I seemed to become Hagar myself, and when my little one, from the wagon behind me, called out, "Mamma I want a drink"—I stopped, gave her some, noted that there were but a few swallows left, then mechanically pressed onward again, alone, repeating, over and over, the words, "Let me not see the death of the child."

Just in the heat of noon-day we came to where the sage bushes were nearer together; and a fire, left by campers or Indians, had spread for some distance, leaving beds of ashes, and occasionally charred skeletons of bushes to make the scene more dreary. Smoke was still sluggishly curling up here and there, but no fire was visible; when suddenly just before me to my right a bright flame sprang up at the foot of a small bush, ran rapidly up it, leaped from one little branch to another till all, for a few seconds, were ablaze together, then went out, leaving nothing but a few ashes and a little smouldering trunk. It was a small incident, easily accounted for, but to my then over-wrought fancy it made more vivid the illusion of being a wanderer in a far off, old time desert, and myself witnessing a wonderful phenomenon. For a few moments I stood with bowed head worshiping the God of Horeb, and I was strengthened thereby.

Wearily passed the hottest noon-day hour, with many an anxious look at the horned-heads, which seemed to me to bow lower and lower, while the poor tired hoofs almost refused to move. The two young men had been out of sight for sometime; when, all at once, we heard a shout, and saw, a few hundred yards in advance, a couple of hats thrown into the air and four hands waving triumphantly. As soon as we got near enough, we heard them call out, "Grass and water! Grass and water!" and shortly we were at the meadows. The remainder of that day was spent chiefly in rest and refreshment. The next day the men busied themselves in cutting and spreading grass; while I sorted out and re-arranged things in the wagon so as to make all possible room for hay and water; and also cooked all the meat we had left, and as much of our small stock of flour, rice, and dried fruits, as might last us till we could again find wood.

The day after that was Sunday, and we should have had a very quiet rest, had we not been visited by a party of some eight or ten Indians, who came from the Humboldt Mountains on Saturday afternoon, and remained near us till we left. They professed to be friendly; but were rather troublesome, and evidently desirous of getting something out of us if they could. Two or three of them had rifles; and when the young men went to talk to them they began to show off their marksmanship by firing at particular objects. The young men felt this to be rather of the nature of a challenge; and thought it would be safer to accept than to ignore it. So they got the arms from the wagon, set up a mark, and, as one of them—the gentleman of the two—proved to be a remarkable shot, the Indians were struck with surprise, which, as time after time W——'s ball hit within an inch of his aim, grew to admiration, and ended in evident awe; for not one of their party could quite equal him. How much our safety, and exemption from pillage, were due to that young man's true aim we might not be quite sure; but I have always been very willing to acknowledge a debt of gratitude to him.

On Monday morning we loaded up, but did not hurry, for the cattle had not rested any too long; another day would have been better; but we dared not linger. So, giving them time that morning thoroughly to satisfy themselves with grass and water, we once more set forward toward the formidable desert, and, at that late season, with our equipment, the scarcely less formidable Sierras. The feeling that we were once more going forward instead of backward gave an animation to every step which we could never have felt but by contrast.

There was no moon yet, but by starlight we had for some time seen, only too plainly, the dead bodies of cattle lying here and there on both sides of the road. As we advanced they increased in numbers, and presently we saw two or three wagons. At first we thought we had overtaken a company but, coming close, no sign of life appeared. We had candles with us, so, as there was not the least breeze, we lit one or two and examined. Everything indicated a complete break down, and a hasty flight. Some animals were lying nearly in front of a wagon, apparently just as they had dropped down, while loose yokes and chains indicated that part of the teams had been driven on, laden probably with some necessaries of life; for the contents of the wagons were scattered in confusion, the most essential articles alone evidently having been thought worth carrying. "Ah," we said, "some belated little company has been obliged to pack what they could, and hurry to the river. Maybe it was the little company we met the other day." It was not a very encouraging scene but our four oxen still kept their feet; we would drive on a little farther, out of this scene of ruin, bait them, rest ourselves, and go on. We did so, but soon found that what we had supposed an exceptional misfortune must have been the common fate of many companies; for at still shortening intervals, scenes of ruin similar to that just described kept recurring till we seemed to be but the last, little, feeble, struggling band at the rear of a routed army.

Soon we came upon a scene of wreck that surpassed anything preceding it. As we neared it, we wondered at the size of the wagons, which, in the dim light, looked tall as houses against the sky. Coming to them, we found three or four of them to be of the make that the early Mississippi Valley emigrants used to call "Prairie Schooners": having deep beds, with projecting backs and high tops. One of them was specially immense, and, useless as we felt it to be to spend time in examining these warning relics of those who had gone before us, curiosity led us to lift the front curtain, which hung down, and, by the light of our candle that we had again lit, look in. There from the strong, high bows, hung several sides of well-cured bacon, much better in quality than that we had finished at our last resting place. So we had but a short interval in which to say we were destitute of meat, for, though warned by all we saw not to add a useless pound to our load, we thought it wise to take a little, to eke out our scanty supply of food. And as to the young men, who had so rarely, since they joined us, had a bit of meat they could call their own, they were very glad to bear the burden of a few pounds of bacon slung over their shoulders.

After this little episode, the only cheering incident for many hours, we turned to look at what lay round these monster wagons. It would be impossible to describe the motley collection of things of various sorts, strewed all about. The greater part of the materials, however, were pasteboard boxes, some complete, but most of them broken, and pieces of wrapping paper still creased, partially in the form of packages. But the most prominent objects were two or three, perhaps more, very beautifully finished trunks of various sizes, some of them standing open, their pretty trays lying on the ground, and all rifled of their contents; save that occasionally a few pamphlets or, here and there, a book remained in the corners. We concluded that this must have been a company of merchants hauling a load of goods to California, that some of their animals had given out, and, fearing the rest would, they had packed such things as they could, and had fled for their lives toward the river. There was only one thing (besides the few pounds of bacon) that, in all these varied heaps of things, many of which, in civilized scenes, would have been valuable, I thought worth picking up. That was a little book, bound in cloth and illustrated with a number of small engravings. Its title was "Little Ella." I thought it would please Mary, so I put it in my pocket. It was an easily carried souvenir of the desert; and more than one pair of young eyes learned to read its pages in after years.

Morning was now approaching, and we hoped, when full daylight came, to see some signs of the river.... I had again, unconsciously, got in advance; my eyes scanning the horizon to catch the first glimpse of any change; though I had no definite idea in my mind what first to expect. But now there was surely something. Was it a cloud? It was very low at first and I feared it might evaporate as the sun warmed it. But it became rather more distinct and a little higher. I paused, and stood till the team came up. Then walking beside it I asked my husband what he thought that low dark line could be. "I think," he said, "it must be the timber on Carson River." Again we were silent and for a while I watched anxiously the heads of the two leading cattle. They were rather unusually fine animals, often showing considerable intelligence, and so faithful had they been, through so many trying scenes, I could not help feeling a sort of attachment to them; and I pitied them, as I observed how low their heads drooped as they pressed their shoulders so resolutely and yet so wearily against the bows. Another glance at the horizon. Surely there was now visible a little unevenness in the top of that dark line, as though it might indeed be trees. "How far off do you think that is now?" I said. "About five or six miles I guess," was the reply. At that moment the white-faced leader raised his head, stretched forward his nose, and uttered a low "Moo-o-oo." I was startled, fearing it was the sign for him to fall, exhausted. "What is the matter with him?" I said. "I think he smells the water" was the answer. "How can he at such a distance?" As I spoke, the other leader raised his head, stretched out his nose, and uttered the same sound. The hinder cattle seemed to catch the idea, whatever it was; they all somewhat increased their pace, and from that time, showed renewed animation.

But we had yet many weary steps to take, and noon had passed before we stood in the shade of those longed-for trees, beside the Carson River. As soon as the yokes were removed the oxen walked into the stream, and stood a few moments, apparently enjoying its coolness, then drank as they chose, came out, and soon found feed that satisfied them for the present, though at this point it was not abundant. The remainder of that day was spent in much needed rest....We had conquered the desert.

from DEATH VALLEY IN '49

WILLIAM L. MANLY

West of Fort Bridger, Wyoming, overland routes were unmapped and thus more danger-
ous, resulting in an abundance of possible paths. William L. Manly (1820–1903), a
Wisconsin silver miner, led his company of emigrants down the Green and Colorado
Rivers by boat, hoping to float all the way to California. Forced to abandon that route,
they struck out overland for Salt Lake City. In Utah, Manly joined a group called the
Sand Walking Company that headed southward but splintered into separate groups as
the trip wore on. The party Manly was with ended up with a desperately short supply of
food and water on the wrong side of Death Valley. Death Valley in '49, an account of
his harrowing experiences, was written in 1894 and incorporated the stories of several
others who survived Death Valley.

WE TALKED OVER OUR PRESENT POSITION pretty freely, and every one was
asked to speak his unbiased mind, for we knew not who might be right or
who might be wrong, and some one might make a suggestion of the utmost
value. We all felt pretty much downhearted. Our civilized provisions were
getting so scarce that all must be saved for the women and children, and the
men must get along some way on ox meat alone. It was decided not a scrap of
anything that would sustain life must go to waste. The blood, hide, and intes-
tines were all prepared in some way for food. This meeting lasted till late at
night. If some of them had lost their minds I should not have been surprised,
for hunger swallows all other feelings. A man in a starving condition is a
savage. He may be as bloodshed and selfish as a wild beast, as docile and gentle
as a lamb, or as wild and crazy as a terrified animal, devoid of affection, reason,
or thought of justice. We were none of us as bad as this, and yet there was a
strange look in the eyes of some of us sometimes, as I saw by looking round,
and as others no doubt realized, for I saw them making mysterious glances
even in my direction.

When in bed I could not keep my thoughts back from the old home I had
left, where good water and a bountiful spread were always ready at the proper
hour. I know I dreamed of taking a draft of cool, sweet water from a full
pitcher and then woke up with my mouth and throat as dry as dust. The good

107

home I left behind was a favorite theme about the campfire, and many a one told of the dream pictures, natural as life, that came to him of the happy Eastern home with comfort and happiness surrounding it, even if wealth was lacking. The home of the poorest man on earth was preferable to this place. A board of twenty dollar gold pieces could stand before us the whole day long with no temptation to touch a single coin, for its very weight would drag us nearer death. We could purchase nothing with it and we would have cared no more for it as a thing of value than we did the desert sands. We would have given much more for some of the snow, which we could see drifting over the peak of the great snow mountains over our heads like a dusty cloud.

Deeming it best to spare the strength as much as possible, I threw away everything I could, retaining only my glass, some ammunition, sheath knife, and tin cup. No unnecessary burden could be put on any man or beast, lest he lie down under it, never to rise again. Life and strength were sought to be husbanded in every possible way.

[The next] night we had another meeting to decide upon our course and determine what to do. At this meeting no one was wiser than another, for no one had explored the country and knew what to expect. The questions that now arose were "How long can we endure this work in this situation?" "How long will our oxen be able to endure the great hardship on the small nourishment they receive?" "How long can we provide ourselves with food?"

We had a few small pieces of dry bread. This was kept for the children, giving them a little now and then. Our only food was in the flesh of the oxen, and when they failed to carry themselves along we must begin to starve. It began to look as if the chances of leaving our bones to bleach upon the desert were the most prominent ones.

One thing was certain: we must move somewhere at once. If we stay here we can live as long as the oxen do, and no longer, and if we go on it is uncertain where to go, to get a better place. We had guns and ammunition to be sure, but of late we had seen no living creature in this desert wild. Finally Mr. Bennett spoke and said—

"Now I will make you a proposition. I propose that we select two of our youngest, strongest men and ask them to take some food and go ahead on foot to try to seek a settlement, and food, and we will go back to the good spring we have just left and wait for their return. It will surely not take them more than ten days for the trip, and when they get back we shall know all about the road and its character and how long it will take us to travel it. They can secure some other kind of food that will make us feel better, and when the oxen have rested a little at the spring we can get out with our wagons and animals and be safe. I think this is the best and safest way. Now what do you all say?"

After a little discussion all seemed to agree that this was the best, and now it remained to find the men to go. No one offered to accept the position of advance messengers. Finally Mr. Bennett said he knew one man well enough to know that he would come back if he lived, and he was sure he would push his way through. "I will take Lewis (myself) if he will consent to go." I consented, though I knew it was a hazardous journey, exposed to all sorts of things, Indians, climate, and probable lack of water, but I thought I could do it and would not refuse. John Rogers, a large strong Tennessee man, was then chosen as the other one and he consented also.

Now preparations began, Mr. Arcane killed the ox which had so nearly failed, and all the men went to drying and preparing meat. Others made us some new moccasins out of rawhide, and the women made us each a knapsack.

Our meat was closely packed, and one can form an idea how poor our cattle were from the fact that John and I actually packed seven-eighths of all the flesh of an ox into our knapsacks and carried it away. They put in a couple spoonfulls of rice and about as much tea. This seemed like robbery to the children, but the good women said that in case of sickness even that little bit might save our lives. I wore no coat or vest, but took half of a light blanket, while Rogers wore a thin summer coat and took no blanket. We each had a small tin cup and a small camp kettle holding a quart. Bennett had me take his seven-shooter rifle, and Rogers had a good double-barreled shot gun. We each had a sheath knife, and our hats were small brimmed, drab affairs fitting close to the head and not very conspicuous to an enemy as we might rise up from behind a hill into possible views. We tried on our packs and fitted the straps a little so they would carry easy. They collected all the money there was in camp and gave it to us. Mr. Arcane had about thirty dollars and others threw in small amounts from forty cents upward. We received all sorts of advice ... and then we bade them all good-bye. Some turned away, too much affected to approach us, and others shook our hands with deep feeling, grasping them firmly and heartily, hoping we would be successful and be able to pilot them out of this dreary place into a better land.... Mrs. Bennett was the last, and she asked God to bless us and bring some food to her starving children.

We were so much affected that we could not speak and silently turned away and took our course again up the canyon we had descended the night before. After a while we looked back and when they saw us turn around, all the hats and bonnets waved us a final parting.

Those left in camp were Asabel, Bennett and Sarah, his wife, with three children, George, Melissa, and Martha; J. B. Arcane and wife with son Charles.

The youngest children were not more than two years old. There were also the two Earhart brothers, and a grown son, Captain Culverwell, and some others I cannot recall; eleven grown people in all, besides a Mr. Wade, his wife, and three children, who did not mingle with our party, but usually camped a little distance off, followed our trail, but seemed to shun company. We soon passed round a bend of the cañon, and then walked on in silence.

By night we were far up the mountain, near the perpendicular rough peak, and far above us on a slope we could see some bunches of grass and sage brush. We went to this and found some small water holes. No water ran from them they were so small. Here we staid all night.

Through this gap came a cold breeze, and we had to look round to get a sheltered place in which to sleep. We lay down close together, spoon fashion, and made the little blanket do as cover for the both of us. In the morning we filled our canteens, which we had made by binding two powder cans together with strips of cloth, and started for the summit near by. From this was the grandest sight we ever beheld. Looking east we could see the country we had been crawling over since November 4th. "Just look at the cursed country we have come over!" said Rogers as he pointed over it. To the north was the biggest mountain we ever saw, peaks on peaks and towering far above our heads, and covered with snow which was apparently everlasting.

After looking at this grand but worthless landscape long enough to take in its principal features, we asked each other what we supposed the people we left behind would think to see mountains so far ahead. We knew that they had an idea that the coast range was not very far ahead, but we saw at once to go over all these mountains and return within the limits of fifteen days which had been agreed upon between us would probably be impossible, but we must try as best we could, so down the rocky steep we clambered and hurried on our way.

Part way down the mountain a valley or depression opened up in that direction, up which it seemed as if we could look a hundred miles. Near by and a short distance north was a lake of water and when we reached the valley we crossed a clear stream of water flowing slowly toward the lake.

Being in need of water, we rushed eagerly to it and prepared to take a big drink, but the tempting fluid was as salt as brine and made our thirst all the more intolerable. Nothing grew on the bank of this stream and the bed was of hard clay, which glistened in the sun.

In the morning we started on, and near the summit we came to the dead body of Mr. Fish, laying in the hot sun, as there was no material near here with which his friends could cover the remains. This Mr. Fish was the man who left camp some two weeks before in company with another and who carried the long whiplash wound about his body, in hope he could somewhere be able to trade it for bread. No doubt in this very place where he breathed his last, his bones still lie.

We turned now west again, making for a cañon, up which we passed in the hope we should at some turn find a little basin of rain water in some rock. We traveled in it miles and miles, and our mouths became so dry we had to put a bullet or a small smooth stone in and chew it and turn it around with the tongue to induce a flow of saliva. If we saw a spear of green grass on the north side of a rock, it was quickly pulled and eaten to obtain the little moisture it contained.

Thus we traveled along for hours, never speaking, for we found it much better for our thirst to keep our mouths closed as much as possible, and prevent the evaporation. The dry air of that region took up water as a sponge does.

We were so nearly worn out that we tried to eat a little meat, but after chewing a long time, the mouth would not moisten it enough so we could swallow, and we had to reject it. It seemed as if we were going to die with plenty of food in our hand, because we could not eat it.

We tried to sleep but could not, but after a little rest we noticed a bright star two hours above the horizon, and from the course of the moon we saw the star must be pretty truly west of us. We talked a little, and the burden of it was fear that we could not endure the terrible thirst a while longer. The thought of the women and children waiting for our return made us feel more desperate than if we were the only ones concerned. We thought we could fight to the death over a water hole if we could only secure a little of the precious fluid. No one who has ever felt the extreme of thirst can imagine the distress, the despair, which it brings. I can find no words, no way to express it so others can understand.

The moon gave us so much light that we decided we would start on our course, and get as far as we could before the hot sun came out.

In order to not miss a possible bit of water we separated and agreed upon a general course, and that if either one found water he should fire his gun as a signal. After about a mile or so had been gone over I heard Roger's gun and went in his direction. He had found a little ice that had frozen under the clear sky. It was not thicker than window glass. After putting a piece in our mouths we gathered all we could and put it into the little quart camp kettle to melt. We gathered just a kettle full, besides what we ate as we were gathering, and kindled a little fire and melted it.

I can but think how providential it was that we started in the night for an hour after the sun had risen that little sheet of ice would have melted and the

"Emigrant Party on the Road to California," 1849

water sunk into the sand. Having quenched our thirst we could now eat, and found that we were nearly starved also. In making this meal we used up all our little store of water, but we felt refreshed and our lives renewed so that we had better courage to go on.

In the morning the trail led us toward the snow, and as we went along, a brave old crow surprised us by lighting on a bush near the trail, and we surprised him by killing him with a charge of shot. "Here's your fresh meat," said Rogers as he put it into his knapsack to cook for supper, and marched on. As we approached the summit we could see, on the high mountains south of us, some trees, and when we came near the highest part of our road there were some juniper trees near it, which was very encouraging. We crossed over several miles of hard snow, but it moistened up our moccasins and made them soft and uncomfortable. After we had turned down the western slope we killed a small hawk. "Here's your meat," said I, as the poor thin fellow was stowed away for future grub, to cook with the crow.

While eating our stew of crow and hawk, we could see willows, alders, and big sage brush around and we had noticed what seemed to be cottonwoods

112

farther down the cañon, and green trees on the slope of the mountain. We were sure we were on the edge of the promised land and were quite light hearted....As to these birds ... the hawk was pretty fair and quite good eating; but that abominable crow! His flesh was about as black as his feathers and full of tough and bony sinews. We concluded we did not want any more of that kind of bird, and ever since that day, when I have heard people talk of "eating crow" as a bitter pill, I think I know all about it from experience.

There seemed to be no other way for us but to push on in the morning and try to obtain some relief for the poor women and children and then get back to them as fast as ever we could, so we shouldered our packs and went on down the cañon as fast as we could.

About ten o'clock I felt a sudden pain in my left knee, keen and sharp, and as we went along it kept growing worse. I had to stop often to rest, and it was quite plain that if this increased or continued I was sure enough disabled, and would be kept from helping those whom we had left.

We worked along through the tangled brush, [which] got worse and worse as we descended, and at times we walked in the bed of the stream in order to make more headway, but my lameness increased and we had to go very slow indeed.

Before us now was a spur from the hills that reached nearly across our little valley and shut out further sight in that direction and when we came to it we climbed up over it to shorten the distance. When the summit was reached a most pleasing sight filled our sick hearts with a most indescribable joy. I shall never have the ability to adequately describe the beauty of the scene as it appeared to us, and so long as I live that landscape will be impressed upon the canvas of my memory as the most cheering in the world. There before us was a beautiful meadow of a thousand acres, green as a thick carpet of grass could make it, and shaded with oaks, wide branching and symmetrical, equal to those of an old English park, while all over the low mountains that bordered it on the south and over the broad acres of luxuriant grass was a herd of cattle numbering many hundreds if not thousands. They were of all colors, shades, and sizes. Some were calmly lying down in happy rumination, others rapidly cropping the sweet grass, while the gay calves worked off their superfluous life and spirit in vigorous exercise or drew rich nourishment in the abundant mother's milk. All seemed happy and content, and such a scene of abundance and rich plenty and comfort bursting thus upon our eyes, which for months had seen only the desolation and sadness of the desert, was like getting a glimpse of Paradise, and tears of joy ran down our faces. If ever a poor mortal escapes from this world where so many trials come, and joys of a happy Heaven are opened up to him, the change cannot be much more that this which was suddenly opened to us on that bright day which was either one of the very last of December, 1849, or the first of January, 1850. I am inclined to think it was the very day of the new year, but in our troubles, the accuracy of the calendar was among the least of our troubles.

The morning was clear and pleasant. We had our knapsacks filled with good food we had prepared, and were enjoying the cool breeze which came up the valley, when we heard faintly the bark of a dog, or at least we thought we did. If this were true there must be some one living not very far away and we felt better. I was still very lame and as we started along the walking seemed to make it worse again, so that it was all I could do to follow John on the trail down the valley. As we went along a man and woman passed us some distance on the left, and they did not seem to notice us, though we were in plain sight. They were curiously dressed. The woman had no hoops nor shoes, and a shawl wound about her neck and one end thrown over her head was a substitute bonnet. The man had sandals on his feet, with white cotton pants, a calico shirt, and a wide-brimmed, comical, snuff-colored hat. We at once put them down as Spaniards, or then descendants of Mexico, and if what we had read about them in books was true, we were in a set of land pirates, and bloodthirsty men whom we might have occasion to be aware of. We had never heard a word of Spanish spoken, except perhaps a word or two upon the plains which some fellow knew, and how we could make ourselves known and explain who we were was a puzzle to us.

[*After several more days, Manly and Rogers arrived at the Mission of San Fernando and received assistance. They immediately began their arduous return trip to rescue their stranded companions.*]

We were some seven or eight miles along the road when I stopped to fix my moccasin while Rogers went slowly along.... When I had started up again I saw Rogers ahead leaning on his gun and waiting for me, apparently looking at something on the ground. As I came near enough to speak I asked what he had found and he said—"Here is Captain Culverwell, dead." He did not look much like a dead man. He lay upon his back with arms extended wide, and his little canteen, made of two powder flasks, lying by his side. This looked indeed as if some of our saddest forebodings were coming true. How many more bodies should we find? Or should we find the camp deserted, and never find a trace of the former occupants.

About noon we came in sight of the wagons, still a long way off, but in the clear air we could make them out, and tell what they were, without being able to see anything more. Half a mile was the distance between us and the camp before we could see very plainly, as they were in a little depression. We could see the covers had been taken off, and this was an ominous sort of circumstance to us, for we feared the depredations of the Indians.

We surely left seven wagons. Now we could see only four and nowhere the sign of an ox. They must have gone ahead with a small train, and left these four standing, after dismantling them.

No signs of life were anywhere about, and the thought of our hard struggles between life and death to go out and return, with the fruitless results that now seemed apparent, was almost more than human heart could bear. When should we know their fate? When would we find their remains, and how learn of their sad history if we ourselves should live to get back again to settlements and life? If ever two men were troubled, Rogers and I surely passed through the furnace.

One hundred yards now to the wagons and still no sign of life, no positive sign of death, though we looked carefully for both. We fear that perhaps there are Indians in ambush, and with nervous irregular breathing we counsel what to do. Finally Rogers suggested that he had two charges in his shot gun and I seven in the Coll's rifle, and that I fire one of mine and await results before we ventured any nearer, and if there are any of the red devils there we can kill some of them before they get to us. And now both closely watching the wagons I fired the shot. Still as death and not a move for a moment, and then as if by magic a man came out from under a wagon and stood up looking all around, for he did not see us. Then he threw up his arms high over his head and shouted—"The boys have come! The boys have come!" Then other bare heads appeared, and Mr. Bennett and wife and Mr. Arcane came toward us as fast as ever they could. The great suspense was over and our hearts were first in our mouths, and then the blood all went away and left us almost fainting as we stood and tried to step. Some were safe, perhaps all of those nearest us, and the dark shadow of death that had hovered over us, and cast what seemed a pall upon every thought and action, was lifted and fell away, a heavy oppression gone. Bennett and Arcane caught us in their arms and embraced us with all their strength, and Mrs. Bennett when she came fell down on her knees and clung to me like a maniac in the great emotion that came to her, and not a word was spoken. If they had been strong enough they would have carried us to camp upon their shoulders. As it was they stopped two or three times, and turned as if to speak, but there was too much feeling for words, convulsive weeping would choke the voice.

from THE WORLD RUSHED IN

J. S. HOLLIDAY

Sabrina Swain (1825–1912) experienced a very different side of the gold rush—she was one of the thousands of eastern women abandoned by treasure-seeking husbands. Her husband, William, read about California gold in a local Youngstown, New York, newspaper and was convinced he had to see it for himself. Sabrina argued against the idea, especially in light of their newborn daughter. But in the spring of 1849, William joined the now steady stream of wagon trains headed for California. He returned two years later; Sabrina's letters, collected in J. S. Holliday's The World Rushed In, *reveal how difficult and lonely those two years were for her.*

SUNDAY EVENING, APRIL 15, 1849

Dear, dear William,

I want very much to describe my feelings as near as I can, but in doing so I hope not to crucify yours. I feel as though I was alone in the world. The night you left home I did not, nor could not, close my eyes to sleep. Sis slept very well, awoke in the morning, and looked over at me seemingly to welcome a spree with her father, but to her disappointment the looked-for one was absent. She appears very lonesome, and seems to miss you very much. She is very troublesome and will not go to anyone, but cries after me and clings to me more than ever.

I received your daguerrian.... I think I never saw anything but life look more natural. I showed it to Little Cub, and to my astonishment and pleasure she appeared to recognize it. She put her finger on it, looked up at me and laughed, put her face down to yours, and kissed it several times in succession. Every time it comes in her sight she will cry after it.

William, if I had known that I could not be more reconciled to your absence than I am, I never could have consented to your going. However, I will try to reconcile myself as well as I can, believing God will order all things for the best.

Sabrina Swain

YOUNGSTOWN, SUNDAY: JUNE 24, 1849

Dear William,

I have seated myself by the stand in my bedroom to write a line to my absent but much loved husband. It is now twelve o'clock; all is still around me except for the stomping feet and prattling noise of our dear little daughter, who is trotting around and now and then comes to chat a bit with her Ma. Mother is in her rocking chair reading the Bible. George is upstairs on the bed, unwell with the headache.

Eliza is better and grows like a weed. She is rather troublesome nights yet and needs a great deal of care and attention both day and night, more than I feel able to do many times.

I have not been to church today, not being able to go to [choir] practice.... Mother has just been out in the garden and brought in a handful of strawberries, and Sis is running after her crying for them. She is now sitting on the floor eating them. They are not sweet yet, but taste very well.

It is now Monday morning, and I have again attempted to finish this scrawl. I had a very bad night, being this morning anything but a fit subject to write. I was up with Sis till twelve and sick the rest of the night myself.

O! William, I wish I could see you this morning. I dreamed about you last night with my eyes wide open, which I often do, and sometimes with them shut. However, I cannot derive pleasure from my dreams, for you will not have anything to say to me.

We received your letter of the 29th of May on June 22nd. I was somewhat surprised at your slow progress, but was glad to hear of good health and good luck. May God grant that it might be so until your journey is through.

The next morning [Tuesday] After getting your letters, I took them and went down to see Mrs. Bailey, and I read some parts of them to her. She said Mr. Bailey had mentioned some sickness amongst them, but from what she said, I took it to be nothing serious. I hope you will not keep anything back, let it be ever so bad. Nothing could make me feel worse than I do now. I am all the time framing up something that will befall you. I do not place that confidence in God that I ought to; still, I feel that His arm is able to protect you in your absence. But the loss of your society is great, and the longer you are gone the less reconciled I feel.

I assure you of one thing, and that is, if God spares you to get home again, I shall hang on to you as long as there is any of you left. However, my dear, I never have been sorry that I acted the part I did in letting you go, but I think I should act otherwise were it to be done again. This may, as I hope and trust,

117

be a good lesson for us both. It may learn us to be contented with what we have and to enjoy ourselves better when together. I, however, have one thing to comfort me, that we always did live agreeably when together, and often does my mind revert to the times and places that we have been and enjoyed ourselves together. Yet with all this, we cannot realize our attachments and fondness for one another until we are deprived of the society of those fond ones.

Mrs. Bailey and child are well; we see them often. We have not had cholera any nearer than Lockport, and only one case there. I do not give myself uneasiness about it. I only think of it on your part. As for myself I think nothing about it.

It is getting time for the mail, and I must say adieu.

From your affectionate wife,
Sabrina Swain

YOUNGSTOWN, AUGUST 24, '49

Dear William,

I again seat myself to write a line to an absent husband, and it is as usual in a hurry—only half an hour to write all I would like to say.

Little Eliza C. has been bad with diarrhea this week past, but I have at last succeeded in checking it in a small degree. She is not by any means a healthy child, although she appears to be pretty well and grows. She has three double teeth, which she has cut through lately, which may be the cause of her diarrhea. She tries to talk a great deal and does in her fashion. She can say "poor Pa" as plain as any one. She is a great deal of company for me, and I often think if she should be taken away, I could not be reconciled to it under my present affliction. May God grant that I may not be called to pass through the trial.

I often think what a tedious summer you have spent; makes me shudder and think you have had to exercise a great deal of patience to endure all you must have had to pass through. May God grant that this absence and journey may prove to be a wise lesson to us both. O! William, if I could see you this morning, I would hug and kiss you till you would blush.

When you get where you can write with comfort, write me a great, long letter and tell me just how you feel, all the hardships of your journey. Do not keep anything back.

Father's people join in love to you.

So good-bye for this time.
Sabrina Swain

Letters from Home

RACHEL ANN BROWN

Rachel Ann Brown's husband, David, was one of the five thousand African-Americans who had joined the rush to California by 1860. While he was gone, Brown struggled alone in Lancaster, Ohio, supporting herself as a launderess and servant. As the years passed, she remained hopeful that David would earn enough money to bring her out to California, but he never did. He instead bought a house in Downieville and settled there without her. Her melancholy letters to her husband illustrate the concerns of those the gold rush left behind.

LANCASTER OHIO
October 18th, 1852

My dear husband,

I recived your kind letter which found us enjoying good health. I was glad to heare that you was well & that you have arived there safe, you was no longer on the road than I expected you would be, but I am glad that you got through safe. You must not think strange of me not writing sooner, you did not tell me to write to any point on the way & I thougt it not expediant to write until you would get through as I heard so many reports, but I told you in the other letter I want you to write me a letter as soon as you recived this, so I will get a letter every month.

I would like to have you home for I am very lonely without you. Provisions are high here, in this place, I never knew it so high before, they are selling at city prices. My pigs are fine order, I must buy some more corn this week, they cost me great deal....We cannot get any one to saw your wood half the time & it cost so much. We have a good garden this summer, cabbage firstrate, sweet potatoes very fine. We raised a barrel of Irish potatoes, the tree was very full of appels. I told you all about mother visit in the other letter. Woodruff has not come yet, he was detained on account of Samuel has been very low ever since he went with Shaffer, seven months that he has been sick & he is not able to sit up yet but as soon as he can ride Woodruff will bring him home. James Bankes will be here this week or next, he intends to live in this place. Woodruff wife is here & baba. I don't know weather he will stay here or not but they will stay until spring. I told you in my other letter that mother intended to visit Canada but she has declined this winter—perhaps in the Spring she may go with him on a visit. Best I writ & let you know we have worked very hard this summer.

I am so lonesome, tired & discouraged & everything. I suppose that you do your washing yourself. I have had one tooth drawn since you left but my health other wise has been very good. You did not tell me about the dog.

You must not fail to write me when you get this, you must excuse bad writing as I have been washing all day & my hands is stiff. I must now close my leter for it is dark and I must send it to the office.

You must not think that I will forget you, for I think more of every day so I hope that you will have a better opinion of your wife then that.

I remain your affectionate wife. Write soon.

Mrs R A Brown to Mr D Brown

LANCASTER, OHIO
March 4th, '55

My Dear Husband,

I take this method to inform you that I received your kind favor this evening which found me enjoying tolerable health. I have a very bad pain in my head. It is Cold. I have written you several letters quit recently every mail except one when I did not received any frome you. I am going to look for a situation before long as soon as the weather brake up, then I will let you know what I can buy for & where, then I will let you know all about it. You are excuseable for what you said in your last. I suppose you feel freted sometimes as I do. I will strive to get a place without fail.

Mrs. Lennet is going to start next month. Uncle John Jones expect to start in May. Mr. Matson family is giving to move back again to Chillcothe, they will be quit a turn around here in the Spring. If you could this Spring or not you must let me know the precise time. I have nothing very perticular this time but I hope that I will be able to tell you all about a home in the next. Little Sis Johnson send her love to her uncle Brown & you must send her a prestant. Eliza Johnson send her love to you. Don't you forget Turner to send him some money whatever you do. Bill Peck is going to farming. He has bought part of the Clark farm. They are about to begin a school here but they want white teacher & the Col. [colored] want a Col. one. I don't know how they will make it yet.

My dear husband, if you had your business arrainged so you could come home I would be glad so we could get fix to housekeep. If you had I do think that if we could get a place improved it would be better but perhaps we would have to pay more for it, perhaps it may have trees on & other conveniences but I will see. The weather is getting mild again but very dry & dusty. I think that we will have another hot summer.

Mother said that you must come soon. She send her best respects to you. You must excuse this short letter & believe me to be your affectionate wife. Good night. Write more than I have when you write.

Rachel Ann Brown to Mr. David Brown

"The Independent Gold Hunter on the Way to California," c. 1850

from PIONEER DAYS IN CALIFORNIA

JOHN CARR

Gold's siren song proved hard to resist. John Carr (1827–1896), an Irishman who came to the United States as a child, left Peoria, Illinois, for California at age twenty-two. Like so many other hopeful Argonauts, Carr found it difficult to make a living in the mines and turned to another trade—blacksmithing—and prospered on the northern coast of California. But in 1880 the promise of gold seduced him once again, sending him this time from Eureka to Arizona, where he became the first mayor of the town of Tombstone. Four years later he was back in Eureka, where his autobiography, Pioneer Days in California, *was published in 1891.*

FROM FORT BRIDGER our objective point was Salt Lake City. We found the road very mountainous and rough, and it was with much pleasure that we finally found ourselves at the top of the mountain ridge overlooking the great Salt Lake Valley. The road down to the valley was very steep. Locks on the wheels were of very little account, and we cut a small bushy tree and tied it to the hind axle of the wagon, which acted as a capital brake, and we got down all right.

We were now safe in Brigham's dominions, and had to put on our good behavior. We found the city to be one of magnificent distances. The town lots were very large—two or three acres in extent; broad streets, with ditches of water running through them, and rows of trees set out on each side, gave the city a very neat and home-like appearance.

The houses were principally one-story, and built of adobe. Brigham's house was the largest in the city, two stories in height, and it was not much of a house at that. The temple was a large, round house, capable of seating a large number of people. Here the elders and bishops every Sunday preached to the faithful, and abused Uncle Sam and his government. We drove to the city and camped about a mile out of town on the emigrant road, intending to remain about one week to rest and recruit our team for the remainder of the trip.

Being the "kid" of the camp, I was sent on a foraging expedition for fresh "grub," such as butter, milk, eggs, cheese, and fresh vegetables. I had no trouble in buying such things at reasonable prices. We lived on the fat of the land while we sojourned with the followers of Joseph. When laying in our stores before we started from Fort Leavenworth, we bought only sufficient flour to last until we should arrive at Salt Lake, expecting to replenish our stock there for the remainder of the trip. When we got to Salt Lake, however, we found we could not buy anything in the shape of bread-stuff on account of an order Brigham Young had made that no bread-stuff should be sold until the new crop came in. This left us in a bad fix, for we would have to lie over six or seven weeks, much against our will, and the faithful would not, or dare not, disobey the orders of their prophet, priest, and king.

On one of my foraging expeditions I met Brigham himself. I had become acquainted with an old Vermont lady who made excellent butter, and who was a splendid talker on her side of the question. She tried hard to convert me, and told me I would make a splendid Mormon. During one of my visits to her house I met a gentleman of about forty years of age, very pleasing in his address. About the first question he put to me was: "Young man, are you as anxious for the salvation of your soul as you are to go to California and get gold?"

My answer was that the salvation of my soul did not bother me much about that time.

He wanted to know my name, where I was from, what religion I professed, my occupation, and if I had any prejudice against the Mormons. All of the questions were properly answered. As regards prejudice against the Mormons I had none, as I had never seen a Mormon to my knowledge until I arrived at Salt Lake.

He then proposed to me to stay at Salt Lake and he would give me employment until fall at five dollars per day, and if we liked each other, he would then start me in business; and as further inducement, if I would join the Church I would no doubt rise to eminence as a servant of the Lord and a pillar of the Church. All of which I respectfully declined.

The next day I called on my Vermont lady friend. She wanted to know how I liked the Governor.

"Governor who?" I asked.

"Why, Governor Young—the gentleman you were talking to yesterday!"

"Great Scott! Was that Governor Young?"

"Yes, indeed it was, and he has taken a liking to you. You had better stay here and take his offer."

I have often thought what a fine old Mormon elder I would have made, or maybe a bishop, with half a dozen wives, and no end of young Mormons. But Brigham and the saints lost an elder or a bishop, and California gained a blacksmith.

from THE LIFE AND ADVENTURES OF JAMES P. BECKWOURTH

JAMES P. BECKWOURTH

James P. Beckworth (1798–c. 1867) was a Virginia-born, African-American fur trapper and mountain man who found opportunity in the wide open spaces of the West. He visited California in the 1830s and '40s and lived for several years as a member of the Crow Indians. During the gold rush, he led emigrant wagon trains through a pass he discovered in the Sierra Nevada. Colorful and garrulous, in 1856 he dictated his memoirs to Thomas Bonner, a justice of the peace in gold country. Bonner polished up Beckworth's story and published it as The Life and Adventures of James P. Beckworth.

BECOMING TIRED of my business in Sonora, for inactivity fatigued me to death, I disposed of my interest in it for six thousand dollars, and went on to Sacramento City with the money in my pocket.... Thence I proceeded to Greenwood Valley to establish my winter quarters, but I was seized with an attack of inflammatory rheumatism, and I had a nice time of it that winter. Before I was able to get about, I was called on by the inhabitants to go several miles to shoot a grizzly bear, and as I was unable to walk the distance, several of them volunteered to carry me. The bear was in the habit of walking past a row of cabins every morning on his return to his den, he having issued forth the preceding night to procure his evening meal. They had fired several shots at Bruin as he passed, but he had never deigned to pay any attention to the molestation. I mounted a horse, and rode some distance to his customary path, until I came to a tree which offered a fair shelter to await his approach. I place my back against it as a support while I awaited his coming, the neighbors drawing off to a safe distance to witness the sport. By-and-by Grizzly came in sight, walking along as independently as an alderman elect. I allowed him to approach till he was within twenty paces, when I called out to him; he stopped suddenly, and looked around to ascertain whence the sound proceeded. As he arrested himself, I fired, and the ball entered his heart. He advanced ten or fifteen paces before he fell; observers shouted to me to run, they forgetting in their excitement that I had not strength to move. The bear never stirred from where he fell, and he expired without a groan. When dressed, he weighed over fourteen hundred pounds.

The next spring I engaged in mining and prospecting in various parts of the gold region. I advanced as far as the American Valley, having one man in my company, and proceeded north into the Pitt River country, where we had a slight difficulty with the Indians. We had come upon a party who manifested the utmost friendship toward us; but I, knowing how far friendly appearances could be trusted to, cautioned my partner on no account to relinquish his gun, if the Indians should attempt to take it. They crowded round us, pretending to have the greatest interest in the pack that we carried, until they made a sudden spring, and seized our guns, and attempted to wrest them from our grasp. I jerked from them, and retreated a few steps; then, cocking my gun, I bade them, if they wished to fight, to come on. This produced a change in their feelings, and they were very friendly again, begging caps and ammunition of us, which, of course, we refused. We then walked backward for about one hundred and fifty yards, still keeping our pieces ready should they attempt further hostilities; but they did not deem it prudent to molest us again.

While on this excursion I discovered what is now known as "Beckwourth's Pass" in the Sierra Nevada. From some of the elevations over which we passed I remarked a place far away to the southward that seemed lower than any other. I made no mention of it to my companion, but thought that at some future time I would examine into it farther.

It was the latter end of April when we entered upon an extensive valley at the northwest extremity of the Sierra range. The valley was already robed in freshest verdure, contrasting most delightfully with the huge snow-clad masses of rock we had just left. Flowers of every variety and hue spread their variegated charms before us; magpies were chattering, and gorgeously-plumaged birds were caroling in the delights of unmolested solitude. Swarms of wild geese and ducks were swimming on the surface of the cool crystal stream, which was the central fork of the Rio de las Plumas [Feather River], or sailed the air in clouds over our heads. Deer and antelope filled the plains, and their boldness was conclusive that the hunter's rifle was to them unknown. Nowhere visible were any traces of the white man's approach, and it is probable that our steps were the first that ever marked the spot.

We struck across this beautiful valley to the waters of the Yuba, from thence to the waters of the Truchy [Truckee], which latter flowed in an easterly direction, telling us we were on the eastern slope of the mountain range. This, I at once saw, would afford the best wagon-road into the American Valley approaching from the eastward, and I imparted my views to three of my companions in whose judgment I placed the most confidence. They thought highly of the discovery, and even proposed to associate with me in opening the road. We also found gold, but not in sufficient quantity to warrant our working it; and, furthermore, the ground was too wet to admit of our prospecting to any advantage.

On my return to the American Valley, I made known my discovery to a Mr. Turner, proprietor of the American Ranch, who entered enthusiastically into my views; it was a thing, he said, he had never dreamed of before. If I could but carry out my plan, and divert travel into that road, he thought I should be a made man for life. Thereupon he drew up a subscription-list, setting forth the merits of the project, and showing how the road could be made practicable to Bidwell's Bar, and thence to Marysville, which latter place would derive peculiar advantages from the discovery. He headed the subscription with two hundred dollars.

When I reached Bidwell's Bar and unfolded my project, the town was seized with a perfect mania for the opening of the route. The subscriptions toward the fund required for its accomplishment amounted to five hundred dollars. I then proceeded to Marysville, a place which would unquestionably derive greater benefit from the newly-discovered route than any other place on the way, since this must be the entrepôt or principal starting-place for emigrants.

The mayor entered warmly into my views, and pronounced it as his opinion that the profits resulting from the speculation could not be less than from six to ten thousand dollars; and as the benefits accruing to the city would be incalculable, he would insure my expenses while engaged upon it.

I mentioned that I should prefer some guarantee before entering upon my labors, to secure me against loss of what money I might lay out.

"Leave that to me," said the mayor; "I will attend to the whole affair. I feel confident that a subject of so great importance to our interests will engage the earliest attention."

I thereupon left the whole proceeding in his hands, and, immediately setting men to work upon the road, went out to the Truchy to turn emigration into my newly-discovered route. While thus busily engaged I was seized with erysipelas, and abandoned all hopes of recovery; I was over one hundred miles away from medical assistance, and my only shelter was a brush tent. I made my will, and resigned myself to death. Life still lingered in me, however, and a train of wagons came up, and encamped near to where I lay. I was reduced to a very low condition, but I saw the drivers, and acquainted them with the object which had brought me out there. They offered to attempt the new road if I thought myself sufficiently strong to guide them through it. The women, God bless them! came to my assistance, and through their kind attentions and excellent nursing I rapidly recovered from my lingering sickness, until I was soon able to mount my horse, and lead the first train, consisting of seventeen wagons, through "Beckwourth's Pass." We reached the American Valley without the least accident, and the emigrants expressed entire satisfaction with the route. I returned with the train through to Marysville, and on the intelligence being communicated of the practicability of my road, there was quite a public rejoicing. A northern route had been discovered, and the city had received an impetus that would advance her beyond all her sisters on the Pacific shore. I felt proud of my achievement, and was foolish enough to promise myself a substantial recognition of my labors.

I was destined to disappointment, for that same night Marysville was laid in ashes. The mayor of the ruined town congratulated me upon bringing a train through. He expressed great delight at my good fortune, but regretted that their recent calamity had placed it entirely beyond his power to obtain for me any substantial reward. With the exception of some two hundred dollars subscribed by some liberal-minded citizens of Marysville, I have received no indemnification for the money and labor I have expended upon my discovery. The city had been greatly benefited by it, as all must acknowledge, for the emigrants that now flock to Marysville would otherwise have gone to Sacramento. Sixteen hundred dollars I expended upon the road is forever gone, but those who derive advantage from this outlay and loss of time devote no thought to the discoverer; nor do I see clearly how I am to help myself, for every one knows I can not roll a mountain into the pass and shut it up.

In the spring of 1852 I established myself in Beckwourth Valley, and finally found myself transformed into a hotel-keeper and chief of a trading-post. My house is considered the emigrant's landing-place, as it is the first ranch he arrives at in the golden state, and is the only house between this point and Salt Lake. Here is a valley two hundred and forty miles in circumference, containing some of the choicest land in the world. Its yield of hay is incalculable; the red and white clovers spring up spontaneously, and the grass that covers its smooth surface is of the most nutritious nature. When the weary, toil-worn emigrant reaches this valley, he feels himself secure; he can lay himself down and taste refreshing repose, undisturbed by the fear of Indians. His cattle can graze around him in pasture up to their eyes, without running any danger of

129

being driven off by the Arabs of the forest, and springs flow before them as pure as any that refreshes this verdant earth.

When I stand at my door, and watch the weary, way-worn travelers approach, their wagons holding together by a miracle, their stock in the last stage of emaciation, and themselves a perfect exaggeration of caricature, I frequently amuse myself with imagining the contrast they must offer to the *tout ensemble* and general appearance they presented to their admiring friends when they first set out upon their journey.

We will take a fancy sketch of them as they start from their homes. We will fancy their strong and well-stored wagon, bran-new for the occasion, and so firmly put together that, to look at it, one would suppose it fit to circum-rotate the globe as many times as there are spokes in the wheels; then their fat and frightened steers, so high-spirited and fractious that it takes the father and his two or three sons to get each under the yoke; next, the ambitious emigrant and his proud family, with their highly-raised expectations of the future that is before them: the father, so confident and important, who deems the Eastern States unworthy of his abilities, and can alone find a sufficiently ample field in the growing republic on the Pacific side; the mother, who is unwilling to leave her pleasant gossiping friends and early associations, is still half-tempted to believe that the crop of gold that waits their gathering may indemnify her for her labors; so they pull up stakes, and leave town in good style, expecting to return with whole cart-loads of gold dust, and dazzle their neighbors' eyes with their excellent good fortune.

The girls, dear creatures! put on their very best, as all their admiring beaux assemble to see them start, and to give them the last kiss they will receive east of the Nevada Mountains; for their idea is that they will be snatched up and married the moment they step over the threshold into California by some fine young gentleman who is a solid pile of gold, and they joyously start away, in anticipation of the event, their hats decked with ribbons, their persons in long-flowing riding-dresses, their delicate fingers glittering with rings, and their charming little ankles incased in their fashionable and neatly-laced gaiters.

At the close of day, perhaps amid a pelting rain, these same parties heave wearily into sight: they have achieved the passage of the Plains, and their pleasant Eastern homes, with their agreeable, sociable neighbors, are now at a distance it is painful to contemplate. The brave show they made at starting, as the whole town hurried them off, is sadly faded away. Their wagon appears like a relic of the Revolution after doing hard service for the commissariat: its cover burned into holes, and torn to tatters; its strong axles replaced with rough pieces of trees hewn by the wayside; the tires bound on with ropes; the

130

iron linchpins gone, and chips of hickory substituted, and rags wound round the hubs to hold them together, which they keep continually wetted to prevent falling to pieces. The oxen are held up by the tail to keep them upon their legs, and the ravens and magpies evidently feel themselves ill treated in being driven off from what they deem their lawful rights.

The old folks are peevish and quarrelsome; the young men are so headstrong, and the small children so full of wants, and precisely at a time when every thing has given out, and they have nothing to pacify them with. But the poor girls have suffered the most. Their glossy, luxuriant locks, that won so much admiration, are now frizzled and discolored by the sun; their elegant riding-habit is replaced with an improvised Bloomer, and their neat little feet are exposed in sad disarray; their fingers are white no longer, and in place of rings we see sundry bits of rag wound round, to keep the dirt from entering their sore cuts. The young men of gold, who looked so attractive in the distance, are now too often found to be worthless and of no intrinsic value; their time employed in haunting gaming-tables or dram-shops, and their habits corrupted by unthrift and dissipation.

I do not wish to speak disparagingly of my adopted state, and by no means to intimate the slightest disrespect to the many worthy citizens who have crossed the Plains. I appeal to the many who have witnessed the picture for the accuracy of my portraiture. So much good material constantly infused into society ought to improve the character of the compound, but the demoralizing effects of transplantation greatly neutralize the benefits.

Take a family from their peaceful and happy homes in a community where good morals are observed, and the tone of society exercises a salutary influence over the thoughts of both old and young, and put them in such a place as this, where all is chaotic, and the principles that regulate the social intercourse of men are not yet recognized as law, and their dignity of thought and *prestige* of position is bereft from them. They have to struggle among a greedy, unscrupulous populace for the means of living; their homes have yet acquired no comfort, and they feel isolated and abandoned; and it is even worse upon the children; all corrective influence is removed from them, and the examples that surround them are often of the most vicious and worst possible description. All wholesome objects of ambition being removed, and money alone substituted as the reward of their greed, they grow up unlike their fathers; and it is only those in whom there is a solid substratum of correct feeling that mature into good citizens and proper men.

The girls, too, little darlings, suffer severely. They have left their worthy sweethearts behind, and can not get back to them; and those who now offer themselves here are not fit to bestow a thought upon. Every thing is strange to them. They miss their little social reunions, their quilting-parties, their winter quadrilles, the gossip of the village, their delightful summer haunts, and their dear paternal fireside. They have no pursuits except of the grosser kinds, and all their refinements are roughed over by the prevailing struggle after gold.

Numbers have put up at my ranch without a morsel of food, and without a dollar in the world to procure any. They never were refused what they asked for at my house; and, during the short space that I have spent in the Valley, I have furnished provisions and other necessaries to the numerous sufferers who have applied for them to a very serious amount. Some have since paid me, but the bills of many remain unsettled. Still, although a prudent business man would condemn the proceeding, I can not find it in my heart to refuse relief to such necessities, and, if my pocket suffers a little, I have my recompense in a feeling of internal satisfaction.

from GOLD RUSH

J. GOLDSBOROUGH BRUFF

J. Goldsborough Bruff (1804–1889), born in Washington, D.C., was forced to resign from West Point in 1822 after wounding a classmate in a pistol duel. After sailing through Europe and South America for several years as a cabin boy, Bruff got a job with the U.S. Bureau of Topographical Engineers and made the first state map of Florida in 1846. A self-styled military commander, he formed the Washington City Mining Company in 1849 and led its sixty-six members overland to the Sierra Nevada, where his men abandoned him on the Lassen Trail as winter set in. Luckily, a fellow Mason named Poyle rescued him and together they made it to California the following spring. The grueling experience apparently dimmed Bruff's appetite for excitement because he soon caught a ship back to New York. His remarkably detailed, thousand-page journal was finally published in 1944.

[MARCH] 29TH. COMMENCES CLEAR AND CALM, temp. 54°—Hunger awakened me at dawn, and though exceedingly feeble, I must endeavor to preserve my life, [not] for its value to me at all, but for those who now little dream of my sad circumstances. I took my gun, and walked down the hollow again; the robins were crying & hopping about among the cedars, but flew before I could get near them. Saw a bald eagle and several vultures soaring over head. Fever and acid stomach. A flock of geese flew over to the Northward,—they were low enough to shoot, but I was too weak to raise my gun in time. The blue woodpeckers are as shy as the robins. Cannot get nearer than 200 yards of either, and have no fine shot.—I am compelled to charge with heavy loads of buck-shot any how, in case of meeting deer or other beast. Returned exhausted: threw myself down, and rested. I then made coffee, drank a pint, put a teaspoonful of salt in ¹/₂ pint grounds, and eat that. I hunted around the cabin, and found several naked leg-bones of deer, long since stripped by the dogs and wolves;—these I gladly gathered, and carried to my abode. I cracked a couple, and found in each a yellow shrivelled string of marrow. I warmed some water, washed them some, & boiled them, producing a very *cheesy*-tasting broth.—This, seasoned with pepper and salt, I greedily swallowed, at 11 AM. A large mixed flock, of geese & swan, flew over, to the N.W.

Robins are chirping, but they are not for me to eat. At dusk a flock of geese passed,—going to the N. and flew high.—Their gabbling startled me, as has happened before. Geese and cranes, when distant, sound very much like human voices,—and always sets my pup barking, as no doubt he is thus deceived also.—Must I eat my faithful watch?—My poor little Nevada, who has shared my sufferings?—for one meal, and then die regretting it?—I will not! Drank balance of bone broth. Have a few bones left for to-morrow.

Night clear and mild;—Wild fowl flying over all night. I got on the roof of the cabin, at night, with great difficulty, and lay there some time, looking for a grizzler to come along. The night breeze moans through the dells and among the tall trees; the howl of a distant wolf is heard, and in an adjacent tree, an old owl is hooting his monotonous ditty. All else is still, here, in this lovely spot.— Hush! I hear music! a sweet pathetic air, on the flute, &c!—Am I dreaming? No! There! I heard a cock crow! and a child laugh! What does all this mean?— Am I crazy?—certainly not. Pshaw! Of course there must be queer sounds here, caused by the various obstructions to the passage of the light breeze up these hollows, through trees, &c. I asked myself, audibly, (while peering around, with my hand upon my rifle,) if I was not too philosophical to allow my mind to give way, and sinking into imbecility, frustrate my struggles to save my life for the benefit of my wife and children? I rose, clenched my teeth, and said "Yes!" I was chilled;—walked over to lonely couch, and fell asleep.

MARCH 30TH. Commences clear, light W. wind, temp. 50°—A flock of geese just flew over to the N.W. Weakness and acid stomach annoying. If Clough does not return to-day, he is undoubtedly gone forever! I had a number of deer-skins hanging on a line, to dry.—I examined them, & found, where the flesh side adhered, there were some very small strips of dry meat, and these places were full of worms; I carefully opened them, and with my butcher-knife, scraped out the *skippers*, and tore off the bits of meat; resulting in giving me about a gill of very *gamey* venison. This boiled with two old cracked leg-bones, and another inch of tallow candle, made me broth, which with coffee had to serve for breakfast. I then shouldered my gun, and pouch, and started to go ahead, on the road as far as I dare, to look for game, and maybe to find the remains of my friend. I started several deer, many grouse, and numerous small birds;—all seemed to know that I was a doom'd man— Proscribed by Heaven!—An outlaw; and they must not allow me to come near enough to shoot them; must not contribute to support me, against the will of Heaven!—Such thoughts ran through my brain; I staggered, and sank against a huge pine. Here I fell in a trance, and thought I was most comfortable at home,—my little boy was at my side, and parting my long and matted hair with his little hands.—Was brought to consciousness by a nose, and heard a wolf bark.—I now raised myself with difficulty; and retraced my weary feeble steps, to my melancholy-looking lodge, set my gun against the side, and threw myself down exhausted on my pallet; where I lay about ¹/₂ hour. I suppose I travelled about five miles.

Sun-set clear, moderate W.N.W. wind, temp. 56°— The road, as far as I went to-day, is nearly clear of snow. The tracks of grizzly-bears and wolves are thick upon it, going & coming this way, and some of them very recent. A grizzler must have gone on a very short time on the road before me. His track was perfectly fresh in the mud and snow. Deer tracks in all directions.

I made coffee and eat the grounds, with salt, for supper.

MARCH 31ST. I slept little, but soundly last night—latter part, and this morning. Just before I awoke, this morning, dreamt of having just arrived at home, and embracing my family. Spoiled venison tea & coffee, for breakfast, and I again took my gun and went to try for game of any kind.—It commenced drizzling ere I reached 300 yards, and I found myself too feeble to proceed, so returned.

I recollected that Roberts had put a deer's head under the eaves of the cabin, a long time since, where it became wedged in the logs, and he could not conveniently extricate it, to give the dogs—This I sought.—Ha! I have food! I thought. On reaching it, I with much difficulty got it down by the aid of a pole; and found it half-decayed, and consumed by worms & insects.— However, I took it to a stump, near my tent, chopped it up with a hatchet, and cut out the shrivelled tongue. Gave the head and root of the tongue to my faithful pup, and put the small half of the tongue in a kettle to cook. While this was boiling, I overhauled the skins again, and found one, of a fawn, with the hoofs and fetlock-joints attached.—These I cut off, scraped out the worms, singed off most of the hair, and threw them also in the kettle. Then I made coffee, and thank God! had another meal, with some solid food; which possessed a queer taste; and would have been, probably, in different circumstances, quite disgusting!

Attacked with what I at first conceived to be a whooping noise in my chest, on breathing when walking; it annoyed me much, and I thought several times that it was the howl of a distant wolf. On walking out to-day, this low wolf-howl haunted me, for go where I would, in every position, and in calm or breeze, still the same monotonous low howl of a wolf was heard; and though so low as to sound like the voice of a wolf at least two miles off, yet it seemed to be near me! I tried my breathing, and ascertained that it was not thus produced! I reflected on it; what could it be? When at rest it rested also! I asked myself if I was becoming superstitious? or crazy? I then recollected that prolonged hunger produced insanity; and I reasoned with my own mind on that subject. Can I not stave off these dreadful consequences of starvation & weakness? Can I not rally my mind to struggle against such disastrous results?—"It must be done!" said I;—gritting my teeth and clenching my fist!—There is a reasonable and philosophical cause for this annoyance, this mysterious, and now painful sound. It shall haunt me no more! And I will be rendered miserable no longer, in mind, when I walk out, by this strange bogee of the winds! Could the breeze passing through my pouch-belt cause it? I walked a few paces, disproving that. Then I thought there might be something about my old felt hat—No! Maybe there was something in my ear; I tried them, nothing in my ears! I sat down in a tremor of nervousness; could not rationally account for the irksome sound! My gun fell over, and that suggested the truth;—the air passing over the muzzle!—I arose, and walked, holding my gun at a trail, so as the breeze or motion of walking would cause the current of air to pass obliquely across the muzzle.—This was the cause!—My anxiety was relieved;—it felt almost as serviceable as a good meal! I am not weak-minded! I am yet sane!—Thank God!

Reflecting on the crisis, I see but one chance of saving myself. The impediment to attempt travelling in to the settlements existed in disability to walk, from rheumatic pains in my spine & loins, and legs,—particularly the latter; to say naught about debility. At present, if I attempted it, prostration would leave me on the route for the bears & wolves to devour; and there is as much chance to kill game here as any where. And there is nothing on the road to subsist on. Now I have, in reserve, two tallow candles, and likewise a dozen acorns, which I had preserved for specimens.—These have just occurred to my memory. The candles will answer to travel on, when I can walk; and in order to relieve the pain in my legs, I shall at once set to and rub them, and continue to do so every day several times with camphor and cayenne, both of which I am so lucky as to possess. I got up and prepared a mixture accordingly, and rubbed my back & legs, the latter several times; then laid down, and felt better.

APRIL 2D. [Meridian] Clear, light S. wind, temp. 60°—Below my knees my legs are very stiff. Rub them again. Still think the rubbing serviceable, and if no succor arrives, and strength & weather permit, I am determined to attempt going in to-morrow, let the issue be what it may. Now I know, when I leave this, what I have to encounter, and how great is the risk;—at least three nights' exposure to cold, beasts, and Indians, in my feeble condition; and liable also to be overtaken by a storm; but prudence dictates it as the last hope of salvation from the imminent perils thickening around me, so I commenced making the necessary preparations.—Collected my note-books, & papers,—quite a parcel.—Put ammunition, the two tallow candles, matches, flint & steel, a memorandum book & pencil in a haversack. A clean shirt, pair of socks, comb, towel, soap, pouch of tobacco & pipe—which I have not dared to smoke since I gave Clough up as lost; my journal-books, my watch, one belonging to Mr. Goodrich, and his draught; a gold chain & seal, found in Dr. Caldwell's wagon, and a case of sewing materials, made by my wife, I put in a knapsack.... Laid out my rifle pouch and horn, bowie-knife, pistols, and belt, and double-barrel'd gun, all ready. I transferred all our property from the camp over to the cabin, and stowed them up snugly in a bunk. My pack, arms, &c. I fear much are more than I will be able to carry.

APRIL 5TH. Commences with flying clouds, light N.E. wind, temp. 53°—I am very lame, & enfeebled this morning. Must try to reach water, any how. Travelled about 300 yards, & found a small muddy rivulet. Threw off my pack, lighted up a fire, and made coffee. Drank a cup full, and shot another small bluebird. Gave the head, feet, and entrails to my pup, slightly grilled the bird, and eat it. Now, having had a *breakfast*, I proceeded,—exceedingly stiff & weak—very hard travelling; having to rest every twenty paces, on stones, &c. I had now to descend a very rugged & crooked road, to a stream, which I barely managed to cross without falling in: springing from rock to rock, by the aid of a pole. Then ascended a hill, on the Western side, about 300 yards, and in 100 yards more gave out and fell. When I recovered so that I could set up, I thought of the candles, and got one out of my pack,—and eat about 1/4 of it, with pepper & salt; it tasted bitter. (It was of that manufacture called the diamond candle.) Cut up a piece of raw hide & some leather strings, soaked and gave them to the poor pup to gnaw on. Gave her also the candle wick.

Nearly all the afternoon cloudy, with occasional sprinkes of rain.... Found here a camp place, of about October '49, and where some seed had been spilt. I noticed a few very small sprouts of cabbages, lettuce, and reddishes, none over two inches long. I carefully gathered them, on my hands and knees,—procured about a gill, and eat them greedily, roots, and all—some grains of sand. I thought it was the sweetest cold salad I ever eat in my life. Travelled on till again exhausted, and fell near a wagon under a tree. Put my pack &c, in the wagon. Sun-set drizzles, and strong S.S.W. wind, temp: 60°. Found a large piece of old oil-cloth, and covered my things in wagon with it. I now made a fire beside the wagon, and crawled under the wagon out of the wet. Another sleepless night—lay in the wagon, wet and cool all night, and the howling of wolves, and my dog barking at them, awoke me when otherwise I might have slept.

APRIL 6TH. [This morning I proceeded, excessively weak,] halting at every stone and stump where I could sit and support my knapsack: every twenty paces at the most. Oak trees scattered about looking much like an old apple-orchard.

I threw down my packs, was about to draw my bowie-knife, when something caused me to look ahead, and on the left of the road, under a tree, I perceived a group of men, one in the act of charging a gun.—I at first thought them Indians, and resolved to visit them, and obtain food, or die. I cocked my gun, and walked with considerable energy some 300 yards, and reached the spot, found they were white men; I saluted them, staggered, fell, and asked in the name of God for some thing to eat, that I was starving! One of them said he believed they had a piece of cold bread, and soon handed it to me, with a little salt pork grease. It soon disappeared. I now ascertained that this was a *prospecting* party, from neighborhood of Lassen's, bound to the vicinity of the Cabin: they were Messrs. Barton, Collier, Darrow, Warren, Boston, O'Neil, and Bateman. It was about 3:30 PM and they informed that this spot is about sixteen miles from Davis' rancho. So then I have travelled fourteen miles— seven to "Steep Hollow," and seven this side of it. Surely my mind has dragged my feeble body on; physically alone, it were impossible! The rain prevented these men from pursuing their journey, and they fastened blankets up for a sort of tent to sleep under.

Sun-set cloudy, fresh S.E. breeze, temp. 60°—At dusk I had the luxury of a pipe, but it rendered me so nervous I dare not repeat it. Two of this party had known me, and also knew before meeting me that I was in the hills. They huddled together under the shelter, from the rain, and invited me to do so, but there was no room, and I was satisfied to rest my weary head and shelter my shoulders only, between their legs. I gave my dog a pork bone.

Observed on the right of road, a grave—

C. FORMAN

DIED SEP: 25.—1849

AGED 21 YEARS

APRIL 7TH. Commences drizzly, moderate S.E. wind, temp. 50°—The party dried their blankets, cooked breakfast, of flour cakes, fried pork, and coffee, inviting me to partake.—I needed not pressing to do so. They cut up and equally divided the cakes, handing each his share. They, no doubt, eat a hearty breakfast, but it seemed to me to be only a mouthful. I briefly related my recent sufferings, and that I feared much I had not sufficient strength to carry me in, *having nothing to eat*, and was growing weaker every hour. "Oh! Captain!" said one, "you can soon get in now; you needn't be alarmed." And they shouldered their blankets and *sacks of flour*, said "good bye, Captain," and resumed their journey! It was about 10 AM when my *charitable* friends left me. I say charitable, for unless I had just then obtained such succor, I never could have survived that night.—Nature had done wonders, but she was exhausted. I rested some time after they left, & warmed myself. I thought how differently I would have acted toward one of them, had our positions been reversed.— They saw my pale & haggard face, and my weakness; yet not one said "here's a hand-full of flour, to go in upon." They hearty and robust, with eight or ten days full rations, and I an emaciated starveling! Such is human nature! Oh selfishness, thou makest wolves of mankind! I will not, however, be ungrateful—they fed me, and saved my life;—for this, I am very thankful. A small grey wolf, this morning early, came near camp, and Nevada run him off.

APRIL 9TH. Commences clear, with a light N. wind, temp. 44°—Warmed my coffee, drank & eat it, and prepared to ford the creek and cross the plains; some eight miles to the settlements. I am so weak, I fear I have suffered all this travel for naught, to give myself to the beasts & birds of the valley, instead of leaving my body for those of the hills.

In a quarter mile more; I met a low square-built Indian, very dark, and had slight mustache; he had just emerged from a deep gulch on the left. He was nude, except a kind of fig-leaf, had a knife, a quiver full of arrows on his back, and a bow in his hand. He was accompanied by a small black Indian dog. I spoke to him in Spanish, but he did nor understand me. I then made signs that I was hungry—starving, and wanted something to eat, which he comprehended but gave me to understand he had nothing, and was on his way to Dry Creek, to shoot birds. My pup was following his dog, and I worried myself much to get her along; so glad was she to meet one of her own specie, I had to make signs to the Indian to drive her back—beat her with his bow—which he did.—While he was going off I turned round, thought of eating him; he was then about thirty or forty paces; but I could not shoot the poor wretch in the back: besides, he had done me a favor.... I managed to get probably two miles farther when I found the shrivelled carcass of an ox; on this I rested, looking to see if the Indian visited my cache, but he kept lower down, crossing the road some distance this side of it. While I rested here, poor little Nevada was gnawing and pulling about the hard withered remains I sat upon. Arose, and continued on the muddy, rough, winding road, till I at length reached ... the banks of Deer Creek, at the ford; now a raging flood, a perfect cataract, and deep.

The stream here runs Westerly. I followed a path, keeping down near the stream, turned an elbow, and reached a prostrate oak. I sat down, aching, feeble and weary, fell back in the branches, fitting like the back of an easy chair; and fell into a lethargy, from which I would never have awakened in this world had I remained undisturbed two hours.

The bark of my pup aroused me, but I found myself unable to arise; and turning my head, beheld Poile approaching! He was as much astonished, and affected at my circumstances and appearance, as I was delighted to see him. After shaking hands, I asked for something to eat, when he handed me part of a hard ship-biscuit, which I at once commenced devouring, like a starved wolf.—This devoted friend, this true *Brother*, was on his way out to the camp, to succor me. He had some flour and meal, and a piece of pork for me. Had failed seeing any one I wrote to; and intended to assist me till I could walk in.... He wished to light a fire, make coffee, and broil a piece of pork; but when I learnt that Davis's house was only about 300 yards off, around a point of timber, I resolved, with his assistance, to reach it. Poile assisted me, I arose, and went on, and in fifteeen minutes was at Davis's rancho, greeted cordially by him, Colonel Ely, Captain Potts, Davis's sons, &c: but feeling faint, I was taken in the house; and on recovering, eat a *very* hearty dinner! And Mrs. D most kindly gave me a glass of toddy. My back was so weak and ached so much that I could not sit up on a chair or bench, and had to sit flat, in a corner of the room.—I asked some person to get my pipe and tobacco out of my pouch, and filling my pipe, and taking a whiff, I said "Well! I'm not dead yet!" "Oh, No!" replied the bystanders, "You're worth several dead men yet, Captain!" Colonel Ely most kindly mounted his horse, and brought in the knapsack & quilt I left near Dry Creek.

The bunks were full of lodgers, so Poile and I made a pallet before the fire, and there slept.—The soundest night's rest I have enjoyed for a long time.

GOLD RUSH LIFE

Gold mining is nature's great lottery scheme.
—Dame Shirley

The language now spoken in our country, the laws which govern us, the faces which we encounter daily, are those of the masters of this land, and of course antagonistic to our interests and rights, but what does that matter to the conqueror?
—Mariano Guadalupe Vallejo

Truly the events of years in other countries transpire here in days.
—Daniel Wadsworth Coit

Miners at Spanish Flat near Placerville, 1852

THE ARRIVAL OF WHITES

ANDREW FREEMAN

The Native American residents of California experienced a brutal side of the gold rush—one marked by disease, oppression, and death. California's Indian population, already diminished by a century of Spanish intrusion, dropped from 150,000 at the time of the gold rush to 30,000 by 1870 as hundreds of thousands of Anglo gold rushers methodically mined, hunted, and logged even the Indians' most remote hiding places. When Native Californians retaliated by raiding white camps for subsistence, Americans organized war parties and slaughtered entire Indian groups. Andrew Freeman, affiliated with the Nomlaki tribe, gave this account in 1936— passed down from older tribe members—of the arrival of whites.

WE HAD A MAN at Thomas Creek that had power given to him. He was young. He sang all the time. He drank water and ate once a month. He ate a little of everything, then took one swallow of water and smoked. He stayed in the sweat-house all the time.

Now our captain [chief] used to get out early every morning on top of the sweat-house and, calling everybody by name, would tell them what to do.

This fortuneteller from Thomas Creek would tell the people just how much game they would get and whether any mishaps would fall. He lived across from our present reservation at Paskenta. One day he said, "There are some people from across the ocean who are going to come to this country." He looked for them for three years. "They have some kind of boat with which they can cross, and they will make it. They are on the way." Finally he said that they were on the land and that they were coming now. He said that they had fire at night and lots to eat. "They cook the same as we do; they smoke after meals, and they have a language of their own. They talk, laugh, and sing, just as we do. Besides, they have five fingers and toes, they are built like we are, only they are light." He said their blood was awfully light.

"They have a four-legged animal which some are riding and some are packing. They haven't any wives, any of them. They all are single. They are bringing some kind of sickness."

So everybody was notified. The night watch and day watch were kept. He said that they had something long which shoots little round things a long distance. They have something short that shoots just the same.

Finally the whites came in at Orland; many of them. When they came in they started shooting. There were thousands of Indians in the hills who went to fighting the whites. The Indians went after them but they couldn't do anything to them. Finally they got to Newville, and the man who was telling these fortunes said the whites were going to be there. The Indians were ready for them. The whites came by Oakes' place and down the flat at one o'clock in the morning. They killed the first Indian that showed himself. The captain told the others to stay in the house and get their bows and arrows ready.

The captain yelled to the whites that he was ready inside the house. He told his men, "When you get ready, run out and crowd into it." The captain sent them to fight at close range. He said, "We are dead anyway." The whites couldn't load their muzzleloaders, so they used revolvers. The captain told his men to spear them. They fought from morning till afternoon. The Indians had come all the way from Colusa. They killed all those whites. The Indians were afraid of gray horses. They killed the horses. They examined everything. They divided everything up. One old man from south of the Tapscott place took away a lot of their money. His children used to take the money and play with it. Finally he took it up the canyon and hid it. The whites are looking for that money today but can't find it.

Another group of whites came to Mountain House [*lopom*]. They killed many of the Indians. White people hit women and children in the head. One Indian shouted from a rock when the white men started back. The whites came up there, and that Indian went into the rock cave, and they shot one white man from there. But the whites threw fire into the cave and killed all the Indians in there.

They had been hiding in the hills. Indians couldn't get to the salt. They got very weak—they say salt keeps a person fit. There was no rain for three years, and fighting going on every day. No clover, no acorn, juniper berries, or peppergrass. Nothing for three years. Very little rain.

Finally the Indians got smallpox, and the Indian doctor couldn't cure them. They died by the thousands. Gonorrhea came among the Indians. That killed a lot of them. My grandfather said that if he had fought he would have been killed too. But he went up to Yolla Bolly Mountain with about six hundred others and stayed three years. On the third winter there was a heavy snowstorm. The snow was over his head. He said women can stand more starvation than men. They singed the hair off a deerhide shoulder strap and ate it.

Men died every day from starvation. That was in Camp of Dark Canyon in the winter. Women would find a little bunch of grass and eat it and would bring a handful back for their husbands. The women would have to chew it for the men. The man was too weak to swallow it. She would take a mouthful of water and pour it into his mouth. That was the way they saved a lot of them.

After that the whites began to gather up the Indians. They made the Nome Lackee Reservation in Tehama County. They take a tame Indian along when they bring Indians together on a reservation. They worked the Indians on the reservation. Old Martin was given a saddle mule and clothes. He wouldn't wear anything but the shirt—the overalls hurt his legs. He was a kind of foreman. Every Saturday they killed four or five beef and divided it among the Indians. They ground wheat and made biscuits. The women shocked hay. They had to examine all the men and women for disease.

Garland on the present Oakes' place wouldn't let them take the Indians off of his land, and that's what saved them. When they took the Indians to Covelo [in Round Valley, on the Nome Cult Reserve] they drove them like stock. Indians had to carry their own food. Some of the old people began to give out when they got to the hills. They shot the old people who couldn't make the trip. They would shoot children who were getting tired. Finally they got the Indians to Covelo. They killed all who tried to get away and wouldn't return to Covelo.

Letter to James Buchanan

Thomas O. Larkin

Thomas O. Larkin (1802–1858) was born in Massachusetts and came to California in 1832 haunted by a string of failed business endeavors. Through trade with Mexico and the Sandwich Islands, Larkin soon grew wealthy and prominent in pre-annexation California. He served as a consul for the U.S. government and when gold was discovered near Los Angeles in 1842, Larkin was quick to boast of his new home's abundant mineral resources. In 1845 he agreed to act covertly for Secretary of State James Buchanan in order to promote a peaceable transfer of California to the United States' control. Despite Larkin's propaganda campaign, war broke out. He continued to correspond with U.S. government officials, providing detailed appraisals of California's gold supply.

San Francisco, Upper California
June 1, 1848

Sir: I have to report to the State Department one of the most astonishing excitements and state of affairs now existing in this country that, perhaps, has ever been brought to the notice of the Government. On the American fork of the Sacramento and Feather rivers, another branch of the same, and the adjoining lands, there has been, within the present year, discovered a placer, a vast tract of land containing gold in small particles. This gold, thus far, has been taken on the bank of the river from the surface to eighteen inches in depth, and is supposed deeper, and to extend over the country. On account of the inconvenience of washing, the people have, to this time, only gathered the metal on the banks, which is done simply with a shovel, filling a shallow dish, bowl, basket, or tin pan, and washing out the sand by movement of the vessel. It is now two or three weeks since the men employed in those washings have appeared in this town with gold, to exchange for merchandise and provisions.

I am confident that this town (San Francisco) has one-half of its tenements empty, locked up with the furniture. The owners—storekeepers, lawyers, mechanics, and laborers—all gone to the Sacramento with their families. Several United States volunteers have deserted. United States bark *Anita*, belonging to the army, now at anchor here, has but six men. One Sandwich Island vessel in port lost all her men; engaged another crew at fifty dollars ($50) for the run of fifteen days to the islands.

A merchant, lately from China, has even lost his China servants. Should the excitement continue through the year, and the whale ships visit San Francisco, I think they will lose most all their crews. How Colonel Mason can retain his men, unless he puts a force on the spot, I know not. I have seen several pounds of this gold, and consider it very pure, worth, in New York, seventeen to eighteen dollars per ounce; fourteen to sixteen dollars, in merchandise, is paid for it here. What good or bad effect this gold region will have on California, I cannot foretell. It may end this year; but I am informed that it will continue many years. I have seen some of the black sand, as taken from the bottom of the river (I should think in the States it would bring twenty-five to fifty cents per pound), containing many pieces of gold; they are from the size of the head of a pin to the weight of the eighth of an ounce. I have seen some weighing one-quarter of an ounce (four dollars). Although my statements are almost incredible, I believe I am within the statements believed by every one here. Ten days back, the excitement had not reached Monterey. I shall, within a few days, visit this gold mine, and will make another report to you. Enclosed you will have a specimen.

I have the honor to be, very respectfully,

Thomas O. Larkin

P.S. This placer, or gold region, is situated on public land.

from MEMOIRS OF GENERAL
WILLIAM T. SHERMAN

WILLIAM TECUMSEH SHERMAN

William Tecumseh Sherman (1820–1891) was born in Ohio and served as an aide to General Stephen Kearney during the Mexican War. Relieved of his military duties in 1850, he toured California's gold country, preparing a series of dispatches for General Winfield Scott and President James Polk. He managed a San Francisco bank for four years until the bank went under in 1857, whereupon he left California. During the Civil War, Sherman rose to national fame as Ulysses S. Grant's successor as supreme commander in the West. "General Sherman," the world's largest redwood in Sequoia National Park, was named for him by a former soldier. Sherman's journal was first published in 1875.

AS SOON AS THE FAME of the gold discovery spread through California, the Mormons naturally turned to Mormon Island, so that in July, 1848, we found about three hundred of them there at work. Sam Brannan was on hand as the high-priest, collecting the tithes. Clark, of Clark's Point, an early pioneer, was there also, and nearly all the Mormons who had come out in the Brooklyn, or who had staid in California after the discharge of their battalion, had collected there.

I recall the scene as perfectly to-day as though it were yesterday. In the midst of a broken country, all parched and dried by the hot sun of July, sparsely wooded with live-oaks and straggling pines, lay the valley of the American River, with its bold mountain-stream coming out of the Snowy Mountains to the east. In this valley is a flat, or gravel-bed, which in high water is an island, or is overflown, but at the time of our visit was simply a level gravel-bed of the river. On its edges men were digging, and filling buckets with the finer earth and gravel, which was carried to a machine made like a baby's cradle, open at the foot, and at the head a plate of sheet-iron or zinc, punctured full of holes. On this metallic plate was emptied the earth, and water was then poured

148

on it from buckets, while one man shook the cradle with violent rocking by a handle. On the bottom were nailed cleats of wood. With this rude machine four men could earn from forty to one hundred dollars a day, averaging sixteen dollars, or a gold ounce, per man per day.

While the sun blazed down on the heads of the miners with tropical heat, the water was bitter cold, and all hands were either standing in the water or had their clothes wet all the time; yet there were no complaints of rheumatism or cold. We made our camp on a small knoll, a little below the island, and from it could overlook the busy scene. A few bush-huts near by served as stores, boarding-houses, and for sleeping; but all hands slept on the ground, with pine-leaves and blankets for bedding. As soon as the news spread that the Governor was there, persons came to see us, and volunteered all kinds of information, illustrating it by samples of the gold, which was of a uniform kind, "scale-gold," bright and beautiful. A large variety, of every conceivable shape and form, was found in the smaller gulches round about, but the gold in the river-bed was uniformly "scale-gold."

I remember that Mr. Clark was in camp, talking to Colonel [Richard] Mason about matters and things generally, when he inquired, "Governor, what business has Sam Brannan to collect the tithes here?" Clark admitted that Brannan was the head of the Mormon church in California, and he was simply questioning as to Brannan's right, as high-priest, to compel the Mormons to pay him the regular tithes.

Colonel Mason answered, "Brannan has a perfect right to collect the tax, if you Mormons are fools enough to pay it."

"Then," said Clark, "I for one won't pay it any longer."

Colonel Mason added: "This is public land, and the gold is the property of the United States; all of you here are trespassers, but, as the Government is benefited by your getting out the gold, I do not intend to interfere."

I understood, afterward, that from that time the payment of the tithes ceased, but Brannan had already collected enough money wherewith to hire Sutter's hospital, and to open a store there, in which he made more money than any merchant in California, during that summer and fall. The understanding was, that the money collected by him as tithes was the foundation of his fortune, which is still very large in San Francisco. That evening we all mingled freely with the miners, and witnessed the process of cleaning up and "panning" out, which is the last process for separating the pure gold from the fine dirt and black sand.

The next day we continued our journey up the valley of the American Fork, stopping at various camps, where mining was in progress; and about noon we reached Coloma, the place where gold had been first discovered. The hills were higher, and the timber of better quality. The river was narrower and bolder, but few miners were at work there, by reason of Marshall's and Sutter's claim to the site. There stood the sawmill unfinished, the dam and tail-race just as they were left when the Mormons ceased work. Marshall and [his assistant Peter] Wimmer's family of wife and half a dozen children were there, guarding their supposed treasure; living in a house made of clapboards. Here also we were shown many specimens of gold, of a coarser grain than that found at Mormon Island.

The next day we crossed the American River to its north side, and visited many small camps of men, in what were called the "dry diggings." Little pools of water stood in the beds of the streams, and these were used to wash the dirt; and there the gold was in every conceivable shape and size, some of the specimens weighing several ounces. Some of these "diggings" were extremely rich, but as a whole they were more precarious in results than at the river. Sometimes a lucky fellow would hit on a "pocket," and collect several thousand dollars in a few days, and then again he would be shifting about from place to place, "prospecting," and spending all he had made. Little stores were being opened at every point, where flour, bacon, etc., were sold; every thing being a dollar a pound, and a meal usually costing three dollars. Nobody paid for a bed, for he slept on the ground, without fear of cold or rain.

We spent nearly a week in that region, and were quite bewildered by the fabulous tales of recent discoveries, which at the time were confined to the several forks of the American and Yuba Rivers. All this time our horses had nothing to eat but the sparse grass in that region, and we were forced to work our way down toward the Sacramento Valley, or to see our animals perish.

Crossing the Sacramento again by swimming our horses, and ferrying their loads in that solitary canoe, we took our back track as far as the Napa, and then turned to Benicia, on Carquinez Straits. We found there a solitary adobe-house, occupied by Mr. Hastings and his family, embracing Dr. Semple, the proprietor of the ferry. This ferry was a ship's boat, with a latteen-sail, which could carry across at one tide six or eight horses.

It took us several days to cross over, and during that time we got well-acquainted with the doctor, who was quite a character. He had come to California from Illinois, and was brother to Senator Semple. He was about seven feet high, and very intelligent. When we first reached Monterey, he had a printing-press, which belonged to the United States, having been captured at the custom-house, and had been used to print custom-house blanks. With this Dr. Semple, as editor, published the *Californian,* a small sheet of news, once a week; and it was a curiosity in its line, using two *v*'s for a *w*, and other combinations of letters, made necessary by want of type.

After some time he removed to Yerba Buena with his paper, and it grew up to be the *Alta California* of to-day. Foreseeing, as he thought, the growth of a great city somewhere on the Bay of San Francisco, he selected Carquinez Straits as its location, and obtained from General Vallejo a title to a league of land, on condition of building up a city thereon to bear the name of Vallejo's wife. This was Francisca Benicia; accordingly, the new city was named "Francisca." At this time, the town near the mouth of the bay was known universally as Yerba Buena; but that name was not known abroad, although San Francisco was familiar to the whole civilized world. Now, some of the chief men of Yerba Buena, [rancher Joseph] Folsom, [merchant William] Howard, [U.S. vice-consul William] Leidesdorff, and others, knowing the importance of a *name,* saw their danger, and, by some action of the *ayuntamiento,* or town council, changed the name of Yerba Buena to "San Francisco."

Dr. Semple was outraged at their changing the name to one so like his of *Francisca,* and he in turn changed his town to the other name of Mrs. Vallejo, viz., "Benicia"; and Benicia it has remained to this day. I am convinced that this little circumstance was big with consequences. That Benicia has the best natural site for a commercial city, I am satisfied; and had half the money and half the labor since bestowed upon San Francisco been expended at Benicia, we should have at this day a city of palaces on the Carquinez Straits. The name of "San Francisco," however, fixed the city where it now is; for every ship in 1848–'49, which cleared from any part of the world, knew the name of San Francisco, but not Yerba Buena or Benicia; and, accordingly, ships consigned to California came pouring in with their contents, and were anchored in front of Yerba Buena, the first town. Captains and crews deserted for the gold-mines, and now half the city in front of Montgomery Street is built over the hulks thus abandoned. But Dr. Semple, at that time, was all there was of Benicia; he was captain and crew of his ferry-boat, and managed to pass our party to the south side of Carquinez Straits in about two days.

from THREE YEARS IN CALIFORNIA

WALTER COLTON

Walter Colton (1797–1851), born in Vermont, was shipped to California in 1846 as a chaplain with the U.S. Navy. He was named consular agent of Monterey and soon won the confidence of the town's Spanish-speaking residents; in fact, they elected him alcalde two months after his arrival. A Protestant minister in a Catholic stronghold, Colton nonetheless preached every Sunday. After the Mexican War, he built Monterey's stone capitol and started its first newspaper. In Three Years in California, *published in 1850, he depicted the effect of the gold discovery on sleepy Monterey in 1848.*

MONDAY, MAY 29 [1848]. Our town was startled out of its quiet dreams to-day by the announcement that gold had been discovered on the American Fork. The men wondered and talked, and the women too; but neither believed. The sibyls were less skeptical; they said the moon had, for several nights, appeared not more than a cable's length from the earth; that a white raven had been seen playing with an infant; and that an owl had rung the church bells.

MONDAY, JUNE 5. Another report reached us this morning from the American Fork. The rumor ran that several workmen, while excavating for a mill-race, had thrown up little shining scales of a yellow ore that proved to be gold; that an old Sonoranian, who had spent his life in gold mines, pronounced it the genuine thing. Still the public incredulity remained, save here and there a glimmer of faith, like the flash of a fire-fly at night. One good old lady, however, declared that she had been dreaming of gold every night for several weeks, and that it had so frustrated her simple household economy that she had relieved her conscience by confessing to her priest—

Absolve me, father, of that sinful dream.

TUESDAY, JUNE 6. Being troubled with the golden dream almost as much as the good lady, I determined to put an end to the suspense, and dispatched a messenger this morning to the American Fork. He will have to ride, going and returning, some 400 miles, but his report will be reliable. We shall then know whether this gold is a fact or a fiction—a tangible reality on the earth, or a fanciful treasure at the base of some rainbow, retreating over hill and water-fall, to lure pursuit and disappoint hope.

TUESDAY, JUNE 20. My messenger sent to the mines has returned with specimens of the gold; he dismounted in a sea of upturned faces. As he drew forth the yellow lumps from his pockets, and passed them around among the eager crowd, the doubts, which had lingered till now, fled. All admitted they were gold, except one old man, who still persisted they were some Yankee invention, got up to reconcile the people to the change of flag. The excitement produced was intense; and many were soon busy in their hasty preparations for a departure to the mines. The family who had kept house for me caught the moving infection. Husband and wife were both packing up; the blacksmith dropped his hammer, the carpenter his plane, the mason his trowel, the farmer his sickle, the baker his loaf, and the tapster his bottle. All were off for the mines, some on horses, some on carts, and some on crutches, and one went in a litter. An American woman, who had recently established a boarding-house here, pulled up stakes and was off before her lodgers had even time to pay their bills. Debtors ran, of course. I have only a community of women left, and a gang of prisoners, with here and there a soldier, who will give his captain the slip at the first chance. I don't blame the fellow a whit; seven dollars a month, while others are making two or three hundred a day! that is too much for human nature to stand.

SATURDAY, JULY 15. The gold fever has reached every servant in Monterey; none are to be trusted in their engagement beyond a week, and as for compulsion, it is like attempting to drive fish into a net with the ocean before them. Gen. Mason, Lieut. Lanman, and myself form a mess; we have a house, and all the table furniture and culinary apparatus requisite; but our servants have run, one after another, till we are almost in despair: even Sambo, who we thought would stick by from laziness, if no other cause, ran last night; and this morning, for the fortieth time, we had to take to the kitchen, and cook our own breakfast. A general of the United States Army, the commander of a man-of-war, and the Alcalde of Monterey, in a smoking kitchen grinding coffee, toasting a herring, and pealing onions! These gold mines are going to upset all the domestic arrangements of society, turning the head to the tail, and the tail to the head. Well, it is an ill wind that blows nobody any good: the nabobs have had their time, and now comes that of the "niggers."

TUESDAY, JULY 18. Another bag of gold from the mines, and another spasm in the community. It was brought down by a sailor from Yuba River, and contains 136 ounces. It is the most beautiful gold that has appeared in the market; it looks like the yellow scales of the dolphin, passing through his rainbow hues at death. My carpenters, at work on the school-house, on seeing it threw down their saws and planes, shouldered their picks, and are off for the Yuba. Three seamen ran from the Warren, forfeiting their four years' pay; and a whole platoon of soldiers from the fort left only their colors behind. One old woman declared she would never again break an egg or kill a chicken, without examining yolk and gizzard.

THURSDAY, JULY 27. I never knew mosquitoes turned to any good account save in California; and here it seems they are sometimes ministers of justice. A rogue had stolen a bag of gold from a digger in the mines, and hid it. Neither threats nor persuasions could induce him to reveal the place of its conceal- ment. He was at last sentenced to a hundred lashes, and then informed that he would be let off with thirty, provided he would tell what he had done with the gold; but he refused. The thirty lashes were inflicted, but he was still stubborn as a mule.

He was then stripped naked and tied to a tree. The mosquitoes with their long bills went at him, and in less than three hours he was covered with blood. Writhing and trembling from head to foot with exquisite torture, he ex- claimed, "Untie me, untie me, and I will tell where it is." "Tell first," was the reply. So he told where it might be found. Some of the party then, with wisps, kept off the still-hungry mosquitoes, while others went where the culprit had directed and recovered the bag of gold. He was then untied, washed with cold water, and helped to his clothes, while he muttered, as if talking to himself, "I couldn't stand that anyhow."

SATURDAY, AUGUST 12. My man Bob, who is of Irish extraction, and who had been in the mines about two months, returned to Monterey four weeks since, bringing with him over $2000, as the proceeds of his labor. Bob, while in my employ, required me to pay him every Saturday night, in gold, which he put into a little leather bag and sewed into the lining of his coat, after taking out just 12 $1/2$ cents, his weekly allowance for tobacco. But now he took rooms and began to branch out; he had the best horses, the richest viands, and the choicest wines in the place. He never drank himself, but it filled him with delight to brim the sparkling goblet for others. I met Bob to-day, and asked him how he got on. "Oh, very well," he replied, "but I am off again for the mines." "How is that, Bob? you brought down with you over $2000...." "Oh, yes," replied Bob, "...but the $2000 came easily by good luck, and has gone as easily as it came." Now Bob's story is only one of a thousand like it in Califor- nia, and has a deeper philosophy in it than meets the eye. Multitudes here are none the richer for the mines. He who can shake chestnuts from an exhaust- less tree won't stickle about the quantity he roasts.

THURSDAY, AUGUST 16. Four citizens of Monterey are just in from the gold mines on Feather River, where they worked in company with three others. They employed about thirty wild Indians, who are attached to the rancho owned by one of the party. They worked precisely seven weeks and three days, and have divided $76,844—nearly $11,000 to each. Make a dot there, and let me introduce a man, well known to me, who has worked on the Yuba River sixty-four days, and brought back, as the result of his individual labor, $5356. Make a dot there, and let me introduce another townsman, who has worked on the North Fork fifty-seven days, and brought back $4534. Make a dot there, and let me introduce a boy, fourteen years of age, who has worked on the Mokelumne fifty-four days, and brought back $3476. Make another dot there, and let me introduce a woman, of Sonoranian birth, who has worked in the dry diggings forty-six days, and brought back $2125. Is not this enough to make a man throw down his ledger and shoulder a pick? But the deposits which yielded these harvests were now opened for the first time; they were the accumulation of ages; only the foot-prints of the elk and wild savage had passed over them. Their slumber was broken for the first time by the sturdy arms of the American emigrant.

SATURDAY, SEPTEMBER 16. The gold mines are producing one good result; every creditor who has gone there is paying his debts. Claims not deemed worth a farthing are now cashed on presentation at nature's great bank. This has rendered the credit of every man here good for almost any amount. Orders for merchandise are honored which six months ago would have been thrown into the fire. There is none so poor, who has two stout arms and a pickaxe left, but he can empty any store in Monterey.... I met a man to-day from the mines in patched buckskins, rough as a badger from his hole, who had $15,000 in yellow dust swung at his back. Talk to him of brooches, gold-headed canes, and Carpenter's coats! Why he can unpack a lump of gold that would throw all Chesnut-street into spasms. And there is more where this came from. *His* rights in the great domain are equal to yours, and his prospects of getting it out vastly better. With these advantages, he bends the knee to no man, but strides along in his buckskins, a lord of earth by a higher prescriptive privilege than what emanates from the partiality of kings. His patent is medallioned with rivers which roll over golden sands, and embossed with mountains which have lifted for ages their golden coronets to heaven. Clear out of the way with your crests, and crowns, and pedigree trees, and let this democrat pass. Every drop of blood in his veins tells that it flows from a great heart, which God has made and which man shall never enslave. Such are the genuine sons of California; such may they live and die.

from A Tour of Duty in California

JOSEPH WARREN REVERE

Joseph Warren Revere (1812–1880), the grandson of Paul Revere, was born in Boston and joined the Navy at age sixteen. A lifelong military man, he was assigned to California in 1845, raised the U.S. flag at Sonoma, and later served as a brigadier general in the Civil War. In A Tour of Duty in California, *published in 1849, he offered advice to new emigrants and made a few surprisingly accurate predictions about the future of California.*

TO THOSE WHO INTEND TO SETTLE in California, I would respectfully offer a few words of advice. You are mostly young men, full of hope and energy. You leave behind you a land where liberty is regulated by law, and where you have witnessed the practical effects of good government. You leave behind you a happy, prosperous, and enlightened people, whose free institutions are the glory of the age, and whose devotion to public order is the best guaranty of the perpetuity of those institutions. You go to a comparatively uncivilized country, where you will be beyond the reach of those salutary restraints, which are imposed at home by custom, religion, law, the example of all good men, and the benign influences of family and friends. You go as adventurers among adventurers, and it cannot be otherwise than that you will encounter many dangerous, lawless, and unprincipled men.... I pray you to beware of the dangers which will beset your path, and to shun with resolute determination everything which may bring upon you dishonor and the scorn of honorable men. If you meet with a lax system of public morals, be it your aim to elevate the tone of society; if you be tempted to sully an honorable name by dishonest practices, resist to the last the lures of avarice and corruption; if dissipation prevail and you see men popular who are sunk in vice and depravity, be assured that their day will be short, and stand firmly on the Rock of Right. Virtue is the same everywhere; Truth is the same everywhere; God is the same everywhere;—and be it your aim to act, even in the midst of sin and pollution, as if the eyes of a purer society, the eyes of friends and kindred, of sisters and mothers, were ever upon you.... Maintain, and next to God, reverence *character.* Let it be to you a real presence—a tangible existence—whose preservation is of infinitely greater importance than all the gold the whole world contains. The perils of the sea safely surmounted, make not a moral shipwreck; but while pursuing the shadow which men call wealth, aspire to be something better than that most poverty-stricken of mortals—a mere rich man. The destiny of man is onward and upward, and let not the future generations of California have cause to say that the sins of the fathers are visited upon the children; but rather let them celebrate the good deeds of their ancestry.

Perhaps a hundred years hence, some curious book-worm, while exploring a musty library, may alight upon this then forgotten volume, and will be tempted to find out what was said and predicted of California at the eventful period of her annexation to the United States, and the discovery of her mineral wealth. The poor Indians will then have passed away; the rancheros will be remembered only as the ancient proprietors of broad lands, which will have passed into the possession of the more enterprising race who are about to succeed them; the Grizzly Bear will live only in books and in tradition; the Elk will have become extinct; the wild horse will be seen no more; author, editor, publishers, readers, all will have passed away and mingled with the dust; and perchance new philologists will have so marred our noble English language that these poor pages will be intelligible only to the learned.

CHILD OF THE FUTURE! what wilt thou then see? Will not a hundred million free and happy human beings inhabit the great Republic then still known as the United States of America—their habitations extending from the shores of the boisterous Atlantic to those of the placid Pacific? Will not the arts of peace flourish beyond example, and the majestic tread of man still press onward towards a yet more glorious Destiny? And California—what will she then be? Will she have fulfilled the promises of this our day, and be the highway of a mighty commerce, and replete with enterprise and opulence? Will she have become populous and enlightened, the seat of arts and learning, the generous rival of her elder sisters in all that is lovely and of good report among men? SON OF A HOPEFUL AGE! thy response may not reach "the dull, cold ear of death"; but Heaven grant it may be such as, if living, we should most wish to hear!

from THE GLORIES OF A DAWNING AGE

WILLIAM NEWELL

Eastern ministers, alarmed as increasing numbers of young men left their congregations for godless California, earnestly preached against the gold rush. When this had little effect, they switched tactics—go to California, they said, but as missionaries, not as fortuneseekers. In 1853, Presbyterian reverend William Newell delivered this sermon in Liverpool, New York, to a group of his flock about to sail to San Francisco.

I KNOW THAT THE WORLD is now in open rebellion. Satan, with his shouting legions, is armed at every point, all ready to receive us. His standards are fixed on every hill, his banners are waving over every valley; he has the vantage ground. But, hark! a trumpet blast is heard on high. Jesus, with ten thousand times ten thousand saints, is hastening to this last great conflict. The word is given—they rush to the strife of battle—the clash of arms and dying groans are mingled. But the reeling foe gives way, and hurrying back to hell's deep caverns, they fly, and this work of Christian victory goes on, and on, and on; while Christ, upon the ruins of Satan's fall, is rolling in his victorious car; every head is bared, every knee is bent, every tongue has confessed, and one continued shout of "blessing and honor, glory and power, to Him that sitteth upon the throne, and to the Lamb forever," goes *up to Heaven,* and echoes round our globe.

And who would not gather to this contest? Who is faint of heart when Jesus calls? He is now abroad, marshalling his hosts; and what matters it whether the clash of our arms is heard on the Atlantic or on the Pacific shore? But all this has seemed so dark and distant; we have moved so slow, that it was all of faith; but now we have indications of progress. The rapid spread of the English language; the prodigious activity and restless sway of the Anglo Saxon mind are greatly encouraging.

Twenty-eight years ago the American Home Missionary Society was not born; now there are in the field 1100, mostly accompanied by their wives, preaching in near 2000 districts; reporting for the year, sixty-one revivals, and near 4000 converts received to the church. And how strange the Providence that extends our rule and rears our spires on the Pacific coast.

God waited till the Jesuits were driven from that land—He waited till it became American soil; then he uncapped those mountains of gold, and then, as one has said: "The busy dreamers of the world are aroused—cold, dead, lethargic masses, are raised to life. The fire of youth, the restlessness of enterprise, the lust of gain, the decrepitude of age, are all hurrying and jostling on together to the scene; and highways will be cut, and railroads made, and oceans forever parted will now join hands and kiss each other."

Arise then, my brethren! Go forth toward the setting sun, and there be sure *you shine.*

Let the light of your Christian life spread through the valleys of the Sacramento and San Joaquin; let it gild Sierra Nevada's tops. Come down the slope of the stony mountains, and stream away "o'er China's plains and India's coral strand."

Leave not your stamp in the gold and granite, the hills and valleys of California that crumble away, but leave it in something vastly more valuable and lasting. Let it lie deeply imbedded in the souls that are gathered there. Then it shall be borne at the judgment day—then shall it be read of all men to the ages of eternity.

Go, then, dearly beloved of the Lord! May it be yours to wave the banner of the cross over the El Dorado of our world.

from DISCOURSES

BRIGHAM YOUNG

The first Mormons to arrive in California did so in the 1840s at the behest of Brigham Young (1801–1877), Joseph Smith's replacement as president of the Church of Jesus Christ of Latter-Day Saints. Young, after leading the Church to Utah and establishing Salt Lake City, dreamt of a Mormon nation in the West. His missionaries founded more than 350 towns in Utah, Idaho, Nevada, Arizona, and California. After the gold discovery, Young publicly preached against greedy materialism but privately urged hundreds of Mormons into the goldfields, hoping they would return laden with treasure. Some returned; the rest stayed and integrated. Young became the first governor of Utah in 1849 and had children with sixteen women and married many others. Discourses, *published in 1925, collected snippets from his public speeches from 1851 to his death in 1877.*

EARTHLY RICHES ARE CONCEALED in the elements God has given to man, and the essence of wealth is power to organize from these elements every comfort and convenience of life for our sustenance here, and for eternal existence hereafter. The possession of all the gold and silver in the world would not satisfy the cravings of the immortal soul of man. The gift of the Holy Spirit of the Lord alone can produce a good, wholesome, contented mind. Instead of looking for gold and silver, look to the heavens and try to learn wisdom until you can organize the native elements for your benefit; then, and not until then, will you begin to possess the true riches.

There is no happiness in gold, not the least. It is very convenient as an article of exchange, in purchasing what we need; and instead of finding comfort and happiness in gold, you exchange it to obtain happiness, or that which may conduce to it. There is no real wealth in gold. People talk about being wealthy—about being rich; but place the richest banking company in the world upon a barren rock, with their gold piled around them, with no possible chance of exchanging it, and destitute of the creature comforts, and they would be poor indeed. Where then is their joy, their comfort, their great wealth? They have none.

I am not for hoarding up gold and other property to lie useless, I wish to put everything to a good use. I never keep a dollar lying idly by me, for I wish all the means to be put into active operation.

Do you want wealth? If you do, do not be in a hurry. Do you want the riches pertaining to this world? Yes, we acknowledge we do. Then, be calm, contented, composed; keep your pulses correct, do not let them get up to a hundred and twenty, but keep them as high as you can, ranging from seventy to seventy-six; and when there is an appointment for a meeting be sure to attend that meeting. If there is to be a two-day meeting, come to it; spend the time here and learn what is going on. Watch closely, hear every word that is spoken, let every heart be lifted to God for wisdom, and know and understand every word of prophecy, every revelation that may be given, every counsel that may be presented to the people, that you may be able to weigh, measure, comprehend, and decide between that which is of God and that which is not of God. Refuse the evil, learn wisdom, and grow in grace and in the knowledge of the truth.

My policy is to get rich; I am a miser in eternal things. Do I want to become rich in the things of this earth? Yes, if the Lord wishes me to have such riches, and I can use them to good advantage. My policy is to keep every man, woman, and child busily employed, that they may have no idle time for hatching mischief in the night, and for making plans to accomplish their own ruin.

I told you the other day what makes me rich, it is the labor of those whom I feed and clothe; still I do not feel that I have a dollar in the world that is my own, it is the Lord's and he has made me a steward over it; and if I can know where the Lord is pleased to have it appropriated, there it shall go.

All the real business we have on hand is to promote our religion. If you come naked and barefooted (I would not care if you had naught but a deer skin around you when you arrive here), and bring your God and your religion, you are a thousand times better than if you come with wagon loads of silver and gold and left your God behind.

Some say, "If we had a gold mine, we would do well." If I knew where there was a gold mine, I would not tell you. I do not want you to find one, and I do not mean that you shall; or, if you do, it shall be over my faith. We have gold enough in the world, and it is all the Lord's, and we do not deserve more than we get. Let us make good use of that, and send out the Elders.

from Recuerdos Históricos y Personales Tocante a la Alta California

MARIANO GUADALUPE VALLEJO

Late in life, Mariano Guadalupe Vallejo, living on his Sonoma rancho, Lachryma Montis, with his wife and enormous family, became a symbol of "Old California" to a generation of Anglos regretful about the vanishing Californio culture. In 1875, Vallejo gave this scathing account of what the gold brought to California.

GOLD IN THE MINES! This cry, resounding throughout the length and breadth of California, created a veritable revolution, social and financial. The farmer left his plough in the furrow, the schoolmaster abandoned his books and blackboards, the sailor deserted his ship, the barber flung down his razor and the tailor his shears. Even the lover relinquished the hand of his sweetheart to clutch the pick and shovel and rush forth in search of the longed-for metal.

At this time, when the populous cities of the southern part of the state were deserted by their inhabitants, the frontier town of Sonoma, an essentially agricultural community which up to that time had figured only as an outpost against the raids of the heathen savages, rose to the first rank among the cities of Alta California.

All the caravans from Monterey and other parts of the state, and even those which arrived from the state of Sonora, broke their journey at Sonoma, where they rested the wearied animals, repaired harness and wagons, shod their saddle horses, and bought fresh provisions before resuming their march. On the other hand, the miners who had met with good fortune in the diggings came, for the most part, to Sonoma to dispose of their gold, to buy new clothing and to make other necessary preparations for their return to the mines.

In December, 1848, and during all of the year 1849, gold in dust or flakes was so abundant in Sonoma that it was difficult to obtain six dollars an ounce in exchange for coined money. This low rate was attributed in part to the large amount of gold brought in by the Indians.

At the diggings, the food consisted of the flesh of wild animals, of ship biscuit or bread made by the miners, onions, potatoes, dried beans, salt pork, and, from time to time, of salmon. This fish abounded in the Sacramento River, and at that time could be caught with astonishing ease. The fishermen loaded great carts with salmon and, traveling day and night, brought them still fresh to the mining camps, where they sold them for twenty *reales* ($2.50) a pound. As a rule, a four-horse wagon carried to the mines a ton of salmon, which produced for its owner, when he had sold it to the miners, about $5000. When it is taken into consideration that the round trip could be made in eight days, and sometimes in even shorter time, it can be seen that the earnings of the fisherman were on a level with those of the miners, without the exposure to the calamitous and unpleasant experiences peculiar to the life of the gold diggers.

When the rainy season drew near, the miners who had been fortunate came down from the diggings to spend the winter in Sacramento, which, by reason of its proximity to San Francisco, offered a thousand comforts which one would have sought in vain in the towns of the interior. There were undoubtedly many cases of miners, owners of rich placers, who feared to lose their claims if they abandoned them during the winter, and so remained in the diggings during the rainy season. Some of these men lost their lives, buried under the snow, some were drowned in the rivers and some were devoured by wild beasts. Misfortunes of this sort were very frequent in the district behind Downieville, where in the winter the snow lies to a depth of eight, ten, or twelve feet, and wild animals are abundant.

In the winter Sacramento was always crowded, since it was there that the gamblers assembled in droves to fleece the unwary. Gaming tables were set up everywhere; faro, monte, rouge et noire, and lasquinet were the favorite games. The amounts wagered on a single card were very great, and there were times when they reached five or six hundred ounces of gold.

In the neighborhood of the gambling houses appeared, as by magic, pawn-shops. Their sole business was to lend money to the victims of the gamblers, who, after losing their gold, pledged their jewelry, arms, and clothes in order to seek revenge and of course returned to lose again, eventually finding themselves stripped of their last possession. Many Californians, drawn by the novelty of the spectacle (for gambling in public was not permitted under Mexican rule, although in private the common people played until they lost the clothes off their backs) and deluded into believing that they could easily enrich themselves by guessing the cards, lost in half an hour cattle and ranches that had been owned, for half a century perhaps, by their ancestors. Blinded by the passion for the game, they did not awaken to the truth of the situation until it was already too late to remedy.

It is well to note that in '49 the Americans classed as Chileans all the citizens of the other South American republics. They fell into this error because all the ships arriving from South America were cleared at Valparaíso, where they took on board flour and beans. As the flag covered the cargo, whenever a ship from Chile carrying passengers dropped anchor in the port of San Francisco, the miners shouted, "Here are some more Chileans for you!" although frequently most if not all the passengers belonged to other nationalities.

In California in 1849 there was no asylum in which to care for the insane, and the miners and emigrants who lost their reason during the first years of North American rule in California were treated more like wild beasts of the desert than like human beings. The raving maniacs were fastened with chains to trees or posts in the stables, and the harmless lunatics were locked up on deserted ships in the harbor. It is in truth with profound sadness that we reflect that from '48 until '52 the sick and insane received at our hands treatment that very ill befitted the boasted civilization of the century and our humanitarian sentiments.

When gold was discovered, the flag of stars already waved above Alta California. No longer were we ruled by the Mexican laws, under whose shadow some had advanced while others fell back, but under which no one had perished of hunger, and only two individuals had been by law deprived of their lives, a very common event during the early years of the North American domination in California.

The language now spoken in our country, the laws which govern us, the faces which we encounter daily, are those of the masters of the land, and of course antagonistic to our interests and rights, but what does that matter to the conqueror? He wishes his own well-being and not ours!

Although the treaty of Guadalupe Hidalgo imposed on the North Americans an obligation to respect established rights, the Americans, always astute and filled with cunning, placed the owners of valuable lands in such a position that they often saw themselves obliged to expend the value of their properties to obtain valid titles to them. There were times when, after obtaining in San Francisco, at great cost, a favorable verdict in the federal courts established by the Attorney-General, an order, issued to favor some protégé, would come from Washington that the case must be reviewed by the Supreme Court of the United States at Washington, in which tribunal the California owner was almost certain to lose his lands.

This method of procedure was not in harmony with the honeyed words of the American orators, who announced in the public squares, in the churches, at the corners of the streets, and from the balconies of their houses that they had come to close the jails and to abolish the gibbets and the bloody laws set up by the Mexican Government.

Australia sent us a swarm of bandits who, on their arrival in California, dedicated themselves exclusively to robbery and assault. The Mormons, lascivious but very industrious people, sent the ship *Brooklyn* loaded with emigrants who professed a religion which is in open conflict with good taste and with moral and political soundness. Peru sent us a great number of rascals, begotten in idleness and schooled in vice, who debased themselves for lucre. Mexico inundated us with a wave of gamblers who had no occupation save that of the card table, no motive but the spoliation of the unwary.

France, desiring to be rid of several thousand lying men and corrupt women, embarked them at the expense of the government on ships which brought them to San Francisco. Italy sent us musicians and gardeners. The former, of course, lost no time in fraternizing with the keepers of gambling-houses and brothels, while the latter, poor but industrious folk, settled in huts or dark caves near the Mission, cultivated gardens, raised poultry, and in a short time became rich, since vegetables brought fabulous prices from '48 to '53, and eggs sold at from six to twelve dollars a dozen.

Germany sent us its contingent. Some of them, on arriving among us, opened barber shops, some laundries, and some dairies, while a few became hunters. This occupation was then very profitable, as wild beasts were abundant and brought high prices.

Chile sent us many laborers who were very useful and contributed not a little to the development of the resources of the country. Their favorite occupations were wood cutting and farm labor. There is no doubt that this group of citizens was highly desirable, and it is only to be regretted that so many of them were addicted to drink and gambling.

China poured upon our shores clouds and more clouds of Asiatics and more Asiatics. These, without exception, came to California with the determination to use any means of enriching themselves "by hook or crook" and returning immediately to their own country.

I believe that the great Chinese immigration which invaded California in '50–1–2 was very harmful to the moral and material development of the country, to the spread of the white race and to the healthfulness of San Francisco, the spot in which were congested most of the Chinese women, who, it seems, had made it a duty to keep the hospitals always filled with syphilitics.

But all these evils became insignificant in comparison with the swollen torrent of shysters, who came from Missouri and other states of the Union.

165

No sooner had they arrived than they assumed the title of attorney, and began to seek means of depriving the Californians of their farms and other properties. The escaped bandits from Australia stole our cattle and our horses; but these legal thieves, clothed in the robes of the law, took from us our lands and our houses and without the least scruple enthroned themselves in our homes like so many powerful kings. For them existed no law but their own will and caprice, they recognized no right but that of force. It was our misfortune that these adventurers of evil law were so numerous that it was impossible for us to defend our rights in the courts, since the majority of the judges were squatters and the same could be said of the sheriffs and the juries. I believe it would be superfluous to say that to all these, justice was only a word used to sanction robbery.

The number of California families despoiled of their lands under one pretext or another by means of the arbitrary actions of the courts ran into hundreds. Some of the defrauded Californians devoted themselves to useful enterprises and sought the welfare of themselves and their families, but the majority of the young men who had been so unjustly despoiled, burning for revenge, swelled the ranks of Joaquín Murieta, and under command of this much feared outlaw were able to pay off some of the wrongs which the North Americans had inflicted upon them. A large number of these rash of individuals, who disregarded the counsels of wisdom and tried to avenge themselves by illegal and reprehensible methods, came to an untimely end. Some received passports to the other world at the hands of Judge Lynch and now rest in graves dug by the peace officers. Others have gone to dwell at San Quentin in the home which the government maintains for those who commit major crimes. The asylum for the insane also received as guests several Californians, a circumstance which caused much wonder among us born in the country, since, with the exception of two lunatics whom the general government had sent from Mexico, insane persons had been unknown among us since the settlement of Alta California.

I believe that they do not stray from the truth who assure us that madness is caused by liquor. Here, before the coming of Frémont, we drank only pure liquor, and that in small quantities, and everyone enjoyed good health, tenacious memories, and lively intelligence. But after the country came to form part of the great federation of the United States of North America, from France and Germany were introduced great supplies of liquors made up of chemical ingredients and noxious herbs, and these affected the nervous system, clouded the intelligence, and undermined the most robust constitutions, sowing the fatal seeds of a multitude of diseases which were not long in sending to premature graves young men in the flower of their lives.

In conclusion, I say that in my humble opinion the change of government which took place in California on July 7, 1846, has resulted in benefit to the commerce and agriculture of the young state, but in damage to the morale of the people, whose patriarchal customs have broken down little by little through contact with so many immoral persons who came to this my country from every nook and corner of the known world.

The time has not yet come to make a final judgment of the actions of the authority which now governs the country, but the coming generation will perform this task and I have no doubt that it will agree with me when I assert that, in carrying out the treaty of Guadalupe Hidalgo, the North Americans have treated the Californians as a conquered people and not as citizens who voluntarily joined to form part of the great family dwelling beneath the glorious flag which flamed so proudly from Bunker Hill, and braved the attacks of the European monarchs, who, from their tottering thrones, cast covetous eyes toward California and the other territories which compose the great federation of the sons of liberty.

Mining Camps of the Gold Country

The uncertain nature of gold mining led to dozens of hastily named mining camps littered up and down the state's riverbeds, ravines, and canyons. The peripatetic miners clambered after rumored rich spots, leaving behind the skeletal remains of forgotten camps.

Paradise
Dead Mule Cañon
Christmas Hill
Humbug Cañon
Grizzly Flat
Rat Trap Slide
Seven-by-nine Valley
Gas Hill
Mad Cañon
French Corral
Chucklehead Diggings
Red Dog
Poor Man's Creek
Relief Hill
Nutcake Camp
Puppytown
Blue-Belly Ravine
Wild Goose Flat
Bogus Thunder
Fine Gold
Humpback Slide
Greasers' Camp
Christian Flat
Blue Tent
Rough and Ready
Stud-Horse Cañon
Gomorrah
Centipede Hollow
Barefoot Diggings

Ground Hog's Glory
Jackass Gulch
Delirium Tremens
Shinbone Peak
Gouge Eye
Seven-up Ravine
Chicken-Thief Flat
Coon Hollow
You Bet
Hell's Delight
Angels' Camp
Pancake Ravine
Paint-Pot Hill
Brandy Flat
Scotch Hill
Miller's Defeat
Quack Hill
Newtown
Ladies' Cañon
Shirt-tail Cañon
Hungry Camp
Grizzly Hill
Hog's Diggings
Indian Flat
Git-up-and-git
Graveyard Cañon
Alpha
Omega
Guano Hill

from SIXTEEN MONTHS AT THE GOLD DIGGINGS

DANIEL B. WOODS

Daniel B. Woods, a Philadelphia school teacher who decided to try his luck in the California diggings in 1849, quickly discovered mining was extremely hard work—not to mention monotonous and physically exhausting. Like the vast majority of miners, he never got rich; after sixteen months he calculated that he had averaged only $7.28 a day. His diary, published in 1851, described his frustration as golden dreams faded into leaden realities.

JULY 8TH, SUNDAY. All the miners upon the bar, with the exception of one man, who is working by himself below, have laid aside their labors for the day. This is partly at least, owing to a regard for its sacredness. And when may we be so much sustained by the encouragements, cheered by the promises, or influenced by the restraints of religion, as in the circumstances in which we are now placed? Religion—Heaven's most precious gift to man—comes and offers to lead us, and to be with us in all our weary exile from home.

JULY 9TH. To-day we have made $20 each. One of the conclusions at which we are rapidly arriving is that the chances of our making a fortune in the gold mines are about the same as those in favor of our drawing a prize in a lottery. No kind of work is so uncertain....Two foreigners, who had been some time in the mines, began to work their respective claims, leaving a small space between them. The question arose to which of them this space belonged. As they could not amicably settle the dispute, they agreed to leave it to the decision of an American who happened by, and who had not yet done an hour's work in the mines. He measured off ten feet—which is allowed by custom—to each of the claimants, taking for his trouble the narrow strip of land lying between them. In a few hours, the larger claims, belonging to the old miners, were abandoned as useless, while the new miner discovered a deposit which yielded him $7435.

JULY 10TH. We made three dollars each to-day. This life of severe hardship and exposure has affected my health. Our diet consists of hard bread, flour,

Mexican, Native American, and white miners at Taylorsville, c. 1850

which we eat half-cooked, and salt pork, with occasionally a salmon which we purchase of the Indians. Vegetables are not to be procured. Our feet are wet all day, while a hot sun shines down upon our heads, and the very air parches the skin like the hot air of an oven. Our drinking water comes down to us thoroughly impregnated with the mineral substances washed through the thousand cradles above us.

After our days of labor, exhausted and faint, we *retire*—if this word may be applied to the simple act of lying down in our clothes—robbing our feet of their boots to make a pillow of them, and wrapping our blankets about us, on a bed of pine boughs, or on the ground, beneath the clear, bright stars of night. Near morning there is always a change in the temperature of the air, and several blankets become necessary. Then the feet and the hands of the novice in this business become blistered and lame, and the limbs are stiff. Besides all these causes of sickness, the anxieties and cares which wear away the life of so many men who leave their families to come to this land of gold contribute, in no small degree, to this same result. It may with truth be said, "the whole head is sick, and the whole heart faint." I have to-day removed to the top of the hill above the encampment, and beneath a large oak-tree, for the benefit of a cooler air and shade during the intense heat of noon.

AUG. 20TH. After my last date I was prostrated at once by the acclimating disease of the country, and rendered as helpless as a child. All day and all night long I was alone under my oak, and without those kind attentions so necessary in sickness, and which can not be had here. I was reduced to a very low state, with but little hope, under the circumstances, of recovery. It did seem hard to lie down to die there, and to think that I was no more to see my beloved family. Yet I feared not to die. Indeed, I marked off the spot under the oak where my grave should be, and prayed for submission to God's righteous will, and that his love would protect and bless those dear to me.

At this critical time, a gentleman from New Orleans, hearing of my case, came up to see me, and gave me a few pills, which, fortunately, he had with him. They checked the disease, and after a few hours I could eat a bird shot and cooked for me by a kind friend. Not soon shall I forget this noble-hearted friend, B. Rough as a grisly bear, he was yet one of nature's noblemen. At home he filled, at one time, the office of sheriff. He said that the office cost him too much, and was making him poor. If he was sent to seize a destitute woman's effects for rent, he would be sure to pay that rent, and then would send her a bag of flour from his own farm. Thus we learn that many of the most valuable traits of character and excellencies of heart lie, like the purest gold, concealed beneath a rough surface.

Yesterday morning we reached Weaver's Creek, and, after prospecting some hours, located ourselves on the spot where we now are at work, with some good prospect of success. Just below us is a Georgia miner, who showed me to-day nine pounds of gold he made last week with the assistance of two hired men. The mountains here are very precipitous and abrupt, hanging over our heads in wild grandeur. The creek is only accessible through wild ravines and over steep mountains. Owing to their great depth, and their being shut up on all sides by mountains so lofty that the sun rises two hours later and sets two hours earlier than upon the plains, the heat is most intense. We have spent our first day in making preparations for our work. W. is now putting up a brush arbor, to guard us more effectually against the heat of the sun.

WEAVER'S CREEK, AUG. 21ST. Our mining company has been to-day increased, two others having joined us, making our number five. One of these has been engaged in walling in a spring where we obtain our drinking-water—another is making a cradle. The others have been employed in removing the stones and top soil, and carrying the auriferous dirt on hand-barrows, made of hides, down to the edge of the water, ready to be washed. From every indication, we have "struck a rich lead." We find much gold on the rocks: on one I counted twenty-five scales.

AUG. 22ND. We have finished our cradle, and washed a little dirt this forenoon, which yielded us about $10 in all. Our hopes are bright for the morrow.

AUG. 23D. How is "the gold become dim!" After all our preparations and hopes, our toil early and late, toil of the most laborious kind, digging, down in the channel of the river till the water was up to our knees, giving ourselves barely time to eat, we have made but $4 each. We sat down upon the rocks, and looked at the small ridge of gold in the pan, and then at each other. One fell to swearing, another to laughing; I tried to say some encouraging things. Our way indeed is dark, and great are our difficulties, and oft-repeated our failures, and we experience the bitterness of the "Hope deferred which maketh the heart sick," but our motto must be *press on*. The motives which induced us to come here were good—our object is good—then, trusting in God's merciful providence, let us *persevere.*

One young man near us has just died. He was without companion or friend—alone in his tent. Not even his name could be discovered. We buried him, tied down his tent, leaving his effects within. Thus is a home made doubly desolate. Years will pass, and that loved son, or brother, or husband still be expected, and the question still repeated, Why don't he come? Right below me, upon a root of our wide-spreading oak, is seated an old man of three-score and ten years. He left a wife and seven children at home, whose memory he cherishes with a kind of devotion unheard of before. He says when he is home-sick he can not cry, but it makes him sick at his stomach. He is an industrious old man, but has not made enough to buy his provisions, and we have given him a helping hand. Is it surprising that many fly to gambling, and more to drink, to drown their disappointments? To-day I have weighed my little store of gold, after paying all expenses, and find it amounts, after over six weeks of hard labor, to $35.

from CALIFORNIA CORRESPONDENCE

ALONZO DELANO

Humorist Alonzo Delano, exhausted from his punishing overland journey, arrived at Feather River on September 9, 1849, with four dollars in his pocket. He eventually struck it rich in the mines of the Yuba River but sent off this missive to an eastern newspaper during the lean years. His letters were collected as California Correspondence *in 1966.*

INDEPENDENCE, OCTOBER 20, 1850

It is with a kind of desperation that I seize the pen this morning as an antidote to ennui. The miners have been mostly frightened away by a succession of stormy weather, rain in the valleys and snow on the mountains; and I am also preparing to evacuate these diggings in two or three days. I shall remove to the mouth of the creek four miles below, where about two hundred and fifty men are preparing winter quarters where, by the appearance of the trees, the snow falls forty or fifty feet deep.

The miners who are left here are all out at work, and I went out and rocked the cradle an hour or so for pastime, and got only twenty-five cents; so I gave it up, and not to let the time hang heavily on my hands, I take up my pen to make you pay a postage to Uncle Samuel, who never refuses such contributions, although his boys may grumble sometimes at having to make them.

I think when the sufferings of the emigrants both on the plains and after their arrival is known at home, our people will begin to see California stripped of her gaudy robes, her paint and outward adornments, which have been so liberally heaped upon her by thoughtless letter-writers and culpable editors, and they will be content to stay at home and reap their own grain, and enjoy the comforts which they really possess, rather than come here to starve or pick up what would be thrown from their own tables at home to satisfy the cravings of hunger. The *greatness of California!* Faugh! Great for what and for whom? Great at present as an outlet to a portion of the surplus wheat, pork, and clothes, blacklegs, prostitutes, and vicious [?] at home, and for the would-be politicians of the country and the ultras who quarrel over us in Washington.

Oregon will be the greatest of the two, and here is another theme. She will have more wealth in time by selling her potatoes to us at five dollars per bushel, her lumber at thirty dollars per M, her flour, her pork, and soon her woolens, her leather, &c., &c., than we shall have with all our mines. If I was a politician (thank God *I am not*), I would gather statistics enough to satisfy any political economist on this subject.

I am a little curious to learn what effect a residence in California has had upon that portion of emigrants who have returned, whether they have as easily relapsed into steady habits again when surrounded by the moral influences of our old country, as they (not all, be it understood) fell into the snares of vice without any such restraint here. Could not we get up some tall lectures on what we have seen—eh? *The Decline and Fall of the Roman Empire* by that most beautiful of all writers, Gibbon, or the rise and progress of Mormonism, couldn't hold a candle to it; it's the subject I mean, not our style or descriptive powers.

It is noon and near dinnertime. Will you join me? Don't fear a griddle-cake infliction. No, no, just a plain family dinner—fried potatoes and ham. I made some gingerbread yesterday—all but the ginger (that I couldn't get)—it's good, too, and that shall be our dessert. Will you have a glass of wine?—just bring it along, for I haven't got it; but there is chocolate enough left from my breakfast to warm over again. Come, boys, move that monte bank off the table; the Colonel and I want to dine. Hardy, drive that mule out of the tent; let him wait till we get through. There, Colonel, scrape off that old cigar, take that keg, and go to your death. Pshaw! Colonel, don't pick your teeth with the fork; take your bowie knife. What's the use of being so effeminate? Now, tumble down on my mattress and take a siesta, while I talk to the boys.

Adieu,
Alonzo Delano

from CALIFORNIA AS IT IS, AND AS IT MAY BE

FELIX WIERZBICKI

Dr. Felix Wierzbicki (1815–1860) was born in Poland and emigrated to the United States in 1834. He had earned a medical degree and was practicing medicine in Rhode Island when the Mexican War broke out in 1846. Wierzbicki enlisted in Stevenson's Regiment, a motley group of New England farmers, machinists, and self-proclaimed "adventurers" who agreed to fight Mexicans in exchange for a free trip to California. After the war, Wierzbicki set up a doctor's office in gold rush San Francisco and was deluged with patients suffering from typhoid, dysentery, and gunshot wounds. In 1849 he published California as It Is, and as It May Be *to debunk the outrageous rumors about California he heard from Eastern visitors. It was the first English-language book published in California.*

CALIFORNIA HOLDS IN ITS BOSOM resources that no other country can boast of comprised in so small a territory—its mineral wealth, its agricultural capacity, its geographical position conspire to make it in time one of the most favored lands. And it will lie in the power of the government either to accelerate or retard the unfolding of its future importance. When considered in point of mineral productions, if allowed to be developed by capitalists, California is capable of becoming an important centre of the commerce of the Pacific.

Here we find in the neighborhood of the Clear Lake, about a hundred and twenty-five miles north of Sonoma, Lead, Copper, Sulphur, and Saltpetre; on the south side of San Francisco Bay, Silver-mines have been found in the vicinity of Pueblo de San Jose; Quick-silver mines which are pronounced to be richer than those of Spain are already being worked to a great profit in the same region; Coal strata have been also found in the coast range of San Luis Obispo, and near San Diego.

We mention not the gold washings that are being worked so successfully at present, for as respects their duration and the development of the industry of the country, they scarcely deserve the attention of the economist be they ever so rich; as all other mines are more beneficent in their influence to the progress of a country than gold mines. These will become the means of advancing the prosperity of the country only when a regular system of mining by sinking shafts into the rocks shall commence, which it is to be hoped will be done ere long.

The mineral region being under the sole control of mining companies will exclude all private adventurers; thus first benefitting the commerce by checking the now unavoidable desertion of the crews of its shipping, which at this very moment amounts to more than sixty thousand tons, of the finest ships in the world lying in the harbor....And secondly, preventing an influx of all sorts of adventurers into the country, whose presence is more of an nuisance than benefit to any country.

Then a farming population, cured of the gold mania, will seek to enrich itself by more sure means, the product of the soil, and will crowd to the Pacific shores. The arts will take a start—every species of industry will be called into existence; the surplus capital of the commerce will be devoted to the development of internal resources of the country; nay, even capital from abroad may find an employment here; the commerce of the country will be put on a firm footing and will grow daily and steadily. Even the government itself, thus rid of this bother of California gold, will find more leisure to do its duty to this newly acquired territory. In fine, the country will grow steadily in a permanent population, in strength of order and law; and the business of life will unavoidably fall into its natural and proper channels.

This country is particularly fitted for that class of people who once knew what affluence was, and who by a sudden turn of the wheel of fortune found their means reduced to mediocrity. Life in California, although it must have its inconveniences belonging to a thinly inhabited country, yet it cannot be compared to anything like life in new settlements in the Western States or Oregon. If people only were willing to take it easy, they would, ninety-nine out of a hundred, even like it. The population here is much more ready to take at once, or very soon, a more agreeable and polished form than could be expected in any other new country. There is something in the climate—we of course except San Francisco and the Valley of the Sacramento, which predisposes one to contentment. The sunny skies for so long a portion of the year have an exhilarating influence upon the mind, and so much so that we have known cases of Americans who were in the habit of carrying care-worn visages in their own country, acquire here smiling and contented countenances, smoothed by placidity. Indeed, we would recommend, as a medicine, to all vinegar-faced, care-corroded gentry that are well to do in the world, to come and settle in the rich valleys of California, where good health and azure skies can be enjoyed; where winter does not touch you with its freezing hand.

from VIAJE A CALIFORNIA

VICENTE PÉREZ ROSALES

Chileans had easy access to California because San Francisco–bound ships circling Cape Horn often stopped for supplies at the Chilean port of Valparaíso. In fact, Chilean miners were so successful in the gold country that white anti-Chilean sentiment more than once escalated into outright violence. Vicente Pérez Rosales (1807–1886), born in Chile and educated in France, felt the effects of this hatred soon after his arrival in California in 1848. His 1878 memoir, Viaje a California: Recuerdos de 1848, 1849, 1850, *chronicled his financial struggles in gold rush California. Later in life he returned to Chile and served as a diplomat to Europe.*

THE RELATIONS BETWEEN CHILEANS and Americans were anything but cordial. When General Persifer Smith sent a decree from Panamá to the effect that, after that date, no foreigner was to be allowed to exploit gold mines in California, that decree brought to a head all the hostility shown to peaceful and defenseless Chileans.

The ill will of the Yankee rabble against the sons of other nations, and especially Chileans, was rising by that time. They offered a simple and conclusive argument: Chileans were descended from Spaniards; Spaniards were of Moorish ancestry; therefore a Chilean was at the best something like a Hottentot, or, to put it more gently, something like the humbled but dangerous Californio. They could not stomach the fearlessness of the Chilean, who might be submissive in his own country but did not behave that way abroad. A Chilean would face up to a loaded pistol at his chest if he had his hand on the haft of his knife. For his part, the Chilean detested the Yankee and constantly referred to him as a coward. This mutual bad feeling explains the bloody hostilities and atrocities we witnessed every day in this land of gold and hope.

It was not long in San Francisco until an organized group of bandits appeared, called the Hounds. They were vagrants, gamblers, or drunks, drawn together in a fellowship of crime; and they had as their motto, "We can get away with it." Fear and hatred spread in advance of their appearance, and they deliberately generated these feelings by their provocations. Everywhere they went they established their control by quarrelsomeness and violence.

They did not always "get away with it," though. One morning when they were passing by a little point of land to the north of town where a sort of Little Chile had grown up, separated from the center of the city, these vicious Hounds decided to give it a savage going over. Because in California time is money, these merciless ruffians in large numbers charged the Chileans there with pistols and clubs. You can imagine the shouting and uproar this brutal and unprovoked attack brought on. The Chileans rallied and counterattacked by hurling stones. One respectable Chilean gentleman, not being able to escape through the front of his tent because it was jammed with a threatening band of Hounds, brought one of them down with a pistol shot as he came toward him and then, slashing with his dagger the cloth of his tent, managed to escape through that improvised exit and join his friends in safety.

[Sam] Brannan, ... informed by some Chileans of what was happening in Little Chile, climbed up on top of his own house in just indignation and shouted in a loud voice for the people to come. Then in a short but forceful speech he declared it was time to make an example of those who had perpetrated such unheard-of atrocities against the sons of a friendly country, a country that had day after day supplied the city of San Francisco with its best flour, as well as the most skillful arms in the world when it came to making *adobe bricks!* "I propose," he said, "that to take care of this once and for all, the Chileans of good will, led by citizens of the United States, go at once to the scene and arrest these disturbers of the peace!" A general "Hurrah!" was raised, and the almost instantaneous appearance of the defenders of order at the point put an end to the savagery that could have brought on the most terrible consequences.

Eighteen of the bandits were dragged from hideouts by force and were incarcerated on board the flagship of the Yankee American squadron, and with this, peace returned to the new Babylon.

Among the large number of acquaintances and relatives I had run into from time to time was Miguel Ramírez. He had heard me say I was going to buy a launch, and he offered to sell me one of twelve tons' burden that had just been built for $700. He did not need it any more because he was going to become a lumberman instead of a boatman, so he would sell it to me for $300. The deal was made.

Assisted by three young Chileans who were willing to turn sailor to pay their passage to Sacramento, the Dean, once a cook but now captain, formerly an accountant at the Sutter's mill mine but now a retail merchant and shop owner, was soon able to complete the loading of the *Infatigable*. That is what our fine little launch was called.

Her cargo consisted of eight bales of jerky, somewhat reduced through the efforts of moths; twenty hundredweight of Chanco cheese, carefully squared by a knife to remove parts that had been spoiled; four sacks of dried peaches, two barrels of rum at eight gallons each; a small box of candied preserves I had received from Chile; and two sacks of toasted flour.

I was ready to embark when the devil—it could have been no one else—almost ruined the whole business. He appeared in the form of a customs agent who let me know I was not to move from that anchorage. My ship had not been manufactured in North America, and the keel was not of American wood, two indispensable requirements for boats that traded on the rivers. Furious as could be at such a frustrating situation in a land where time is money, I decided this was a case where the saying must be turned around: if time is money, I told myself, then, clearly, money is time. It is not only time; it is everything in the world! So I ran to the former insurance man from Valparaiso who had become, so his sign said, a lawyer or attorney at law.... He said my case was a difficult but not an impossible one. "Charge me whatever you please," I told him, "because if this does not come out right for me, a barrelful of demons will have me." "Well," he said gravely, "you can begin by paying half the cost of my services, and we will get to work." I gave him $450 in gold.

Four days later (which is like a century in California), the counselor at law brought a bundle of papers all covered with scribbling. In them could be found incontestable proof that the wood in my hull had been cut in the "Eggplant" forest of the United States, and that the builder who had carved its keel was actually in San Francisco, on his way to the mines. It appeared that not only was the ship of unclouded ancestry, but so was its name. Instead of *Infatigable*, which Mexicans had called it because they could not pronounce English, its true name was *Impermeable*.

God bless him! I was now the owner, master, and captain of an American ship, having paid $900 for a clear legal title, and I could now proceed to set sail.

The crew of the ship consisted of five persons, from captain to cabin boy. Two from Chiloé were named Velásquez; Valdivia was from Casa-Blanca; and a lad, Martínez, was from the south. Martínez, who was about twenty-two years old, was my favorite. He had good manners and a pleasant appearance. He suffered from a tertian fever, though, and when it attacked him he developed chills and fevers, became extremely weak, and then went into a coma that lasted for over an hour. I wish I had never taken him aboard.

There had been a violent ebb tide that morning and two whale boats had sunk in the swirls and eddies of the Golden Gate with all their men, including

179

three Chileans. I decided not to start out until the high tide. While waiting I had a horrifying demonstration, with poor Martínez as the subject, of the effects such a fever can produce.

For three days in a row the proud *Impermeable* had sailed with winds and tides in her favor, exchanging hurrahs with all the ships she left behind. When we entered the waters of Suisún Bay, however, the wind and tide both turned against us at once. So, about noon, we tied up to a half-submerged tree trunk covered with turtles. The heat forced us to seek some shade ashore while we awaited the return of the tide.

Unfortunately, Martínez had just suffered one of his attacks, so we covered him as well as we could with a sailcloth and placed a jug of water near him. Then, leaving him there unconscious, we went ashore. We regretted having to abandon him that way, but we had no premonition of what we were to find on our return.

I have already described the enormous swarms of poisonous and persistent mosquitoes that infest the swampy shores of the Sacramento and San Joaquín Rivers, especially where the two rivers join.

We protected ourselves as best we could, swatting them with our handkerchiefs and, finally, taking cover under some bushes that faced a dry grassless area. This area was covered with small holes like those made by our *cururos* [Chilean field rats] in the dry area beyond the Maule River. We were there about an hour before we noticed little sticks, about three inches long, that were lying there, one beside each hole, in a manner that could not be accidental. I became curious then and walked out to look at them more closely—then backed up in a fright, yelling, "They are snakes!"

I have roamed through many solitary regions in the course of my life, but I cannot remember seeing anywhere a land with so many vipers and other snakes as golden California possesses.

We spent a good deal of time beating these creatures to death with clubs, and then bombarding with rocks the turtles that were lined up on tree trunks floating in the water. We were at the same time being attacked by such clouds of mosquitoes that they actually blocked our view, as well as tore us to pieces with their bites. They could not be driven off by hand-waving, fanning with branches, or even by smoke. It was late in the afternoon by the time we got back to the ship.

There are certain sights so horrifying you can never forget them. Martínez was lying motionless, monstrously swollen, the blanket at his feet—no doubt kicked there in some convulsive movement. His whole body, including his head, was covered with a disgusting and bloody layer of mosquitoes, hovering, bloated and heavy, over their miserable victim; at least an inch thick, it seemed to us. When we saw that, we ran to him, shook him, and brushed off so many thousands of mosquitoes that our hands were covered with blood. But it was too late: Martínez was dead!

We had no tools to dig a grave for him. There was no point in carrying him on to Sacramento. And the thought of leaving him ashore was, of course, unendurable to us, for he would he eaten by coyotes. After a sad night, the waters of the Sacramento River received, along with our tears, the lifeless body of the unhappy young man who only the day before had been friend and companion.

The life of a California miner closely resembled that of a soldier on a campaign. A tear may sometimes moisten the bronzed face of a soldier as he grimly shakes the hand of a dead comrade for the last time; but that tear quickly dries when he is faced with new dangers, or elated by the enthusiasm victory brings.

The cool breeze of morning, the disappearance of the mosquitoes swept away by the wind, the impressive vision of the tranquil waters of Suisún Bay, the gracious hills and forest of its faraway shore, the screeching of birds, the continuous passing parade of boats filled with happy passengers—and, perhaps, also the thought that tears are useless when shed over misfortunes that cannot be altered—all of these things reawakened in our sad spirits their dormant energies.

Two days later we arrived at Sacramento. I showed my bills of lading to my brothers, and they, full of enthusiasm for the merchandise I had managed to buy during one of those periods of low prices that are so surprising to everyone in California, proceeded immediately to unload the goods and stow them away.

We no longer had a field tent; that luxury had disappeared. A small strip of cotton suspended from stakes formed the roof of our home and warehouse. The walls were made of branches set in a semicircle to protect us from the wind. A box, placed upside down in the opening where the door should be, served us as a counter; and since the merchandise did not all fit inside the shelter, we piled some of it in an open space next to it, and called that our storehouse.

Some curious patrons approached soon after they saw we had set up a scale needed to weigh the gold. Next to it we placed a slice of cheese, a small pile of dried peaches, and a bottle with two fine glasses. The bottle was the first supply we had drawn from the barrels of brandy we were keeping inside as a reserve.

Everything was selling marvellously except the jerky, which could not be exposed to the light of day without some shame. We did not know what to do with it. In addition to everything else, the moths were still in competition with us. So the Board of Directors decided the moth holes had to be filled with lard or tallow to restore the jerky to its original appearance.

The bales were broken open, and the jerky (the pieces of which really looked like sieves) was shaken out and spread on the grass after having been given a coating of hot lard. We let it dry in the sun there. On the day before, Federico had brought us a sack of peppers some Chileans had discarded by a tree trunk, and, since there is nothing human ingenuity cannot accomplish, we took advantage of this. We piled up the sun-heated jerky in an artistic Egyptian pyramid and poured over it a devilishly hot pepper sauce.

The smell wafting away from this exotic offering attracted two wealthy Mexicans from Sonora who asked what in the world this aromatic dish could be. We told them it was the most select jerky, the kind served to the aristocracy in Santiago. We added that we had never offered it before because California people, in spite of their wealth, seemed to buy cheap inferior things rather than good things that were more expensive. We lied like experienced merchants who assure a trusting female customer that they are losing money on an item, and would not sell it at such a low price to anyone but her; she must tell no one else and keep it as a secret, and so on. The accursed shreds were sold at a peso a pound; and, what is more, it was all bought up. The brandy was sold at six *reales* a glass, because "it was of the quality that the Duke of Orleans drank." And so it went with the other items.

from A FRENCHMAN IN THE GOLD RUSH

ERNEST DE MASSEY

In response to the unparalleled flood of Chilean, Peruvian, Australian, Mexican, and European immigrants who arrived daily by the boatload, the California legislature—inundated by complaints from Yankee miners—passed the Foreign Miners' Tax Law of 1850. Its $20 monthly fee was ludicrously high, selectively enforced, and served mostly as an excuse to kick Hispanic miners out of rich diggings. In Sonora, however, a group of French and German miners protested the tax alongside several thousand Mexicans in the "French Revolution," only to be subdued by 500 well-armed Americans hastily called in from nearby camps. The tax was later lowered to $3 a month in an attempt to wring money from the increasing swell of Chinese gold rushers. Ernest de Massey, a French nobleman who came to California hoping to bolster his family fortune, found nothing but hard labor and misery in the mines. He was working as a hired hand on the Trinity River when the Foreign Miners' Tax became law.

ON THE TWENTY-EIGHTH and twenty-ninth [of May, 1850], I worked until evening in the interest of my two Irish bosses, but their claim is not a rich one, and I believe that in these three days they will just about break even, counting the food they have supplied me in the capacity of hired man at the rate of three dollars a day.

The work has been extremely irksome. I had to fill, carry, and empty three hundred buckets of sand. I made one hundred and fifty trips up and down a path as hard to descend as it was to climb—a distance of some seven kilometers in all—carrying a weight of fifteen kilograms in each hand. All this was under a broiling sun! In addition, we were badly treated, badly fed, and poorly housed at night.

Such a life is somewhat strenuous for anyone not accustomed to it. Naturally I was not sorry when my lords and masters told me, on the evening of the third day, that they would have to dispense with my services, for I am afraid I could not have held out much longer. Then, too, I had not been able to please my employers and they were tired of me.

On May thirtieth, as I was taking an enforced rest with Pidaucet who has not yet been able to work, a group of three Americans offered me a job with them. I accepted, for there will be ample time to loaf when work is not available.

These Yankees out here are boorish in the extreme. They have a sinister look and are absolutely uncommunicative. Hard workers, themselves, they believe in making those under them labor. Also, they are very strong physically. I cannot say where they hail from; in all events not from a civilized part of the country. It is from this population out here that squatters and filibusters might be recruited. When my day was over I was paid off, and I was glad to see the last of them.

So ended my thirty-eighth year. This same anniversary I celebrated a year ago on board the *Cérès* in the mid-Atlantic off Lisbon. At that time I was gay, full of enthusiasm, and cheerful over the future. The day was made memorable by meeting an English brig, the *Caroline,* of Sunderland, which had run out of food and water. Her food was almost gone, she had come over to us for assistance. Anyone who is superstitious might have deduced, from this incident, trouble ahead for us. Skeptics like myself, who mock at prophets and events, are now being punished for our levity.

Those, however, who predict calamities and misfortunes nearly always find them and few in this world are completely happy. Such are my thoughts as I am about to begin—on June first, 1850—my thirty-ninth birthday. If my luck gets any worse I shall be dead, or insane, by the time I am forty. I had not counted on any such bad luck as this when, in 1849, I set sail from Hâvre.

Monday, June third. At last we are at work! We have taken out an ounce of gold-dust between us, netting us five dollars and a half apiece for our work. While this is not a large sum yet we are our own masters and this is just the beginning. We have high hopes of making much more.

On Tuesday, June fourth, we had just begun work when, around noontime, an individual who called himself a tax-collector came in and, in the name of the law, demanded from each miner the sum of twenty dollars to be paid once a month. You can readily imagine no one wanted to pay it. Had he been able to collect I doubt if the State of California would have been the richer. All the money received without any control or check would never have reached its destination. The American administration, even though it is quite business-like and carefully supervised, is not entirely free from cupidity, greed, and disloyalty on the part of both of the underlings and chiefs who look after them.

"The French Miner," 1855, by Frank Marryat

Nevertheless, this visit from the tax-collector gave certain jealous and ill-tempered Americans a pretext for picking a quarrel with new miners—and our neighbors have lopped off part of the claim we are working. These bold citizens, who refused to pay the tax, were angry with us for also refusing.

185

from JOURNAL OF LIFE AT SONORA

WILLIAM PERKINS

Sonora, in present Tuolumne County, was named by its first inhabitants, who had emigrated from Sonora in northern Mexico. It became a magnet for foreigners of all nationalities and reached a population of approximately 5,000 by 1849. Because Sonora prospered, it eventually attracted attention from white miners, who drove out most of the foreigners. The journal of William Perkins, a Canadian merchant, offers a lively account of Sonora at the height of its colorful diversity. His journal was first published in 1964.

WHEN I ARRIVED, at the commencement of June, 1849, I thought I had never seen a more beautiful, a wilder, or more romantic spot. The Camp, as it was then termed, was literally embowered in trees. The habitations were constructed of canvas, cotton cloth, or of upright unhewn sticks with green branches and leaves and vines interwoven, and decorated with gaudy hangings of silks, fancy cottons, flags, brilliant goods of every description; the many-tinted Mexican *zarape,* the rich *manga,* with its gold embroidery, Chinese scarfs and shawls of the most costly quality; gold and silver plated saddles, bridles and spurs were strewn about in all directions.

The scene irresistibly reminded one of the descriptions we have read of the brilliant bazaars of oriental countries. Here were to be seen goods of so costly a nature that they would hardly be out of place in Regents' Street. But what article was too costly for men who could pay for it with handfuls of gold dust, the product of a few hours labor!

Here were to be seen people of every nation in all varieties of costume, and speaking fifty different languages, and yet all mixing together amicably and socially; and probably not one in a thousand moralizing on the really extraordinary scene in which he was just as extraordinary an actor.

Here was a John Chinaman with his quilted jacket, his full blue cotton breeches reaching to the knees, and meeting the stocking-shoes with their soles an inch thick; his head covered with the peculiar cap like a small beehive, then scarcely known by Europeans, but since become a fashionable *tile* for both sexes. Under this head covering, coiled up and safely stowed away, lies the

Sonora, 1852

inestimable and dearly cherished pig-tail. This pig-tail is only suffered to grow from two or three inches of surface; the rest of the head is regularly shaved.

Here was a Lascar, known at once, and distinguished from the Chinaman, by the more oval contour of physiognomy, the bright Madras handkerchief wound round the head, and the long *Kreese* stuck in the girdle.

And here was a *Kanacker,* or Sandwich Islander—small eyes, coarse face, and an immense shock of hair. A bright-colored calico shirt is bound about the waist with a gaudy silk sash. He wears no shoes, and his pantaloons are nothing but a pair of cotton drawers. There is a vacancy and stupidity of look about him that contrasts unpleasantly with the intelligent-looking East Indian.

There were plenty of native Indians strolling about, many with a military jacket on, with a shirt barely covering their haunches and without pantaloons or drawers; their huge bushy head enveloped in a red handkerchief, their coarse matted hair always allowed to fall in front to the eyes and there kept cropped in a straight line.

Amongst the Mexicans, some wore only cotton drawers, a shirt, and *zarape,* with a huge *sombrero* hat, black outside and lined with green; the crown decorated with large patines of silver, round and convex. Others wore the *vaquero* dress: a leathern jacket, double, with the outer surface scolloped out into fantastic patterns, showing red or blue figures on the under leather; half-tanned leathern trousers open down the leg on the outside, and adorned with rows of silver buttons; inside a pair of white cotton drawers, very wide and loose, and

187

the leg encased to the knee in *botas* ornamented in the same manner as the jacket. In these *botas* is stuck the knife, the handle of which projects alongside of the leg, and, when the man is mounted, is most conveniently at hand. A pair of silver spurs, with rowels having the diameter of a good sized saucer, with the hat already described, complete the picture of the Mexican *vaquero* or Herdsman (from *vaca,* cow). Others are entirely enveloped in a rich *manga,* which is a *zarape* made of fine cloth, and the space in the centre round the slit for the head to pass through, heavy with gold and silver embroidery.

The dress of the South Americans was something similar to the Mexican; but instead of the long *zarape* of the latter, they have a short one, which is called *poncho,* put over the shoulders in the same way by means of the slit through which the head is passed. The Peruvian *poncho* is generally of thick white cotton, with colored bands along the edge; the Chilian is black, or some dark color, of thick woolen material, with red, blue, and yellow bands. The Peruvians and Chilenos, as well as the Argentinos, who appear to be the most civilized of them all, wear a heavy leather belt about six inches wide, and divided into various pockets, and in which they carry their money, their stock of tobacco, cigarrito paper, and *Mechera* or tinderbox. These belts are fastened by buttons composed of silver dollars and often of gold ounces.

The dress of the Saxon race was generally uniform as to shape. A pair of thick pantaloons, heavy boots worn outside the trowsers, a red or blue flannel shirt also worn outside, and gathered round the waist by a Chinese *banda* or silk scarf, or a black leather belt, perhaps both; and in which a Colts' revolver was invariably stuck. As for the styles of covering for the head, their name was legion. It is scarcely possible for the imagination to conceive of any shape of hat or cap that had not its representative on the *caput* of some rough unshaven Saxon, with the sole exception of the chimney-pot, black beaver; that abominable, ugly, inconvenient, and yet indispensable "tile" of all civilized countries.

At the time I speak of, Sonora was probably the only place in California where numbers of the gentler sex were to be found. I have mentioned that the camp was formed by an immigration of families from Sonora, in Mexico; this accounts for the presence of women in the place.

The men had constructed brush houses and, leaving their wives and children in charge, separated in all directions in search of the richest diggings, where they would work all the week, to return to the camp and their families on Saturday, when they generally commenced gambling and drinking, and continued both until Monday, never thinking of sleep.

When Peruvian or Chilean women arrived in San Francisco, they soon found out that Sonora was the only place where their own sex were congregated in any number, and at once found their way to this vicinity. We have consequently always had an abundance of dark-skinned women amongst us, but white—none; except when some South American without much Indian blood in her veins made her appearance. These were generally *china-blancas,* *mestiza-claras,* or *quinteras,* and they formed our aristocratic society. A lady's social position with the white gentlemen was graduated by shades of color; although we would sometimes give the preferance to a slightly brown complexion, if the race was unmixed with the negro—pure white and pure Indian. Thus the *mestiza* is a child of a white father by an Indian mother; rather dark; preferable, however, to a *china-blanca,* who is the child of a white father, the mother being born of an Indian father, and a negro or mulatto mother. The *quintera* is perfectly white, but comes from negro blood, through the *cuarterona* and mulatto. As for the *Zambas, Zamba-claras, china-oscuras, india-mestizas,* etc. they were not admitted into refined society at all!

It is evident that an intimate knowledge of ethnography was requisite to enable one to move in our society without soiling his dignity.

On Saturdays and Sundays the old camp used to wear, night and day, an almost magic appearance. Besides the numberless lights from the gaily decorated houses, all of them with their fronts entirely open to the streets, the streets themselves were strewn with lighted tapers.

Where there was an open space, a Mexican would take off his variegated *zarape,* lay it on the ground, put a lighted wax or sperm candle at each corner, and pour into the center his *pile* or stock of silver and gold. The *zarape* would soon be surrounded by his countrymen, who, seated on the ground, would stake and generally lose their hard-earned weekly wages.

It would have been difficult to have taken a horse through the crowded streets. As for wheeled carriages, they were not known as yet.

Tables [were] loaded with *dulces,* sweetmeats of every description, cooling beverages, with snow from the Sierra Nevada floating in them, cakes and dried fruits, hot meats, pies, every thing in the greatest abundance. One could hardly believe in his senses, the brilliant scene appeared so unreal and fairy-like.

Almost every house had its band of music, such as it was. Some of the Mexicans display considerable talent in the art, and some bands, composed of a clarionet, a harp, and a base guitar, did much credit to their members.

Mission Indians, with scarlet bandanas round their heads, a richly colored *zarape* over their shoulder, a pair of cotton drawers, and bare-footed, would push their way through the crowd, carrying pails of iced liquor on their heads, crying in the shrill falsetto voice peculiar to most of the savage tribes, "*agua fresco, agua fresco, cuatro reales.*"

Behind portable kitchens were Mexican and Indian women in their picturesque costumes, their heads covered with the omnipresent *rebosa,* occupied in making the national dish of meat and chile pepper, wrapped within two *tortillas* of wheaten flour, a delicacy for which the Mexican *peon* would sell his birthright.

In some less crowded spot might be witnessed the national dances of the Spaniards. That of the Mexicans is simple but energetic. On a board about six feet long and ten or twelve inches broad you may see a couple, fronting each other; the man with the perspiration streaming from every pore, executing the genuine "hoe-down" of the Virginia nigger, but with even more energy (if not with so much skill) than his more joyous rival of the States. It soon becomes a matter of competition between the dancer and the musicians as to who gives in first; and there is often a lively vitality in the former's legs when the latter's arms and lungs are in a state of complete exhaustion. The movements of the woman during all this time are tame, and unexcited, being nothing more than a mere shuffling of the feet and a pirouette now and then.

from Early Recollections of the California Mines

James H. Carson

James H. Carson, a Virginia native whose army regiment landed at Monterey just after the Mexican War ended in 1847, deserted his army duties while on furlough to explore and pan the tributaries of the Stanislaus River. He struck it rich at what was soon called Carson's Creek but developed rheumatism in the process and spent most of his remaining days in the state hospital in Monterey. In early 1852, the Stockton newspaper The San Joaquin Republican *printed thirty-three articles written by Carson from his sickbed describing humorous anecdotes from his mining experiences. His letters were collected later that year as* Early Recollections of the California Mines, *the first book ever published in Stockton. He died in April of 1853—a month before his wife and daughter finally arrived in California.*

In the tide of emigration which set into the mines in the latter part of 1848 and during '49, were to be found every species of the human family; and amongst the other animals, a full-sized live dandy could be seen once in a while, with a very delicate pick, a wash pan made to order in the States, and a fine Bowie knife, perambulating through the diggings in search of "ah very rich hole, whah a gentleman could procure an agreeable shade to work under."

The dandy has always been known to go dressed in the finest and most fashionable apparel—kid gloves that covered lily-white hands, small walking stick, hair usually long and soaped down until his head shines like a junk bottle, feet encased in patent leather boots, speaking a sweet little language of his own, which is faintly tinged in places with the English tongue, was never known to have done an hour's work in his life, and the oldest inhabitants never knew one of them to have a "dem cent."

One of this species came into a ravine on the Stanislaus in which some thirty men were at work; it was the month of June, '49, and the heat of the sun was quite oppressive in the mountains, and most of us were lying in our camps, but were aroused by the arrival of five finely dressed strangers; four of them were professional men, who, after having struggled hard for years in the

191

Forty-niner Joseph Sharp at Sharp's Flat, 1849

Eastern States for a fortune without success, had come to California with the intention of laboring in the mines; they were good-hearted fellows and gentlemen in the true sense of the word; such as these the old miners always instructed, aided, and encouraged by every means in their worthy undertakings. The fifth one was a dandy, who, with his soft talk and foolish questions, soon attracted the miners' attention, and his former companions (the first four mentioned) seemed to wish to get rid of him. For the love of fun, we agreed to take him off their hands, and instruct him in the fine art of handling the pick and spade.

He informed us that he had stopped amongst us because he knew we were "dem foin fellows," and all he desired at present was to be given a rich hole, very easy to dig. Such a place was shown him as was known to consist of the hardest earth in the gulch, and where no gold had ever been found. He set to work with his little pick, which he used about as handy as a ring-tail monkey would. After working by spells for some two hours, he had thrown out about a bushel of dirt without seeing any gold. Disheartened, he threw down his tools, and came up to where some dozen of us were enjoying the rich sight of a "dandy's" first attempt at gold digging. He was in a perfect rage.

And after he had blown off a long stream of fancy indignation gas, we advised him to ... *hire* some men to work for him—that he could get good hands for twenty dollars per day, who, he might rest assured, would get out each three ounces, thus giving him a fine profit. This seemed to please him well, and he set the next day as that on which his future fortunes were to commence.

At the bottom of the gulch, off from the rest, an old mountaineer had erected his brush house; and old trappers generally have about the same regard for a dandy that he has for a skunk; and old M—— was one of the oldest stamp, and was about as pleasant a companion to mankind as a grizzly bear would prove to be. To M's camp our dandy friend was directed, as being a place where he would be sure to get one good man at least. After viewing his toilet for a moment, off he started; the whole population of the hollow was on tiptoe to know the result of his expedition.

A short time elapsed before a loud yell from the vicinity of old M's camp informed us that the beauty "vat wanted to hire gold diggers" was in a tight place. What passed at M's camp between the two, we never learned; but the yells drew nearer, until at length the dandy and old M. were seen coming at rail-road speed: M. had a brush from the side of his shanty, with which he gave the dandy a loving rap at every jump; and as far as we could see them over the hills, the same persuasive power of locomotion was being applied. Old M. returned in a short time, swearing that "that ar 'tarnal varmint never come to his lodge without being sent thar, and if he knew the man, he would have a lock of his 'har' to remember him by." We never saw our dandy digger again, and no doubt he never stopped before San Francisco brought him up.

from A FRONTIER LADY

SARAH ROYCE

Sarah Royce arrived in California in October of 1849. She eventually settled in Grass Valley but first visited a mining camp in the Sierra foothills. She gave this account to her son, historian Josiah Royce, in 1879.

AND NOW BEGAN my first experience in a California mining camp. The sense of safety that came from having arrived where there was no danger of attacks from Indians, or of perishing of want or of cold on the desert, or in the mountains, was at first so restful that I was willing, for awhile, to throw off anxiety; and, like a child fixing a play-house, I sang as I arranged our few comforts in our tent. Indeed, part of the time it was fixing a play-house; for Mary was constantly pattering about at my side; and often, things were arranged for her convenience and amusement.

Still, there was a lurking feeling of want of security from having only a cloth wall between us and out of doors. I had heard the sad story (which, while it shocked, reassured us) of the summary punishment inflicted in a neighboring town upon three thieves, who had been tried by a committee of citizens and, upon conviction, all hung. The circumstances had given to the place the name of Hang-Town. We were assured that, since then, no case of stealing had occurred in the northern mines; and I had seen, with my own eyes, buck-skin purses half full of gold-dust, lying on a rock near the road-side, while the owners were working some distance off. So I was not afraid of robbery; but it seemed as if some impertinent person might so easily intrude, or hang about, in a troublesome manner.

But I soon found I had no reason to fear. Sitting in my tent sewing, I heard some men cutting wood up a hill behind us. One of them called out to another "Look out not to let any sticks roll that way, there's a woman and child in that tent." "Aye, aye, we won't frighten them" was the reply, all spoken in pleasant, respectful tones. A number of miners passed every morning and afternoon, to and from their work; but none of them stared obtrusively. One, I observed, looked at Mary with interest a time or two, but did not stop, till one day I happened to be walking with her near the door when he paused, bowed courteously, and said, "Excuse me madam, may I speak to the little girl? We see so few ladies and children in California, and she is about the size of a little sister I left at home." "Certainly," I said, leading her towards him. His gentle tones and pleasant words easily induced her to shake hands, and talk with him. He proved to be a young physician, who had not long commenced practice at home, when the news of gold discovery in California induced him to seek El Dorado, hoping thus to secure, more speedily, means of support for his widowed mother and the younger members of the family. His partner in work was a well-educated lawyer; and another of their party was a scientist who had been applying his knowledge of geology and mineralogy in exploring; and had lately returned from a few miles south with a report so favorable they intended in a day or two to go and make a claim on his newly discovered ground. Here, then, was a party of California miners, dressed in the usual mining attire, and carrying pick, shovel, and pans to and from their work; who yet were cultured gentlemen.

I soon found that this was by no means a solitary instance. But a much larger number of the miners belonged to other very valuable classes of society. Merchants, mechanics, farmers were all there in large numbers; so that in almost every mining camp there was enough of the element of order to control, or very much influence, the opposite forces. These facts soon became apparent to me, and, ere long, I felt as secure in my tent with the curtain tied in front as I had formerly felt with locked and bolted doors. There was, of course, the other element as elsewhere; but they themselves knew that it was safer for law and order to govern; and, with a few desperate exceptions, were willing to let the lovers of order enjoy their rights and wield their influence. And the desperate exceptions were, for the time, so over-awed by the severe punishment some of their number had lately suffered that, for a while, at least, in those early days, life and property were very safe in the mines; unless indeed you chose to associate with gamblers and desperados, in which case you of course constantly risked your money and your life. But, the same is true in the heart of New York, Philadelphia, or London.

from HUNTING FOR GOLD

WILLIAM DOWNIE

Born in Scotland, Major William Downie heard news of the gold discovery while in a hotel in Buffalo, New York. He arrived in San Francisco in the summer of 1849 and headed for the northern gold fields. He discovered gold on a branch of the North Fork of the Yuba River near what is now known, appropriately, as Downieville. California was not his last adventure—later in life he followed rumors of gold to Canada, Alaska, and Panama. In his playful memoir Hunting for Gold, *published in 1893, he described how the Fourth of July was celebrated in the California mines.*

EVERYTHING LOOKED FESTIVE when the sun appeared over the lofty Sierras on that Fourth of July morning [1850]. On Jersey Flat and up and down the Yuba, all around the Forks wherever tent or cabin served as habitation, the Stars and Stripes had been exhibited, denoting enthusiasm—not only on the part of native Americans, but on the part of the many who had sworn allegiance to the flag, and under its protection were seeking to make themselves and the world richer. As a matter of course, the store-keepers were kept busy, as the day wore on.

At Galloway's an elaborate dinner was prepared. It was not served *à la Russe* or in the so-called French style, there were no gilt-edged *menu* cards to tell us what the next course would be; neither were we waited upon by men in swallow-tails and white shirt fronts; nor did we drink wine from crystal goblets but we had the best that could be procured where money was no object, and where the only impediments were the distance from the market and the difficulties of getting there. Mrs. Galloway had prepared the dinner, and it was pronounced "fit for a prince."

Bottled ale played an important part on that occasion, and it was varied with something stronger of different kinds. The company became animated and toast followed toast. We drank to the Star Spangled Banner, to George Washington, and the galaxy of states—men and soldiers who had shared the laurels with him, to the American nation in general and the Constitution in particular; to absent friends and to everything and anything else that it was possible to toast.

Meanwhile the carousing had been going on in other parts of the settlement, and in the afternoon men began to get hilarious. Shots were fired from guns and pistols, and the racket increased until the general tumult and excitement assumed dimensions which could hardly be exceeded by a modern celebration, when fire crackers, brass bands, and processions are brought into action. Then occurred the first incident of which I am about to speak.

Two men, who had been indulging in the fiery liquid until their brains had become giddy, had a quarrel. It passed from words to blows, and the fight became furious. In the heat of passion one of them drew a knife, and before his adversary could ward off the thrust, or by-standers interfere, he sunk it deep into his opponent's body. The blood spurted out as the wounded man sank to the ground. The wound did not prove a dangerous one, but at the time no one knew the extent of the injury done, and the sight of blood inflamed the crowd with anger towards the man who did the stabbing. He was seized and bound, and while a few attended to the wounded man, the miscreant was at once brought to justice. He was comparatively a stranger and no doubt thought that in these rough surroundings the use of a knife was in order. But the jury saw no extenuating circumstances which could excuse him, and he was sentenced to thirty-nine lashes on the bare back.

There was no reason to postpone the execution of justice, and while the slanting rays of the midsummer sun fell upon the scene, and the hot air filled the valley with an almost stifling atmosphere, the wretched man was brought out to receive his punishment. He was tied hand and foot to a slender tree, and the flogging inflicted with a stout strip of rawhide. It was a sickening sight to behold. "Big" Logan, who wielded the instrument of torture, was a large, muscular man, whose sinewy arms denoted enormous strength. He was a sailor by occupation, but had lately driven an ox team across the plains, and was well practiced in the use of a whip, and moreover he was a cousin of the injured man.... The unfortunate culprit writhed in agony as the heavy strokes fell upon his body, which became more and more lacerated by each blow that tapped the blood from his veins, and at last, Logan seemed the only man in the crowd who was entirely unmoved by the horrible spectacle.

It may be remarked in connection with this that the flogging of that day had a remarkably healthy influence on our community. The miners had established a precedent, and whenever anybody flourished a knife in an angry moment, it was merely necessary to remind him of what happened on the Fourth of July, and for a long time the effect of such a reminder was simply magical.

from A Miner's Sunday in Coloma

CHARLES B. GILLESPIE

Sundays offered a break from the daily drudgery and competitiveness of mining. Along with a chance to rest, read, write letters, bathe, and wash clothes, miners also spent some of their hard-earned gold dust. They congregated at bars, gambling houses, auctions, dances, and even the occasional circus. "A Miner's Sunday in Coloma," from the gold rush journal of Charles B. Gillespie, appeared in Century Magazine *in 1891.*

THE PRINCIPAL STREET of Coloma was alive with crowds of moving men, passing and repassing, laughing, talking, and all appearing in the best of humor: Negroes from the Southern States swaggering in the expansive feeling of run-away freedom; mulattoes from Jamaica trudging arm-in-arm with Kanakas from Hawaii; Peruvians and Chilians claiming affinity with the swarthier Mexicans; Frenchmen, Germans, and Italians fraternizing with one another and with the cockney fresh from the purlieus of St. Giles; an Irishman, with the dewdrop still in his eye, tracing relationship with the ragged Australian; Yankees from the Penobscot chatting and bargaining with the genial Oregonians; a few Celestials scattered here and there, their pigtails and conical hats recalling the strange pictures that took my boyish fancy while studying the geography of the East; last of all, a few Indians, the only indigenous creatures among all these exotics, lost, swallowed up—out of place like "*rari nantes in gurgite vasto.*"

It was a scene that no other country could ever imitate. Antipodes of color, race, religion, language, government, condition, size, capability, strength, and morals were there, within that small village in the mountains of California, all impressed with but one purpose—impelled with but one desire.

A group of half a dozen Indians especially attracted my attention. They were strutting about in all the glory of newly acquired habiliments; but with this distinction—that one suit of clothes was sufficient to dress the whole crowd. The largest and best-looking Indian had appropriated the hat and boots, and without other apparel walked about as proudly as any city clerk. Another was lost in an immense pair of pantaloons. A third sported nothing but a white shirt with ruffled bosom. A fourth flaunted a blue swallow-tailed coat, bespangled with immense brass buttons. A fifth was decked with a flashy vest; while the sixth had nothing but a red bandana, which was carefully wrapped around his neck. Thus what would scarcely serve one white man just as effectually accommodated six Indians.

The street was one continuous din. Thimble-riggers, French monte dealers, or string-game tricksters were shouting aloud at every corner: "Six ounces, gentlemen, no one can tell where the little joker is!" or "Bet on the jack, the jack's the winning card! Three ounces no man can turn up the jack!" or "Here's the place to git your money back! The veritable string game! Here it goes! Three, six, twelve ounces no one can put his finger in the loop!" But rising above all this ceaseless clamor was the shrill voice of a down-east auctioneer, who, perched on a large box in front of a very small canvas booth, was disposing of the various articles in the shebang behind him, "all at a bargain." What a ragged, dirty, unshaven, good-natured assemblage!—swallowing the stale jests of the "crier" with the greatest guffaws, and bidding with all the recklessness of half-tipsy brains and with all the confidence of capacious, well-stuffed bags. Behind a smaller box, to the left of the Yankee, was a Jew in a red cap and scarlet flannel shirt, busy with his scales and leaden weights, to weigh out the "dust" from the various purchasers. There was no fear of the weights being heavier than the law allows, or that the tricky Jew by chance should place the half-ounce on the scales when there was but a quarter due. That there should be a few pennyweights too many made no difference; it is only the hungry purse that higgles about weights or prices. A little bad brandy and a big purse made a miner wonderfully important and magnanimous; and he regarded everything below an ounce as unworthy of attention.

This German Jew was also barkeeper. Beside him were a few tin cups, and a whole army of long and short necked, gaily labeled bottles, from which he dealt out horrible compounds for fifty cents a drink. His eye brightened as he perceived coming up the street a crowd of rollicking, thirsty, sunburned fellows, fresh from their "diggins" among the hills. But the quick eye of the auctioneer also singled them out and read their wants.

"Here's a splendid pair of brand-new boots! cowhide, double-soled, triple-pegged, water-proof boots! The very thing for you, sir, fit your road-smashers exactly; just intended, cut out, made for your mud-splashers alone; going for only four ounces and a half—four and a half! and gone—for four and a half ounces; walk up here and weigh out your dust."

"Wet your boots, old boy!" sang out the companions of the purchaser.

The barkeeper, with his weights already on the scales, exclaimed, "Shtand back, poys, and let de shentlemens to de bar."

The newcomers approached, crowding tumultuously around their companion of the boots, who, drawing out a long and well-filled buckskin bag, tossed it to the expectant Jew with as much carelessness as if it were only dust.

"Thar's the bag, old feller! weigh out the boots and eight lickers. Come, boys, call for what you like; it's my treat—go it big , fellers! all one price."

"Vat ye takes?" asks the barkeeper, after weighing out the amount due and handing the purse back to its owner.

"Brandy straight," "brandy punch," "brandy sling," "gin cocktail," and thus they went on, each calling for a different drink.

Then the bargaining began. Butcher-knives for crevicing, tin pans, shovels, picks, clothing of all colors, shapes, and sizes; hats and caps of every style; coffee, tea, sugar, bacon, flour, liquors of all grades in stiff-necked bottles—in a word, almost everything that could be enumerated—were disposed of at a furious rate; so that in an hour's time the contents of the little grocery were distributed among the jolly crowd.

Suddenly there was a great noise of shouting and hurrahing away up the street, and, the crowd heaving and separating upon either side , on came a dozen half-wild, bearded miners, fine, wiry, strapping fellows, on foaming horses, lashing them to the utmost, and giving the piercing scalp-halloo of the Comanches! They suddenly halted in front of Winter's hotel, and while the greater number dismounted and tumultuously entered the barroom for refreshment, a few of the remainder made themselves conspicuous by acts of daring horsemanship—picking up knives from the ground while at full gallop, Indian-like whirling on the sides of their steeds, then up and off like the wind and, while apparently dashing into the surrounding crowd, suddenly reining in their horses upon their haunches and whirling them upon their hind legs, then without a stop dashing off as furiously in the opposite direction. These few proved to be Doniphan's wild riders, who even excelled the Mexican caballeros in their feats of horsemanship. At last, all together once more they came sweeping down the street, apparently reckless of life and limb. As they passed, the scurrying footmen cheered them on with great good nature. The crowd closed again and in a brief time everything was as restless as ever.

Passing up the street, I came to a large unfinished frame-house, the sashless windows and doorway crowded with a motley crew, apparently intent upon something solemn happening within. After a little crowding and pushing I looked over the numberless heads in front, and saw—could I believe my eyes?—a preacher, as ragged and as hairy as myself, holding forth to an attentive audience. Though the careless and noisy crowd was surging immediately without, all was quiet within. He spoke well and to the purpose and warmed every

Dutch Flat's Main Street, 1850s, by Lawrence and Houseworth

one with his fine and impassioned delivery. He closed with a benediction but prefaced it by saying: "There will be divine service in this house next Sabbath—if, in the meantime, I hear of no new diggin's!"

The audience silently streamed out, the greater part directing their steps to a large, two-story frame-house across the street. This was the hotel *par excellence* of the town; one could easily perceive that by its long white colonnade in front, and its too numerous windows in the upper story.

A large saloon occupied the whole front of the building.... There was a perfect babel of noises! English, French, Spaniards, Portuguese, Italians, Kanakas, Chilians, all were talking in their respective languages. Glasses were jingling, money was rattling, and, crowning all, two fiddlers in a distant corner were scraping furiously on their instruments, seemingly the presiding divinities of this variegated pandemonium!

Crowding, inch by inch, into one of these motley groups, I found myself at last in front of a large table, neatly covered with blue cloth, upon which was a mass of Mexican silver dollars piled up in ounce or sixteen-dollar stacks. Immediately facing me was the banker; a well-dressed, middle-aged, quiet little man, with one of the most demure countenances imaginable. Beside him was the croupier, a very boy, whose duty it was to rake in the winnings and pay out the losses, which he did with wonderful dexterity.

Fronting the dealer, and dividing the silver into two equal portions, was a large Chinese box of exquisite construction. Upon it were ranged half a dozen packs of French and Spanish cards, several large masses of native gold, and a dozen or more buckskin bags of all sizes and conditions containing dust. Dollars and half-dollars were piled upon these purses—some with a few, others with a greater number thereon. One unacquainted with the game might guess for a day and not be able to hit upon the object of this arrangement, but a close observer might read elation or depression in the anxious eyes of the players as the weight upon these bags was either diminished or increased. These purses were in pawn; the dollars and half-dollars were the counters wherewith the banker numbered the ounces or half-ounces that might be owing to the bank.

"There's another millstone on the pile," groaned a thin-faced, watery-eyed little fellow in a hickory shirt and walnut pantaloons, as he saw another dollar added to his dust-bag.

"Take off two o' them air buttons," laughed a fat-faced man in red shirt and Chinese cap.

"I won two ounces on the deuce; another bet like that, and my bag's not for your mill, old feller!"

The cards were all out, and the "old feller" was shuffling them for a new deal; during which operation he cast a furtive glance about the table to see if there were any new customers to bite at his game, or, perhaps, to note if any of those who had bitten seemed to be cooling off—a weakness which he hastened to counteract by singing out: "Barkeeper!" and inquiring "What will the gentlemen take to drink?" This invitation was given in such a quiet and insinuating manner that one hesitated to decline for fear of wounding the delicate sensibilities of the banker. Each called for what he wished, and all concluded to "fight the tiger" a little while longer. The sprightly barkeeper was back in a twinkling, with a large waiter covered with glasses. These he distributed with wonderful dexterity, remembering perfectly what each one had ordered; so that, much to the player's surprise, he found his own glass chosen from among twenty and placed before him. That barkeeper had a niche in his brain for every man at the table.

By this time my appetite began to warn me of the near approach of noon. There were any number of eating-houses and booths, but which to choose I could not tell. However, suffering myself to be guided in a measure by the crowd which was now streaming to the other side of the river, I soon found myself in front of "Little's Hotel," the largest frame building on the right bank of the river, serving in the treble capacity of post-office, store, and tavern. Here I found all my acquaintances, who, like me, were on the search for a good dinner; and who had been induced to go there by the encomiums of "olderhands," who every Sunday had made a custom of visiting Coloma for the express purpose of having one good dinner in the week....The dinner was really excellent, and every one appeared heartily to enjoy it.

When the edge of my appetite had in a measure been ground away, I took occasion to look up and down the table, and I could but wonder how I happened among such a collection of uncouth men. The contrast was certainly startling between the snow-white tablecloth, china dishes, silver forks and spoons and the unwashed, half-famished, sunburnt crowd of hungry and bearded miners. At home, one would associate such a crowd with the deck of a Mississippi steamboat, or the platform of an Alleghany River raft, with iron forks and spoons and tin plates spread on a rough pine board for a table; but here they lorded it over every luxury that money could procure. There was not a single coat in the whole crowd, and certainly not over half a dozen vests, and neither neckties nor collars. But then, to make amends for these deficiencies, there were any number and variety of fancy shirts, from the walnut-stained homespun of the Missourian to the embroidered blouse of the sallow Frenchman. Never before was I so fully impressed with the truth of the old adage that "dress makes the man," for I doubt if the whole world could present to a stranger's eye a crowd of rougher or apparently lower characters than were then seated around that hospitable table. And yet many of these men were lawyers and physicians, and the rest principally farmers and mechanics from the "States"; who now with their long beards and fierce mustaches looked anything else than the quiet citizens they were at home. Men who formerly were effeminacy itself in dress and manners were here changed into rough and swaggering braves, with a carelessness of appearance and language that a semi-civilized condition of society alone could permit.

THE GOLD RUSH SONGBOOK

ANONYMOUS

The songs of the gold rush were often existing eastern tunes adapted to fit the forty-niners'
new circumstances. "Oh, Susanna," for example, became "Oh, California." Popular
songs spread from town to town and campfire to campfire, allowing gold rushers to relieve
their loneliness, voice their hopes, and mock their fears. At turns bawdy and sentimental,
songs such as "Sweet Betsy from Pike" and "Prospecting Dream" mourned old lovers,
complained of past gambling losses, and generally celebrated their western lifestyle.

WHAT WAS YOUR NAME IN THE STATES?

Oh, what was your name in the States?
Was it Thompson, or Johnson or Bates?
Did you murder your wife
And fly for you life?
Say, what was your name in the States?

CLEMENTINE

In a cavern, in a canyon,
Excavating for a mine,
Lived a miner, forty-niner,
And his daughter Clementine.

Chorus: Oh my darlin', oh my darlin',
Oh my darlin' Clementine,
You are lost and gone forever,
Dreadful sorry Clementine.

Light she was and like a fairy,
And her shoes were number nine;
Herring boxes without topses,
Sandals were for Clementine. (*Chorus*)

Drove she ducklings to the water,
Every morning just at nine,
Hit her foot against a splinter,
Fell into the foaming brine. (*Chorus*)

Ruby lips above the water,
Blowing bubbles soft and fine,
Alas for me, I was no swimmer,
So I lost my Clementine. (*Chorus*)

In a churchyard near the canyon,
Where the myrtle doth entwine,
There grow roses and other posies,
Fertilized by Clementine. (*Chorus*)

In my dreams she oft doth haunt me,
With her garments soaked in brine;
Though in life I used to hug her,
Now she's dead I draw the line. (*Chorus*)

Then the miner, forty-niner,
Soon began to peak and pine;
Thought he 'oughter join his daughter,
Now he's with his Clementine. (*Chorus*)

ACRES OF CLAMS

I've wandered all over this country,
Prospecting and digging for gold;
I've tunneled, hydraulicked, and cradled,
And I have been frequently sold.

And I have been frequently sold,
And I have been frequently sold.
I've tunneled, hydraulicked, and cradled,
And I have been frequently sold!

For one who got rich by mining,
I saw there were hundreds grew poor;

I made up my mind to try farming,
The only pursuit that is sure.

I rolled up my grub in my blanket,
I left all my tools on the ground,
I started one morning to shank it,
For the country they call Puget Sound.

No longer the slave of ambition,
I laugh at the world and its shams,
And think of my happy condition,
Surrounded by acres of clams.

Surrounded by acres of clams,
Surrounded by acres of clams.
And think of my happy condition,
Surrounded by acres of clams!

British songsheet, c. 1850, by George Edward Madeley

from THREE YEARS IN CALIFORNIA

J. D. BORTHWICK

John David Borthwick (1825–c.1900), a Scottish artist and journalist living in New York when gold fever ignited the East, took the Panama route to California. Well-traveled and sophisticated, his travelogue Three Years in California, *published in Edinburgh in 1857, offered wry descriptions of nearly every aspect of chaotic gold rush society.*

THE TOWN OF PLACERVILLE—or Hangtown, as it was commonly called—consisted of one long straggling street of clapboard houses and log cabins, built in a hollow at the side of a creek, and surrounded by high and steep hills.

The diggings here had been exceedingly rich—men used to pick the chunks of gold out of the crevices of the rocks in the ravines with no other tool than a bowie-knife; but those days had passed, and now the whole surface of the surrounding country showed the amount of real hard work which had been done. The beds of the numerous ravines which wrinkle the faces of the hills, the bed of the creek, and all the little flats alongside of it were a confused mass of heaps of dirt and piles of stones lying around the innumerable holes, about six feet square and five or six feet deep, from which they had been thrown out. The original course of the creek was completely obliterated, its waters being distributed into numberless little ditches, and from them conducted into the "long toms" of the miners through canvas hoses, looking like immensely long slimy sea-serpents.

The number of bare stumps of what had once been gigantic pine trees, dotted over the naked hill-sides surrounding the town, showed how freely the ax had been used, and to what purpose was apparent in the extent of the town itself, and in the numerous log-cabins scattered over the hills, in situations apparently chosen at the caprice of the owners, but in reality with a view to be near to their diggings and at the same time to be within a convenient distance of water and firewood.

There was a continual noise and clatter, as mud, dirt, stones, and water were thrown about in all directions; and the men, dressed in ragged clothes and big boots, wielding picks and shovels and rolling big rocks about, were all working as if for their lives, going into it with a will and a degree of energy, not usually seen among laboring men. It was altogether a scene which conveyed the idea of hard work in the fullest sense of the words, and in comparison with which a gang of railway navvies would have seemed to be merely a party of gentlemen amateurs playing at working *pour passer le temps.*

The street itself was in many places knee-deep in mud, and was plentifully strewed with old boots, hats, and shirts, old sardine-boxes, empty tins of preserved oysters, empty bottles, worn-out pots and kettles, old ham-bones, broken picks and shovels, and other rubbish too various to particularize. Here and there, in the middle of the street, was a square hole about six feet deep in which one miner was digging, while another was baling the water out with a bucket, and a third, sitting alongside the heap of dirt which had been dug up, was washing it in a rocker. Wagons, drawn by six or eight mules or oxen, were navigating along the street, or discharging their strangely-assorted cargoes at the various stores; and men in picturesque rags, with large muddy boots, long beards, and brown faces, were the only inhabitants to be been seen.

We had many pleasant neighbors, and among them were some very amusing characters. One man, who went by the name of the "Philosopher," might possibly have earned a better right to the name if he had had the resolution to abstain from whisky. He had been, I believe, a farmer in Kentucky, and was one of a class not uncommon in America, who, without much education, but with great ability and immense command of language, together with a very superficial knowledge of some science, hold forth on it most fluently, using such long words, and putting them so well together, that, were it not for the crooked ideas they enunciated, one might almost suppose they knew what they were talking about.

Phrenology was this man's hobby, and he had all the phrenological phraseology at his finger-ends. His great delight was to paw a man's head and to tell him his character. One Sunday morning he came into our cabin as he was going down to the store for provisions, and after a few minutes' conversation, of course he introduced phrenology; and as I knew I should not get rid of him till I did so, I gave him my permission to feel my head. He fingered it all over, and gave me a very elaborate synopsis of my character, explaining most minutely the consequences of the combination of the different bumps, and telling me how I would act in a variety of supposed contingencies. Having satisfied himself as to my character, he went off, and I was in hopes I was done with him, but an hour or so after dark he came rolling into the cabin just as I was going to turn in. He was as drunk as he well could be; his nose was swelled and bloody, his eyes were both well blackened, and altogether he was very unlike a learned professor of phrenology. He begged to be allowed to stay all night; and as he would most likely have broken his neck over the rocks if he had tried to reach his own home that night, I made him welcome, thinking that he would immediately fall asleep without troubling me further. But I was very much mistaken; he had no sooner lain down than he began to harangue me as if I were a public meeting or a debating society, addressing me as "gentlemen," and expatiating on a variety of topics, but chiefly on phrenology, the Democratic ticket, and the great mass of the people. He had a bottle of brandy with him, which I made him finish in hopes it might have the effect of silencing him; but there was unfortunately not enough of it for that—it only made him worse, for he left the debating society and got into a bar-room, where, when I went to sleep, he was playing "poker" with some imaginary individual whom he called Jim.

In the morning he made most ample apologies, and was very earnest in expressing his gratitude for my hospitality. I took the liberty of asking him what bumps he called those in the neighborhood of his eyes. "Well, sir," he said, "you ask me a plain question, I'll give you a plain answer. I got into a 'muss' down at the store last night, and was whipped; and I deserved it too." As he was so penitent, I did not press him for further particulars; but I heard from another man the same day that when at the store he had taken the opportunity of an audience to lecture them on his favorite subject, and illustrated his theory by feeling several heads, and giving very full descriptions of the characters of the individuals. At last he got hold of a man who must have had something peculiar in the formation of his cranium, for he gave him a most dreadful character, calling him a liar, a cheat, and a thief, and winding up by saying that he was a man who would murder his father for five dollars.

The natural consequence was that the owner of this enviable character jumped up and pitched into the phrenologist, giving him the whipping which he had so candidly acknowledged, and would probably have murdered him without the consideration of the five dollars if the bystanders had not interfered.

While at this camp [in Slate Range], I went down the river two or three miles to see a place called Mississippi Bar, where a company of Chinamen were at work. After an hour's climbing along the rocky banks, and having crossed and recrossed the river some half-dozen times on pine logs, I at last got down among the Celestials.

There were about a hundred and fifty of them here, living in a perfect village of small tents, all clustered together on the rocks. They had a claim in the bed of the river, which they were working by means of a wing dam. A "wing dam," I may here mention, is one which first runs half-way across the river, then down the river, and back again to the same side, thus damming off a portion of its bed without the necessity of the more expensive operation of lifting up the whole river bodily in a "flume."

The Chinamen's dam was two or three hundred yards in length, and was built of large pine trees laid one on the top of the other. They must have had great difficulty in handling such immense logs in such a place; but they are exceedingly ingenious in applying mechanical power, particularly in concentrating the force of a large number of men upon one point.

There were Chinamen of the better class among them, who no doubt directed the work, and paid the common men very poor wages—poor at least for California. A Chinaman could be hired for two or at most three dollars a day by any one who thought their labor worth so much; but those at work here were most likely paid at a still lower rate, for it was well known that whole shiploads of Chinamen came to the country under a species of bondage to some of their wealthy countrymen in San Francisco, who, immediately on their arrival, shipped them off to the mines under charge of an agent, keeping them completely under control by some mysterious celestial influence, quite independent of the accepted laws of the country.

They sent up to the mines for their use supplies of Chinese provisions and clothing, and thus all the gold taken out by them remained in Chinese hands, and benefited the rest of the community but little by passing through the ordinary channels of trade.

In fact, the Chinese formed a distinct class, which enriched itself at the expense of the country, abstracting a large portion of its latent wealth without contributing, in a degree commensurate with their numbers, to the prosperity of the community of which they formed a part.

The individuals of any community must exist by supplying the wants of others; and when a man neither does this, nor has any wants of his own but those which he provides for himself, he is of no use to his neighbors; but when, in addition to this, he also diminishes the productiveness of the country, he is a positive disadvantage in proportion to the amount of public wealth which he engrosses, and becomes a public nuisance.

What is true of an individual is true also of a class; and the Chinese, though they were no doubt, as far as China was concerned, both productive and consumptive, were considered by a very large party in California to be merely destructive as far as that country was interested.

They were, of course, not altogether so, for such a numerous body as they

211

were could not possibly be so isolated as to be entirely independent of others; but any advantage which the country derived from their presence was too dearly paid for by the quantity of gold which they took from it; and the propriety of expelling all the Chinese from the State was long discussed, both by the press and in the Legislature; but the principles of the American constitution prevailed; the country was open to all the world, and the Chinese enjoyed equal rights with the most favored nation. In some parts of the mines, however, the miners had their own ideas on the subject, and would not allow the Chinamen to come among them; but generally they were not interfered with, for they contented themselves with working such poor diggings as it was not thought worthwhile to take from them.

This claim on the Yuba was the greatest undertaking I ever saw attempted by them.

They expended a vast deal of unnecessary labor in their method of working, and their individual labor, in effect, was as nothing compared with that of other miners. A company of fifteen or twenty white men would have wing-dammed this claim and worked it out in two or three months, while here were about 150 Chinamen humbugging round it all the season, and still had not worked one half the ground.

Their mechanical contrivances were not in the usual rough straightforward style of the mines; they were curious, and very elaborately got up, but extremely wasteful of labor, and, moreover, very ineffective.

Their camp was wonderfully clean: when I passed through it, I found a great many of them at their toilet, getting their heads shaved, or plaiting each other's pigtails; but most of them were at dinner, squatted on the rocks in groups of eight or ten round a number of curious little black pots and dishes, from which they helped themselves with their chopsticks. In the center was a large bowl of rice. This is their staple article, and they devour it most voraciously. Throwing back their heads, they hold a large cupful to their wide-open mouths, and, with a quick motion of the chopsticks in the other hand, they cause the rice to flow down their throats in a continuous stream.

I received several invitations to dinner, but declined the pleasure, preferring to be a spectator. The rice looked well enough, and the rest of their dishes were no doubt very clean, but they had a very dubious appearance, and were far from suggesting the idea of being good to eat. In the store I found the storekeeper lying asleep on a mat. He was a sleek dirty-looking object, like a fat pig with the hair scalded off, his head being all close-shaved excepting the pigtail. His opium-pipe lay in his hand, and the lamp still burned beside him, so I supposed he was already in the seventh heaven. The store was like other

Black, Chinese, and white miners at Auburn Ravine, 1852

stores in the mines, inasmuch as it contained a higgledy-piggledy collection of provisions and clothing, but everything was Chinese excepting the boots. These are the only articles of barbarian costume which the Chinaman adopts, and he always wears them of an enormous size, on a scale commensurate with the ample capacity of his other garments.

In the evening, a ball took place at the hotel I was staying at [in Angels Camp], where, though none of the fair sex were present, dancing was kept up with great spirit for several hours. For music the company were indebted to two amateurs, one of whom played the fiddle and the other the flute. It is customary in the mines for the fiddler to take the responsibility of keeping the dancers all right. He goes through the dance orally, and at the proper intervals his voice is heard above the music and the conversation, shouting loudly his directions to the dancers, "Lady's chain," "Set to your partner," with other dancing-school words of command; and after all the legitimate figures of the dance had been performed, out of consideration for the thirsty appetites of the dancers, and for the good of the house, he always announced, in a louder voice than usual, the supplementary finale of "Promenade to the bar, and treat your partners." This injunction, as may be supposed, was most rigorously obeyed, and the "ladies," after their fatigues, tossed off their cocktails and lighted their pipes just as in more polished circles they eat ice-creams and sip lemonade.

It was a strange sight to see a party of long-bearded men, in heavy boots and flannel shirts, going through all the steps and figures of the dance with so much spirit, and often with a great deal of grace, hearty enjoyment depicted on their dried-up sunburned faces, and revolvers and bowie-knives glancing in their belts; while a crowd of the same rough-looking customers stood around, cheering them on to greater efforts, and occasionally dancing a step or two quietly on their own account. Dancing parties such as these were very common, especially in small camps where there was no such general resort as the gambling-saloons of the larger towns. Wherever a fiddler could be found to play, a dance was got up. Waltzes and polkas were not so much in fashion as the lancers which appeared to be very generally known, and, besides, gave plenty of exercise to the light fantastic toes of the dancers; for here men danced, as they did everything else, with all their might; and to go through the lancers in such company was a very severe gymnastic exercise.

The absence of ladies was a difficulty which was very easily overcome, by a simple arrangement whereby it was understood that every gentleman who had a patch on a certain part of his inexpressibles should be considered a lady for the time being. These patches were rather fashionable, and were usually large squares of canvas, showing brightly on a dark ground, so that the "ladies" of the party were as conspicuous as if they had been surrounded by the usual quantity of white muslin.

A *pas seul* sometimes varied the entertainment. I was present on one occasion at a dance at Foster's Bar, when, after several sets of the lancers had been danced, a young Scotch boy, who was probably a runaway apprentice from a Scotch ship—for the sailor-boy air was easily seen through the thick coating of flour which he had acquired in his present occupation in the employment of a French baker—was requested to dance the Highland fling for the amusement of the company. The music was good, and he certainly did justice to it; dancing most vigorously for about a quarter of an hour, shouting and yelling as he was cheered by the crowd, and going into it with all the fury of a wild savage in a war-dance. The spectators were uproarious in their applause. I daresay many of them never saw such exhibition before. The youngster was looked upon as a perfect prodigy, and if he had drunk with all the men who then sought the honor of "treating" him, he would never have lived to tread another measure.

from PHOENIXIANA

GEORGE HORATIO DERBY

George Horatio Derby (1823–1861), an early California humorist, was born in Mas-
sachusetts and graduated from West Point in 1846. He came to California in 1849 and
conducted military expeditions into gold country and the San Joaquin Valley. Under the
pseudonyms "Squibob" and "John Phoenix," Derby published dozens of wildly popu-
lar sketches in the San Diego Herald *and* San Francisco's Pioneer. *A legendary*
practical joker, he was adept at blending satire, nonsense, and exaggeration to poke fun at
other people's arrogance and staid traditions. Phoenixiana, *a collection of his sketches for*
the Pioneer, *was published in 1855.*

BENICIA, OCTOBER 1ST, 1850

Leaving the metropolis last evening by the gradually-increasing-in-popularity
steamer, *West Point,* I "skeeted" up Pablo Bay with the intention of spending a
few days at the world-renowned sea-port of Benicia. Our Captain (a very
pleasant and gentlemanly little fellow by the way) was named Swift, our passengers were emphatically a fast set, the wind blew like well-watered rose-
bushes, and the tide was strong in our favor. All these circumstances tended
to impress me with the idea that we were to make a wonderfully quick passage, but alas, "the race is not always to the Swift," the *Senator* passed us ten
miles from the wharf, and it was nine o'clock, and very dark at that, when we
were roped in by the side of the "ancient and fishlike" smelling hulk that forms
the broad wharf of Benicia.

As I shouldered my carpet-bag, and stepped upon the wharf among the
dense crowd of four individuals that were there assembled, and gazing upon
the mighty city whose glimmering lights, feebly discernible through the
Benician darkness, extended over an area of five acres, an overpowering sense
of the grandeur and majesty of the great rival of San Francisco affected me.—
I felt my own extreme insignificance, and was fain to lean upon a pile of
watermelons for support. "Boy!" said I, addressing an intelligent specimen of
humanity who formed an integral portion of the above-mentioned crowd,
"Boy! can you direct me to the best hotel in this city?"—"Ain't but one,"

responded the youth, "Winn keeps it; right up the hill thar." Decidedly, thought I, I will go in to Winn, and reshouldering my carpet-bag, I blundered down the ladder, upon a plank foot-path leading over an extensive morass in the direction indicated, not noticing, in my abstraction, that I had inadvertently retained within my grasp the melon upon which my hand had rested. "*Saw yer!*" resounded from the wharf as I retired—"*Saw yer!*" repeated several individuals upon the foot-path. For an instant my heart beat with violence at the idea of being seen accidentally appropriating so contemptible an affair as a watermelon; but hearing a man with a small white hat and large white mustache shout "Hello!" and immediately rush with frantic violence up the ladder, I comprehended that Sawyer was his proper name, and by no means alluded to me or my proceedings; so slipping the melon in my carpet-bag, I tranquilly resumed my journey.

A short walk brought me to the portal of the best and only hotel in the city, a large two-story building dignified by the title of the "Solano Hotel," where I was graciously received by mine host, who welcomed me to Benicia in the most *winning* manner. After slightly refreshing my inner man with a feeble stimulant, and undergoing an introduction to the oldest inhabitant, I calmly seated myself in the bar-room, and contemplated with intense interest the progress of a game of billiards between two enterprising citizens; but finding, after a lapse of two hours, that there was no earthly probability of its ever being concluded, I seized a candle-stick and retired to my room. Here I discussed my melon with intense relish, and then seeking my couch, essayed to sleep. But, oh! the fleas! skipping, hopping, crawling, biting! "Won't someone establish an agency for the sale of D. L. Charles & Co.'s Fleabane, in Benicia?" I agonizingly shouted, and echo answered through the reverberating halls of the "Solano Hotel," "Yes, they won't!" What a night!

But everything must have an end (circles and California gold excepted), and day at last broke over Benicia. Magnificent place! I gazed upon it from the attic window of the "Solano Hotel," with feelings too deep for utterance. The sun was rising in its majesty, gilding the red wood shingles of the U.S. Storehouses in the distance; seven deserted hulks were riding majestically at anchor in the bay; clothes-lines, with their burdens, were flapping in the morning breeze; a man with a wheelbarrow was coming down the street!—Everything, in short, spoke of the life, activity, business, and bustle of a great city. But in the midst of the excitement of this scene, an odoriferous smell of beefsteak came, like a holy calm, across my olfactories, and hastily drawing in my *cabeza,* I descended to breakfast. This operation concluded, I took a stroll in company with the oldest inhabitant, from whom I obtained much valuable information

216

Forty-niner Thomas Drew, 1849

(which I hasten to present), and who cheerfully volunteered to accompany me as a guide to the lions of the city.

There are no less than forty-two wooden houses, many of them two stories in height, in this great place—and nearly 1200 inhabitants, men, women and children! There are six grocery, provision, drygoods, auction, commission, and where-you-can-get-almost-any-little-thing-you-want stores, one hotel, one school-house—which is also a *brevet* church—three billiard-tables, a post-

217

office—from which I actually saw a man get a letter—and a tenpin-alley, where I am told a man once rolled a whole game, paid $1.50 for it, and walked off chuckling. Then there is a "monte bank"—a Common Council, and a Mayor, who, my guide informed me, was called "*Carne,*" from a singular habit he has of eating roast beef for dinner.—But there isn't a tree in all Benicia. "There was one," said the guide, "last year—only four miles from here, but they chopped it down for firewood for the 'post.' Alas! why didn't the woodman spare that tree?" The dwelling of one individual pleased me indescribably—he had painted it a vivid green! Imaginative being. He had evidently tried to fancy it a tree, and in the enjoyment of this sweet illusion, had reclined beneath its grateful shade, secured from the rays of the burning sun, and in the full enjoyment of rural felicity even among the crowded streets of this great metropolis.

As I sit here looking from my airy chamber upon the crowds of two or three persons thronging the streets of the great city; as I gaze upon that man carrying home a pound and a half of fresh beef for his dinner; as I listen to the bell of the *Mary* (a Napa steam packet of four cat power) ringing for departure, while her captain in a hoarse voice of authority requests the passengers to "step over the other side, as the larboard paddle-box is under water"; as I view all these unmistakable signs of the growth and prosperity of Benicia, I cannot but wonder at the infatuation of the people of your village, who will persist in their absurd belief that San Francisco will become a *place,* and do not hesitate to advance the imbecile idea that it may become a successful rival of this city. Nonsense! Oh Lord! at this instant there passed by my window the—prettiest—little—I can't write any more this week; if this takes, I'll try it again.

Yours for ever, Squibob

SONOMA, OCTOBER 10, 1850

I arrived at this place some days since, but have been so entirely occupied during the interval, in racing over the adjacent hills in pursuit of unhappy partridges, wandering along the banks of the beautiful creek, whipping its tranquil surface for speckled trout, or cramming myself with grapes at the vineyard, that I have not, until this moment, found time to fulfil my promise of a continuation of my traveling adventures. I left Benicia with satisfaction. Ungrateful people! I had expected, after the very handsome manner in which I had spoken of their city; the glowing description of its magnitude, prosperity, and resources that I had given; the consequent rise in property that had taken place; the manifest effect that my letter would produce upon the action of

Congress in making Benicia a port of entry; in view of all these circumstances I had, indeed, expected some trifling compliment—a public dinner, possibly, or peradventure a delicate present of a lot or two—the deeds enclosed in a neat and appropriate letter from the Town Council. But no!—the name of Squibob remains unhonored and unsung, and, what is far worse, unrecorded and untaxed in magnificent Benicia. "How sharper than a serpent's thanks it is to have a toothless child," as Pope beautifully remarks in his *Paradise Lost*. One individual characterized my letter as "a d——d burlesque." I pity that person, and forgive him.

Yours for ever.

OCTOBER 15, 1850

Sonoma *is* a nice place. As my Sabbath-school instructor (peace to his memory) used to add, by way of a clincher to his dictum—Piety is the foundation of all Religion—"thar can't be no doubt on't." Situated in the midst of the delightful and fertile valley which bears its name, within three miles of the beautiful creek upon whose "silvery tide, where whilom sported the *tule* boats of the unpleasant Indians," the magnificent (ly little) steamer *Georgina* now puffs and wheezes tri-weekly from San Francisco; enjoying an unvarying salubrious climate, neither too warm nor too cold. With little wind, few fleas, and a sky of that peculiarly blue description that Fremont terms the Italian, it may well be called, as by the sentimentally struck traveling snob it frequently is, the Garden of California. I remained there ten whole days—somewhat of a marvel for so determined a gadabout as myself—and don't remember of ever passing ten days more pleasantly.

It is useless for me to occupy time and trespass upon your patience by a lengthy description of Sonoma. If any of your readers would know the exact number of houses it contains, the names of the people who dwell therein, the botanical applications of the plants growing in its vicinity, or anything else about it that would be of any mortal use to anyone, without being positively amusing, let them purchase Revere, or some other equally scientific work on California, and inform themselves; suffice it to say that there is delightful society, beautiful women, brave men, and most luscious grapes to be found there; and the best thing one can possibly do, if a tired and *ennuyeed* resident of San Francisco, Benicia, or any other great city of all work and no play, is to take the *Georgina* some pleasant afternoon and go up there for a change. He'll find it!

Write me by the post orifice. *Au reservoir.*

from BOYHOOD DAYS

YGNACIO VILLEGAS

The Mexican residents of Baja and Alta California suffered many changes after the American conquest in 1846. Dispossessed of their land, approximately 5,000 Californios settled in Sonora in the Sierra foothills. After the discovery of gold, white forty-niners were eager to learn all they could from the more experienced Mexican miners, but cooperation soon gave way to anti-Hispanic discrimination and violence. Ygnacio Villegas (1840–1914) was born in Baja California and emigrated with his parents to Monterey in 1848. He followed his father into cattle ranching and loved to help drive the cattle up the California coast. In 1895 he wrote Boyhood Days, *a series of reminiscences of his childhood days in Monterey and in Rancho San Felipe, describing how his life was touched by the violence of gold rush.*

WHILE I WAS ONLY A BOY my father and family left Mexico and came over-land, following the coast as closely as possible. A cart with huge wooden wheels was used to carry my mother, who was sick, and when the squeak of the wheels became unbearable, we poured hot tallow onto the wooden axles. Those of us on horseback who were riding ahead could hear the squeak of the carts for miles. San Diego, Los Angeles, Santa Barbara, and San Luis Obispo were the only villages or habitations between the Gulf of California and Monterey. We arrived in Monterey in 1846, and it was just like the sleepy village we had left in Mexico. Nothing worried or disturbed the people, and life was just one *fiesta* to another. Game of all kinds could be killed in the pine woods back of town, and the swamps swarmed with ducks and water fowl, so eating was an easy matter.

When I crossed the Salinas Valley in 1849, and for many years thereafter, there was not a town between Monterey and the San Felipe *rancho,* excepting the Mission San Juan Bautista, founded in 1797 and situated on a plateau overlooking the San Juan Valley below. Besides the mission church there were a few dwellings scattered about, only two streets and three alleys.

The big event for San Juan every year was June 24, St. John's Day. The town was then full of life, activity, and stir, people coming from as far south as San Luis Obispo, and from the Pueblo of San Jose. The Tulare Indians, which were the most bloodthirsty and thieving of all California Indians, often sneaked into town on these occasions, and robbed and pillaged. None of these Indians would ever take up Christianity, nor would they settle around a mission.

Horse racing, in which those interested bet everything they owned, were frequent, and of course feats of horsemanship and throwing of the lariats. Then at nights dancing was enjoyed, and they always continued all night long. At these dances all were on an equal footing, there being no social lines drawn.

Regarding the floating population in and about San Juan, from 1850 to 1856 there were among them some criminals guilty of theft, robbery, and murder. Most of these bad men were the outcasts from the mining camps, who came to San Juan to hide while their crimes would be forgotten at the diggings. I saw one of these men hanging from a limb of a tree by the neck, his death being caused by others who were fearful he would tell on them. Then, to be on the safe side, one of the executioners shot down the man who had helped him in the hanging. "Dead Indian good. Dead men tell no tales," was the cry of the killing. I also came across a horse thief hanging from a tree a few miles west of the Pacheco pass. He was still twitching when I rode up. He was caught by a posse led by the sheriff of Monterey County, mounted on a horse, a rope placed around his neck, and the animal driven from under him. He made good food for the coyotes.

There were, besides, many men shot, killed, and hanged by a self-styled vigilante committee in Monterey County. The leader of this committee is credited with the death of eight men by hanging and shooting. He, however, finally died with his boots on and paid the penalty for his reckless killing. After that there was no more wholesale murdering under the guise of a secret organization in Monterey County. Some of the most atrocious murders took place on the highway between what is now Watsonville and San Juan. The Las Aromas *rancho,* located near the south side of the Pajaro River, saw many men bite the dust. Some were killed for robbery and others for spite. In the hills southwest of Aromas, which are thickly wooded, were many human skeletons and corpses with dismembered limbs, thighs, legs, arms, and heads detached from the bodies, many partly gnawed over by the wild animals. It was a veritable charnel house and a ghastly sight to view the corpses in the secluded spots—especially when one had known some of them and realized that the killing was a thirst for blood.

All the murdered men were Americans. Who killed these men will never be known. Some believed it was the bandit Murieta's vengeance. The deeds are shrouded in the folds of mystery and in the cold, grim shadows of the past.

from THE LIFE AND ADVENTURES OF JOAQUÍN MURIETA

JOHN ROLLIN RIDGE

Unsolved murders and robberies in the California mines were said to be the handiwork of Joaquín Murieta, a swashbuckling bandit who was most likely an amalgamation of several Mexican desperadoes all named Joaquín. Someone (perhaps Murieta himself) was beheaded by Captain Harry Love in 1853 for a huge reward from the California legislature. John Rollin Ridge (1827–1867), a half-white, half-Cherokee writer who came from Georgia to San Francisco during the gold rush, was the first to put the Joaquín Murieta myth on paper. His The Life and Adventures of Joaquín Murieta, *published in 1854, portrayed Murieta as a martyred Mexican hero who struck back at American injustices. As a Cherokee, Ridge identified with the oppressed Mexican peoples and offered them a champion.* Joaquín Murieta *was the first novel publiished by a Native American author.*

JOAQUÍN MURIETA was a Mexican, born in the province of Sonora of respectable parents and educated in the schools of Mexico. While growing up, he was remarkable for a very mild and peaceable disposition, and gave no sign of that indomitable and daring spirit which afterwards characterized him.

The first that we hear of him in the Golden State is that, in the spring of 1850, he is engaged in the honest occupation of a miner in the Stanislaus placers, then reckoned among the richest portions of the mines. He was then eighteen years of age, a little over the medium height, slenderly but gracefully built, and active as a young tiger. His complexion was neither very dark or very light, but clear and brilliant, and his countenance is pronounced to have been, at that time, exceedingly handsome and attractive. His large black eyes, kindling with the enthusiasm of his earnest nature, his firm and well-formed mouth, his well-shaped head from which the long, glossy, black hair hung down over his shoulders, his silvery voice full of generous utterance, and the frank and cordial bearing which distinguished him made him beloved by all with whom he came in contact. He had the confidence and respect of the whole community around him, and was fast amassing a fortune from his rich mining claim. He had built himself a comfortable mining residence in which he had domiciled his heart's treasure—a beautiful Sonorian girl, who had followed the young adventurer in all his wanderings with that devotedness of passion which belongs to the dark-eyed damsels of Mexico.

It was at this moment of peace and felicity that a blight came over the young man's prospects. The country was then full of lawless and desperate men, who bore the name of Americans but failed to support the honor and dignity of that title. A feeling was prevalent among this class of contempt for any and all Mexicans, whom they looked upon as no better than conquered subjects of the United States, having no rights which could stand before a haughtier and superior race. They made no exceptions. If the proud blood of the Castilians mounted to the cheek of a partial descendant of the Mexiques, showing that he had inherited the old chivalrous spirit of his Spanish ancestry, they looked upon it as a saucy presumption in one so inferior to them. The prejudice of color, the antipathy of races, which are always stronger and bitterer with the ignorant and unlettered, they could not overcome, or if they could, would not, because it afforded them a convenient excuse for their unmanly cruelty and oppression.

A band of these lawless men, having the brute power to do as they pleased, visited Joaquín's house and peremptorily bade him leave his claim, as they would allow no Mexicans to work in that region. Upon his remonstrating against such outrageous conduct, they struck him violently over the face, and, being physically superior, compelled him to swallow his wrath. Not content with this, they tied him hand and foot and ravished his mistress before his eyes. They left him, but the soul of the young man was from that moment darkened. It was the first injury he had ever received at the hands of the Americans, whom he had always hitherto respected, and it wrung him to the soul as a deeper and deadlier wrong from that very circumstance. He departed with his weeping and almost heart-broken mistress for a more northern portion of the mines; and the next we hear of him, he is cultivating a little farm on the banks of a beautiful stream that watered a fertile valley, far out in the seclusion of the mountains. Here he might hope for peace—here he might forget the past, and again be happy.

But his dream was not destined to last. A company of unprincipled Americans—shame that there should be such bearing the name!—saw his retreat, coveted his little home surrounded by its fertile tract of land, and drove him from it, with no other excuse than that he was "an infernal Mexican intruder!" Joaquín's blood boiled in his veins, but his spirit was still unbroken, nor had the iron so far entered his soul as to sear up the innate sensitiveness to honor and right which reigned in his bosom. Twice broken up in his honest pursuit of fortune, he resolved still to labor on with unflinching brow and with that true *moral* bravery which throws its redeeming light forward upon his subsequently dark and criminal career. How deep must have been the anguish of that young heart and how strongly rooted the native honesty of his soul, none can know or imagine but they who have been tried in a like manner. He bundled up his little movable property, still accompanied by his faithful bosom-friend, and again started forth to strike once more, like a brave and honest man, for fortune and for happiness.

He arrived at "Murphy's Diggings" in Calaveras County, in the month of April, and went again to mining, but, meeting with nothing like his former success, he soon abandoned that business and devoted his time to dealing "monte," a game which is common in Mexico, and has been almost universally adopted by gamblers in California. It is considered by the Mexican in no manner a disreputable employment.... Having a very pleasing exterior and being, despite of all his sorrows, very gay and lively in disposition, he attracted many persons to his table, and won their money with such skill and grace, or lost his own with such perfect good humor, that he was considered by all the very beau ideal of a gambler and the prince of clever fellows. His sky seemed clear and his prospects bright, but Fate was weaving her mysterious web around him, and fitting him to be by the force of circumstances what nature never intended to make him.

[One day] he had gone a short distance from Murphy's Diggings to see a half-brother, who had been located in that vicinity for several months, and returned to Murphy's upon a horse which his brother had lent him. The animal proved to have been stolen, and being recognized by a number of individuals in town, an excitement was raised on the subject. Joaquín suddenly found himself surrounded by a furious mob and charged with the crime of theft. He told them how it happened that he was riding the horse and in what manner his half-brother had come in possession of it. They listened to no explanation, but bound him to a tree, and publicly disgraced him with the lash. They then proceeded to the house of his half-brother and hung him without judge or jury. It was then that the character of Joaquín changed, suddenly and irrevocably. Wanton cruelty and the tyranny of prejudice had reached their climax. His soul swelled beyond its former boundaries, and the barriers of honor, rocked into atoms by the strong passion which shook his heart like an earthquake, crumbled around him. Then it was that he declared to a friend that he would

Joaquín Murieta, 1859, by Charles Nahl

live henceforth for revenge and that his path should be marked with blood. Fearfully did he keep his promise, as the following pages will show.

It was not long after this unfortunate affair that an American was found dead in the vicinity of Murphy's Diggings, having been cut to pieces with a knife. Though horribly mangled, he was recognized as one of the mob engaged in whipping Joaquín. A doctor, passing in the neighborhood of this murder, was met, shortly afterward, by two men on horseback, who fired

225

their revolvers at him, but, owing to his speed on foot, and the unevenness of the ground, he succeeded in escaping with no further injury than having a bullet shot through his hat within an inch of the top of his head! A panic spread among the rash individuals who had composed that mob, and they were afraid to stir out on their ordinary business. Whenever any one of them strayed out of sight of his camp or ventured to travel on the highway, he was shot down suddenly and mysteriously. Report after report came into the villages that Americans had been found dead on the highways, having been either shot or stabbed, and it was invariably discovered, for many weeks, that the murdered men belonged to the mob who publicly whipped Joaquín. It was fearful and it was strange to see how swiftly and mysteriously those men disappeared. "Murieta's revenge was very nearly complete," said an eyewitness of these events, in reply to an inquiry which I addressed him. "I am inclined to think he *wiped out* the most of those prominently engaged in whipping him."

Thus far, who can blame him? But the iron had entered too deeply in his soul for him to stop here. He had contracted a hatred to the whole American race, and was determined to shed their blood, whenever and wherever an opportunity occurred.

Among the many thrilling instances of the daring and recklessness of spirit which belonged to Joaquín, there is one which I do not feel at liberty to omit— especially as it comes naturally and properly in this connection. Shortly after he parted from Reis and Luis Vulvia, he went up into the extreme north of the country. There, at the head of a branch of the South Fork of the Mokelumne River, in a wild and desolate region near the boundary line of Calaveras and El Dorado Counties, were located a company of miners, consisting of twenty-five men. They were at a long distance from any neighbors, having gone there well-armed on a prospecting tour which resulted in their finding diggings so rich that they were persuaded to pitch their tents and remain.

One morning while they were eating their breakfast on a flat rock—a natural table which stood in front of their tents—armed as usual with their revolvers, a young fellow with very dark hair and eyes rode up and saluted them. He spoke very good English and they could scarcely make out whether he was a Mexican or an American. They requested him to get down and eat with them, but he politely declined. He sat with one leg crossed over his horse's neck very much at his ease, conversing very freely on various subjects, until Jim Boyce, one of the partners who had been to the spring after water, appeared in sight. At the first glance on him, the young horseman flung his reclining leg back over the saddle and spurred his horse.

Boyce roared out: "Boys, that fellow is *Joaquín;* d——n it, shoot him!" At the same instant, he himself fired but without effect.

Joaquín dashed down to the creek below with headlong speed and crossed with the intention, no doubt, to escape over the hills which ran parallel with the stream, but his way was blocked up by perpendicular rocks, and his only practicable path was a narrow digger-trail which led along the side of a huge mountain, directly over a ledge of rocks a hundred yards in length, which hung beatling over the rushing stream beneath in a direct line with the hill upon which the miners had pitched their tents, and not more than forty yards distant. It was a fearful gauntlet for any man to run. Not only was there danger of falling a hundred feet from the rocks, but he must run in a parallel line with his enemies, and in pistol-range, for a hundred yards. In fair view of him stood the whole company with their revolvers drawn. He dashed along that fearful trail as if he had been mounted upon a spirit-steed, shouting as he passed:

"I am Joaquín! Kill me if you can!"

Shot after shot came clanging around his head, and bullet after bullet flattened on the wall of slate at his right. In the midst of the first firing, his hat was knocked from his head, and left his long black hair streaming behind him. He had no time to use his own pistol, but, knowing that his only chance lay in the swiftness of his sure-footed animal, he drew his keenly polished bowie-knife in proud defiance of the danger and waved it in scorn as he rode on. It was perfectly sublime to see such super-human daring and recklessness. At each report, which came fast and thick, he kissed the flashing blade and waved it at his foes. He passed the ordeal, as awful and harrowing to a man's nerves as can be conceived, untouched by a ball and otherwise unharmed. In a few moments, a loud whoop rang out in the woods a quarter of a mile distant, and the bold rider was safe!

from THE NARRATIVE OF A JAPANESE

JOSEPH HECO

Joseph Heco was just a boy when he was picked up by an American ship bound for San Francisco after his father's trading boat was wrecked by a storm in 1850. He was among the extremely small number of Japanese immigrants who participated in the gold rush. Heco later made several return trips to California. His memoir, written mostly in English, was first published in 1895.

AFTER THE BARQUE had been put upon her proper course, and the excitement of getting us on board had subsided, the Captain summoned the cook to the quarter-deck. He came to where we were, bringing with him a writing brush, India-ink, and paper, and at the Captain's orders he wrote something on the paper in Chinese characters. This we read "Gold mountain." Then he wrote something more but we could not make out anything except "Rice," "Interest," and "*Ka,*" to increase or to add, and did not at all understand what was meant.

When he wrote "Gold Mountain," he pointed to the ship. Some of our party said this meant that the vessel was called by this name—for we did not truly comprehend his meaning, viz: that the vessel was bound to California, the country of gold mountains—until we reached San Francisco long afterwards.

In the forenoon, while we were on deck looking at the ship sliding nicely along the water, with yards almost squared and all sails set before the westerly wind, the second Mate came to us with a large book under his arm and squatted down beside us. He opened the book and began to explain something, pointing to the picture of a large tract of land—and saying "America, America," and then pointing to himself and to the ship. This we understood to mean that the ship and he belonged to that country, so we nodded. Then he smiled and seemed much pleased at our understanding him. Again he pointed to the vessel and then towards the East, or ship's head, and said "California." This too we understood; that the vessel was bound to a country called by that name. So we smiled and nodded again; but just at this moment he was called forward for some duty, and he went off, and our lesson was suspended.

A little before noon the second Mate brought some old clothes out of his room and made a sign to me to come and take off the Japanese clothing I had on. I obeyed him, and he put on me a flannel shirt, a pair of cloth trousers, and a cloth jacket. All of these were of course much too large for me, although he was smaller than the average man of his race. He marked the clothes here and there with some white stuff and told me by a sign to take them off again. This I did, and he took them away to his room to alter them by cutting and sewing. By the next afternoon he had completed the alterations and I put the clothes on again, when he found that they fitted me nicely. He looked at me and exclaimed, "Now you one Yankee boy!" and he smiled. I did not understand what he said at the time, but I remembered the sound of the words and afterward I learned their meaning. This was the first time in my life that I had ever put on foreign clothing, and I felt much tightness about my body; still they were much warmer than my own garment, besides being more convenient for working. I thanked the Mate by nodding and bowing for thus making me a comfortable dress. Then he patted my shoulder, said, "all right," and beckoned me to follow him to the cabin, which I did. When we entered we found the Captain and first Mate seated and busily writing. The second Officer said something to them and at the same time pointed at me; they looked at me and smiled and the Captain came up to me and shook hands, at the same time saying something which I did not understand, except that they both said at the end "very nice."

On the following morning, while we were all on the quarter deck talking amongst ourselves my new friend—the second Mate—came to me and said something; pointing at my head and pulling his own hair. I did not know at all what it was that he said, but I nodded—thinking that perhaps he meant to say my hair was darker than his, or that he wore his hair in a different style from mine. No sooner did he see me nodding at him, agreeing as he supposed, to what he said, than he went to his room, and in a few seconds came back with a pair of scissors and a stool. He signed to me to sit down upon it.

I did so and he then cut off my top-knot, and clipped my hair short all round my head. Then he brought sweet oil and rubbed it into my hair, and combed it and brushed it. When I saw the scissors, I wanted to stop his cutting off my top-knot, in that whilst on the wreck I had made a vow to our gods that if ever happily I might reach our native-land in safety, I should offer that top-knot up as an offering. But I was afraid to stop him, on account of not understanding his tongue, for he might misconstrue my meaning even as he had misunderstood what my thoughts were when I had nodded a few moments before.

But what that Mate had just done vexed me sorely. Though he had been kind and had acted with no ill intention on his part, still he had no right to cut that top-knot off,—that top-knot which I had vowed to the gods, if perchance I should once more get back to my country. And now before ever that vow could be fulfilled the stranger goes and cuts it off!

However I reflected that had we known each other's language this misunderstanding would not have happened. Wherefore I went forward and washed my hands and my mouth and prayed to the gods and begged their forgiveness for the sin that had been unwittingly committed.

26TH DAY OF THE 12TH MOON. About 9:30 AM we heard a loud screaming forward, so we went to find out what was the matter. To our amazement and horror we found that Chinese cook in the very act of killing one of these pigs on board for food! Such a thing we had never witnessed with our eyes before, although we had heard that in some of the far-off provinces of our country such as Satsuma and Loochoo the people ate pigs and rats. But we as dwellers on the mainland and religious men never did such cruel deeds.

After seeing the gruesome work of that Chinese cook, we began to talk among ourselves and to be afraid of the strangers. One of our elders solemnly shook his head and affirmed that if our course across the deep should be long these strangers would assuredly fall upon us and slay us and devour us.

2ND DAY OF 2ND MOON. During the night the weather cleared, but being so near port, the vessel was compelled to heave to till day-break. Then she set sail again end stood for the harbour of San Francisco.

Next morning we were early astir looking eagerly for the land, for we had not seen it for nearly 100 days. About 7 AM we were near the entrance to the port. Several vessels of all classes were standing in and out while numerous smaller craft with three-cornered sails were rushing about like racers. These were pilot-boats I was afterward told.

Soon we were within a few miles of the Golden Gate. Two of the little craft above mentioned (pilot schooners) bore down upon us. On board of them were several persons dressed differently from anything we had seen, in tall black hats. One of them on the schooner nearest to the *Auckland* called out something to our vessel through a trumpet, and the Captain of our barque replied. Shortly after the schooner lowered a boat and a gentleman and a sailor got into it. It pulled toward us and in a few minutes it was alongside, when the gentleman came on board and the sailor pulled back to the schooner.

Our Captain went forward and shook hands with the new comer. The latter brought lots of papers which he handed to the Captain, and both went on the quarter deck. In a few minutes more the new man took charge of the vessel while the Captain went below and began to read those papers he had got from the other. We did not know then what these documents were, but we afterward heard that they were called newspapers. All this time the schooner had hoisted her boat on board and sailed out seaward while we stood on in toward the port.

The stranger who had just come on board was dressed in a suit of black, with a great gold chain dangling in front of him just below his chest. His head was covered with something that looked like a black box with a wide bottom. I afterward was told that this was a beaver hat. He was a large well-built man, with dark hair, a thick bushy beard running all over his face, and black eyes and seemed about forty-five years of age. He spoke quickly and in a loud resonant voice. He had a trumpet under his arm, and whenever he spoke or gave an order to the men he spoke through that trumpet. He wailed briskly to and fro on the quarter-deck with one hand in his trouser's pocket, and looked as if our ship and everything on it belonged to him.

About 10 AM our good old barque came to anchor at the North Beach close under Telegraph Hill.

[Four days after our arrival] we had landed and walked up to the town. Here for the first time I saw what a foreign city was like. The streets were broad and paved with stones and tiles, with side-walks for foot-passengers, and the centre of the way for horses and wheeled traffic. The houses were much larger than in our country, some of them two or three storeys high, built of brick and stone, and though some of them were of wood, still even they were large and spacious. There were numerous shops of all kinds, with goods displayed in large glass windows, hotels, restaurants, drinking places, horses, carts, and carriages. And all the people looked busy and the place seemed lively and prosperous. And in fact it appeared to me much like the City of Yedo with the exception of the carts which were here drawn by horses instead of by men or cows and bullocks as they are in our country.

As we walked up the street from the Wharf, I observed over fifty men with chains on their legs all working hard at digging and carting the earth from the hill close by. This I afterward learned was called the "chain-gang." It consisted of criminals serving their terms for the various crimes they had committed. As I gazed at the carts passing, I was greatly frightened to see a black object driving a goods-cart or dray. It wore a blue and red flannel shirt, dark blue pants, long boots into which its pants were stuck, suspenders over its shoulders, a red comforter round its neck, and a felt hat on its head. Its black face and white teeth and huge red lips, which formed such a contrast with its soot-like face were fearful and dreadful. I thought it was not human, and fancied it must be more akin to *Oni* (a devil) than anything else. Though I had heard of the existence of folks with short bodies and long legs and arms, yet I had never heard tell of such a creature as this. Therefore it came into my mind that it could be nothing but *Oni*.... And if it was so he must come from *Jigoku* (Hell), as we are taught that in *Jigoku* are many red, and black and white *Oni*. And if such was the case *Jigoku* must be near. Thus thinking I gripped the Mate's hand fast and looked at the black man steadily until he had passed safely out of sight.

By this time we had reached a shoe-shop. We entered it, and the gentleman said something to the shop-keeper. Then he brought several pairs of boots and shoes and the gentleman signed that I should put them on. I tried one or two pairs and at last one pair which fitted me nicely. Then the stranger felt my feet and asked me how that would do. I nodded "All right!" Then he paid for the shoes and told me to keep them on. After this we walked across to a bar, or drinking-place, where I saw cakes and pies besides. Here the Mate and the stranger took a drink together, and gave me some cakes and pies to eat. I ate some and kept the rest for my companions. By-and-by the stranger bade us good-bye. I thanked him for the shoes and we parted, and the Mate and myself returned on board. When I got the new shoes on I felt quite proud of them. When I got on board I told my companions of all that I had seen, and especially about the object that looked so like the *Oni* we had seen in pictures of *Jigozku.*

[A few days later] as I was handling my presents and counting my money the first Mate observed me and coming up said something to me. At the same time he pointed to the shore, to my clothes, and to the money I was then counting, and to his own clothes. From this I understood that if I went ashore with him, he would buy me other clothing. So I nodded and he said "all right."

When evening came we went ashore and wended our way to the city. We came to a street where there were several drinking saloons, and the Mate entered one of those and beckoned to me to follow. He went to the bar, called for a drink, lit a cigar, and entered into conversation with the bar-keeper and with some people seated in the front room. He told me to sit down on the side settee. Presently he had another drink and then two females came from behind the bar with whom he chatted away and in a few minutes they all began to dance to the music of a violin which the bar-keeper came out and played for them. At the end of the first dance he had another drink and a smoke, and then there was another dance and so on till about twelve.

Then he came and asked for my money. I handed it to him, and he paid for all his drinks and cigars with it. Meanwhile I sat in my corner, looking on half-asleep, taking no interest in the proceedings whatsoever. A female of the place brought me some pie, cakes, and a cup of coffee. She began to chat, but I did not understand a word she said, and felt more inclined to go to sleep than anything else.

At last I went up to the Mate and asked him to go home as it was getting late. Besides the man had misled me, for I understood him to mean that he was to buy me a coat and vest with my money, instead of which he had spent it all to pay for his drinks and cigars, at which I was greatly vexed. At this point he said "All right," and paid the bill, and we started for our ship and got on board about 1 AM.

When I appeared my companions asked me where I had been and why I was so late. I told them what the Mate had said to me, and how he had misled me. At this they all waxed very wroth, and promised to help me to recover the money he had taken from me. Next day two of my companions and myself went to the first Mate and asked him for the money he had taken away from me the night before. He pretended not to understand what we wanted. But when we kept on persistently signifying to him by signs that he had to return the money he at length went into his cabin and opened his clothes-chest and brought out a China-made dark-blue crepe summer frock-coat which might have cost him about $3.50 in China, and handed it to me to put on. And he was a man of six foot two inches and I was a Japanese boy of thirteen or fourteen, but this old coat was all I got in return for my $15.50. After this we began to mistrust that first Mate.

from MOUNTAINS AND MOLEHILLS

FRANK MARRYAT

Frank Marryat (1826–1855) was a British adventurer, artist, playwright, and sports-man who headed to San Francisco in 1850 looking for a locale as exotic as Borneo, the subject of his first popular travelogue. His perspective on California was markedly amoral, exempt from the outraged tone present in many gold rush narratives. The more than two years he spent exploring California resulted in Mountains and Molehills, *an imme-diate bestseller when published in 1855. Marryat, however, could not enjoy his success for long—he died of a ruptured blood vessel a few months after his book appeared, not yet thirty years old.*

I MUST CONFESS I felt great delight when we made the mountains at the entrance of San Francisco Bay; I had been cooped up for forty-five days on board a small barque, in company with 165 passengers, of whom 160 were noisy, quarrelsome, discontented, and dirty in the extreme.

As we open the bay, we observe dense masses of smoke rolling to leeward; the town and shipping are almost undistinguishable, for we have arrived at the moment of the great June Fire of 1850, and San Francisco is again in ashes!

The fire was fast subsiding; and as the embers died away, and the heavy smoke rolled off to leeward, the site of the conflagration was plainly marked out to the spectator like a great black chart. There is nothing particularly im-pressive in the scene, for although 400 houses have been destroyed, they were but of wood, or thin sheet-iron, and the "devouring element" has made a clean sweep of every thing, except a few brick chimneys and iron pots. Every body seems in good-humor, and there is no reason why the stranger, who has lost nothing by the calamity, should allow himself to be plunged into melancholy reflections! Planks and lumber are already being carted in all directions, and so soon as the embers cool, the work of rebuilding will commence.

I found it amusing next day to walk over the ground and observe the effects of the intense heat on the articles which were strewed around. Gun-barrels were twisted and knotted like snakes; there were tons of nails welded together by the heat, standing in the shape of the kegs which had contained them; small lakes of molten glass of all the colors of the rainbow; tools of all descriptions, from which the wood-work had disappeared, and pitch-pots filled with melted lead and glass. Here was an iron house that had collapsed with the heat, and an iron fire-proof safe that had burst under the same influence; spoons, knives, forks, and crockery were melted up together in heaps; crucibles even had cracked; preserved meats had been unable to stand this second cooking, and had exploded in every direction.

On the "lot" where I had observed the remains of gun-barrels and nails, stands its late proprietor, Mr. Jones, who is giving directions to a master-carpenter, or "boss," for the rebuilding of a new store, the materials for which are already on the spot. The carpenter promises to get every thing "fixed right off," and have the store ready in two days. At this juncture passes Mr. Smith, also in company with a cargo of building materials; he was the owner of the iron house; he says to Jones, interrogatively—

"*Burnt* out?"

JONES. "Yes, and burst up."

SMITH. "Flat?"

JONES. "Flat as a d—d pancake!"

SMITH. "It's a great country."

JONES. "It's nothing shorter."

And in a couple of days both Smith and Jones are on their legs again, and with a little help from their friends live to grow rich perhaps, and build brick buildings that withstand the flames.

This fire was attributed to incendiarism, but when the general carelessness that existed is considered, it is quite as probable that it resulted from accident. It is much to be regretted that these fires did not sweep off the gambling-houses; but these buildings were now constructed of brick, and were tolerably well secured against all risk. When the burnt portion of the city was again covered with buildings, I had an opportunity of judging of the enormous strides the place had made since two years back, when it was, by all accounts, a settlement of tents. Three fires had checked its growth in this short space; but a daring confidence had laughed as it were at these obstacles, and any one who knew human nature might see that, so long as that spirit of energy animated every breast, the city would increase in size and wealth, in spite even of conflagrations so calamitous....Twelve months back there was little else but canvas tents here, and a small, shifting, restless, gambling population: who was it then, when all looked *uncertain in the future,* that sent away so many thousand miles for steam excavators, and tramways, and railway trucks? who were those, again, who sent from this hamlet of shanties for all the material for large foundries of iron and brass, for blocks of granite, bricks, and mortar, for pile-drivers and

San Francisco's Sacramento Street, c. 1852

steamboats? I don't know—but these things all arrived; and now, in 1850, the sand-hills tumble down as if by magic, and are carried to the water's edge on a railroad where the pile-drivers are at work....The clang of foundries is heard on all sides, as machinery is manufactured for the mines—brick buildings are springing up in the principal thoroughfares, steamers crowd the rivers, and thousands of men are blasting out huge masses of rock to make space for the rapid strides of this ambitious young city.

The stranger in San Francisco at this time is at once impressed with the feverish state of excitement that pervades the whole population; there is no attention paid to dress, and every one is hurried and incoherent in manner. Clubs, reading-rooms, and the society of women are unknown; and from the harassing duties of the day's business, there is nothing to turn to for recreation but the drinking-saloons and gambling-houses.

Drinking is carried on to an incredible extent here; not that there is much drunkenness, but a vast quantity of liquor is daily consumed.

From the time the habitual drinker in San Francisco takes his morning gin-cocktail to stimulate an appetite for breakfast, he supplies himself at intervals throughout the day with an indefinite number of racy little spirituous compounds that have the effect of keeping him always more or less primed. And where saloons line the streets, and you can not meet a friend, or make a new acquaintance, or strike a bargain, without an invitation to drink, which amounts to a command; and when the days are hot, and you see men issuing from the saloons licking their lips after their iced mint juleps; and where Brown, who has a party with him, meets you as he enters the saloon, and says, "Join us!" and where it is the fashion to accept such invitations, and rude to refuse them, what can a thirsty man do?

The better description of drinking-bars are fitted up with great taste, and at enormous expense. Order and quiet are preserved within them during the day; they are generally supplied with periodicals and newspapers, and business assignations are made and held in them at all hours. Every body in the place is generous and lavish of money; and perhaps one reason for so many drinks being consumed is in the fact that there is ever some liberal soul who is not content until he has ranged some twenty of his acquaintances at the bar; and when each one is supplied with a "drink," he says, "My respects gentlemen!" and the twenty heads being simultaneously thrown back, down go "straight brandies," "Queen-Charlottes," "stone-fences," "Champagne-cocktails," and "sulky sangarees," while the liberal entertainer discharges the score, and each one hurries off to his business. There is no one in such a hurry as a Californian, but he has always time to take a drink.

from STORY OF MY LIFE

WILLIAM TAYLOR

Methodist minister William Taylor (1821–1902) was sent to San Francisco in 1848 by the Methodist General Conference. In Portsmouth Plaza and on the Long Wharf, the young, dynamic orator's sermons soon attracted audiences of thousands. Taylor spent seven years preaching on the streets of San Francisco, using simple words and an honest compassion the gold rushers responded to. Later in life, he served as a missionary to Canada, Europe, Australia, and India, but returned to retire in California. His autobiography, Story of My Life, *published in 1896, described his gold rush experiences and his time spent with the sick and dying in the crowded San Francisco City Hospital, where he made daily visits.*

IN THE FALL OF 1849, as I walked down Clay Street one day, my eye rested on a sign in large red letters, "City Hospital." I stopped and gazed at it till my soul was thrilled with horror. The letters looked as if they were written with blood, and I said to myself, "Ah, that is the depot of death, where the fast adventurers of California, young men in manhood's strength, stricken down by the hand of disease, are cast out of the train and left to perish. There all their bright hopes and visions of future wealth and weal expire and are buried forever. There are husbands and sons and brothers thousands of miles from sympathizing kindred and friends dying in destitution and despair. Shall I not be a brother to the sick stranger in California, and tell him of that heavenly Friend 'that sticketh closer than a brother?' " The cross of intruding myself into strange hospitals and offering my services to the promiscuous masses of the sick and dying of all nations and creeds was, to my unobtrusive nature, very heavy, but I there resolved to take it up; a decision which I have never regretted.

The most prevalent and fatal disease in California at that time was chronic diarrhea and dysentery, a consumption of the bowels, very similar in its debilitating effect on the constitution to consumption of the lungs. Men afflicted with this disease have been seen moping about the streets, looking like the personification of death and despair, for weeks, till strength and money and friends were gone, and then, as a last resort, they were carried to the hospital to pass a few miserable weeks more in one of those filthy wards, where they often died in the night without anyone knowing the time of their departure. In the morning when the nurses passed round they found and reported the dead. A plain coffin was immediately brought, for a supply was kept on hand, and laid beside the cot of the deceased, and he was lifted from the cot just as he died, laid in the coffin, and carried out to the dead cart, the driver of which was seen daily plodding through the mud to the graveyard near North Beach, with from one to three corpses at a load.

To transcribe in detail the hospital scenes which have been daguerreotyped on the tablets of my memory during a period of seven years in San Francisco would make a volume. My purpose, therefore, in these reminiscences is simply to present a few specimen scenes and individual cases of hope and despair occurring at different periods in the history of that city.

[One] very genteel-looking man ... died with cholera in the hospital during the fall of 1850. He was in a collapsed state when I found him. I said to him, "My dear brother, have you made your peace with God?"

"No, sir," said he; "I can't say that I have."

"Do you not pray to the Lord sometimes to have mercy on you, and for the sake of Jesus to pardon your sins?"

"No, sir."

"Have you never prayed?"

"No, sir, never in my life."

"You believe in the divine reality of religion and that we may have our sins all forgiven and enjoy the conscious evidence of pardon, do you not?"

"Yes, sir; I believe in religion, and think it a very good thing to have."

He was calm and composed; his dreadful paroxysms had passed, and the fatal work was done. He was then poised on an eddying wave of death's dark tide, which on its next swell would whirl him out of the bounds of time into the breakers of eternal seas beyond. I saw his peril, and pulled with all my might to bring the lifeboat of mercy by his side. I got very near to him, and entreated him to try to get into it and save his soul, but I could not prevail on him to make an effort; under the force of the ruling habit of his life he coolly said, "Well, I'll think about it."

I have seen hundreds of poor fellows sleeping away their lives without any apparent consciousness of danger, and I have heard men call this peaceful dying!

A great many, however, of those whom I have seen in the death struggle shook off the apathy I have described and awoke to the keenest sensibilities of conscience and the most dreadful forebodings of future ill; but a large majority of such wrapped themselves in the mantle of despair, so dark and impervious that no ray of hope could reach their souls.

from CALIFORNIA ILLUSTRATED

JOHN M. LETTS

Approximately 90,000 forty-niners left California in the early 1850s and returned to their homes. All went by ship; there are no known gold rushers who returned east on an overland trail. Less was written about this trip back, partly because the optimism that had spurred their pens on the journey to California had been replaced for so many with disillusionment, poverty, and illness. New Yorker John M. Letts arrived in San Francisco in the summer of 1849 intent on chronicling the gold rush for an eastern publisher. Fewer than six months later he was on a boat headed out of California. His 1852 travel book, California Illustrated, *described his dramatic sea ride home.*

I HAD DESIGNED to leave San Francisco for home in the steamer of the 1st December ... [but I] was induced to sell my ticket, and take passage in the ship *Edward Everett,* which was to sail on the 28th November, and which, I felt confident, would reach Panama in advance of the steamer. We were notified to be on board at 9 AM; and when Mr. Fairchild and myself reached the shore with our baggage, we saw the ship two miles out just preparing to swing from her moorings. We engaged two hardy "tars," and were soon pulling off for her; we threaded our way through the shipping, and were doing our utmost as we saw the anchor of the *Everett* already up, her foresail aback, and she "turning on her heel," preparatory to standing out to sea. We boarded her as she was under way.... The passengers, eighty in number, were all on deck to take a last look at the receding landscape.

It had been but a few short days since they first beheld this scene—since they first entered through this "Gate," into the land of promise. They now look upon the same narrow passage, the same bold rocky coast, they had looked for with so much anxiety, and greeted with so much enthusiasm. But how different the feelings now! what a change! They were then accompanied by a brother or a friend, with high hopes and vigorous constitutions, looking forward with brilliant anticipations. But now the brother and friend are sleeping quietly at the base of yonder snow-capped mountain, and they are bearing the sad intelligence to the bereaved parents, brothers, and sisters. Instead of the vigorous constitutions, they are obliged to cling to the rigging for support, while they gaze for the last time upon the scene. With many it is the last time they are to view such a scene; their eyes are about to close upon the earth forever, to sleep beneath the bosom of the ocean. Many have not only sacrificed health, but are also destitute of means, and are now reeling about the ship, endeavoring to earn their passage by their labor. Our ship seemed a hospital; three-fourths of all the passengers were invalids, some of them helpless.

The 30th was ushered in with a fine breeze, and we were standing on our course. At noon we found the table supplied with hard bread (sea-biscuit) and salt beef; dainties that our stomachs did not relish; the same table was kept standing for supper. Captain Smith was interrogated in reference to his supply of provisions, for which we had paid him extra; he replied that he was abundantly supplied with the above, which, if we chose, we could have served up every day during the voyage; when too late we learned that the delicacies for the sick, with which he had by public notice proclaimed his ship abundantly supplied, were "*non est.*" He had not even a pound of fruit on board; the invalids felt this privation most sensibly, many of whom had come on board without supplies, having been led to believe by advertisements that the ship had been furnished with a direct view to the comforts of those returning in ill-health. From the fare with which our table was supplied, it was impossible for a weak stomach to extract sufficient nutriment to sustain life. This was soon manifest, as those who were destitute immediately commenced to decline, and were soon confined to their berths. We could plainly see that the lives of some were fast ebbing away.

On the 6th December, in latitude 22° 50' North, it was announced that G. W. Ray, of Maine, was dead. He died at 10 AM; the gang-plank was placed, one end extending over the side of the ship, supported by the rail, the other supported by a cask, over this was thrown a piece of canvas, upon which was placed the corpse. A rope was tied around the body, thence passing down was tied around the ankles, and to the end was attached a canvas bag, filled with sand. The body was then sewed up in the canvas, over which was thrown the ensign of California. The passengers now surround the corpse, with heads uncovered. A prayer is read by the captain, the ensign is removed, and at the word one end of the plank is raised, and the body passes gently into its grave. We are under a full press of canvas with an eight-knot breeze; the last bubble rises to the surface, and the wind passes mournfully through the shrouds, as if sighing his last requiem.

At 8 PM, of the same day, another death was announced. Deceased, Mr. Cook, was a young man from Sag Harbor, where he left a wife and child. One hour after the announcement of his death, he was consigned to the grave that had so recently opened to receive his unfortunate companion. He was buried in latitude 20° 50' North.

On the morning of the 14th another death was announced; the deceased, Dr. Reed, of Massachusetts, had been, for some days, conscious of his approaching end, and manifested a strong desire to have his remains conveyed to his friends. This was his last and almost only request; the fear that this might not be complied with seemed to linger with him to the last, and died only with his last pulsation. He received some encouragement from the captain, but one short hour after his death he followed his unfortunate companions to the grave. He was buried in latitude 16° 3' North.

A report is in circulation that there are dead bodies on board. On inquiry, we learn that there are three—a man, a woman, and child; they were preserved in casks of spirits, and are being conveyed to the States. This created the greatest consternation in the minds of the sailors, and they unanimously resolved to leave the ship at the first port. They have a superstitious idea that vessels cannot be safely navigated with dead bodies on board. Many of the passengers were confined to their berths, some of them destined never again to leave them, until removed by death. The scurvy had appeared in its worst form, and there was nothing on board to relieve its victims. The food served out was most execrable; those in robust health were pining away, and for the invalids, there was no hope. Among the latter there were five who were deranged; they were all confined to their berths, and seemed waiting to be relieved by death. There is a physician on board, (whose father and Captain Smith are sole owners of the ship), his services, however, are not at the disposition of all. The captain has flour, but pretends it does not belong to the ship, and refuses to serve it out to the passengers. He, however, offered to sell it, and two or three of us joined and bought a quantity of him, together with a quantity of sugar; all to be paid for in Panama, at Panama prices, and for all of which we *never had the most distant idea* of paying him a farthing. We hired the cook to prepare it for us, and thereafter were wellserved. With this supply, we were in a condition to invite the invalids to our table, where we could furnish them something more palatable than sea-biscuit and salt beef.

My attention was attracted to one of the passengers, who, upon my inquiring for Spanish books, offered me one of Spanish comedy; there was something polished in his manners, yet something wayward, which very much excited my interest. His clothes were good, still, in his helplessness, they had become extremely filthy. He commenced conversation, but soon stopped for a moment, as if trying to recollect himself; and said he believed he had entirely lost his mind, that his ideas were so incoherent, he feared he could not make himself understood. He first inquired where the ship was bound; I informed him, and asked him how he came on board. He did not know, but said he was informed that he was to be sent home; he did not know why, nor from whom he received the information.

He wished me to converse with him, and try to set him right; he gave me the keys to his trunks, and wished me to open them. I found them stored with clothing of the best quality, together with a well-selected library of books, mathematical instruments, and materials for drawing: everything indicating a man of refinement and education. In his writing desk I found a patriotic poem, composed and read by him on board the ship in which he sailed for California: on the anniversary of our national independence. I also found a daguerreotype; the sight of this seemed to awaken pleasing emotions. It contained the portraits of a lady and child; these he recognized as his wife and little daughter. By the sight of these, he was at first overcome; his wife appeared natural to him, but he had not the most distant idea of the age of his little daughter; he wondered if it was of a sufficient age, when he left home, to call him father, and whether it would remember and greet him when he returned. He now realized, most painfully, the gloom that hung like a pall over his memory.... I requested him to run back in his memory, if possible, to the time when he first became deranged. He said that he was attacked with the fever at Benicia, and carried on board a ship that was then lying at anchor. There were several sick on board, and during his sickness, one was brought and placed on a table in front of his berth. He watched him day after day, until one night, as the light fell dimly on his pallid features, a slight convulsion passed over him, and his jaw fell. This closed the scene; from this moment his mind had been wandering in the dark labyrinths of forgetfulness. The fever had left him, and given place to that dreaded malady, the scurvy, with which he had now become reduced almost to helplessness. His feet and limbs were swollen to double their usual size, their purple hue denoting the fearful state to which his system was reduced. The name of this unfortunate man was E. W. Clark, Jr., of West Boylston, Massachusetts. He gave me his name, and the address of his friends, at a time when he had but little hope of ever seeing them, with the request that I should write them the particulars of his death.

from DIGGING FOR GOLD
WITHOUT A SHOVEL

DANIEL WADSWORTH COIT

*Daniel Wadsworth Coit (1787–1876) was a sixty-one-year-old American banker liv-
ing in Mexico City when news of gold in California broke out in the summer of 1848.
Sensing a fortune in the making, Coit moved to San Francisco and set up an investment
office where he bought miners' gold dust in exchange for cheap but easily transferable gold
and silver coins. This life of relative ease afforded him time for a series of letters and
drawings that reflected a middle-aged man's view of bustling gold rush society. His letters,
including this account of the celebration over California's admission as the thirty-first
state, were later collected as* Digging for Gold Without a Shovel *in 1967.*

SAN FRANCISCO, OCTOBER 31, 1850

My very dear Harriet,

We have had some very exciting events here within the past few days,
joyous on the one hand, and most sad on the other. The news from Washington which reached us recently of the admission of California into the Union
of States was received on all hands with demonstrations of joy. Balls, processions, illuminations, fireworks, all testified to the general sentiment which
prevailed, but in the very midst of this rejoicing a loud explosion was heard at
one of the principal wharves. Half the population who were in the streets
rushed to the spot only to witness one of the most appalling sights. A steamboat bound up the river with about 120 or 130 souls on board, just in the act
of hauling out, had blown up with a frightful loss of life. You may well suppose
that the scene presented at the moment was revolting and shocking beyond
anything that language can describe. I send a newspaper containing some
particulars if you can make up your mind to read such sickening details.

The following night after this accident we were again alarmed by the cry of
fire. It was found to proceed from a house owned and occupied by a notorious
courtesan who is said to have accumulated here no less than $50,000. The fire
was directly in our rear, and I hastened to it, presuming at first that we were in

Great Seal of the State of California, adopted Oct. 2, 1849

some danger. It being rather remote from the more thickly settled part of the town, people were rather slower than usual in arriving at the spot. When I got there not many were present and I approached near the building, from the doors and windows of which the flames were just beginning to issue.

The scene which presented itself to my view was a curious one, to say the least of it. The house had been furnished at great cost with the richest description of bedroom and drawing-room furniture, and here it lay, thrown on the ground in one promiscuous heap—French bedsteads, mirrors, carpets, silk curtains, hangings, toilet furniture, rich female apparel, etc., etc. On one side

245

and occasionally moving about with perfect composure and affected dignity, the proprietor of all this rich furniture—a tall, showy woman, not very youthful or very pretty, but yet in a full rich plain black satin dress with the light shining strongly upon her, a very striking object at the moment. It was not many minutes before the sparks and burning shingles or pieces of them began to shower down upon the rich furniture and trappings. When they were roughly removed to a greater distance by the crowd, something in this new movement suddenly disturbed the equanimity of the frail lady. The mock dignity was lost sight of and the cauldron of rage, which was boiling but stifled within, burst forth and vented itself upon a most inoffensive glass chandelier, which was kicked and trampled to pieces in a moment.

What sufferings do not men hastily rush into, wherever there is a prospect of collecting a little gold without the ordinary industry, economy, and labor which is generally called for in its accumulation? The vicissitudes and exposures to which men are sometimes called in this "El Dorado" are strikingly exemplified in the case of some of these invalids I have been speaking of. Not a week ago they were here in high health and spirits, bound for the mines. Well, probably with all their worldly effects (it might be so), they went aboard one of the steamers bound up the river. This steamer was run into by another larger coming down and instantly sank, barely giving time for the passengers to escape with their lives. Arriving here, some of them immediately took passage on another steamer just about leaving for their destination. This was the unfortunate one blown up at the wharf already referred to, and now those of our adventurers who were not killed outright are carried, scalded and maimed, to the hospital where, within forty-eight hours, they have another hairbreadth escape. What a succession of disasters—truly the events of years in other countries transpire here in days.

D.W.C.

from PIONEER DAYS IN CALIFORNIA

JOHN CARR

Irish gold rusher John Carr reached California in August of 1850. He wandered through San Francisco and Sacramento before joining the 1851 mini-rush to the northern mines of Trinity County. His Pioneer Days in California *was published in 1891.*

IN THE MONTH OF MARCH, 1851, one of those cases occurred which bring disgrace to our civilization and dishonor to our manhood. Nearly every miner owned a mule or some other sort of animal to pack his tools, blankets, and provisions on when moving from one gulch or diggings to another. Those animals caused the miners a great deal of trouble to hunt up when wanted for use. Generally when new diggings were found and sufficient animals were in the neighborhood, some enterprising individual would start a herd: that is, he would gather up all the animals in the neighborhood and herd them during the day. Feed was abundant. At night he would have a corral that was considered Indian-proof to keep the herd in. The charge was four dollars per month for each animal. The Indians on the Trinity and its tributaries were very fond of "mule-beef," and never failed to obtain a supply of it, when they had an opportunity, from the honest miner, and the miner never failed to fill Mr. Indian's skin with lead when he was caught helping himself to any of the miners' property, especially to mules.

Uncle Joe Strudivant and his partner, John W. Carter, and Jerry Whitmore, were then running a pack-train between Shasta and Trinity River.

They had a large pack-train to look after. They built a corral and herded the stock on a flat, where Strudivant's ranch is now located. One night the animals were all properly corralled, but the next morning they had all disappeared—forty or forty-five head, all told.

Four men immediately started on their track, and followed them for several days. At last they overtook them at the head of the Sacramento Valley—three white men and the stolen mules in their possession. Before the thieves were aware, the pursuers opened fire on them and killed all three of them. The pursuing party was led by a fellow called "Texas," a man who held human life very lightly. After killing the thieves they scalped them, and brought the scalps and the animals back with them. "Texas" showed me one of the scalps he had in his belt when in Weaverville on his way back to the ranch on Trinity. They not only took the thieves' scalps, but skinned their whiskers off and brought them back, and nailed both scalps and whiskers on the gateposts of the corral as a warning to others. That herd was not troubled by white thieves any more that season.

In those days horse-stealing was the crime of crimes. If two men got into trouble and one killed the other in a fight, there was very little said about it; but if a man was caught stealing a horse or a mule, his days were short, or else he got whipped and banished from the diggings, sometimes branded.

from NARRATIVE OF A JOURNEY ROUND THE WORLD

FRIEDRICH GERSTÄCKER

Friedrich Gerstäcker (1816–1872), a German writer who made tales of the gold rush popular to a European audience, moved to the United States in 1837 and traveled extensively throughout the South. In 1849 the excitement of the gold rush drew him to San Francisco and, inevitably, gold country. Although he left California a little more than a year later, he used it for the setting of six books. He offered this description of his encounters with California Indians in his autobiography, Narrative of a Journey Round the World, *published in 1853.*

OUR LITTLE PARTY consisted of seven souls, and a motley company it was, three of them being merchant's clerks, one an apothecary, one a sailor, one a locksmith (the locksmith and one of the merchants' clerks were brothers), and myself. We had only taken with us what little luggage we could not do without, but, besides this, nearly all of us carried some kind of weapon or other. But I had better give the reader at once a true description of all of us, he'll get acquainted in that way with a great number of such parties that started and even yet start in a similar way to the mountain—for gold.

We had been, as I have said, seven, but one of the young merchantmen gave up the second day, and staid behind; the weather was too hot for him, and he was not able to undergo so many hardships as he thought we would be obliged to do from the first start—and he was not far wrong in that.

The two brothers, to commence with the most interesting part of the group—Jews from Berlin, seemed not to have had much idea about working hard, but like a good many of the new comers thought they should find the gold easily enough in the mountains, they wanted at least to make the trial, and were equipped accordingly.

The little apothecary wore a green Polish cap, with four corners, a strip of black fur around it, and a red beard below it, carrying upon his back a kind of soldier's black knapsack, with a rolled-up blanket laid over it, and a short, stout walking-stick in his hand. His trowsers were also tucked up half-way to his knee, and he had a peculiar way of holding the stick in walking far away from his body. His name was Kunitz, the two brothers name Meyer.

The fourth, Hulme, was a stout young fellow, of about twenty years of age, with a green hunting-cap, yellow overcoat, trowsers, and half boots, a striped bag over one shoulder, a rolled-up blanket over the other, and a double-barreled gun in his hand.

The young sailor wore his sea-clothes, but with the addition of a double-barreled gun, and a rolled-up blanket.

I myself wore my old leathern hunting-shirt, with hunting-pouch, rifle, and bowie-knife, with a Scotch cap and high water-boots, and also a small pouch buckled round me, which contained the most necessary medicines for the mines.

Such was our equipments for the diggings, and with the mule among us, which one of us always had to lead, the reader may be assured we formed a perfect picture.

[Several days into our travels] we determined on taking the northern route: we crossed Feather River by wading it, and camped on the other side. On this day we came to the first Indian village, built on the banks of the river, and consisting of at least thirty or thirty-five well-made huts, dug half in the ground, and walled and roofed very much like those of the Mandan Indians of North America. The huts were dug about four feet deep into the ground, strong posts being set up in the inside and the middle, with rafters and beams across them, which were overlaid and connected with branches, and finally covered with a thick and well-beaten coat of earth, which was of a perfectly round shape and turned off the rain completely.

At the entrance of a great many huts we found squaws sitting, with large piles of roasted acorns spread out on a blanket by their side, while they were crack-ing the hard shell of the acorn with their ivory teeth, dropping the kernel without touching it with their lips into a piece of cloth upon their laps, and throwing the shell away. The dress of the women consisted of a blanket thrown round the shoulders, and a short but thick kind of mat, or rather apron, made out of reeds or rushes. The men, on the contrary, sported nearly every fashion in the world; some were entirely naked without even a waist-coat, merely with some ornament in the hair, others had a blanket wrapped around them, while others again wore a perfectly European dress with every thing belong-ing to it, except shoes. Their national ornaments seemed to be of a very simple kind; they all had, both men and women, their ears pierced, and wore in these a simple piece of wood or quill ornament and painted. They also tattoo, but I only saw a few of them with these marks, and then on the chin, only, with fine blue stripes running down from the corners of the mouth.

The first village we passed seemed very thickly inhabited, or else every body was before his own door or upon the roof of his hut, where the men were principally sitting, and seemingly enjoying the warm sun with a great deal of pleasure. They were nearly all naked, squatting with their backs together, and appearing not to take the least notice of the white passers. Only upon one hut four fellows were stationed, three naked and one wrapped up in a fiery red blanket, who seemed to find peculiar amusement in our appearance, talking, arguing with each other, and laughing. The women were nearly all busy, diving though, wherever they got a chance, away into their huts as soon as the white strangers approached them. We saw a singular kind of ornament in one of these villages; it was a long pole, upon the upper part of which five or six very well-stuffed wild geese were fastened just as if they were running up the pole with outstretched necks. Not speaking the language, I could not inquire of the natives for what purpose they had set up such a sign, for there was no wild goose hotel in the neighborhood; but what I heard afterward of the tribe makes me think it was a kind of national emblem, the favorite animal of the tribe, and as likely as not that from which the whole tribe derives its name, as other tribes in California are called *cayotas,* and also in the Atlantic States "Wolves and Foxes."

One of our party, the oldest Meyer, poor fellow, got a dreadful tooth-ache, after we were a few days out, and in consequence of it a swelled face, but such a face I never saw before in my life; his head really seemed to be double its proper size, and his countenance was in fact most doleful. Tooth-ache is at the same time an extraordinary pain, and whoever has suffered from it, will know it—with some teeth cold water held on to them will cease the pain.... Some teeth require you to hold your head up, while others make you bend it down to let the blood rush to it, or even stand upon your head, sometimes in its worst paroxysms. This was the sort of tooth Meyer had, and the mad aching seemed to ease as soon as he held down his head, perhaps for half a minute to the ground; and as much as we pitied the poor fellow, it was sometimes really impossible to refrain from laughing at his maneuvers.

The wagon road led right through the third Indian village we reached, and following it, we entered the little town where the natives were sitting in their surly silence on the houses, only once in a while throwing a dark look upon the strangers who pressed in more and more, filling the country with their multitudes. Suddenly right in the very centre of the place, and surrounded on every side by the crowded huts—for tooth-ache never cares for place nor time—Meyer had one of his worst fits; and without even looking round to see where he was, he placed both his hands upon the ground, and dropping his head down as far as he could, he lifted, partly to bring the upper portion of his body farther forward, and partly to balance it, his right leg as high up as he could get it. The cap fell from his head, all the things he carried, slipped forward over his shoulders, and the hanger had caught in some fold or other, and was now standing, just as it had hung before, right upright into the air, increasing of course the oddity of the whole figure.

The effect was, however, extraordinary, which this posture had upon the at first so indolent natives. At the first moment, a couple of women, who had been setting close by, cleaning a crous, jumped up, dropped whatever they held in their laps, and ran as quickly as they could into their huts, and even the men rose up suddenly, looking in mute astonishment and wonder at the extraordinary stranger who presented himself in the heart of their homes in such a peculiar and perhaps hostile posture. The thick red face that now became visible between his arms and just above the ground did not serve to reassure them; but when we ourselves could hold on no longer, but burst out, in spite of our compassion for the poor fellow, into loud and perfect roars of laughter, they seemed to drop every idea of hostility on his part, and thinking, as likely as not, the whole only a performance the kind stranger had got up for their own and sole amusement, they also set up a perfect scream of delight; and the women on every side coming out of their caves again, and other natives jumping upon the nearest hut, we were surrounded in a few seconds by swarms of Indians, poor Meyer, with his dreadful pain and desperate posture, forming the centre of this merry crowd.

At last he rose up again, greeted this time by a perfect cheer; but he was not in the humor to favor the grinning savages with another performance, which they seemed really desirous to have, but throwing a wild and angry look around him, he shook his luggage in order, and traveled on.

In the neighborhood of Murphey's New Diggings, a large tribe of the Wynoot Indians camped; and though Americans not unfrequently tell dreadful stories about the treacherous character of these natives, I never found a more quiet and peaceable people in any country than they were.

When I reached the camp, the squaws—and a little warm water and soap would have decidedly improved their complexion—were busied in getting the sumptuous meal ready for their lords and husbands, and I had a beautiful chance of seeing the simple but also most peculiar way in which they prepare their dinners. The main part of this seemed to consist of a soft mush of pounded

Wealthy Nisenan bride, c. 1870

acorns. They had dug—or, I rather believe, stamped—a small flat hole in the ground, in the shape of a round and deep dish, or a Java hat, or also something like a Californian washing-pan, beaten this as hard as possible, and filled it with the acorn-mush, already beaten up in one of their waterproof baskets. Upon this they had placed some light twigs, as I soon found, to protect the bowl itself, as they placed hot stones into it, which they put upon the twigs to make them sink slowly to the bottom. As they also poured some water in, to make the mush thinner, these twigs prevented the fluid from damaging the bottom of the vessel.

This kind of poe was soon prepared, and I now went toward a small family, to see it also devoured. Of course, I looked around for a spoon; for I had thought up to this time that such a thin, soup-like mush could not be eaten in any other way but with some instrument at least resembling a spoon: but a fat, jovial native soon taught me better. He was, of course, the husband of the lady who brought him the basket filled with the soup, which she had ladled out with a flat calabash; and taking the basket between his knees, and trying first, rather carefully with one finger, if the mush had cooled enough to be eaten, he shoved the four fingers of his right hand into it, and then put them, apparently with the utmost satisfaction, into his wide and hospitably-opened organ of mastication, out of which they came directly afterward clean and shining, and ready to repeat the operation, till he had nearly finished half the basket. The thumb looked on all the time, accompanying the other four fingers down and up again, and only acting as a kind of preventative to hinder the hand from disappearing entirely.

While I was standing there a couple of pretty young girls came from the woods, with flat baskets full of flower-seed emitting a peculiar fragrance, which they also prepared for eating. They put some live coals among the seed, and swinging it and throwing it together, to shake the coals and the seed well, and bring them in continual and close contact without burning the latter, they roasted it completely, and the mixture smelled so beautiful and refreshing that I tasted a good handful of it, and found it most excellent.

They also brought great pine-apples—that is, real pine-apples—with a nut-like kernel, and many other delicacies, such as roasted grasshoppers and baked wasps, &c., which I was too poor a connoisseur to do justice to.

On the second of July, 1850, a black fellow—that is, not a negro, but a Bombay-man, of rather dark complexion for that race—came running into a little mining place, Douglas Flat, on the same creek Murphey's New Diggings lay on; two Indians were following him, but when they saw he had taken shelter with the whites, they left off their pursuit, and walked back. But the India-man now told a dreadful story, how the natives had taken hold of him, and robbed him of $1900 in gold dust. Some Texans, who were accidentally in the trader's tent the Bombay-man had sought shelter in, and possibly guided more by the hope of getting the $1900 than of helping the "nigger," as they called him, gave chase directly; and the natives hardly saw white men with their rifles in their hands start after them before they knew only too well what they had to expect from their mild pursuers, and fled to the hills and their own camp. But they had some old Texan woodmen after them, with legs as tough and strong as their own, to follow even through the rough and uneven ground of the hills; and on reaching the camping-place of their tribe, and thinking perhaps that far more whites were on their track than there really were, they only called to their comrades to take up their arms and flee with them farther into the thicket. Even the women had hardly time to snatch up their babies and save themselves from a hostile attack for which they could assign no cause.

Several other whites had followed the first, and while the Texans ran after the two natives, who, as they madly and foolishly thought, must have the gold, the others without even inquiring if the poor wretches, who were now chased like beasts of the forest, had done any harm, set fire to their little camping-place, and maliciously burned the provisions and blankets, as well as the only shelter the poor natives had raised for themselves in the woods; and had it not been for some other men, and American and a German, who had also followed to see what was the matter, and who scattered the fire before it had destroyed more than about half of the little village, every thing that tribe before possessed would have been devoured by the greedy flames.

The Texans, at last, when they saw they could not overtake the fleeter natives, fired several times at them, and they sent back a shower of arrows, but of course without doing the least harm, as they had to keep off as far as they could for fear of the bullets, and a distance of seventy or eighty yards made their light arrows powerless. At last, one of the Texans, heading the tribe as they followed up a narrow gulch to the top of the hill, got in shooting distance, and taking deliberate aim at one, shot him in the back from the low hill where he was standing. The poor fellow fell, but the others carried him off; and as the wood became thicker here, the Texans returned to the camp.

Next day a delegation from the Indians came into Stoutenburgh, to inquire what they had done that the whites should make war upon them, and to tell the alcalde there—for they knew he was the capitano of the whites—one of their number had been shot, and their village burnt by some of their white brethren.

A jury was sworn to go up to the ridge on which the Indians had now taken shelter; and when we reached the spot, where the women looked at us in fear and despair, and the men in hate and anger, though they did not use their weapons against us, we found the poor fellow who had been shot the day before, standing upright under a tree. He had just raised himself when he heard of our coming, for I could see the bloody spot where he had lain a little while before. His wife was supporting him, and death was written on his countenance. The bullet had entered his back close to the back-bone, and seemed to have lodged inside, and had followed a slanting direction from a higher place, somewhere on the hip-bone. We had a doctor with us (as the man called himself), but he could do nothing for the poor fellow; and after hearing what account the Indians could give of the whole matter, and seeing on our return the burned camp with our own eyes, a trial was to be held next day upon the Bombay-man.

When we left the hill, and the wife of the poor Indian, who had probably thought white men sufficiently skilled in the art of medicine to heal the wounds they had inflicted, now saw them give him up, she commenced wailing over the murdered man; and while the wounded native again lay down under the tree, her shrill cries filled the air. I ran down the hill as fast as I could, to be out of hearing of those dreadful sounds. I was ashamed of being a white man at that moment.

Next day a jury sat; but the Bombay-man understood no English, at least, he pretended not to do so now. Still every thing was proved against him, and some traders from the next camp stood up as witnesses against him, stating on their oath that the nigger had not even money enough with him the night before to pay for his drink, and they had kicked him out of the tent. As it now appeared, the fellow had reached the night before the Indian camp, where he was hospitably received; but insulting the women, he was first repulsed, and then, not being satisfied with a first lesson, driven out of the camp by the men. Afterward, I believe, he had again returned, and the natives had followed to chastise, but not to rob the rascal.

The trial of the Bombay-man was interesting, for nobody spoke his language, while he himself pretended not to understand a word of English; though one of the Yankees, a raw down-easter, tried once to play the interpreter, by bawling to him in English—which he thought the foreigner must understand, because he himself understood nothing else. But it was no go, and with circumstantial proof enough, they condemned him to twenty-five lashes, of which the sheriff gave him thirteen the next morning—accidentally the Fourth of July—and one of the Indians the rest. But the natives were not satisfied with this, and swore they would kill him for raising a false cry against them; and the sheriff had to keep him that night after the punishment in his own tent. When they led him out to receive his lashes though, the poor devil was perfectly convinced they were going to hang him, and he begged for his life bitterly.

This was one of the common Indian wars. "The natives had shot with arrows at the whites, and were driven back into their mountains," so the accounts ran; though, in reality, the whites behaved worse than the cannibals toward the poor, inoffensive creatures, whom they had robbed nearly of every means of existence, and now sought to trample under foot.

But enough of this misery. The time is not far distant when the Indians of this immense territory will have ceased to exist; and it will then be interesting, at least, to know something of the tribes, if we did not care for them when living.

Indian Boy Hanged for Stealing Gold

WILLIAM JOSEPH

As California's new populace appropriated more and more land from the Indians, inevitable conflict quickly led to violence. Fifteen thousand Native Californians were murdered by 1860. The following reminiscence was transcribed by linguist Hans Jørgen Uldall from Nisenan tribe member William Joseph in 1930 or 1931. Joseph was seventy-five years old at the time and living on a Nisenan reservation near Auburn, California.

LONG AGO THE INDIANS had a camp on the north side of the oke'm mountain, the white people call that Mt. Oakum. The bluff by the river at the north side of that, they call that pu'lak' Bluff, and the white people call that Buck's Bar, in that river Indians and white men prospected for gold.

On the west side of Mt. Oakum two white men had their home in a small log cabin. From there they used to go to work at the river every day. The door of their house being left open, an Indian boy who was hunting around felt hungry and went to that house to eat. When he had finished eating he saw two buckskin sacks full of gold, and silver money on that table. He took it, put it in his pocket, and went off with it.

When the two men came home from work they missed the gold and the money. They followed that Indian's tracks. They tracked him to the Indian's camp. They saw him playing cards and putting down sackfuls of gold.

The white men took him right there. They took back all the money. But they took him all the same to a little valley on the west side of Mt. Oakum.

The white men gathered. From there, afterwards, they summoned all the Indian chiefs. They kept him there all day, waiting for one chief. When it was about three o'clock, they put a rope around his neck.

At length, the chief arrived. The Indians said, "They are waiting for you, they are going to hang the boy, go and prevent it."

That chief went in the center of the group of people. He talked, speaking white language, "Captain he says, Lowas he says, Hemas he says, 'Hang him up!'" he said.

The white people said to the mule, "Get up!" The mule pulled him up by the rope and hanged him. All the Indians hollered and cried. When he was dead, they let him back down. They gave him to the Indians. The Indians took the body along and burned it.

After that the Indians did not burgle or steal anything belonging to white people. "That is the way they will treat us if they catch us," they said.

When the chiefs made speeches they said, "Do not take anything from them, do not steal from them, they will treat you that way if they catch you! Those white men are different men, they are not our relatives." They said, "They will hang you without mercy."

All the chiefs preached that. They talked about that at every big time. The Indians were very much afraid of the whites in the early days. That is what was done, the whites were bad in the old days, those who prospected for gold.

Those who have come now brought women along, white women, those ones were good, they gave us all kinds of food when we went to their houses. That was bad whites in the early days, those who prospected for gold. Those who came next were good whites, married people, that was how it was in the old days.

from San Francisco Vigilance Committees

WILLIAM T. COLEMAN

The Committee of Vigilance, formed by some of San Francisco's most prominent leaders and businessmen, emerged from the social unrest of the gold rush in 1851. Led by William T. Coleman (1824–1893), a wealthy Kentucky-born merchant, the Committee sought to curb robbery, murder, and arson in under-policed San Francisco. During its one-hundred-day reign, the Committee members lynched four suspects, deported twenty-eight, and whipped at least one. Twice more, in 1856 and 1877, the vigilantes regrouped to deliver hasty retribution to perceived murderers and to quash riots. In Century Magazine *in 1891, Coleman explained the atmosphere of fear and lawlessness that spawned the Committee's mob violence.*

ON THE 14TH OF AUGUST, 1849, my brother and I rode from the Sierra foothills into the Sacramento Valley, intending to reach Sutter's Fort that night. Early in the forenoon we were overtaken by a horseman, a finely mounted, handsome fellow, who asked if we were immigrants. We answered, Yes. He welcomed us into the new country, and said he had arrived some months earlier. I told him that my brother, who was near by, and I were just arriving overland; that we had come from Salt Lake alone in about twenty days, for being well equipped we had made quick time; that he was the first Californian we had met, and, indeed, the first person we had seen in several days. I asked him if gold in California was a reality or a romance. He said it was an assured reality, and, as a ready proof, loosened his waistcoat and revealed a large, long, leather bag strapped securely to his person, in which he said was about $3000 in gold-dust, the result of his labor for a short time. He stopped his horse, opened his purse, and showed us the glittering metal.

Enjoying my surprise and interest, he gave me several handsome specimens as a souvenir. I asked him if it was not hazardous to make such a display of his wealth. He answered, No, it was perfectly safe; that people were honest, or made to be honest; that there was no room in this country for thieves, and there was no such thing as highway robbery; there had been troubles in the

259

country, but the worst men had been summarily punished, the others had learned better, and there was plenty for all who would work. He gave me many particulars about the country, the new population, the gold product; described the new towns, especially Sacramento, which had grown up on the river near Sutter's Fort, and whither he was then going; gave me the distances, and advised me of the best camping-grounds, and, his animal being fresher than ours, bade us good-bye, and galloped on.

The second day, after having rested, I went to the new city of Sacramento, and found it a scene of activity and vitality. It was a town of tents, with a few frame buildings altogether strongly resembling a huge camp-meeting, with many people camping in the open air. The streets were filled with men coming and going, wagons and pack animals loading from the well-filled stores; many vessels were discharging on the river banks cargoes of mining supplies and provisions of all kinds, and there was everywhere a full display of prosperous business and earnest life.... I noticed large piles of goods outside the stores and tents, unprotected, and I asked if they were left out at night and were safe. The answers were all affirmative. The doors of houses had no locks, or they were unused; the tents had no fastenings, yet there were no losses of property, as every trespasser knew that in theft he would hazard his life.

This I afterward found was the condition all over the country. The miner without fear or hesitation would leave his bag of gold-dust under his pillow and go to his camp for a day's work. He would leave his gold-diggings and rocker with hundreds of dollars exposed without fear of loss: all, or chiefly, the result of very summary punishment inflicted upon lawless men in San Francisco the year before, and of the trial and quick execution of a few throughout the country when found appropriating to their own use what did not belong to them. This was the common law of the country.

This condition of affairs continued through the winter of 1849 and the spring and early summer of 1850, during which time a large additional immigration came in, embracing numbers of our best people, and including many families of early pioneers, all bringing a sense of home-life and sanguine anticipation of future comfort and happiness. But unfortunately this tide was met by a flow of the worst element in the world, chiefly from Sydney and other Pacific Ocean ports, and, as a little foul matter will taint a large stream, so this matter seriously changed and endangered current affairs in California. Reports of robberies and assaults soon became common; again the public mind began to be excited over the general lawlessness. Wealth was increasing, business prospering, solid improvements progressing throughout the city and State; people were hopeful on the one hand, and fearful on the other, for while our golden era was bright, we had many sad proofs that our halcyon days had departed. This was no longer Arcadia.

The rapid and continued increase of crime in San Francisco impressed on every thinking man the conviction that some more vigorous action of the legal authorities was imperative, and must be stimulated and insisted upon, or self-preservation would make it necessary for the people to take the matter into their own hands, and assert the law and establish order in their own way. The police were notoriously inadequate and inefficient; the courts had been accused of corruption; the prisons were small and insecure, and it was boldly proclaimed through the streets that with packed juries and venal judges, false witnesses and dishonest officials, our criminal courts had become a failure and a reproach.

On the third of May, 1851, a great fire occurred that destroyed almost the entire city and in which a hundred lives were lost. There were good reasons for believing that the fire was the work of incendiaries who had sacrificed these valuable lives and millions of dollars' worth of property for the sake of plunder, and a very strong and bitter feeling grew up against the newly arrived population of criminal classes. The conviction grew stronger every day that something should be done by the people themselves to rid the city of incendiaries and robbers.

The want of a strong organization among those who wished to preserve peace and enforce the laws was severely felt. Those who had the largest interests at stake felt that unless there could be united action and control, there might be introduced a system of mob law, which would ultimately be more dangerous than the existing state of affairs. It was for this reason that, on the tenth of June, 1851, an organization of prominent business men was effected, and about 200 names were enrolled under what was styled "The Committee of Vigilance of San Francisco." The objects of the committee were "to watch, pursue, and bring to justice the outlaws infesting the city, through the regularly constituted courts, if possible, through more summary process, if necessary." Each member pledged his word of honor, his life, and his fortune for the protection of his fellow-members, and for purging the city of its bad characters. After arranging for a concert of action, watchwords, and a signal to call the members to the rendezvous, which was three taps of a fire-bell, the committee adjourned for the evening.

Scarcely half an hour had passed before the bell was tapped. On reaching headquarters I found a number of gentlemen, and soon after there was brought in a very large, rough, vicious-looking man called Jenkins, an ex-convict from

261

Sydney, who had been caught in the theft of a safe from a store. He was well known as a desperate character who had frequently evaded justice. The committee was organized immediately into a court, and Jenkins was tried for the offense within an hour. The evidence was overwhelming; he was promptly convicted and sentenced to be hanged that night. Jenkins's bearing throughout the trial was defiant and insulting, and he intimated that his rescue by his friends might be expected at any moment. We were notified by our officers that already the roughest and worst characters throughout the city were mustering in force to resist the committee. At the same time scores of our best citizens came forward and enrolled themselves as members, while others pledged their support in anything we might do.

I strenuously resisted the proposition to execute Jenkins that night, as I held it cowardly to hang him in the dark in such hot haste. I proposed he should be held till next morning and then hanged in broad daylight as the sun rose. Only a few agreed with me; there was much nervousness; the very circumstances of his crime having been committed at the moment of our organization and in defiance of it, and the threatened attack on us by abandoned criminals, all tended to impress the committee with the necessity of prompt action. Seeing that he must be hanged, I moved that the prisoner have the benefit of clergy. This was granted, but when the minister was left with him, the hardened criminal heaped the vilest insults on his venerable head. This hastened his doom, and his career was quickly closed.

The next morning the work of the Vigilance Committee was heralded throughout the State, and hundreds of citizens came forward and tendered their approval of our acts and asked to be enrolled in our ranks. The unexpected arrest and quick execution of Jenkins spread consternation among all his class. The Governor of the State, McDougal, issued a proclamation and maintained a nominal opposition to the committee, but took no active measures against it. Many arrests were made of desperate characters, and where clear proof of murder within the State was lacking, it was decided that banishment or corporal punishment should be the penalty. During the active operations of the committee, four men were hanged, and about thirty were banished. Nearly all were from Sydney or other British colonies, and as far as possible they were returned to the places from which they had come.

After a session of about thirty days the committee, finding that the country had been purged of a goodly number of the worst people, determined to adjourn quietly. It was decided not to disband, but to preserve the organization ready for any emergency. Happily there was no call for its services for some time; in fact, it was four years before the necessity of such a committee was again felt by the people of California, and brought forth finally the famous Vigilance Committee of 1856.

As contemporary testimony to the value of the work of the first Vigilance Committee, and its significance as an example of self-government, I quote the following editorial from the New York "Daily Tribune" of July 19, 1851.

"...The summary proceedings of the San Francisco Committee of Vigilance, in the trial, condemnation, and execution of the thief Jenkins, are not to be regarded in the light of an ordinary riot, much less as an example of hostility to the established laws, heralding disorganization and anarchy. Seen from the proper point of view, it is a manifestation, violent, it is true, of that spirit of order which created the State of California.... San Francisco presents, therefore, the singular spectacle of a community governed by two powers, each of which is separate and distinct from the other. They cannot come in conflict, since there is no aggressive movement against the law on the part of the committee, and no attempt on the part of the regular authorities to interfere with the action of the latter. Public opinion universally upholds the course pursued by the committee. This course, under the circumstances, cannot be called mob law or lynch law, in the common acceptation of the term. It more nearly resembles the martial law which prevails during a state of siege.

"At this distance we will not venture to judge whether the circumstances demand so merciless a code. But we are sufficiently familiar with the characters of the men composing the Committee of Vigilance, to acquit them of any other motive than *that of maintaining public order and individual security.* We believe they will exercise the power they have assumed no longer than is absolutely necessary to subserve these ends, and that their willing submission to the authority of the law, when the law shall be competent to protect them, will add another chapter to the marvelous history of their State. In spite of these violent exhibitions of popular sentiment, the instinct of order, *the capacity for self-government, is manifested more strongly in California, at this moment, than in other part of the world.*"

from SHADOW AND LIGHT

MIFFLIN WISTAR GIBBS

Like most forty-niners, the first African-American gold rushers had no intention of settling in California—they wanted to return home with pockets bursting with gold dust. But as word spread east of California's favorable living conditions, the state's African-American community grew. Not that they found life free from discrimination in the West. During the gold rush, African-Americanss were not allowed to testify in California courts and many schools would not accept their children. The First State Convention of Colored Citizens of California convened in 1855 to combat these unjust laws, as well as to fight for African-American suffrage and equal rights.

Mifflin Wistar Gibbs (1823–1915), one of California's first African-American civil rights leaders, was born in Pennsylvania. He spent several years lecturing with abolitionist Frederick Douglass. Gibbs moved to San Francisco during the gold rush, finding work as a shoe seller. He soon became involved in the city's burgeoning civil rights movement, helping to found the San Francisco Athenaeum Institute (an African-American library and debating society) and start the state's first African-American news-paper. He also organized protests to respond to a fugitive slave law case involving former slave Archy Lee and to fight the racist California poll tax. Gibbs left California in 1858 to become active in southern Reconstruction-era politics. He eventually served as the country's first elected African-American municipal judge. He described his arrival in San Francisco in 1850 in his autobiography, Shadow and Light, *published in 1902.*

HAVING MADE MYSELF somewhat presentable upon leaving the steerage of the steamer, my trunk on a dray, I proceeded to an unprepossessing hotel kept by a colored man on Kearny Street. The cursory view from the outside, and the further inspection on the inside, reminded me of the old lady's descrip-tion of her watch, for she said, "It might look pretty hard on the outside, but the inside works were all right." And so thought its jolly patrons. Seated at tables, well supplied with piles of gold and silver, [were] numerous disciples of that ancient trickster Pharaoh, [and] being dubious perhaps of the propriety of adopting the literal orthography of his name, [had] abbreviated it to Faro.

Getting something for nothing, or risking the smaller in hope of obtaining the greater, seems a passion inherent in human nature, requiring a calm sur-

Miner at Auburn Ravine, 1852, by Dressler

vey of the probabilities, and oftimes the baneful effects to attain a moral resistance. It is the *ignus fatus* that has lured many promising ones and wrecked the future of many lives.

The effervescent happiness of some of the worshipers at this shrine was conspicuous. The future to them seemed cloudless. It was not so with me. I had a secret not at all complacent, for it seemed anxious to get out, and while unhappy from its presence, I thought it wise to retain it.

When I approached the bar I asked for accommodation, and my trunk was brought in. While awaiting this preparatory step to domicile ... my eye caught a notice, prominently placed, in gilt letters. I see it now, "Board twelve dollars a week in advance." It was not the price, but the stipulation demanded that appalled me. Had I looked through a magnifying glass the letters could not have appeared larger. With the brilliancy of a search light they seemed to ask "Who are you and how are you fixed?" I responded by "staring fate in the face," and, going up to the bar, asked for a cigar. How much? Ten cents. I had sixty cents when I landed; had paid fifty for trunk drayage, and I was now moneyless man—hence my secret.

I approached a house in course of construction and applied to the contractor for work. He replied he did not need help. I asked the price of wages. Ten dollars a day. I said you would much oblige me by giving me if only a few days' work, as I have just arrived. After a few moments' thought, during which mayhap charity and gain held conference, which succumbed, it is needless to premise, for we sometimes ascribe selfish motives to kindly acts, he said that if I choose to come for nine dollars a day I might. It is unnecessary for me to add that I chose to come.

When I got outside the building an appalling thought presented itself; whoever heard of a carpenter announcing himself ready for work without his tools. A minister may be without piety, a lawyer without clients, a politician impolitic, but a carpenter without tools, never! It would be prima facie evidence of an impostor. I went back and asked what tools I must bring upon the morrow; he told me and I left. But the tools, the tools, how was I to get them? My only acquaintance in the city was my landlord. But prospects were too bright to reveal to him my secret. I wended my way to a large tent having an assortment of hardware and was shown the tools needed. I then told the merchant that I had no money, and of the place I had to work the next morning. He said nothing for a moment, looked me over, and then said: "All right take them." I felt great relief when I paid the merchant and my landlord on the following Saturday.

Why do I detail to such length these items of endeavor; experiences which have had similarity in many lives? For the reason that they seem to contain data for a moral, which if observed may be useful. Never disclose your poverty until the last gleam of hope has sunk beneath the horizon of your best effort, remembering that invincible determination holds the key to success, while advice and assistance hitherto laggard, now with hasty steps greets you within the door.

I was not allowed to long pursue carpentering. White employees finding me at work on the same building would "strike." On one occasion the contractor came to me and said, "I expect you will have to stop, for this house must be finished in the time specified; but, if you can get six or eight equally good workmen, I will let these fellows go. Not that I have any special liking for your people. I am giving these men all the wages they demand, and I am not willing to submit to the tyranny of their dictation if I can help it." This episode, the moral of which is as pertinent today as then, and more apparent, intensifies the necessity of greater desire upon the part of our young men and women to acquire knowledge in skilled handicraft, reference to which I have hitherto made. But my convictions are so pronounced that I cannot forbear the reiteration. For while it is enobling to the individual, giving independence of character and more financial ability, the reflex influence is so helpful in giving the race a higher status in the industrial activities of a commonwealth. Ignorance of such activities compel our people mostly to engage in the lower and less remunerative pursuits. I could not find the men he wanted or subsequent employment of that kind.

All classes of labor were highly remunerative, blacking boots not excepted.

I after engaged in this, and other like humble employments, part of which was for Hon. John C. Frémont, "the pathfinder overland to California."

Saving my earnings, I joined a firm already established in the clothing business. After a year or more so engaged, I became a partner in the firm of Lester & Gibbs, importers of fine boots and shoes. Just here a thought occurs which may be of advantage to ambitious but impecunious young men. Do not hesitate when you are without choice to accept the most humble and menial employment. It will be a source of pleasure, if by self-denial, saving your earnings, you keep a fixed intent to make it the stepping stone to something higher.

The genius of our institutions, and the noblest of mankind will estimate you by the ratio of distance from the humblest beginning to your present attainment; the greater the distance the greater the luster; the more fitting the meed of praise.

In 1851, Jonas P. Townsend, W. H. Newby, and other colored men with myself, drew up and published in the *Alta California,* the leading paper of the State, a preamble and resolutions protesting against being disfranchised and denied the right of oath, and our determination to use all moral means to secure legal claim to all the rights and privileges of American citizens.

It being the first pronouncement from the colored people of the State, who were supposed to be content with their status, the announcement caused much comment and discussion among the dominant class. For down deep in the heart of every man is a conception of right. He cannot extinguish it, or separate it from its comparative. What would I have others do to me? Pride, interest, adverse contact, all with specious argument may strive to dissipate the comparison, but the pulsations of a common humanity, keeping time with the verities of God never ceased to trouble, and thus the moral pebble thrown on the bosom of the hitherto placid sea of public opinion, like its physical prototype, creating undulations which go on and on to beat against the rock and make sandy shores, so this our earnest but feeble protest contributed its humble share in the rebuilding of a commonwealth where "a man's a man for all that."

LETTERS TO TSI CHOW-CHOO

TSE CHONG-CHEE

Widespread economic depression in China's Kwangtung province and the unrest follow-ing the Taiping Rebellion sent more than 25,000 Chinese emigrants to California beginning in 1852. To pay for the long ship voyage, many agreed to dock their future earnings, virtually rendering themselves indentured servants in their new home. Because of their unfamiliar appearance, language, and culture, the Chinese were targets for white hostility and xenophobia.

This series of letters appeared in Stockton's San Joaquin Republican *in 1853, supposedly written by immigrant Tse Chong-Chee to his cousin in China. Historian Chris Burchfield has suggested that Chong-Chee was most likely the fictional creation of an imaginative white newspaper writer. Nevertheless, the letters do reveal an obvious consciousness of East/West differences, using the guise of Chinese culture to mock American idiosyncrasies.*

CELESTIAL COUSIN

In further compliance with my promise, I proceed to give you some insight into the barbarians among whom I now live. Like most savages they are very fond of the trinkets and even valuables produced by our race. There is scarcely anything of our manufacture, however worthless in itself or silly in its charac-ter, but they covet with much eagerness. Their wow-wows, or women, are especially fond of swinging over their shoulders and swaying around their persons our Chinese-made shawls.

They are remarkable for the length of their feet, which results, I presume, from their incessant travel on foot from their very infancy. And what is very strange about it is, they consider their feet and the fixture to the extremity of their leg a beautiful portion of their persons; and they have a most captivating and sly way of displaying beauty in this respect.

Many of their wow-wows could be considered extremely beautiful if it were not for the largeness of their feet, and the want of angularity in the mode in which their eyes are set in their heads. The squarish set of their eyes is far from being agreeable.

Chinese man in San Francisco, c. 1851, by Isaac Baker

These barbarians, you must know, worship but once a week; and their women, especially, dress in the most extravagant manner to attend the gods. They do this to make a show of greater respect to compensate for their beastly negligence for the remainder of the time.

But it is strange, yet in keeping with their inconstant character, that they should excite their vanity and pride to the highest pitch when they ... prostrate

269

themselves in the dust of humility and reverence. These people exhibit no feeling in their worship.... There is one class among them which they call Methodists that sometimes groan a little in their worship ... yet ... a moment after they leave their temples, all distinction in manner and discharge of duties ceases as soon as they can get out of sight of their gods.

If the gods of this country are as capricious and inconstant as the people, I do not wonder at the badness of their government and the general ignorance of the place.

Your illustrious kinsman,
Tse Chong-Chee

Celestial Cousin

If the barbarians among whom I now sojourn are to be admired for their rare mode of worship they are no less remarkable for their taste in their amusements. One of the most curious I must describe to you.

This exhibition is in the open streets, and is performed by little boys, who seize a dog and fasten a string of fire-crackers to his tail, which are then made to explode. Of course the poor animal sets upon a great howling, while running at a rapid rate along the street, heedless of what he may meet. At this, boys and men run together and set up all sorts of yells and laughs fairly tip toe and leap for joy, in the wildest and most exultant excitement. You would be astonished to see the number [in the] crowd who assemble to witness and enjoy these savage spectacles.

Another barbaric amusement in which this people much delight, closely allied to the other, is a dog-fight.... [Crowds] of these people will gather around exhibiting intense interest in the result.

You can form some crude idea of the wonderful debasement of this people when I tell you that they sometimes fall to fighting together alone from the example of their dogs!... [Yet they] think themselves the most enlightened men in the world. They are so full of this self delusion, they have organized missionary societies which send agents to the distant parts of the earth, to proselytyze the inhabitants ... even ... in our Celestial Empire. You can readily judge of the success they are likely to have from the samples of their morals, religion, and refinement which I have given you.

Your illustrious cousin,
Tse Chong-Chee

Celestial Cousin

In this country, like all lands of the barbarians, the fiercest passions and most deadly strifes and bitter hatreds are produced from the most trifling circumstances. A short time since, a universal civil war was on the point of being kindled about what color was the most Christian and gentlemanly for a menial servant. One party asserted that only the African was fit for a slave, and that a gentleman should have no other. Another party was equally bold in the opinion that to retain a colored menial in servitude was dishonoring to their gods, and that no gentleman should be served by another, other than a white slave. This may seem strange to you, who if color were to be taken into the account in estimating a menial's value, would prefer a servant of celestial tint.

It is more probable, on this end of the continent, by a more frequent association with men of celestial origin, that they will soon prefer celestial menials to any other, if they can get such to serve them, which is very doubtful.... I do not expect "cooleyism" to prevail to any great extent here, unless we should drive off the barbarians and annex their country to the Chinese Empire.

This I do not think advisable at present, as humanity would not allow us to extirpate them; and unless we did, such an infusion of the barbaric element would surely beget much trouble and create a necessity of a great increase in the police department of the kingdom ... for the wildness and ferocity of these people is such that I am quite sure it would take two celestial policemen to hold one barbarian. And if the barbarians are succeeding in the propagation of their race as fast as they boast they are, it would be but a few scores of years before all China would be found in the condition and proportion of two celestials herding one barbarian.

Tse Chong-Chee

LETTERS FROM SAN FRANCISCO

JERUSHA MERRILL

Jerusha Merrill, with her husband and three children, left her home in Newington, Connecticut, for San Francisco in 1848. Like many gold rushers, Merrill wrote frequent letters home to dispel her loneliness and maintain connections with loved ones left behind. She mourned the lack of churches and the arts in San Francisco but expressed optimism about her future.

SAN FRANCISCO MARCH 1ST 1848

Dear Brother and Sister,

Yesterday your welcom letter came to hand. I was much gratified to hear you wer all well. You informed me you had previously written all particulars. We have received but one letter from you which was written soon after ouncle Levi died. It would be very gratifying to me to hear all particulars from home. You say you hear so many stories it is diffecult to tell what is true. Almost evry one tells a differant story. Many times it creates much excitement among us but I shall endeavor to tell you what you may rely upeon. A very great excitement is existing among us at this time. People are daily ariving from all parts by the hundreds. Many land with not one penny to help themselves with. Immagin for one moment what their situation must be. Board at eighteen dollars per week. Not one half can get accommodations at that rate or any other rate. A room just large anough to turn around in rents for onely twenty and thirty dolors per month. You may immagin me in a house with elevon rooms on the first floor, nine on the second, in the midst of sixty boarders, transient ones not mentioned, with hourly applications for more. You can then have onely a faint idea of my situation. Some times I have sevon servants, at others but one or two. With my family it is quite an item to be placed in this situation. Our house is quite a resort for most of the parties, we having the largest room in town. My boarders consist [of] American, English, French, Polls, [Chileans], and some from no country at all, yet a more orderly set could not be obtained in a place like this.

Never was there a better field for making money than now presents itself in this place at this time. Yet many leave with less than they bring. If any one thinks to get gold and keep his hands white he had better be off in the first boat. It is not to be obtained without hard labor. Any thing that is business will sucksead, labour of all kinds being very high. Carpenters from six to ten dollars per day. Lumber is selling at four and five hundred dollars a thousand feet. We got ours in the nick of time and are now reaping our reward. Property is daily rising. Lots that wer sixteen dollars when we arived have been sold at thre, four, and even fifteen thousand according to the location and still rising. We have had some hard rubs to contend with; we trust the worst is over. As to this place seeming like home to me it does not. The uncultivated state of society and the many inconveniencies render it extreemly unpleasant. In the summer we have cold unpleasent winds from the north west but no rain. The first winter very pleasant. The winter past very cold and insesant rain. Our rainy season is now nearly over.

We are satisfied to dig our gold in San Francisco. A man's washing is no small item in this place, it being onely from five to eight dollars per doz just diped in to the water and rung out at that. Female labour is above evry thing else. Many get one ounce a day, servants obtain from fifty to one hundred and fifty per month. If you had the produse of your term in this place one year you would realise a small fortune. I would like to see some corn onse more that is what is called corn at home. Also some of that good cider and apples. A few hickory nuts would not come amis. Farmes are becoming neglected for the mines. At what is Sutter's fort they have what they call a citty of canvas houses.

[MARCH] 2ND: I think if I laid my penn down onse yesterday while writing the above it was somewhear near twenty. In the evening we had a ball which was well represented by my sixty boarders. If you could step in about meal times and hear the clatering you would think I would be crazy. At times I am not far from it. We have written to you several times by different ways. When a young man by the name of Griswould left I did not have timely notes to write. He promised to call on you, I therefore thought he would give you all particulars conserning us.

When he left I had a lovely little boy that any mother would be happy to own but alas he has taken his flight to a better world to be transplanted in more congenial climes. He was too sweet a bud to bloom on earth. He was always happy; all faces afforded him pleasure. He was the pet of evry one that saw him. My friends have told me sinse his death they thought him an uncomon child. He had arived at a verry interesting age—elevon months—but them dear little armes will never entwine themselves around my neck again. He departed this life the sixth of January. I had antisipated much pleasure in bring-

Smith and Porter's coffee house on the corner of Sansome and Sacramento Streets, San Francisco, 1850, by Shaw & Johnson

ing him to the United States. Alas how vain are all things here below. In a moment when least expected they vanish from our view. I think in a former letter we informed you his name was John Selden. The measles have made great mortality among children. Many mothers have been left childless. Four have lain dead in one day.

I remain your ever affectionate sister
J D Merrill

SAN FRANCISCO OCT 28TH 1849

Dear Brother and Sister,

I have been much gratified to hear from you by persons that have so recently seen you.... I have not heard from Rodgers sinse he left for the mines. I hope he is doing well but many are not. The number of deaths is beyond all calculation. Many have no friend to put them under the turf. Yet those that take care [of] themselves and are regular in their habits enjoy good health. I warn all against the gaming house and grog shop. We have rented our place. I am therefore more at liberty than I have been at any time sinse we arived here. Time would fail to tell the wonderful changes that are constantly taking place in this far off country and without doubt a wonderful revolution awaits it. The excited state of things cannot long exist. That large fortunes are being made is true but in the end many must suffer. Many goods sent to this place will never be accounted for. Could you spend a week with us you would almost doubt your eyes and ears. This place is not fit for any thing but business. No one has time to spend a minet for any thing else. Could I be with you a week I could not begin to tell you of the wonders I daily hear and see. Numbers are constantly ariving; what they are going to do this winter I cannot tell. It costes a fortune for a man to live here. Therefore emty purses are useless property.

As we are about moving it is impossible for me to say much. At this time we are all together and enjoying good health. Wish much to viset old friends. My best love to yourself and family; also to enquiring friends.

Believe me sincerely yours
Jerusha D Merrill

SAN FRANCISCO, JANUARY 8TH, 1851

My Dear brother and sister,

Having a good opertunity to send direct I will pen a few hasty lines. I have previously writen several letters but have received no answers. I think it is owing to some delay of the mails. We have just heard of the bad management of some of the agents on the Isthmus and it is thought it will not go right untill Americans manage the whole. I am at preasent a grass widow—my husband has taken up a tract of land and commensed a farm. It is about fifty or sixty miles from this place. He has two yoak of cattle, two mules, an a lot of chickings. Eggs are six dol per doz. It is in a valey well watered and wood[ed]. He has eight men. Each one has a lot. All are to join and assist one another. I have no[t] yet visited it.

Another man came over the mountains with over three hundred cows an has gone six miles beyond. He is going into the butter business. Farming is great in thi[s] country I can assure you. We have renovated our garden and have any quantity of plants to transplant. We have had the largest and best potatoes in our garden I ever saw. I would like to get some of your seed if it wer possible to get it. The seed you sent out the worms got in and distroyed most of it. I shall make out a list and send by Rogers which I wish you to put in a tin box and send by express. Had I known he was going so soon I should have made a package but have but little time now.

I have not been verry well of late. Little Laura has been verry sick. We did not think she would live but is better now. She has four teeth. I would like you to see her and I would like to see your little ones.... I often think of the good apples and things that make the long winter evenings pass away so pleasantly and would like an old fashion sleigh ride again. It is so sandy around us that we cannot have any rides to enjoy. The horse can only walk. We are soon to have a plan[k] road from the town out to an old mision about three miles. Most of our principle streets are already planked.

The cholera has visited us. Most of the cases wer those of intemperate habits. Great rascality is caried on and some of the most daring roberies. They are so bold that they trip a man in the principle streets in the day time and take his bag of gold.... I shall send but a small trifle because I have not the time to look around. Give my love to all and except a good share to yourselves.

In haste I remain your affectionate sister
J D Merrill

from THE SHIRLEY LETTERS

LOUISE CLAPPE

Louisa Amelia Knapp Smith Clappe (1819–1906) was born in Elizabeth, New Jersey, and grew up in Massachusetts. In 1849, she and her young husband sailed around the Horn to California, settling first in Marysville and later along the Feather River in the heart of gold country. In a series of twenty-three letters to her sister in the East, Clappe took on the persona of Dame Shirley, a self-consciously whimsical "Dame" who dissected masculine gold rush society with clear prose and a vivid sense of humor. The letters, written in 1851 and 1852, were published in 1854 in San Francisco's Pioneer *magazine, where they influenced the later writing of gold rush chronicler Bret Harte. The Clappes' marriage foundered after the couple left the mines in 1852. Dame Shirley divorced her husband and taught school in San Francisco for twenty years before returning to her native New Jersey in 1878.*

FROM OUR LOG CABIN, Indian Bar, October 7, 1851

As we approached Indian Bar, the path led several times fearfully near deep holes, from which the laborers were gathering their yellow harvest; and "Dame Shirley's" small head swam dizzily as she crept shudderingly by.

The first thing which attracted my attention, as my new home came in view, was the blended blue, red, and white of the American banner, undulating like a many-colored snake amid the lofty verdure of the cedars which garland the brown brow of the hill behind our cabin. This flag was suspended on the Fourth of July last by a patriotic sailor, who climbed to the top of the tree to which he attached it, cutting away the branches as he descended until it stood among its stately brethren, a beautiful moss-wreathed Liberty pole flinging to the face of Heaven the glad colors of the Free.

This bar is so small that it seems impossible that the tents and cabins scattered over it can amount to a dozen; there are, however, twenty in all, including those formed of calico shirts and pine boughs. With the exception of the paths leading to the different tenements, the entire level is covered with mining holes, on the edges of which lie the immense piles of dirt and stones which have been removed from the excavations.

The first artificial elegance which attracts your vision is a large rag shanty, roofed, however, with a rude kind of shingles, over the entrance of which is painted in red capitals, ("to what base uses do we come at last,") the name of the great Humboldt spelt without the *d*. This is the only hotel in this vicinity, and as there is a really excellent bowling alley attached to it, and the bar-room has a floor upon which the miners can dance, and, above all, a cook who can play the violin—it is very popular. But the clinking of glasses, and the swaggering air of some of the drinkers, reminds us that it is no place for a lady, so we will pass through the dining room and, emerging at the kitchen, in a step or two reach our log cabin. Enter my dear; you are perfectly welcome; besides, we could not keep you out if we would, as there is not even a latch on the canvas door, though we really intend in a day or two to have a hook put on to it.

The room into which we have just entered is about twenty feet square. It is lined over the top with white cotton cloth, the breadths of which being sewed together only in spots stretch apart in many places, giving one a bird's-eye view of the shingles above. The sides are hung with a gaudy chintz, which I consider a perfect marvel of calico printing. The artist seems to have exhausted himself on *roses;* from the largest cabbage, down to the tiniest Burgundy, he has arranged them in every possible variety of wreath, garland, bouquet, and single flower; they are of all stages of growth, from earliest budhood up to the ravishing beauty of the "last rose of summer."

The fireplace is built of stones and mud, the chimney finished off with alternate layers of rough sticks and this same rude mortar; contrary to the usual custom, it is built inside, as it was thought that arrangement would make the room more comfortable; and you may imagine the queer appearance of this unfinished pile of stones, mud, and sticks. The mantle-piece—remember that on this portion of a great building, some artists, by their exquisite workmanship, have become world renowned—is formed of a beam of wood covered with strips of tin procured from cans, upon which still remain in black hieroglyphics the names of the different eatables which they formerly contained. Two smooth stones—how delightfully primitive—do duty as fire-dogs. I suppose that it would be no more than civil to call a hole two feet square in one side of the room a window, although it is as yet guiltless of glass. F. tried to coax the proprietor of the Empire to let him have a window from that pine and canvas palace; but he of course declined, as to part with it would really inconvenience himself; so F. has sent to Marysville for some glass, though it is the general opinion that the snow will render the trail impassable for mules before we can get it. In this case, we shall tack up a piece of cotton cloth, and should it chance at any time to be very cold, hang a blanket before the opening. At present the weather is so mild that it is pleasanter as it is, though we have a fire in the mornings and evenings, more, however, for luxury than because we really need it. For my part, I almost hope that we shall not be able to get any glass, for you will perhaps remember that it was a pet habit of mine, in my own room, to sit by a great fire in the depth of winter, with my window open.

I must mention that the floor is so uneven that no article of furniture gifted with four legs pretends to stand upon but three at once, so that the chairs, tables, etc., remind you constantly of a dog with a sore foot.

At each end of the mantle-piece is arranged a candlestick, not, much to my regret, a block of wood with a hole in the centre of it, but a real brittania-ware candlestick; the space between is gaily ornamented with F.'s meerschaum, several styles of clay pipes, cigars, cigaritos, and every procurable variety of tobacco; for you know the aforesaid individual is a perfect devotee of the Indian weed. If I should give you a month of Sundays you would never guess what we use in lieu of a bookcase, so I will put you out of your misery by informing you instantly that it is nothing more nor less than a candle-box, which contains the library, consisting of a bible and prayer-book, Shakespeare, Spenser, Coleridge, Shelley, Keats, Lowell's *Fable for Critics,* Walton's *Complete Angler,* and some Spanish books—spiritual instead of material lights, you see.

There, my dainty Lady Molly, I have given you, I fear, a wearisomely minute description of my new home. How would you like to winter in such an abode? in a place where there are no newspapers, no churches, lectures, concerts, or theaters; no fresh books, no shopping, calling, nor gossiping little tea-drinkings; no parties, no balls, no picnics, no *tableaux,* no charades, no latest fashions, no daily mail (we have an express once a month), no promenades, no rides nor drives; no vegetables but potatoes and onions, no milk, no eggs, no *nothing?* Now I expect to be very happy here. This strange, odd life fascinates me.

OUR LOG CABIN, INDIAN BAR, NOVEMBER 25, 1851

Nothing of importance has happened since I last wrote you, except that I have become a *mineress;* that is, if the having washed a pan of dirt with my own hands, and procured therefrom $3.25 in gold dust (which I shall inclose in this letter), will entitle me to the name. I can truly say, with the blacksmith's apprentice at the close of his first day's work at the anvil, that "I am sorry I learned the trade"; for I wet my feet, tore my dress, spoilt a pair of new gloves, nearly froze my fingers, got an awful headache, took cold, and lost a valuable breastpin in this my labor of love. After such melancholy self-sacrifice on my part, I trust you will duly prize my gift. I can assure you that it is the last golden handiwork you will ever receive from "Dame Shirley."

Apropos, of lady gold-washers in general—it is a common habit with people residing in towns in the vicinity of the "Diggings" to make up pleasure parties to those places. Each woman of the company will exhibit on her return at least twenty dollars of the *oro*, which she will gravely inform you she has just "panned out" from a single basinfull of the soil. This, of course, gives strangers a very erroneous idea of the average richness of auriferous dirt. I myself thought (now don't laugh) that one had but to saunter gracefully along romantic streamlets, on sunny afternoons, with a parasol and white kid gloves, perhaps, and to stop now and then to admire the scenery, and carelessly rinse out a small panfull of yellow sand (without detriment to the white kids, however, so easy did I fancy the whole process to be), in order to fill one's workbag with the most beautiful and rare specimens of the precious mineral. Since I have been here, I have discovered my mistake, and also the secret of the brilliant success of former gold-washeresses.

The miners are in the habit of flattering the vanity of their fair visitors by scattering a handful of "salt" (which, strange to say, is *exactly* the color of gold dust, and has the remarkable property of often bringing to light very, curious lumps of the ore) through the dirt before the dainty fingers touch it; and the dear creatures go home with their treasures, firmly believing that mining is the prettiest pastime in the world.

I had no idea of permitting such a costly joke to be played upon me; so I said but little of my desire to "go through the motions" of gold washing, until one day, when, as I passed a deep hole in which several men were at work, my companion requested the owner to fill a small pan, which I had in my hand, with dirt from the bedrock. This request was, of course, granted, and, the treasure having been conveyed to the edge of the river, I succeeded, after much awkward maneuvering on my own part, and considerable assistance from friend H., an experienced miner, in gathering together the above speci-fied sum. All the diggers of our acquaintance say that it is an excellent "pros-pect," even to come from the bedrock, where, naturally, the richest dirt is found. To be sure, there are now and then "lucky strikes"; such, for instance, as that mentioned in a former letter, where a person took out of a single basinfull of soil $256. But such luck is as rare as the winning of $100,000 prize in a lottery. We are acquainted with many here whose gains have *never* amounted to much more than "wages"; that is, from six to eight dollars a day. And a "claim" which yields a man a steady income of ten dollars *per diem,* is consid-ered as very valuable.

Last week there was a *post mortem* examination of two men who died very suddenly in the neighborhood. Perhaps it will sound rather barbarous when I tell you that, as there was no building upon the Bar which admitted light enough for the purpose, it was found necessary to conduct the examination in the open air, to the intense interest of the Kanakas, Indians, French, Spanish, English, Irish, and Yankees, who had gathered eagerly about the spot. Paganini Ned, with an anxious desire that Mrs.—— should be *amused* as much as possible in her mountain home, rushed up from the kitchen, his dusky face radiant with excitement, to inform me "that I could see both the bodies by just looking out of the window!" I really frightened the poor fellow by the abrupt and vehement manner in which I declined taking advantage of his kindly hint.

MAY 25, 1852

Last week I rode on horseback to a beautiful Bar called the Junction, so named from the fact that at that point the East Branch of the North Fork of Feather River unites itself with the main North Fork.

The Junction is the most beautiful of all the Bars. From the store, one can walk nearly a mile down the river quite easily. The path is bordered by a row of mingled oaks and firs—the former garlanded with mistletoe, and the latter embroidered with that exquisitely beautiful moss which I tried to describe in one of my first letters.

The little Kanaka woman lives here. I went to see her. She is quite pretty—with large, lustrous eyes, and two great braids of hair, which made me think of black satin cables, they were so heavy and massive. She has good teeth, a sweet smile, and a skin not much darker than that of a French brunette. I never saw any creature so proud as she, almost a child herself, was of her baby. In jest, I asked her to give it to me, and really was almost alarmed at the vehement burst of tears with which she responded to my request. Her husband explained the cause of her distress. It is a superstition among her people that he who refuses to give another anything, no matter what—there are no exceptions which that other may ask for—will be overwhelmed with the most dreadful misfortunes. Her own parents had parted with her for the same reason. Her pretty, girlish face soon resumed its smiles when I told her that I was in jest, and, to console me for the disappointment which she thought I must feel at not obtaining her little brown treasure, she promised to give me the *next* one! It is a Kanaka custom to make a present to the person calling upon them for the first time; in accordance with which habit, I received a pair of dove-colored boots three sizes too large for me.

From our Log Cabin, Indian Bar, August 4, 1852

We have lived through so much of excitement for the last three weeks, dear M., that I almost shrink from relating the gloomy events which have marked their flight. But if I leave out the darker shades of our mountain life, the picture will be very incomplete.

I think that even among these beautiful hills, I never saw a more perfect "bridal of the earth and sky" than that of Sunday the eleventh of July. On that morning, I went with a party of friends to the head of the "Ditch," a walk of about three miles in length. I do not believe that Nature herself ever made anything so lovely as this artificial brooklet. It glides like a living thing, through the very heart of the forest; sometimes creeping softly on, as though with muffled feet, through a wilderness of aquatic plants; sometimes dancing gaily over a white pebbled bottom; now making a "sunshine in a shady place," across the mossy roots of the majestic old trees—and anon leaping with a grand anthem, adown the great, solemn rocks, which lie along its beautiful pathway.... We returned about three in the evening, loaded with fragrant bundles which, arranged in jars, tumblers, pitcher, bottles, and pails (we are not particular as to the quality of our vases in the mountains, and love our flowers as well in their humble chalices as if their beautiful heads lay against a background of marble or porcelain), made the dark old cabin "a bower of beauty for us."

Shortly after our arrival, a perfectly deafening volley of shouts and yells elicited from my companion the careless remark, "that the customary Sabbath-day's fight was apparently more serious than usual." Almost as he spoke, there succeeded a death-like silence, broken in a minute after by a deep groan, at the corner of the cabin, followed by the words, "Why Tom, poor fellow, are you really wounded?" Before we could reach the door, it was burst violently open by a person who inquired hurriedly for the Doctor—who, luckily, happened at that very moment to be approaching. The man who called him then gave us the following excited account of what had happened. He said that in a *melee* between the Americans and the foreigners, Domingo—a tall, majestic-looking Spaniard, a perfect type of the novelistic bandit of Old Spain—had stabbed Tom Somers, a young Irishman, but a naturalized citizen of the United States—and that at the very moment, said Domingo, with a *Mejicana* hanging upon his arm, and brandishing threateningly the long, bloody knife with which he had inflicted the wound upon his victim, was parading up and down the street unmolested. It seems that when Tom Somers fell, the Americans, being unarmed, were seized with a sudden panic and fled. There was a rumor (unfounded, as it afterwards proved) to the effect that the Spaniards had on this day conspired to kill all the Americans on the river. In a few moments, however, the latter rallied and made a rush at the murderer, who immediately plunged into the river and swam across to Missouri Bar; eight or ten shots were fired at him while in the water, not one of which hit him. He ran like an antelope across the flat, swam thence to Smith's Bar, and escaped by the road leading out of the mountains from the Junction. Several men went in pursuit of him, but he was not taken, and without doubt is now safe in Mexico.

In the meanwhile, the consternation was terrific. The Spaniards, who, with the exception of six or eight, knew no more of the affair than I did, thought that the Americans had arisen against them; and our own countrymen equally ignorant, fancied the same of the foreigners. About twenty of the latter, who were either sleeping or reading in their cabins at the time of the *emeute,* aroused by the cry of "Down with the Spaniards!" barricaded themselves in a drinking-saloon, determined to defend themselves as long as possible against the massacre, which was fully expected would follow this appalling shout. In the bake-shop, which stands next door to our cabin, young Tom Somers lay straightened for the grave (he lived but fifteen minutes after he was wounded), while over his dead body a Spanish woman was weeping and moaning in the most piteous and heart-rending manner. The Rich Barians, who had heard a most exaggerated account of the rising of the Spaniards against the Americans, armed with rifles, pistols, clubs, dirks, etc., were rushing down the hill by hundreds. Each one added fuel to his rage by crowding into the little bakery to gaze upon the blood-bathed bosom of the victim, yet warm with the life which but an hour before it had so triumphantly worn. Then arose the most fearful shouts of "Down with the Spaniards!" "Drive every foreigner off the river!" "Don't let one of the murderous devils remain." "Oh, if you have a drop of American blood in your veins, it must cry out for vengeance upon the cowardly assassins of poor Tom." All this, mingled with the most horrible oaths and execrations yelled up, as if in mockery, into that smiling heaven, which in its fair Sabbath calm bent unmoved over the hell which was raging below.

After a time, the more sensible and sober part of the community succeeding in quieting, in a partial degree, the enraged and excited multitude. During the whole affair I had remained perfectly calm, in truth, much more so than I am now, when recalling it. The entire catastrophe had been so unexpected, and so sudden in its consummation, that I fancy I was stupefied into the most exemplary good behavior. F. and several of his friends, taking advantage of the lull in the storm, came into the cabin and entreated me to join the two women who were living on the hill. At this time, it seemed to be the general opinion that there would be a serious fight, and they said I might be wounded accidentally if I remained on the Bar. As I had no fear of anything of the kind, I plead hard to be allowed to stop, but when told that my presence would increase the anxiety of our friends, of course, like a dutiful wife, I went on to the hill.

We three women, left entirely alone, seated ourselves upon a log, overlooking the strange scene below. The Bar was a sea of heads, bristling with guns, rifles, and clubs. We could see nothing, but fancied from the apparent quiet of the crowd that the miners were taking measures to investigate the sad event of the day. All at once, we were startled by the firing of a gun, and the next moment, the crowd dispersing, we saw a man led into the log cabin, while another was carried, apparently lifeless, into a Spanish drinking-saloon, from one end of which were burst off instantly several boards, evidently to give air to the wounded person. Of course, we were utterly unable to imagine what had happened; and to all our perplexity and anxiety, one of the ladies insisted upon believing that it was her own husband who had been shot, and as she is a very nervous woman, you can fancy our distress. It was in vain to tell her—which we did over and over again—that that worthy individual wore a *blue* shirt, and the wounded person a *red* one; she doggedly insisted that her dear M. had been shot, and having informed us confidentially and rather inconsistently that "she should never see him again, never, never," plumped herself down upon the log in an attitude of calm and ladylike despair, which would have been infinitely amusing, had not the occasion been so truly a fearful one. Luckily for our nerves, a benevolent individual, taking pity upon our loneliness, came and told us what had happened.

It seems that an Englishman, the owner of a house of the vilest description, a person who is said to have been the primary cause of all the troubles of the day, attempted to force his way through the line of armed men which had been formed at each side of the street. The guard very properly refused to let him pass. In his drunken fury, he tried to wrest a gun from one of them, which being accidentally discharged in the struggle, inflicted a severe wound upon a Mr. Oxley, and shattered in the most dreadful manner the thigh of Señor Pizarro, a man of high birth and breeding, a *porteño* of Buenos Ayres. This frightful accident recalled the people to their senses, and they began to act a little less like madmen than they had previously done. They elected a Vigilance Committee, and authorized persons to go to the Junction and arrest the suspected Spaniards.

The first act of the Committee was to try a *Mejicana,* who had been foremost in the fray. She has always worn male attire, and on this occasion, armed with a pair of pistols, she fought like a very fury. Luckily, inexperienced in the use of fire-arms, she wounded no one. She was sentenced to leave the Bar by day-light, a perfectly just decision, for there is no doubt that she is a regular little demon. Some went so far as to say she ought to be hung, for she was the *indirect* cause of the fight. You see always, it is the old, cowardly excuse of Adam in Paradise: "The *woman* tempted me, and I did eat." As if the poor, frail head, once so pure and beautiful, had not sin enough of its own, dragging it forever downward, without being made to answer for the wrong-doing of a whole community of men.

The next day, the Committee tried five or six Spaniards, who were proven to have been the ringleaders in the Sabbath-day riot. Two of them were sentenced to be whipped, the remainder to leave the Bar that evening; the property of all to be confiscated to the use of the wounded persons. Oh Mary! imagine my anguish when I heard the first blow fall upon those wretched men. I had never thought that I should be compelled to hear such fearful sounds, and, although I immediately buried my head in a shawl, nothing can efface from memory the disgust and horror of that moment. I had heard of such things, but heretofore had not realized that in the nineteenth century men could be beaten like dogs, much less that other men not only could sentence such barbarism, but could actually stand by and see their own manhood degraded in such disgraceful manner. One of these unhappy persons was a very gentlemanly young Spaniard, who implored for death in the most moving terms. He appealed to his judges in the most eloquent manner—as gentlemen, as men of honor; representing to them that to be deprived of life was nothing in comparison with the never-to-be-effaced stain of the vilest convict's punishment—to which they had sentenced him. Finding all his entreaties disregarded, he swore a most solemn oath that he would murder every American that he should chance to meet alone, and as he is a man of the most dauntless courage, and rendered desperate by a burning sense of disgrace, which will cease only with his life, he will doubtless keep his word.

Although in my very humble opinion, and in that of others more competent to judge of such matters than myself, these sentences were unnecessarily severe, yet so great was the rage and excitement of the crowd that the Vigilance Committee could do no less. The mass of the mob demanded fiercely the death of the prisoners, and it was evident that many of the Committee took side with the people. I shall never forget how horror-struck I was (bombastic as it *now* sounds) at hearing no less a personage than the Whig candidate for representative say, "that the condemned had better fly for their lives, for the Avenger of Blood was on their tracks!" I am happy to say that said very worthy

285

but sanguinary individual, "The Avenger of Blood!"—represented in this case by some half dozen gambling rowdies—either changed his mind or lost scent of his prey; for the intended victims slept about two miles up the hill, quite peacefully until morning.

The following facts, elicited upon the trial, throw light upon this unhappy affair: Seven miners from Old Spain, enraged at the cruel treatment which their countrymen had received on the "Fourth," and at the illiberal cry of "Down with the Spaniard," had united for the purpose of taking revenge on seven Americans whom they believed to be the originators of their insults. All well armed, they came from the Junction, where they were residing at the time, intending to challenge each one his man, and in fair fight, compel their insolent aggressors to answer for the arrogance which they had exhibited more than once towards the Spanish race. Their first move on arriving at Indian Bar was to go and dine at the Humboldt, where they drank a most enormous quantity of champagne and claret. Afterwards, they proceeded to the house of the Englishman, whose brutal carelessness caused the accident which wounded Pizarro and Oxley, when one of them commenced a playful conversation with one of his countrywomen. This enraged the Englishman, who instantly struck the Spaniard a violent blow and ejected him from the shanty. Thereupon ensued a spirited fight, which, through the exertion of a gentleman from Chili, a favorite with both nations, ended without bloodshed. This person knew nothing of the intended duel, or he might have prevented, by his wise counsels, what followed. Not suspecting for a moment anything of the kind, he went to Rich Bar. Soon after he left, Tom Somers, who is said always to have been a dangerous person when in liquor, without any apparent provocation struck Domingo (one of the original seven) a violent blow, which nearly felled him to the earth. The latter, a man of "dark antecedents" and the most reckless character, mad with wine, rage, and revenge, without an instant's pause drew his knife and inflicted a fatal wound upon his insulter. Thereupon followed the chapter of accidents which I have related.

On Tuesday following the fatal Sabbath, a man brought the news of the murder of a Mr. Bacon, a person well known on the river, who kept a ranch about twelve miles from Rich Bar. He was killed for his money, by his servant, a negro, who not three months ago was our own cook. He was the last one anybody would have suspected capable of such an act.

A party of men, appointed by the Vigilance Committee, left the Bar immediately in search of him. The miserable wretch was apprehended in Sacramento and part of the gold found upon his person. On the following Sunday he was brought in chains to Rich Bar. After a trial by the miners, he was

Miner Mary McCloskey, c. 1850

sentenced to be hung at four o'clock in the evening. All efforts to make him confess proved futile. He said, very truly, that whether innocent or guilty, they would hang him; and so he "died and made no sign," with a calm indifference, as the novelists say, "worthy of a better cause." The dreadful crime and death of "Josh," who having been an excellent cook and very neat and respectful was a favorite servant with us, added to the unhappiness which you can easily imagine that I was suffering under all these horrors.

from THE DIARY OF A FORTY-NINER

CHAUNCEY L. CANFIELD, EDITOR

The Diary of a Forty-Niner, *one of the funniest and oddest gold rush memoirs, was purportedly the work of one Alfred T. Jackson, a miner who worked a claim in Rock Creek in Nevada County, California, from 1850 to 1852. Published in 1906, the book's editor, Chauncey L. Canfield, claimed "the diary gives a veracious, faithful, and comprehensive picture of the pioneer miner's life in the early Fifties." Some historians now suspect that the diary was completely cooked up by Canfield, perhaps with the help of a real miner or two. Fiction or not, it addressed one of the most overlooked aspects of the gold rush—the escape from traditional sexual roles it provided.*

MARCH 23, 1852. Out of curiosity I rode over to see the couple who live on Round Mountain, and I made a funny discovery. If one of them is not a woman dressed in men's clothes, then I don't know a woman when I see one. The cabin is a queer sort of shanty, about thirty feet long, built into the bank so that the roof comes down even with it. There are two doors, one narrow and the other five feet wide. There is a wheelbarrow track leading out of the wide door to a dump-pile of waste dirt and a Tom set in the ravine below, where, evidently, the pay dirt is washed. I could see at once that they were tunneling into the hill from the back of the cabin, although if it had not been for the dump-pile, Long Tom, and wheelbarrow track no one would have suspected that any mining was going on in the vicinity. While I was sitting on my horse taking in all this, a slight young fellow came out wheeling a barrow of dirt. He seemed startled to see me, turned his head away, dumped his dirt, pulled his hat down over his eyes, and went back through the door without even saying good morning. I started to ride away when another man appeared at the door—a long-whiskered, stout-built fellow who did not seem to be at all pleased at my being there—and asked me roughly what I wanted. I replied that I wanted nothing, was riding around the country, happened to come across the place, had halted a minute, and that was all. He turned to go back, hesitated, then looked around and asked me to get down and hitch the horse. I was so curious that I accepted the invitation and in a few minutes we were sitting out on the dump-pile in the sun chatting away like old friends.

I think he is a Western man by his accent, not that I asked any questions, not having the chance. He did the questioning, and kept me busy answering, not seeming to know anything about what was going on anywhere, neither in his own neighborhood nor abroad, and although he did not appear to be an ignorant man in a general way, he certainly lacked information on current happenings. The young fellow failed to show up, and, after an hour or so, the man excused himself for a minute—it was past noon—came back, and asked me if I would not stop for dinner. I was dying to see the inside of the cabin and accepted. Well, you never saw a neater place. Twenty feet of it was partitioned off. There was a board floor, swept and clean, a curtain to the window, paper, the edges cut in scallops, on the shelves, a home-made double bed nicely made up, and pillows. The table was covered with a table-cloth made of flour sacks sewn together, but white and clean, and the crockery all washed since breakfast. I wondered what sort of finicky miners these could be, so different in their housekeeping from the rest of us, when the young fellow began to put the grub on the table. That settled it. He had his hat off, and "he" was a woman dead sure. If there had been nothing else, the cooking would have proved it: hot biscuit, fried quail with a thin strip of bacon wrapped around them, beans, of course, but not greasy beans, a fine cup of coffee, and doughnuts. Gracious! That was the first doughnut I had eaten since leaving Connecticut.

He just introduced her as his partner without any explanation and I did not ask for any, although it looked funny to see a pretty, black-haired, black-eyed woman dressed up in a woolen shirt, overalls, and boots. I had sense enough to keep my mouth shut on the subject and we ate our dinner as if there was nothing strange in the situation. After it was over and we had smoked our pipes, she in the meantime clearing off the table and washing the dishes.... He came out with me when I got ready to go away, shook hands, and asked me to ride over again, and then said that he knew that he had the reputation of being unsociable and eccentric; that maybe he was, but if I got acquainted I would find out he was not a bad sort; that while it seemed as if there was a mystery there really wasn't, and there was not much to tell. If I made him another visit he would explain, not because he had to, but that he could understand how it looked queer to an outsider. Then he got sort of gruff and said it was nobody's business but his own, and I rode away. Pard and I talked it over and we agreed that the woman was without doubt his wife, who preferred to live with her husband in this way rather than be separated. If they wanted to lead hermit lives they had the right. Really, the only strange part of it is her dressing in men's clothes and working in the mine. I would not let any wife of mine do that sort of thing.

THE MINERS' TEN COMMANDMENTS

JAMES M. HUTCHINGS

James M. Hutchings (1818–1902), an English-born forty-niner who failed at mining, struck it rich a different way in 1853: his letter sheet "The Miners' Ten Commandments" captured the imaginations of his fellow gold rushers. Designed to be folded up and sent home as stationery, Hutchings' souvenir letter sheet sold 100,000 copies throughout California. He used his profits to launch Hutchings' California Magazine, a mix of local writing and scenic illustrations that reached a circulation of 8,000. In the 1860s Hutchings, one of the first white settlers of Yosemite, opened the valley's first hotel.

A MAN SPAKE THESE WORDS, and said: I am a miner, who wandered "from away down east," and came to sojourn in a strange land, and "see the elephant." And behold I saw him, and bear witness, that from the key of his trunk to the end of his tail, his whole body has passed before me; and I followed him until his huge feet stood still before a clapboard shanty; then with his trunk extended, he pointed to a candle-card tacked upon a shingle, as though he would say Read, and I read the

MINERS' TEN COMMANDMENTS

I. Thou shalt have no other claim than one.

II. Thou shalt not make unto thyself any false claim, nor any likeness to a mean man, by jumping one; whatever thou findest on the top above or on the rock beneath, or in a crevice underneath the rock; —or I will visit the miners around to invite them on my side; and when they decide against thee, thou shalt take thy pick and thy pan, thy shovel and thy blankets, with all that thou hast, and "go prospecting" to seek good diggings; but thou shalt find none. Then, when thou hast returned, in sorrow shalt thou find that thine old claim is worked out, and yet no pile made thee to hide in the ground, or in an old boot beneath thy bunk, or in buckskin or bottle underneath thy cabin; but hast paid all that was in thy purse away, worn out thy boots and thy garments, so that there is nothing good about them but the pockets, and thy patience is likened unto thy garments; and at last thou shalt hire thy body out to make thy board and save thy bacon.

III. Thou shalt not go prospecting before thy claim gives out. Neither shalt thou take thy money, nor thy gold dust, nor thy good name, to the gaming table in vain; for monte, twenty-one, roulette, faro, lansquenet, and poker will prove to thee that the more thou puttest down the less thou shalt take up; and when thou thinkest of thy wife and children, thou shalt not hold thyself guiltless—but insane.

IV. Thou shalt not remember what thy friends do at home on the Sabbath day, lest the remembrance may not compare favorably with what thou doest here.—Six days thou mayest dig or pick all that thy body can stand under; but the other day is Sunday; yet thou washest all thy dirty shirts, darnest all thy stockings, tap thy boots, mend thy clothing, chop thy whole week's firewood, make up and bake thy bread, and boil thy pork and beans, that thou wait not when thou returnest from thy long-tom weary. For in six days' labor only thou canst not work enough to wear out thy body in two years; but if thou workest hard on Sunday also, thou canst do it in six months; and thou, and thy son, and thy daughter, thy male friend and thy female friend, thy morals and thy conscience, be none the better for it; but reproach thee, shouldst thou ever return with thy worn-out body to thy mother's fireside; and thou shalt not strive to justify thyself, because the trader and the blacksmith, the carpenter and the merchant, the tailors, Jews, and buccaneers defy God and civilization by keeping not the Sabbath day, nor wish for a day of rest such as memory, youth, and home made hallowed.

V. Thou shalt not think more of all thy gold, and how thou canst make it fastest, than how thou wilt enjoy it, after thou hast ridden rough-shod over thy good old parents' precepts and examples, that thou mayest have nothing to reproach and sting thee, when thou are left *alone* in the land where thy father's blessing and thy mother's love hath sent thee.

VI. Thou shalt not kill thy body by working in the rain, even though thou shalt make enough to buy physic and attendance with. Neither shalt thou kill thy neighbor's body in a duel; for by "keeping cool," thou canst save his life and thy conscience. Neither shalt thou destroy thyself by getting "tight," nor "slewed," nor "high," nor "corned," nor "half-seas over," nor "three sheets in the wind," by drinking smoothly down—"brandy slings," "gin cocktails," "whisky punches," "rum-toddies," nor "egg nogs." Neither shalt thou suck "mint-julips" nor "sherry-cobblers" through a straw, nor gurgle from a bottle the "raw material," nor "take it neat" from a decanter; for, while thou art swallowing down thy purse, and thy coat from off thy back, thou art burning the coat from off thy stomach; and, if thou couldst see the houses and lands, and gold dust, and home comforts already lying there—"a huge pile"—thou shouldst feel a choking in thy throat; and when to that thou addest thy crooked walkings and hiccuping talkings, of lodgings in the gutter, of broilings in the sun, of prospect-holes half-full of water, and of shafts and ditches, from which thou hast emerged like a drowning rat, thou wilt feel disgusted with thyself, and inquire, "Is thy servant a dog that he doeth these things?" verily I will say, Farewell, old bottle, I will kiss thy gurgling lips no more. And thou, slings, cocktails, punches, smashes, cobblers, nogs, toddies, sangarecs, and julips, forever farewell. Thy remembrance shames me; henceforth, "I cut thy acquaintance," and headaches, tremblings, heart burnings, blue devils, and all the unholy catalogue of evils that follow in thy train. My wife's smiles and my children's merry-hearted laugh shall charm and reward me for having the manly firmness and courage to say *no*. I wish thee an eternal farewell.

VII. Thou shalt not grow discouraged, nor think of going home before thou hast made thy "pile," because thou hast not "struck a lead," nor found a "rich crevice," nor sunk a hole upon a "pocket," lest in going home thou shalt leave four dollars a day, and go to work, ashamed, at fifty cents, and serve thee right: for thou knowest by staying here, thou mightest strike a lead and fifty dollars a day, and keep thy manly self-respect, and then go home with enough to make thyself and others happy.

VIII. Thou shalt not steal a pick, or a shovel, or a pan from thy fellow miner; nor take away his tools without his leave; nor borrow those he cannot spare; nor return them broken, nor trouble him to fetch them back again, nor talk with him while his water rent is running on, nor remove his stake to enlarge thy claim, nor undermine his bank in following a lead, nor pan out gold from his "riffle box," nor wash the "tailings" from his sluice's mouth. Neither shalt thou pick out specimens from the company's pan to put them in thy mouth, or in thy purse; nor cheat thy partner of his share; nor steal from thy cabin-mate his gold dust, to add to thine, for he will be sure to discover what thou hast done, and will straightway call his fellow miners together, and if the law hinder them not, they will hang thee, or give thee fifty lashes, or shave thy head and brand thee, like a horse thief, with "R" upon thy cheek, to be known and read of all men, Californians in particular.

IX. Thou shalt not tell any false tales about "good diggings in the mountains" to thy neighbor that thou mayest benefit a friend who hath mules, and provisions, and tools, and blankets, he cannot sell,—lest in deceiving thy neighbor, when he returneth through the snow with naught save his rifle, he present thee with the contents thereof and, like a dog, thou shalt fall down and die.

X. Thou shalt not commit unsuitable matrimony, nor covet "single blessedness"; nor forget absent maidens; nor neglect thy "first love,"—but thou shalt consider how faithfully and patiently she awaiteth thy return; yea, and covereth each epistle that thou sendest with kisses of kindly welcome—until she hath thyself.

Neither shalt thou covet thy neighbor's wife, nor trifle with the affections of his daughter; yet, if thy heart be free, and thou dost love and covet each other, thou shalt "pop the question" like a man, lest another, more manly than thou art, should step in before thee, and thou love her in vain; and in the anguish of thy heart's disappointment, thou shalt quote the language of the great, and say, "sich is life"; and thy future lot be that of a poor, lonely, despised and comfortless bachelor.

A new Commandment give I unto thee—if thou hast a wife and little ones, that thou lovest dearer than thy life,—that thou keep them continually before thee, to cheer and urge thee onward until thou canst say, "I have enough— God bless them—I will return." Then as thou journiest towards thy much loved home, with open arms shall they come forth to welcome thee, and falling upon thy neck weep tears of unutterable joy that thou art come; then in the fullness of thy heart's gratitude, thou shalt kneel together before thy Heavenly Father, to thank Him for thy safe return. Amen—So mote it be.

FORTY-NINE

from THE HOUSEHOLD NARRATIVE
OF CURRENT EVENTS

CHARLES DICKENS, EDITOR

Foreign newspapers trumpeted the gold rush with enthusiasm. Reports from California, no matter how inaccurate, were hurriedly translated and printed—the more sensationalistic the better. The following news articles appeared in Charles Dickens' London newspaper, The Household Narrative of Current Events, *from 1850 to 1853.*

JANUARY, 1850. The rush for *California* from the United States is described as being immense. No less than three steamers, each filled with passengers, left New York for the golden land a few days before the last mail for England. Emigration to the Pacific also from New England is quite active. It is calculated that there are at present 300 ships in the Bay of San Francisco, mostly without crews; that 500 vessels have sailed from the United States for California, besides steamers; that these vessels have conveyed 50,000 passengers; and that 50,000 more have gone by land, making 100,000 in all.

MARCH, 1851. A dreadful massacre of American gold-diggers by the Indians has been perpetrated near Rattlesnake Creek. The men, seventy-two in number, were working in a chasm, and had stacked their arms, not apprehending any danger. The Indians came upon them by stealth, and having secured their arms, deliberately murdered them one by one.

APRIL, 1851. The American papers mention the repeated occurrence of *Lynch Law* in the California community. A drunken Englishman, who resided at Georgetown, lately murdered his wife by shooting her with a rifle, because she refused to give him money to gamble with. It being Sunday, and the streets full of people, the house instantly filled. The wife was a decent woman, who had supported her family by her industry, and her fate roused the indignation of the multitude. The man was seized, and hurried to an eminence overlooking the town. The people were persuaded to wait till an investigation should take place; the coroner was sent for, and, to save time, a jury was selected to be

"Working in California" as imagined in France, c. 1850

ready for his arrival. But the patience of the mob soon gave way; they dispersed the jury, seized the man, and carried him off to hang from the branch of a tree. At the head of the procession the murderer marched to his gallows, and the body of his wife was borne close behind him. A small box, marked "For the Orphans," was nailed to the tree, and many an ounce was poured into it from the purses of those who followed the father to his death. The body of the murdered woman was lowered into a wide pit, and, even while the wretched man gazed upon it, the cord suddenly tightened around his neck, and he swayed in the air. The mob sat on the hillside, and sternly watched him. At the end of half an hour he was cut down, and laid in the grave by the side of his wife. In the evening the coroner arrived, and, upon hearing the story, summoned his jury for morning. They met at sunrise upon the hill, and stood around the unfilled grave, while the end of a cut cord dangled above their heads. After a few words had been exchanged, and, after laying a slip of paper upon each of the bodies, they proceeded to fill up the grave. Upon one of the slips was written, "Murdered by—Divine, her husband," and upon the other, "Died according to the will of God and justice of men."

SEPTEMBER, 1853. A relic of antiquity has been discovered in *California* which seems to rival the Pyramids of Egypt in age and magnitude. It is thus described in a Californian paper, the *Placerville Herald:*—A party of men, five in number, had ascended the Colorado for nearly 200 miles above the mouth of the Gila, their object being to discover, if possible, some large tributary from the west, by which they might make the passage of the desert, and enter California by a new, more direct, and easier route, inasmuch as there are known to exist numerous small streams upon the eastern slope of the mountains, that are either lost in the sands of the desert or unite with the Colorado, through tributaries heretofore unknown.... An object appeared upon the plain to the west, having so much the appearance of a work of art, from the regularity of its outline and its isolated position, that the party determined upon visiting it. Passing over an almost barren sand plain, a distance of nearly five miles, they reached the base of one of the most wonderful objects, considering its location, it being the very home of desolation, that the mind can possibly conceive of, nothing less than an immense stone pyramid, composed of layers or courses of from eighteen inches to nearly three feet in thickness, and from five to eight feet in length. It has a level top of more than fifty feet square, though it is evident that it was once completed, but that some great convulsion of nature has displaced its entire top, as it evidently now lies a huge and broken mass upon one of its sides, though nearly covered by the sands.

This pyramid differs, in some respects, from the Egyptian pyramids. It is, or was, more slender or pointed; and, while those of Egypt are composed of steps or layers, receding as they rise, the American pyramid was, undoubtedly a more finished structure. The outer surface of the blocks was evidently cut to an angle, that gave the structure, when new and complete, a smooth or regular surface from top to bottom. From the present level of the sands that surround it, there are fifty-two distinct layers of stone, that will average at least two feet; this gives its present height one hundred and four feet, so that before the top was displaced it must have been, judging from an angle of its sides, at least twenty feet higher than at present. How far it extends beneath the surface of the sands it is impossible to determine without great labour. Such is the age of this immense structure that the perpendicular joints between the blocks are worn away to the width of from five to ten inches at the bottom of each joint, and the entire of the pyramid so much worn by the storms, the vicissitudes, and the corrodings of centuries, as to make it easy of ascent, particularly upon one of its sides.

from THE JOURNAL OF HENRY D. THOREAU

HENRY DAVID THOREAU

Henry David Thoreau (1817–1862), born in Concord, Massachusetts, graduated from Harvard in 1837. A transcendentalist and adamant nonconformist, he lived for two years in a self-built cabin at Walden Pond in Massachusetts and was once jailed overnight for protesting slavery by refusing to pay a poll tax. Walden and Civil Disobedience, his two most famous works, resulted from these experiences. Thoreau began keeping a journal in the 1830s at the suggestion of his friend Ralph Waldo Emerson, and it eventually reached more than two million words and filled fourteen volumes. Thoughtful and iconoclastic, Thoreau was not fully appreciated until years after his death. This excerpt from his journal was dated February 1, 1852.

THE RECENT RUSH TO CALIFORNIA and the attitude of the world, even of its philosophers and prophets, in relation to it appears to me to reflect the greatest disgrace on mankind. That so many are ready to get their living by the lottery of gold-digging without contributing any value to society, and that the great majority who stay at home justify them in this both by precept and example! It matches the infatuation of the Hindoos who have cast themselves under the car of Juggernaut. I know of no more startling development of the morality of trade and all the modes of getting a living than the rush to California affords. Of what significance the philosophy, or poetry, or religion of a world that will rush to the lottery of California gold-digging on the receipt of the first news, to live by luck, to get the means of commanding the labor of others less lucky, *i.e.* of slaveholding, without contributing any value to society? And that is called enterprise, and the devil is only a little more enterprising! The philosophy and poetry and religion of such a mankind are not worth the dust of a puffball. The hog that *roots* his own living, and so makes manure, would be ashamed of such company. If I could command the wealth of all the worlds by lifting my finger, I would not pay such a price for it. It makes God to be a moneyed gentleman who scatters a handful of pennies in order to see mankind scramble for them. Going to California. It is only three thousand miles nearer to hell. I will resign my life sooner than live by luck. The world's raffle. A subsistence in the domains of nature a thing to be raffled for! No wonder that they gamble there. I never heard that they did anything else there. What a comment, what a satire, on our institutions! The conclusion will be that mankind will hang itself upon a tree. And who would interfere to cut it down. And have all the precepts in all the bibles taught men only this? and is the last and most admirable invention of the Yankee race only an improved muck-rake?— patented too!

If one came hither to sell lottery tickets, bringing satisfactory credentials, and the prizes were seats in heaven, this world would buy them with a rush.

Did God direct us so to get our living, digging where we never planted,— and He would perchance reward us with lumps of gold? It is a text, oh! for the Jonahs of this generation, and yet the pulpits are as silent as immortal Greece, silent, some of them, because the preacher is gone to California himself. The gold of California is a touchstone which has betrayed the rottenness, the baseness, of mankind. Satan, from one of his elevations, showed mankind the kingdom of California, and they entered into a compact with him at once.

from THE CONDUCT OF LIFE

RALPH WALDO EMERSON

Ralph Waldo Emerson (1803–1882) was born in Boston and studied divinity at Harvard. He became an ordained Unitarian minister before suffering a crisis of faith in 1831. As a lecturer, essayist, and editor he led the New England transcendentalist movement in questioning traditional religion and literature. He was an important influence on a generation of thinkers and authors that included Henry David Thoreau, Walt Whitman, Nathaniel Hawthorne, and Herman Melville. The Conduct of Life *was published in 1860.*

I DO NOT THINK very respectfully of the designs or the doings of the people who went to California in 1849. It was a rush and a scramble of needy adventurers, and, in the western country, a general jail delivery of all the rowdies of the rivers. Some of them went with honest purposes, some with very bad ones, and all of them with the very commonplace wish to find a short way to wealth. But nature watches over all, and turns this malfeasance to good. California gets peopled and subdued, civilized in this immoral way, and on this fiction a real prosperity is rooted and grown. 'Tis a decoy-duck; 'tis tubs thrown to amuse the whale; but real ducks, and whales that yield oil, are caught. And out of Sabine rapes, and out of robbers' forays, real Romes and their heroisms come in fulness of time.

In America the geography is sublime, but the men are not: the inventions are excellent, but the inventors one is sometimes ashamed of. The agencies by which events so grand as the opening of California, of Texas, of Oregon, and the junction of the two oceans, are effected, are paltry,—coarse selfishness, fraud and conspiracy; and most of the great results of history are brought about by discreditable means.

from A LADY'S SECOND JOURNEY ROUND THE WORLD

IDA PFEIFFER

Ida Pfeiffer was born to a wealthy merchant in Vienna, Austria, in 1797. She traveled extensively in her youth and published travelogues of the Holy Land and Iceland before visiting San Francisco in 1853. She made three excursions into gold country and spent a few days in Sacramento and Marysville. Her A Lady's Second Journey Round the World, *published in 1855, provided a sophisticated European perspective on the decidedly unsophisticated gold rush.*

SAN FRANCISCO IS UNANIMOUSLY declared the City of Wonders, and the Americans maintain that its rapid rise, and repeated rebuilding after the fires, are among the most wonderful things the world has seen. There are, indeed, only two forces capable of effecting such wonders—gold and despotism. The former has been the lever in this case; for the thirst of gold, which is the greatest of despots, has drawn people hither from all corners of the earth, and dwellings of wood and stone have arisen for them as if by magic. But what are all these simple works compared with the antique cities of Hindostan, the ruins of which even still attest their magnificence, and which are stated to have been built in a no less incredibly short time. Look, for instance, at Fahpoor Sikri, a town full of the most beautiful palaces, covered with sculptures—of magnificent temples, with minarets, and with high-arched gates, and so forth—the circumference of which, of six miles, was surrounded by a massive stone wall forty feet high; and all this was done in less than ten years. Such works as this are indeed marvelous, for they must have required a whole population of artists and architects for their execution.

The wonders of San Francisco consist of quite ordinary little dwelling-houses, for the building of which the gold-mines of California have furnished, and continue to furnish, sufficient means.

Of the hillocks, holes, and unevenness of all kinds in the streets of this town, no one who has not seen it can form an idea. Here you go up steps, there down steps. In one place the road has been raised, but on going a little further, you find it as nature made it. Some places have been dug out, and whole mountains of bricks, stones, wood, lime, and sand left lying in the road, with no light near them at night to give warning to the unwary. This makes the roads after dark, not only for driving, but even for foot-passengers, positively dangerous; and especially is this the case on the wooden quays, for the sea beneath them has not been filled up, and the boards are so worn and rotten that they often break in.... In the finest and most frequented parts of the town, you see old clothes and rags, crockery, boots, bottles, boxes, dead dogs and cats, and enormous rats (in which the town is particularly rich), and all kinds of filth flung before the doors.

Sometimes the inconveniences are more serious. One morning as I was walking in the street, a passenger who met me suddenly called out "A bear! a bear!" I could not think what he meant; for that it should be really a bear in the streets of a populous town seemed quite incredible. I looked round in all directions, however, and, on looking back, beheld actually a bear running toward me. He was, indeed, fastened to a rope, and the rope to a caravan; but they had allowed him so very long a tether, that he was quite at liberty to introduce himself among the passengers on both sides of the way. The owner was not even troubling himself to warn them, and I had barely time to make my escape.

A walk in San Francisco, in short, either for business or pleasure, is a real penance. In what is called the business part of the town, you can hardly make your way through for the throng of carts, carriages, horsemen, and pedestrians; and where the streets are not paved with boards, you have to wade through sand a foot deep; and all the while you have no better prospect before your eyes than the naked, monotonous sand-hills.

I made three excursions from San Francisco to the interior of California; the first to Sacramento, Marysville, and the gold-mines of the Yuba River.

The American steamers are the finest imaginable, and certainly deserve the title often given them of water-palaces. They look indeed more like houses than ships. The river steamers especially are several stories high, with large doors, windows, and galleries; and the convenience and splendor of the internal fittings and furniture fully correspond with the impression made by the outside view. When you meet one of them at night on the water, they look like enchanted castles, for all their windows are illuminated, and their chimneys vomit fire like volcanoes.

This was the first time I had ever found myself in a large party of Americans, and, as in the gambling houses of San Francisco, the first thing that struck me was the strange contrasts in dress. The ladies were all in grand state, and might have gone into full-dressed parties without changing their traveling costume; but the case was widely different with the gentlemen. Some few were well dressed, but the majority wore jackets, often torn ones, dirty boots pulled up over their trowsers, and had hands so extraordinarily coarse and burned—even the best-dressed gentlemen among them—that they looked as if they belonged to the commonest plowman.

The company passed the time in playing cards and chewing tobacco, without excepting even boys of ten and twelve years old; but they did not spit about at the dreadful rate described by many travelers. They had another practice, however, if possible still more abominable—namely, though they carried a pocket-handkerchief, of making use of their fingers instead of it.

I actually saw this atrocity committed by quite elegantly dressed men.

If, however, in these points they fell grievously short, in another they maintained without any exception the character of gentlemen.

The men, one and all, showed the utmost attention and politeness to our sex. Old or young, rich or poor, well or ill dressed, every woman was treated with respect and kindness; and in this the Americans are far in advance of my countrymen, and indeed of Europeans in general, who usually keep their civilities for youth, beauty, and fine clothes.

The company remained a very little while at table, and spoke scarcely a word. They really did not give themselves time to eat their food properly, but bolted it burning hot and not half-chewed, although nobody had any thing to do when the meal was over. They seem to have got into the habit of regarding every thing as business, and therefore to be performed with the utmost possible dispatch.

from IN CAMP AND CABIN

JOHN STEELE

John Steele (1832–1905), a Methodist minister and Union soldier during the Civil War, came overland to California in 1850. His commentary on colorful gold rush society, In Camp and Cabin, *was published in 1901 and included this account of mail delivery at the eternally crowded Sacramento post office.*

MONDAY, MARCH 24 [1851]. I am quite sure that at this time there was not a post office in the mines. Letters for miners were addressed to Sacramento, and of course the mail arriving here was immense, and when we reached the office the crowd was too great for us to approach the delivery during the day.

The next morning we were there an hour before the time of opening, but the crowd seemed just as great as ever, so we retired again, and spent part of the day in visiting Sutter's Fort.

The condition of this post office is altogether unique. It opens at eight in the morning and closes at eight in the evening. There is a delivery window for nearly every letter of the alphabet, and at each there is a row of people, often reaching more than around the block. When so many come in person for their mail it is simply overwhelming, and when it comes time to close the office, the lines break up, each to take his chances another day. But as hope deferred makes the heart sick, so, many who came a great distance and waited long are compelled to turn away still enduring their anxious suspense.

Recently people have adopted the plan of having their mail addressed, "By express to Nevada, Coloma," or wherever they may be. Thus the postmaster at Sacramento can send the mail by responsible express agents to the various mining towns and greatly relieve the office.

MONDAY, MARCH 31. This morning about one o'clock we arrived at the post office and found a large number in waiting. The line facing the *S* delivery window already extended halfway around the block.

Taking my place in the line, I waited until the office opened, and as the line in front melted away, moved forward. Of course each one of our little company sought the delivery according to name. This put us into different lines, and as we approached the window men came and tried to buy a place in the

Nevada City, c. 1855

line, offering twenty-five and fifty dollars, and I was told that even a hundred dollars had been paid for a place near the delivery. The one who sold his place stepped from the line and went to the extreme rear, or else waited until the office closed and night had shortened the line, and again found a place. Many who were near the delivery when the office closed, remained, holding their place until it opened in the morning.

At last I reached the delivery, and the busy clerk, after looking over a vast pile of mail matter, handed out what belonged to me. Gladly I got out of the way and, hurrying to our room, scanned the familiar writing, and with a strange tremor read the first letters I had received from home and friends since leaving them more than a year before. My companions also received considerable mail, and we spent a portion of the day in answering letters.

from I HEAR THE HOGS IN MY KITCHEN

MARY BALLOU

Gold rush women discovered they could make a living in California using the skills they already possessed from their lives in the east. They worked as cooks, teachers, laundresses, stage coach drivers, entertainers, merchants, and miners. Mary Ballou left two sons in New Hampshire and sailed with her husband to California in 1851. According to her journal, they stopped at Panama for two weeks and Ballou made twelve dollars sewing pants. They arrived in San Francisco in 1852 and settled in "Negrobar" near Sacramento, where she kept a boarding house for miners. Her letters, written to her sons, illustrate the daily concerns of one of the gold rush's many working women.

CALIFORNIA NEGROBAR
OCTOBER 30, 1852

My Dear Selden,

We are about as usual in health. Well I suppose you would like to know what I am doing in this gold region. Well I will try to tell you what my work is here in this muddy Place. All the kitchen that I have is four posts stuck down into the ground and covered over the top with factory cloth—no floor but the ground. This is a Boarding House kitchen. There is a floor in the dining room and my sleeping room coverd with nothing but cloth. We are at work in a Boarding House.

OCT. 27. This morning I awoke and it rained in torrents. Well I got up and I thought of my House. I went and looket into my kitchen. The mud and water was over my Shoes. I could not go into the kitchen to do any work to day but kept perfectly dry in the Dining, so I got along verry well. Your Father put on his Boots and done the work in the kitchen.

I will try to tell you what my work is in this Boarding House. Well sometimes I am washing and Ironing, somtimes I am making mince pie and Apple pie and squash pies. Somtimes frying mince turnovers and Donuts. I make Buiscuit and now and then Indian jonny cake and then again I am making minute puding filled with rasons and Indian Bake pudings and then again a nice Plum Puding and then again I am Stuffing a Ham of pork that cost forty cents a pound. Somtimes I am making gruel for the sick now and then cooking oisters, somtimes making coffee for the French people strong enough for any man to walk on that has Faith as Peter had. Three times a day I set my Table which is about thirty feet in length and do all the little fixings about it such as filling pepper boxes and vinegar cruits and mustard pots and Butter cups. Somtimes I am feeding my chickens and then again I am scareing the Hogs out of my kitchen and driving the mules out of my Dining room.

Last night there a large rat came down pounce down onto our bed in the night. Somtimes I take my fan and try to fan myself but I work so hard that my Arms pain me so severely that I kneed some one to fan me so I do not find much comfort anywhere. I made a Bluberry puding to day for Dinner. Somtimes I am making soups and cramberry tarts and Baking chicken that cost four Dollars a head and cooking Eggs at three Dollars a Dozen. Somtimes boiling cabbage and Turnips and frying fritters and Broiling stake and cooking codfish and potatoes. I often cook nice Salmon trout that weigh from ten to twenty pound apiece. Somtimes I am taking care of Babies and nursing at the rate of Fifty Dollars a week but I would not advise any Lady to come out here and suffer the toil and fatigue that I have suffered for the sake of a little gold— neither do I advise any one to come. Clarks Simmon wife says if she was safe in the States she would not care if she had not one cent. She came in here last night and said, "Oh dear I am so homesick that I must die," and then again my other associate came in with tears in her eyes and said that she had cried all day. She said if she had as good a home as I had got she would not stay twenty five minutes in California. I told her that she could not pick up her duds in that time. She said she would not stop for duds nor anything else but my own heart was two sad to cheer them much.

Now I will tell you a little more about my cooking. Somtimes I am cooking rabbits and Birds that are called quails here and I cook squrrels. Occasionly I run in and have a chat with Jane and Mrs Durphy and I often have a hearty cry. No one but my maker knows my feelings. And then I run into my little cellar which is about four feet square as I have no other place to run that is cool.

I will tell you a little of my bad feelings. On the 9 of September there was a little fight took place in the store. I saw them strike each other through the window in the store. One went and got a pistol and started towards the other man. I never go into the store but your mother's tender heart could not stand that so I ran into the store and Beged and plead with him not to kill him for eight or ten minutes not to take his Life, for the sake of his wife and three little

Woman visiting miners at Auburn Ravine, 1852

children to spare his life and then I ran through the Dining room into my sleeping room and Buried my Face in my bed so as not to hear the sound of the pistol and wept Biterly. Oh I thought if I had wings how quick I would fly to the States. That night at the supper table he told the Boarders if it had not been for what that Lady said to him Scheles would have been a dead man. After he got his pashion over he said that he was glad that he did not kill him, so you see that your mother has saved one Human being's Life. You see that I am trying to relieve all the suffering and trying to do all the good that I can.

There I hear the Hogs in my kichen turning the Pots and kettles upside down so I must drop my pen and run and drive them out. So you [see], this is the way that I have to write—jump up every five minutes for somthing and then again I washed out about a Dollars worth of gold dust the fourth of July in the cradle so you see that I am doing a little mining in this gold region but I think it harder to rock the cradle to wash out gold than it is to rock the cradle for the Babies in the States.

from Voyage Médical en Californie

PIERRE GARNIER

French physician Dr. Pierre Garnier (1819–1901) sailed to Monterey in 1851 with the La Fortune Company, one of the hundreds of privately financed European mining enterprises that hoped to make a fortune in the California mines. Garnier, the company doctor, visited many American hospitals between Monterey and San Francisco. California, which had only eleven trained physicians in the hundred years before U.S. annexation, saw a glut of doctors arrive during the gold rush. Many, as Garnier observed, were unqualified; some were undeniable quacks. He returned to Paris sixteen months after arriving and published Voyage Médical en Californie *in 1854.*

NO LAW REGULATES the healing arts in the land of gold. The practice of medicine and pharmacy is absolutely free and unlimited, and the first comer can take up either or both. The only limitation placed upon those operating public medical shops is the purchase of a monthly license like any other tradesman.

The Americans, in fact, who are in the great majority here, express their natural Yankee predilection for liberty and the free practice of medicine by spontaneously giving the title of doctor to anyone who practices medicine or who desires to be so called. When they are ill they go to the first person with the title of doctor and never require further credentials. Furthermore, ignorant of the true doctor's role, they usually demand a quick cure for a disease which they themselves diagnose. They refuse to permit a complete physical examination to which they are not accustomed, and reject simple manual examinations as well. They prefer a doctor who simply sells them his medicines.

The spread of this easy freedom of medical practice, either by preventing or abolishing any protective or informational public action, is further abetted by another factor: the very nature of the California population. It is almost exclusively composed of foreigners of every country and nationality, ignorant of each other's customs, language, religion, tastes, and habits. They live isolated from one another, with no common ties, sharing nothing in common except the lust for gold which really only divides them the more. Then there is also the egoistic character fostered by this mercenary country, and the unstable and nomadic life which frequent and sudden changes of fortune imposes.

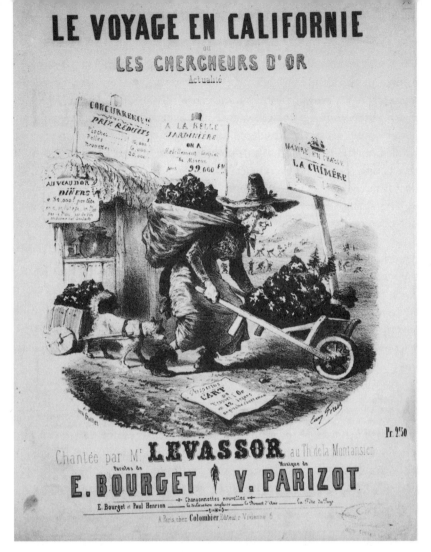

French songsheet "Le Voyage en Californie," c. 1850

These false men of medicine are practically the same everywhere. One of them who owned a "drugstore" at San José also began to sell groceries, oil, and candles. Another kept a rooming house. An Italian wig-maker, improving on tradition, became a doctor and a pharmacist. It is true that he had picked up this tradition of ancient barbers while traveling in South America, where barbers still apply leeches and practice bleeding; I saw several barber's signs in Valparaíso similar to those of our midwives at home.

These tradesmen in the large towns usually operate so-called "drug stores" which look like pharmacies.

Usually they run another business as well, either openly or secretly. Some gamble or run gambling halls; others are money-changers, traders, specula-tors, etc. I saw a drugstore on Commercial Wharf in San Francisco where the pharmacist's symbol of colored waters outside paralleled the shining wine and liquor bottles on the bar inside; a "doctor" held consultations in the bar and handed out medicines at the same counter where he poured his drinks. Simi-lar examples are found everywhere, and especially in the mines where a real doctor rarely practices his profession.

This strange mercantile spirit which Europeans find difficult to accept is not offensive to Americans nor alien to their accustomed views of liberty. Once they are officially approved as a result of a cash payment, which in America is too often the basis for liberty, these self-appointed doctors receive the same protection as men in more useful and more moral employment. They can pursue success by any means. To this end they go to any lengths to advertise and extol their cures through every channel of publicity. Newspaper advertising is very popular and is uncensored by Americans. Next come post-ers, pamphlets, and sign-boards, where the clumsiest of traps are laid to catch the public. Advertisements concerning venereal disease and women's ills are the most prevalent.

Dentists are the greatest charlatans of all. They are very numerous and their task is still the most rewarding of all the healing arts. All dental procedures are highly priced; five to six *piastres* or more are charged for each extraction, although the French barber on the big wharf at San Francisco has lowered his price to four *piastres* (about twenty-one *francs*). This leads me to a brief, prac-tical observation: the Yankees have bad teeth and need frequent dental atten-tion. One seldom finds a jaw among them in good condition. The Spanish, on the other hand, have beautiful and healthy teeth. This unfortunate contrast between the two may result from the fact that, while both smoke excessively, the Yankees chew a great deal of tobacco.

In short, there are no medical associations, societies, or unions, and in San Francisco there is no library or scientific journal, not even a French medical magazine. Intellectual life and stimulation so necessary to the European doc-tor, instead of providing some healthy diversion from his personal privations in these circumstances, are so lacking that his misery and discouragement are only increased and intensified. I cannot better convey the sad state in which most of these doctors find themselves than by repeating the one wish ex-pressed by many of them, a sterile wish, alas, for most: to occupy once more the same position, however precarious, that they formerly held in their own countries.

310

from THE LAND OF GOLD: REALITY VERSUS FICTION

HINTON HELPER

Hinton Helper (1829–1909), a struggling writer from North Carolina, visited California and was unimpressed with what he saw. He viciously attacked gold rush society in The Land of Gold: Reality Versus Fiction, *published in 1855. Lingering over details of California licentiousness and depravity, Helper's tract sold well in the East and launched his writing career.* The Impending Crisis of the South, *written by Helper two years later, argued against slavery on the sole basis of economic benefit to whites. It placed him in the center of a national controversy, bolstered by various charges of embezzlement that followed him his entire life.*

LET US NOW BRIEFLY CONSIDER the moral and religious state of society in California. We know that we are undertaking an ungrateful and painful task—that we shall awaken the animosity of those who have an interest in enticing settlers and that we shall provoke contradiction—but we beseech Heaven to pardon us for speaking the Truth, and challenge our antagonists to disprove our statements.

We cannot pretend to disclose all the terrible iniquity of that society in the compass of a single chapter—the theme is too extensive, the facts too revolting. It requires space to unfold the scroll which records such damning facts, and time is needed for the mind to become sufficiently reconciled to the hideous details, to be able to listen to them without impatience or disgust. Suffice it to say that we know of no country in which there is so much corruption, villainy, outlawry, intemperance, licentiousness, and every variety of crime, folly, and meanness.

How much of this is attributable to the metal which attracts the population, we leave others to determine. It is certain, however, that gold mining districts do not generally enjoy a very enviable reputation in any part of the world and that they attract the most unthrifty and dissolute men who could not be induced to work at any thing else. Hence, the immediate neighborhood of a gold-mine is liable to be a sink for all the idleness and depravity of the surrounding country.

311

In the Atlantic states gold mining is only a branch of industry, and not a very important one compared with the other pursuits of the population. In California it is the chief occupation of the inhabitants of the mining districts. While in the former place the general virtue of the people keeps in check the particular vices of the miner, in the latter the good intentions of the few are overruled and stifled by the many.

We must not, however, commit the mistake of supposing that all the depravity of California is attributable to the nature of its industrial pursuits. This is but one of the elements which assist in producing the deplorable state of affairs under consideration. There are others which spring from the character of the people and the circumstances which brought them together.

It must be borne in mind that all the adventurers to this country have come for the express purpose of making money, and a large majority of them are of a class who are rarely troubled by any qualms of conscience. Mammon is their god and they will worship him.

Another very important cause of this wild excitement, degeneracy, dissipation, and deplorable condition of affairs may be found in the disproportion of the sexes—in the scarcity of women. The women are persecuted by the insulting attentions of the men, and too often fall victims to the arts of their seducers. Nowhere is the sanctity of the domestic hearth so ruthlessly violated as in California. For proof of this we need look no further than the records of the courts of San Francisco. They show that in the course of a single week no less than ten divorces had been granted, while during the same time only two marriages had been solemnized! (It will be seen that, at this rate of divorce and marriage, there will soon be left no married people to obtain divorces, which would probably cause a lot of confusion.)

Not long since, an English gentleman came to me requesting me not to let his wife draw any money from his account inasmuch as she had left him the day before. After finishing his business instructions, he gave us the following history. Listen to it. Said he: "Four years ago, myself and wife and six other men with their wives came together in one vessel to this country. Soon family feuds and jealousies became rife in the domestic circle of one of the parties. The man and his wife separated. Then their example was followed by another couple, and another, and so on, until all the marriage ties of our company were broken except those that happily existed between myself and wife. Having been true to each other so long I cherished the hope that we might remain together and be true to the end. But my fond thoughts and anticipations have proved a sickly dream. My hopes have been blasted, my happiness wrecked, and my children disgraced and deserted. My wife, whom I loved and held dearer than all else on earth, has been basely seduced. The last link that bound the remnant of our seven families together has been severed and we are a disbanded and disreputable people. Cursed be the day that started me to this damnable country!" These were his own words, almost verbatim, and he uttered them as if partly speaking to himself and partly addressing me.

The total disregard of the marriage tie by the majority of the men of California puts the husband, who is foolish enough to take his wife with him to that country, in a painful and embarrassing position.

Should the wife be pretty, she is more liable to the persecution of attentions which will shock her if she be virtuous, and flatter into sin if she is not. She is surrounded by hosts of men who spare neither money, time, nor art to win her affections from her husband. What wonder if they often succeed?

Many women of conceded respectability in California seem to have come out there for the exclusive purpose of selling their charms to the highest bidder. Others, of more honest hearts, have fallen victims to the peculiar seductions of the place.

But I must be allowed to pay a tribute to the sex. They have undoubtedly banished much barbarism, softened many hearts, and given a gentleness to the men which they did not possess before.

from CALIFORNIA IN-DOORS AND OUT

ELIZA FARNHAM

Eliza Farnham (1815–1864) was a feminist, abolitionist, and prison reformer. Her husband left their home in Illinois in 1839 to practice law in Oregon and, later, San Francisco. Farnham, rather than going with him, devoted herself to social reform in the East and served as a matron of women at New York's Sing Sing prison. A year after her husband died in 1848, she distributed a high-profile circular declaring her intent to take one hundred "intelligent, virtuous, and efficient women" to California as proper brides for the unruly forty-niners. News of her plan spread across the globe, resulting in disappointment when she arrived in San Francisco in 1849 with only two women. Fiercely independent, she married again in California, only to divorce and move back to New York in 1858, where she wrote and lectured until her death from tuberculosis at age forty-nine. In California In-Doors and Out *(1856), the second of her three autobiographies, she declared that tales of gold rushers' unfailing respect for women were nothing but myth.*

THERE IS VERY LITTLE valuable addition brought to the mental life by any trait or influence of California at this time. It is rare to meet with a man or woman who seems at all stirred by any but the money phase of the country; and it is almost literally true that there is no conversation except upon that subject, and, among females, upon the adventures of emigration; the different routes and their hardships, and the oppressive sense they suffer from lack of confidence and mutual respect in the communities that surround them. This feature of California life is very painful to large numbers of both sexes, but is especially so to the sensitive and self-respecting of our own who reside in the towns and cities. I have been struck with it, in the conversations I have had with good women in every walk of life here, except the favored few whose lots were cast in homes protected from the approach of suspicion and slander.

Magnificent as is nature here, grand as is the scale of her operations, and lavish as she is of all that can furnish material comfort, or external consolations, there will, I fear, be little in the social and moral life of the country for

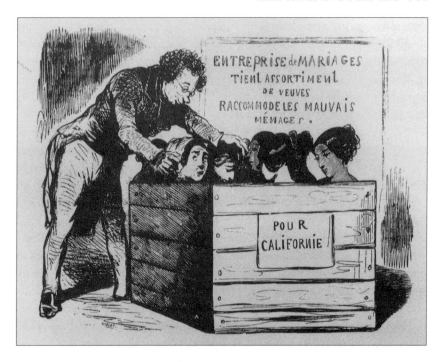

"Mr. Williaume exporting to California what is excessively in demand," c. 1850, by Cham

many years to invite those whose natures expose them to suffering from these causes. And yet only in the presence of women is to be found the efficient remedy for these great evils. The martyr women of California will one day have an honorable place assigned them, when history shall fill her noblest office and truthfully interpret the motives that lead to noble actions. For they come regardless of the trials and dangers that await them; every steamer sends its precious freight throughout the length and breadth of our borders. The home, holiest and purest nursery of what is good in the heart, springs up everywhere before woman. In town and country, cañon and ravine, on mountain and in valley, the sacred temple rises at the bidding of this true missionary of love and purity. Her presence is the guarantee for the best manifestation of his nature of which man is capable, amid the influences which here surround him; and bad as it often is, we may rest assured that without her it would be inconceivably worse.

There is no country in the world where the highest attributes of the female character are more indispensable to the social weal than in California; for nowhere else have the indomitable energies, the quick desires, and the wide-reaching purposes of the Saxon nature been submitted to so severe a test of their self-regulating power. And it is the pride of American women to feel that their countrymen stand first among the nations of men, in their susceptibility to all that is noble and holy in the character of woman. The loyalty that other nations pay to kings and queens, to old institutions, and to superiority of caste, is paid by them to woman—to the wife, mother, sister, daughter, friend, or stranger who is in a position to claim it.

The woman who presided virtuously over a home in the earlier periods of the gold emigration is entitled, I think, to look back from the remainder of her life upon a good work well done; and if, to integrity, she added the charms of gentleness, kindness, and self-restraint under the exposure and toils which were generally shared by the sex in those days, the greater her self-gratulation may be.

There is an exquisite and touching story to be told some day of the unwearied devotion and faithfulness of another woman, whose name I am not at liberty to use, though it ought to be held in honor by all true hearts; who, setting out an invalid from her home in Iowa, became—as her strong husband's will and energies failed under the tremendous sufferings of that terrible journey—the efficient care-taker of him and their three sons; yoked and un-yoked the oxen, gathered fuel, cooked their food, and divided her scanty share, when their supplies were short, with those whose very veins she would have exhausted her own to fill, had it been necessary or possible.

She drove the teams, hunted wood and water in men's boots and tattered clothing, and for months performed all the coarser offices that properly belong to the other sex, and reached her journey's end a gentle, soft-spoken woman, with manners as unsoiled by her hard experience, as truly feminine and sweet, as if the refinements and ease of the drawing-room had surrounded her, instead of the dreary horrors and coarse tasks of those dreadful months. One must love such a woman. When I think of her I can appreciate the feelings which, in early times, exalted characters of such rare beauty to a place in the calendar. Reverence, love, and gratitude ought to flow from the hearts of her family toward her, as richly and freely as odor from the rose, or light from the sun.

I would not invite or encourage any of my sex to emigration without having previously advised them of the pains and perils attendant upon it; but, having done this, I must in faithfulness say to those who leave families here, and who possess sufficient courage, devotion, and firmness to make their presence a blessing instead of a curse to them, that they cannot know how greatly remiss they are in continuing the separation which may already have worked lasting mischief to some of those who have suffered it. Come to the country which is the home of those you are bound to adhere to and save, when they are ready to receive you. Come strong in the resolution to be true to yourselves and to them, under all trials; to put away pining and discontent, and face your hardest fortune bravely, so that they share it with you; so that you find your presence is not without that saving influence which men everywhere more or less need, but which scarcely the strongest and best among them may be safely deprived of here.

Discouraged, hardened, made reckless of the most sacred duties, a man so situated can only be preserved by the rarest purity, self-respect, and firmness from giving himself up to the lawless habits and vile allurements that surround him. If he do not become openly debauched, he finds his former integrity and fidelity to himself and his family superseded by an indifference to all consideration of them, and a readiness to wink at habits and indulgences in others, which, till he felt himself forsaken, he would have regarded and, perhaps, reproved as criminal. I cannot forbear saying, then, to my countrywomen, that if they have the natures which can pass unscathed through the furnace seven times heated, every unselfish consideration, every sentiment of duty binds them to follow here, as they would cleave elsewhere, to those who have the first claim on them. And come not with the expectation of being surrounded by luxury and nursed in the comforts and indulgences of an older social condition. Many of these, many of them, you will lack for a long period, some for your whole life, should it be spent here. But this consideration does not absolve you, nor will it heal your wounded hearts and consciences, when you find those whose earthly salvation you were bound to conserve, quite separated from your ways and influence, quite regardless of their own and your best good.

from THE JOURNAL OF
GEORGIANA BRUCE KIRBY, 1852–1860

GEORGIANA BRUCE KIRBY

Born in England, Georgiana Bruce Kirby (1818–1887) moved to Canada at age sixteen. After several years with the abolitionist and women's suffrage movements in the eastern United States, she joined her longtime friend Eliza Farnham in California in 1850. Georgiana married local tanner Richard Kirby in 1852 and moved with him to rural Santa Cruz. Although San Francisco and the Sierra foothills grew in population fastest during the gold rush, other, more rural areas of California also began to fill up with new settlers. In 1869 Kirby began the area's first chapter of women suffragists and sold short stories to Bret Harte's Overland Monthly. *While in Santa Cruz—lonely despite a new husband and pregnant—she began a journal in 1852, adapted here.*

DECEMBER 14, 1852: The day is blustering and rainy and cold, but I feel in better health and spirits, especially the latter, than for some time. This morning immediately after breakfast I rode my good old Rosea over into the "off hollow" and onto the hills beyond, wishing to see where "Tom" had hauled the new fencing stuff. It always puts me in good spirits to gallop up the hills and view the wild mountain scenery, so on my return, after taking in the clothes and all the wood that was chopped, as the clouds looked ominous, I concluded that today for the first time in my life I would commence a journal. I think that perhaps I may die and my babe live, in which case it would be pleasant for the latter to have some record of my external and spiritual life during these important months; or should I survive this great trial of my physical powers and live to see my child grow up, it will be interesting to me to see how far and in what manner my present and succeeding states of mind may have had influence in forming the character and consequently the external appearance of my child.

Our rancho with its hollows and gulches and noble sweep of hills exactly suits me, but I have been used to mixing in pretty large circles and miss the pleasant and healthy excitement caused by the friction of mind on mind. I long for flowers and fruits and music, too, but one cannot expect every good in the present state of society and I have many as it is—unsurpassed beauty of scenery and climate, good health, neither poverty or riches, and the most devoted friend in my husband. The other day Mr. K. brought home a balm of Gilead tree about 4½ feet high and planted it just opposite the kitchen window. It really gladdened by heart as I watched it constantly during the day as I would a child. It was the first step in the way of *refined* cultivation and gives me faith in the future roses, lilies, dahlias, and so forth, gives me faith that I shall one day gather glorious red currants and Antwerp raspberries and luscious English gooseberries in our own garden on our own Rancho La Salud, near Santa Cruz, California.

In coming to Santa Cruz it was my intention to teach school. There were many girls belonging to these western families of sufficient promise to interest me in them. I could and desired to not only instruct them in books but in their personal habits of cleanliness, neatness, order, courtesy, how to make and mend clothes, and so forth; but the pious young villain who was then keeping the mixed school, one of the cloth who frequently exhorted in the meeting (Methodist), reigned supreme. The regular local minister, Mr. Brier, a self-conceited, bawling brute, without a spark of tenderness, used all his influence against me in this, and, added to the unpopularity of Mrs. Farnham, at whose house I was staying, rendered the entire plan abortive. This teacher afterward seduced some of the young girls and had to leave in the night—went on to the boards in San Francisco and afterwards joined the filibustering expedition to the Sandwich Islands. After giving up the school I took to gardening, much to the benefit of my health and improvement of my pocket. The soil proved too sandy for onions.

For more than a year I did not make one cent. Then I went down with Bryant Hill to the Pajaro Valley to cook for his men. He was the first American that settled there and I remained there six months in a house without a chair or bedstead or table (with the exception of the boards on tressels that we and the men ate off). For three months we had no windows—the light came through the door which was left open—no looking glass, no flat irons. I ironed the bosom and collars of two white shirts with a half-pint tin tumbler kept constantly half-full of boiling water. I worked very hard indeed. My only comfort was a game of whist after eight o'clock with Mrs. Thrift, a young New England woman who had married an illiterate young Southerner who I had with me. She was avowedly an abolitionist and I respected her for this and hoped to find in her a companion and friend, but I found her selfish in the extreme, without a shadow of aspiration, self-willed and wholly wanting in the common traits of New England women—judgment, skill in the various domestic departments, economy, and so forth. I was very sorry to give her up but she obliged me to.

DECEMBER 15TH: Last night there was ice on the pools a quarter of an inch thick and about 10 AM there was quite a brisk shower of snow, which lasted some five minutes and then changed to rain. I believe myself incapable of experiencing pleasure excepting through association. So this snow reminding me of happy days in Canada and Massachusetts fairly made my heart merry.

DECEMBER 22ND: The rain of ten days and nights and the winds that sent seven vessels on shore have at length, so appearances would agree, passed away. The earth is green, the sky fair. Bryant Hill—who had $25,000 worth of produce on board two of the vessels and who supposes his rancho, with $25,000 worth more in bags and heaps of potatoes undug, is for the most part under water and the house blown into the river—left here to return this morning. He came up with his two partners a week ago and, owing to the rise in the San Lorenzo and the Soquel Creek, he could not cross to return. I pray that his affairs be not so desperate as he apprehends, for I long to see Eleanor and the child and she must be so very weary of waiting to join him. I wish also that he may keep the 2000 acres in the Pajaro that so satisfy his farming aspirations.

JANUARY 7th, 1853: The remnants of this remarkable rain storm still hang about us. There cannot have been less than 2 1/2 feet of water fallen during these last six weeks. Farming operations are thus put back—no ploughing done as yet. In former years wheat was sowed in November and December. The upper country must be flooded and all planting necessarily stopped for the present. There must be great suffering in the mines. Provisions, especially the staples, flour and pork, were so high that traders waited for a fall before purchasing their winter stock and now the long rain has cut off communication. A few speculators buy up all the flour and pork and hold it at $35 and $40 and $47 the barrel. If the railroad were built between California and Missouri it would equalize the market.

It is so delightful here when the rain does stop; we have the most glorious summer weather at once. The birds sing, the Bay is covered with a haze of glory, the earth green as emerald.

JANUARY 12th: My health begins to mend. My mind returns to its old picture-making, conversation-holding (imaginary) habits. I regret that I find the exertion of walking disagreeably fatiguing. The various forms of measure (rhythm) that so constantly used to repeat themselves in my mind come back again, also the same vivid conceptions of persons and events as I lie awake at night. Occasionally, too, I have a beautiful dream of being indeed asleep, and the spirit leaving the body finds itself overlooking a noble city, examining its architecture, plan, and so forth, it being cold and solemn and clear at night. Oh, that my best dream nights may be reproduced.

JANUARY 27th: We planted our first potatoes on the 25th. There was so great a press of work (as is usually the case in a California spring) that I volunteered to drop potatoes. I was so anxious to have Mr. Bowman go on with the garden fence. The first day I got along pretty well, but yesterday at noon I completely gave out and went straight to bed dreading a miscarriage after all I had endured for the sake of a future blessing. Today I am rested somewhat but do not like the symptoms at all—regret that I have no arnica to take. Sent off letters to Tacie, Mother, and Paulina Wright, asking particulars about the new association at Raritan Bay, N.J., in which I am interested. Today it rains a little with a prospect of more behind. It is good for our up-hill barley, only I pray that it stop in reasonable time.

FEBRUARY 3rd: Sowing barley below the road.... I am not sure that anything whatever could relieve or comfort me under my present very depressing condition of health, but if anything could it would be a congenial female companion with whom I could chat and be merry—sympathize and advise. The being alone all day from eight in the morning to seven at night ensures a too great seriousness. There is nothing to call out any other faculties of the mind, fancy, imagination, affection, mirthfulness, nothing in fact to kindle or excite a worthy spirit life. I regret this more than I can express, dreading the effect on the little one. Every good woman needs a companion of her own sex, no matter how numerous or valuable her male acquaintances, no matter how close the union between herself and husband; if she have a genial, loving nature, the want of a female friend is felt as a sad void.... For my life, take it all together and considering my natural tendencies, has been one of severe struggle and suffering, only alleviated by the love I found myself able to attract and the sense of power over growing minds. It would be more desirable for me at this time to take a hearty interest in my housekeeping, but I never did feel the slightest in such things and the cooking is most distasteful and irksome to me. All that I do is done of outward necessity and because there would be a worse state of confusion were it left undone. Then being cut off from society out of my natural sphere, since I cannot exert my natural influence and receive those necessary to me in return, I fail in earnestness, concentrativeness, active internal power. If I had a nice friend with me it would recall me from my vague dreaming to the worth of the actual present.

from AN EMIGRANT OF THE FIFTIES

JAMES CLARKE

Southern California, like the rest of the state, experienced a population surge (though on a much smaller scale) as a result of massive immigration during the gold rush. James Clarke, a jack-of-all-trades who arrived in California in 1854, soon headed to Los Angeles after failing to establish a law practice in both San Francisco and Santa Rosa. His letters home in 1854 enthusiastically described a fertile, temperate southern California that contrasted favorably to crowded San Francisco.

SONORA VALLEY, CALIFORNIA, SEPTEMBER 3, 1854

Dear Wife,

I have delaid writing untill I could inform you where to write to me, but even now it is uncertain that Los Angeles will be my future Post Office address & residence,—But to relate what has passed since I wrote—You know I was at Santa Rosa. Where I had hoped to remain, but the scarcity of money in this place has influenced me to give up the most distant idea of receiving anything even if I should stay there; So by taking some $61 in merchandise & about $45 in provision I started in Company with Mr. James Nichols for Los Angeles on the 24 of August, & with a four ox team, one cow, our provision &c. accompanied by his wife, Mrs. Fanny C. Nichols, & little daughter Adestell,—We travel but fifteen miles per day, & the distance is about 400 miles. So it will be six weeks from the time we started to get to that city. You will ask why do I leave the upper part of Cal,—I answer every department of business is overdone no money in circulation and every thing growing worse hard times I assure you— Wheat worth not the cost of growing & men having from 1000 to 5000 bushels of wheat not able to raise money to pay their help same with every other crop potatoes bring nothing stock worth nothing that is comparatively & so on and money is out of the question—The Mines do not afford any better chance so one is worse off here than in the states—I regret very much that I cannot send the money as I had reason to suppose the Mr. Ball whom I expected to get some $300, of failed by reason of being taken sick & the disapointment in obtaining money to buy hogs to drive to the Mines so that sourse of gain is gone. And now I am left only with some sixty Dollars worth of Saddles and provision necessary to take me to Los Angeles where I shall open a school in connection with Mr. Nichols & Wife or go into the business of collecting as an Atty or the purchasing of hides & manufacter of hair ropes & the making of Spanish curled hair for mat rugges &c.

For the past eleven nights we have slept in our blankets [with] three blankets a piece in the open air under some tree where we have camped.... And shall have traveled from some 70m above San Francisco all the circuit of the Bay of San Francisco at the distance of some 20m therefrom through the Vallies of Santa Rosa the Willocas, Sonoma, Suscal, the hills or Mountains to the North of Suscoll som 8m, then the hills between Suscol & Benecia & the Valley of Saisun, then the Valley of Parques then the Valley of San Ramond, the Amedale & Sanjasa, at the head of the sanasa under a large oak I write having camped by the house of a Mr. Randall of Vt. On Monday, Sept. 4 we traveled the remainder of the Valley of San [José] sometimes called Santa Clara & about seven miles in the Valley of Gil Roye which are only sepperated by a creek now dry or mostly so—And camped on the open plain near the house of a Mr. Turner of Vt.... The soil is extremly rich and will produce from thirty to sixty bushels of wheat to the acre—In fact the Valleys we have come through affords oats & grass for the cattle all the year arround and cattle horses hogs hens as well as wheat potatoes Onions Oats barley are so abundant that they are not hardly worth carrying to market, And only bring a fair price when packed on the backs far up into the most remote mining sections where vegitation will not grow—Gardens of the most luxuriant growth florish in all of the mines that are not up among the very extremes—So there is no Market for all of these abundant productions.

We now have a journey of six weeks to reach Los Angeles which with the two weeks past will make the journey of eight weeks & some 400 miles, but I hope to find a country only surpassed by Cuba the choicest parts of China or japan—A country of corn & wine & some money.

James Clarke

NOVEMBER 3, 1854

I now write in the Post Office as we have no table in our sleeping room or other convenience for writing.... Let me say that this City is the place for a poor fellow like me and in a year I hope to make remitances in amt to fully make up for bad luck. The Spanish language is indispensable to success here so I am devoting every evening to the study. Money is worth ten per cent per month Carpenters journeyman get $5 per day laborers $3. Our Climate is that of France yet we have every Tropical production in abundance vis Oranges, Sweet & Sour Limes, Lemmons, figs, prunes, Citron, Peaches, Pears, Apples, Grapes, Quince, Olives &c &c Pepper trees, Sweet potatoes Common potatoes Squash Cabages weighing 50 lb to the head Indian Corn 18 ft high yealding 110 bush per acre, Wheat 40 bush per acre, Onions in any quantyties, Tomatoes beets ten inches in diameter very sweet & nice, Nuts of the best quality. In fact All that heart can wish grows with the slightest cultivation. Now if you will send me some of the best varieties of our plumbs & cherries stones those that are not from grafted stocks. Also some of the clingstone peach stones gooseberries & Strawberry seed you will do me a great favor. Also send me a variety of Apple seeds. Take some pains to get original seed, and label each variety—I shall take a vinyard of five acres to rent to employ my mornings and soon shall take up a lot of five or thirty five acres and as I am determined to remain in this City the five years I came out for & I have no doubt that Lizzie will by that time be ready to come out & live in so beautiful a climate. I suppose you are doing well & well enough should be let alone So Remember me as

Truly, James Clarke

CITY OF LOS ANGELES, DECEMBER 6, 1854

Dear Bro,

You have no idea the exceeding agreeableness of our Climate it is neither too warm or cold, & one is comfortable in his shirt sleves.—The rain since Thursday has wet the ground about six inches, and the Mountains, hills & Valleys are all green with clover, weeds, or Oats,—The Mustard grows wild to the hights of eight or ten feet so that a man on horseback cannot be seen when riding among them.—The wild oats grow down South here best on the high hills & Mountains. & here are most found where trees grow.

James Clarke

[DECEMBER, 1854]

Dear Ella,

How would you like to walk under the orang trees & pick up the ripe oranges as you do apples in the garden!—Beautiful flowrs are on the trees here now & the Olive & the figs are yet ripening.—The Orange will blossom soon & soon the Oranges will be ripe.—The sweet grapes in large clusters are very fine now as it is late in the season for them but now that those we hung up to dry are fit for use & dry we call them raisins, I dried a hundred lb & a half bush of figs, O! how, I wish you and your Mother could be out here in this sunny clime since I came into the Country in April we have had no storms beautiful sunshine & now we are expecting weather like our summer for the rainy season, no cold snow or rain & the trees & the grass ever green & growing.— It is very healthy all along the coast of the Pacific. The residence live to great age and one day this will be the paradise of the United States.—Write me about the strawberries & the plumbs & how Father crop yealded & how you have learned.—I send you a few seeds gathered in the first Orange grove I visited in "Los Angeles" you know the English of *Los Angeles* is " The Angels" so be a una muchacha bueno.

From your loving Father James

LOS ANGELES, MARCH 1, 1855

Dear Bro,

Our vegitables will soon be ready for the market & then another source of income will be available.—Since Jany. We have been at work in the vinyard & have only earned enough to just keep us in provisions tools seed &c. I have one hundred gal of vinegar made from the lees of last years wine and when we shall have finished planting our inventory will stand thus 10,000 grape setings worth some $60, some two hundred peach setings, pears Apple Quince, Figs, Oranges, Cheries about one hundred of each kind.—One acre cultivated as a vegitable garden and one acre in sweet potatoes corn potatoes &c.—And our five acres of vines 1040 trees as they will averedge three inch in diameter & three feet high.—But let me pass to the climate we have had but little rain two days the first of [December] then one rainy day the first of Jany and then the several showery rains of the 21, 23, & 25 of Feb., and in all not more than seven or eight cloudy or unfair days since May last.—The Indians have no houses & in fact need none for one could live comfortably in the open air under a tree all the year round.—This is the case with all Southern Cal if fifteen or [more] miles from the Ocean as on the coast it is unpleasant by reason of the damp cool sea breese of the day commencing about 10 AM. O now that I think of it put some strawberry seeds & flour seeds in your letters & They will be of value to me.

Truly, James Clarke

"Fiddlers of San Francisco," c. 1850

from A California Pioneer

BERNHARD MARKS

Bernhard Marks (c. 1833–1914), a New England Jew who arrived in San Francisco via Panama in 1852, regrettably discovered that anti-Semitism had already permeated Californian society in the few years of rapid influx since the discovery of gold. Marks found work in turn as a miner, railroad land agent, grammar school principal, and land speculator. In a series of letters to his cousin in Massachusetts, he addressed the Jewish stereotypes he encountered in gold rush California.

PLACERVILLE, JUNE 16, 1854

Dear Cousin Jacob,

Were I to measure your interest in my letters by the frequency of yours, and graduate mine accordingly, I should not write more than half the number I now do. Once again have I to complain of neglect on your part, and have already forgiven it in anticipation of the numerous apologies you will make.

I had now been in the country about three months and had saved between three and four hundred dollars. Trade had become distasteful to me, and with my head full of the dignity of labour I resolved on either purchasing or prospecting a mine and going to work as a miner. An old acquaintance of mine who had been here ever since '49 had invested the whole of his hard earned capital, nearly $12,000, in canal stock and lost every dollar of it, [and] was about to start on a prospecting tour of two or three weeks, so that an excellent opportunity was offered me of profiting by the experience of an old miner, it is needless to say that I did not hesitate to avail myself of the proffered occasion. As I before remarked my head was full of the dignity of physical labour, and I really began to feel ashamed of my former avocation, longing, quixotically of course, for the time when with callosed hand, hickory shirt, cowhide boots, and pick on shoulder I could conscientiously call myself a miner.

It is easy to see what influences contributed to bring about this state of things in my mind. An immense population suddenly brought together at an extreme end of the land, distant, virtually thousands of miles from the seat of Government, no hereditary or appointed rulers or authorities, no law and no

327

Two miners with gold nugget stick pins, c. 1853

order, form themselves immediately as it were without confusion, disorder, or violence into an organized state second to none, considering circumstances, in the world. No anarchy, no hierarchy, no oligarchy, individually and collectively free and independent, each man recognized the fundamental principles of democracy, exercised his sovereign right of suffrage, and submitted to the will of the majority. By whom was this affected?—certainly by the mass. And who constituted the mass but the hardy, toilsome miners? But a labouring man in this country is a different thing from one in any other. Here he is what he should be, the world over. Here, he is exempt from the slavery imposed by capital. Here, there is no necessity for cringing to it for the privilege of earning a bare subsistence. Here, the labourer is the corner stone of society. He does not allow himself to be treated with the least contumely for, wherever he strikes his pick, if he has even the poorest kind of fortune, he can earn not only a living but a good one. You will understand all this better however as I proceed.

Contrast then with the miner's independent position the contemptable cringing of the traders, made doubly so by their extraordinary avidity to sell, and more especially, the pedlers, or travelling Jew shops as they are here called, and by whom the country is overrun. But you must not take society in the Atlantic States for a standard by which to judge California life. Because here society, being in a more primitive state, is analyzed with much greater facility and all the minutae of California life tend towards placing the trader and professional man more in the light of what a gambler is considered in the

328

Miner playing a flute, early 1850s

eastern states than a useful member of society. Added to this ... the different shades of society are here more easily distinguishable than in the more thickly populated country of the East and the fact that the Jews are almost exclusively devoted to trade, and that they take so unproportionately small a share in physical labour, is as a consequence more perceptible, and as the theme of the dignity of labour is here a universal favourite, so is or rather was the occupation of trade held in about the same estimation as it was when none but the lowest and oppressed engaged in it, and which was the reason of the intellect and energy of our people being directed so exclusively into that channel. I have made a great number of friends here, was the first and most active in getting up the public library, started a debating club, and after all the controversies had engaged in whenever the subject of "Jews" was introduced, with what bitter, sneering emphasis the word is used by the ignorant brutes of hoosiers, I was ambitious of giving then a practical demonstration that there were at least some Jews who were willing and able to work when that proved as profitable as anything else. All this romantic effervescence evaporated however as soon as I became enabled to take a more practical view of the matter. It was not the hardship of the labour that brought me back to hard sense, for as far as that was concerned I was greatly disappointed, but it was the discovery of the fact that scarce one among those who were first and loudest in prating of the dignity of their occupation, and ranting against all others in which brute strength was not requisite, but would gladly have changed places with those very same lazy, pitiful, little no-bodies, had they but the talent, knowledge, means, or opportunity.

The forty-niners constitute a distinct class, and as I shall very probably allude to them more fully hereafter, I may suffice for the present to say that a forty-niner knows, or supposes he knows, every thing that is worth knowing and some things that are not. He has seen the greatest sights, gone through the most imminent dangers, heard and told the biggest stories, and killed the biggest bears of any other human. Nothing is too extravagant for him to believe, for he has seen greater things himself. According to his opinion, everybody that comes to California is grass green, and if he only had been here in '49 he could have shown them the elephant.

Accompanying this you will receive a Chinese paper published in San Francisco, the heading of which I have translated, and I have endeavored to give you some idea of the sound of the words in the Chinese language. An intelligent Chinaman read the words to me, and fortunately they happened to be such as I understood. I have not taken time to read it but presume you will find much that is interesting in it when you read it. My love to my Aunt, Uncle, Leon, and other cousins, also my particular regard to Mr. and Mrs. Solis, remember me to all friends and believe me

Sincerely Your affectionate cousin,
B. Marks

from Twenty-Four Years After

Richard Henry Dana, Jr.

Twenty-four years after Richard Henry Dana, Jr.'s youthful adventure on a hide-and-tallow ship, the Boston lawyer returned to California in 1859. He published his observations as an epilogue to later editions of Two Years Before the Mast.

It was in the winter of 1835–36 that the ship *Alert,* in the prosecution of her voyage for hides on the remote and almost unknown coast of California, floated into the vast solitude of the Bay of San Francisco. All around was the stillness of nature. One vessel, a Russian, lay at anchor there, but during our whole stay not a sail came or went. Our trade was with remote Missions, which sent hides to us in launches manned by their Indians. Our anchorage was between a small island, called Yerba Buena, and a gravel beach in a little bight or cove of the same name, formed by two small, projecting points. Beyond, to the westward of the landing-place, were dreary sand-hills, with little grass to be seen, and few trees, and beyond them higher hills, steep and barren, their sides gullied by the rains. Some five or six miles beyond the landing-place, to the right, was a ruinous Presidio, and some three or four miles to the left was the Mission of Dolores, as ruinous as the Presidio, almost deserted, with but few Indians attached to it, and but little property in cattle.

Over a region far beyond our sight there were no other human habitations, except that an enterprising Yankee, years in advance of his time, had put up, on the rising ground above the landing, a shanty of rough boards, where he carried on a very small retail trade between the hide ships and the Indians. Vast banks of fog, invading us from the North Pacific, drove in through the entrance, and covered the whole bay; and when they disappeared, we saw a few well-wooded islands, the sand-hills on the west, the grassy and wooded slopes on the east, and the vast stretch of the bay to the southward, where we were told lay the Missions of Santa Clara and San José, and still longer stretches to the northward and northeastward, where we understood smaller bays spread out, and large rivers poured in their tributes of waters. There were no settlements on these bays or rivers, and the few ranchos and Missions were remote and widely separated. Not only the neighborhood of our anchorage, but the entire region of the great bay, was a solitude. On the whole coast of California there was not a light-house, a beacon, or a buoy, and the charts were made up from old and disconnected surveys by British, Russian, and Mexican voyagers. Birds of prey and passage swooped and dived about us, wild beasts ranged through the oak groves, and as we slowly floated out of the harbor with the tide, herds of deer came to the water's edge, on the northerly side of the entrance, to gaze at the strange spectacle.

On the evening of Saturday, the 13th of August, 1859, the superb steamship *Golden Gate,* gay with crowds of passengers, and lighting the sea for miles around with the glare of her signal lights of red, green, and white, and brilliant with lighted saloons and staterooms, bound up from the Isthmus of Panama, neared the entrance to San Francisco, the great centre of a world-wide commerce. Miles out at sea, on the desolate rocks of the Farallones, gleamed the powerful rays of one of the most costly and effective lighthouses in the world. As we drew in through the Golden Gate, another lighthouse met our eyes, and in the clear moonlight of the unbroken California summer we saw, on the right, a large fortification protecting the narrow entrance, and just before us the little island of Alcatraz confronted us,—one entire fortress.

We bore round the point toward the old anchoring-ground of the hide ships, and there, covering the sand-hills and the valleys, stretching from the water's edge to the base of the great hills, and from the old Presidio to the Mission, flickering all over with the lamps of its streets and houses, lay a city of 100,000 inhabitants. Clocks tolled the hour of midnight from its steeples, but the city was alive from the salute of our guns, spreading the news that the fortnightly steamer had come, bringing mails and passengers from the Atlantic world. Clipper ships of the largest size lay at anchor in the stream, or were girt to the wharves; and capacious high-pressure steamers, as large and showy as those of the Hudson or Mississippi, bodies of dazzling light, awaited the delivery of our mails to take their courses up the Bay, stopping at Benicia and the United States Naval Station, and then up the great tributaries—the Sacramento, San Joaquin, and Feather Rivers—to the far inland cities of Sacramento, Stockton, and Marysville.

The dock into which we drew, and the streets about it, were densely crowded with express wagons and hand-carts to take luggage; coaches and cabs for passengers; and with men, some looking out for friends among our hundreds of passengers; agents of the press; and a greater multitude eager for newspapers and verbal intelligence from the great Atlantic and European world. Through this crowd I made my way, along the well-built and well-lighted streets, as alive as by day, where boys in high-keyed voices were already crying the latest New York papers; and between one and two o'clock in the morning found myself comfortably abed in a commodious room, in the Oriental Hotel, which stood, as well as I could learn, on the filled-up cove, and not far from the spot where we used to beach our boats from the *Alert*.

SUNDAY, AUGUST 14TH. When I awoke in the morning, and looked from my windows over the city of San Francisco, with its storehouses, towers, and steeples; its court-houses, theatres, and hospitals; its daily journals; its well-filled learned professions; its fortresses and light-houses; its wharves and harbor, with their thousand-ton clipper ships, more in number than London or Liverpool sheltered that day, itself one of the capitals of the American Republic, and the sole emporium of a new world, the awakened Pacific; when I looked across the bay to the eastward, and beheld a beautiful town on the fertile, wooded shores of the Contra Costa, and steamers, large and small, the ferryboats to the Contra Costa, and capacious freighters and passenger-carriers to all parts of the great bay and its tributaries, with lines of their smoke in the horizon,—when I saw all these things, and reflected on what I once was and saw here, and what now surrounded me, I could scarcely keep my hold on reality at all, or the genuineness of anything, and seemed to myself like one who had moved in "worlds not realized."

Indeed, I found individuals, as well as public bodies, affected in a marked degree by a change of oceans and by California life. One Sunday afternoon I was surprised at receiving the card of a man whom I had last known, some fifteen years ago, as a strict and formal deacon of a Congregational Society in New England. He was a deacon still, in San Francisco, a leader in all pious works, devoted to his denomination and to total abstinence,—the same internally, but externally—what a change! Gone was the downcast eye, the bated breath, the solemn, non-natural voice, the watchful gait, stepping as if he felt responsible for the balance of the moral universe! He walked with a stride, an uplifted open countenance, his face covered with beard, whiskers, and mustache, his voice strong and natural,—and, in short, he had put off the New England deacon and become a human being.

LEGACIES

The 1849 of California, of America, of the world! It was the pivot on which the framework of human progress turned a fresh side to the sun, a side breeding maggots hitherto, but now a new and nobler race of man.

—Hubert Howe Bancroft

The hills have been cut and scalped, and every gorge and gulch and valley torn and disembowled, expressing a fierce and desperate energy hard to understand.

—John Muir

Maidu Traditional Dancers, 1997, by Dugan Aguilar

from CRUSOE'S ISLAND

J. ROSS BROWNE

J. Ross Browne (1821–1875) was born in Ireland and moved to Kentucky at age eleven. By the time he turned thirty-two, he had sailed across the Indian Ocean on a whaling ship, traveled to California with the Revenue Service, conducted a tour of the Mediterranean—and written three books about his experiences. He also served as the official reporter for California's first Constitutional Convention and was an accomplished artist. He settled in Oakland in 1854 and published early muckraking articles in Harper's magazine along with several more travelogues. Crusoe's Island, published in 1864, contained Browne's sardonic look back at the 1859 rush to the silver mines of Washoe County, Nevada.

EVER SINCE 1849, when I first trod the shores of California, the citizens of that Land of Promise have been subject to periodical excitements, the extent and variety of which can find no parallel in any other state of the Union. To enumerate these in chronological detail would be a difficult task, nor is it necessary to my purpose. The destruction of towns by flood and fire; the uprisings and downfallings of vigilance committees; the breaking of banking-houses and pecuniary ruin of thousands; the political wars, senatorial tourna-ments, duels, and personal affrays; the prison and bulkhead schemes; the ex-traordinary ovations to the living and the dead; and innumerable other excite-ments have been too frequently detailed, and have elicited too much com-ment from the Atlantic press not to be still in the memory of the public.

But, numerous as these agitations have been, and prejudicial as some of them must long continue to be to the reputation of the state, they can bear no comparison in point of extent and general interest to the mining excitements which from time to time have convulsed the whole Pacific coast, from Puget's Sound to San Diego. In these there can be no occasion for party animosity; they are confined to no political or sectional clique; all the industrial classes are interested, and in a manner, too, affecting, either directly or incidentally, their very means of subsistence. The country abounds in mineral wealth, and the merchant, the banker, the shipper, the mechanic, the laborer, are all, to some extent, dependent upon its development. Even the gentleman of elegant lei-

sure, vulgarly known as the "Bummer"—and there are many in California—
is occasionally driven by visions of cocktail and cigar-money to doff his "stove-
pipe," and exchange his gold-mounted cane for a pick or shovel. The axiom
has been well established by an eminent English writer that "every man wants
a thousand pounds." It seems, indeed, to be a chronic and constitutional want,
as well in California as in less favored countries.

Few of the early residents of the state can have forgotten the Gold Bluff
excitement of '52, when, by all accounts, old Ocean himself turned miner,
and washed up cartloads of gold on the beach above Trinidad. It was represented, and generally believed, that any enterprising man could take his hat
and a wheelbarrow, and in half an hour gather up gold enough to last him for
life. I have reason to suspect that, of the thousands who went there, many will
long remember their experience with emotions, if pleasant, "yet, mournful to
the soul."

The Kern River excitement threatened for a time to depopulate the northern portion of the state. The stages fom Marysville and Sacramento were
crowded day after day, and new lines were established from Los Angeles, Stockton, San José, and various other points; but such was the pressure of travel in
search of this grand depository, in which it was represented the main wealth of
the world had been treasured by a beneficent Providence, that thousands were
compelled to go on foot, and carry their blankets and provisions on their
backs. From Stockton to the mining district, a distance of more than three
hundred miles, the plains of the San Joaquin were literally speckled with "honest miners." It is a notable fact that of those who went in stages, the majority
returned on foot; and of those who trusted originally to shoe-leather, many
had to walk on their natural soles, or depend on sackcloth or charity.

After the Kern River Exchequer had been exhausted, the public was congratulated by the press throughout the state upon the effectual check now put
upon these ruinous and extravagant excitements. The enterprising miners who
had been tempted to abandon good claims in search of better had undergone
a species of purging which would allay any irritation of the mucous mem-
brane for some time. What they had lost in money they had gained in experience. They would henceforth turn a deaf ear to interested representations and
not be dazzled by visions of sudden wealth conjured up by monte-dealers,
travelers, and horse-jockeys.

Scarcely had the reverberation caused by the bursting of the Kern River
bubble died away, and fortune again smiled upon the ruined multitudes, when
a faint cry was heard from afar—first low and uncertain, like a mysterious
whisper, then full and sonorous, like the boom of glad tidings from the mouth

of a cannon, the inspiring cry of *Frazer River!* Here was gold sure enough! a river of gold! a country that dazzled the eyes with its glitter of gold! There was no deception about it this time.

The steamers, in due course of time, began to return crowded with enterprising miners, who still believed there was gold there if the [frozen] river would only fall. But generosity dictates that I should say no more on this point. It is enough to add that the time arrived when it became a matter of personal offense to ask any spirited gentleman if he been to Frazer River.

There was now, of course, an end to all mining excitements. It could never again happen that such an imposition could be practiced upon public credulity. In the whole state there was not another sheep that could be gulled by the cry of wolf. Business would now resume its steady and legitimate course. Property would cease to fluxuate in value. Every branch of industry would become fixed upon a permanent and reliable basis. All these excitements were the natural results of the daring and enterprising character of the people. But now, having worked off their superabundant steam, they would be prepared to go ahead systematically, and develop those resources which they had hitherto neglected. It was a course of medical effervescence highly beneficial to the body politic. All morbid appetite for sudden wealth was now gone forever.

But softly, good friends! what rumor is this? Whence come these silvery strains that are wafted to our ears from the passes of the Sierra Nevada? What dulcet Æolian harmonies—what divine, enchanting ravishment is it

That with these raptures moves the vocal air?

As I live, it is a cry of Silver! Silver in *Washoe!* Not gold now, you silly men of Gold Bluff; you Kern Riverites; you daring explorers of British Columbia! But *silver*—solid, pure *silver!* Beds of it ten thousand feet deep! Acres of it! miles of it! hundreds of millions of dollars poking their backs up out of the earth ready to be pocketed!

"Sir," said my informant to me, in strict confidence, no later than this morning, "you may rely upon it, for I am personally acquainted with a brother of the gentleman whose most intimate friend saw the man whose partner has just come over the mountains, and he says there never was the like on the face of the earth! The ledges are ten thousand feet deep—solid masses of silver. Let us be off! Now is the time! A pack-mule, pick and shovel, hammer and frying-pan will do. You need nothing more. *Hurrah for Washoe!*"

from CALIFORNIA CULINARY EXPERIENCES

PRENTICE MULFORD

Prentice Mulford (1834–1891), a fixture of the 1860s San Francisco literary scene, came to California from his native New York in 1856. Although a failure at mining, he managed to use those experiences as fodder for dozens of humorous short stories for the Overland Monthly, Golden Era, Californian, *and other local journals. Mulford— or "Dogberry," as he often signed his sketches—portrayed the gold rush as a lively but dangerous place. "California Culinary Experiences" appeared in* Overland Monthly *in 1869.*

I AM A SURVIVOR of all the different eras of California amateur cookery. The human avalanche precipitated on these shores in the rush of "49" and "50" was a mass of culinary ignorance. Cooking had always by us been deemed a part of woman's kingdom. We knew that bread was made of flour, and for the most part so made by woman. It was as natural that it should be made by them as that the sun should shine. Of the knowledge, skill, patience and experience required to conduct this and other culinary operations, we realized nothing. So when the first—the pork, bean, and flapjack—era commenced, thousands of us boiled our pork and beans together an equal period of time, and then wondered at the mysterious hardness of the nutritious vegetable. In the fall of "50" a useful scrap of wisdom was disseminated from Siskiyou to Fresno. It was that beans must be soaked over night and boiled at least two hours before the insertion of the pork. And many a man of mark to-day never experienced a more cheerful thrill of combined pride and pleasure, than when first he successfully accomplished the feat of turning a flapjack.

We soon tired of wheat cakes. Then commenced the bread era; the heavy bread era, which tried the stomach of California. That organ sustained a daily attack of leaden flour and doubtful pork. The climate was censured for a mortality which then prevailed, due, in great measure, to this dreadful diet. With the large majority of our amateur cooks, bread-making proved but a series of disastrous failures. Good bread makers, male or female, are born, not made. In flour we floundered from the extreme of lightness to that of heaviness. We produced our loaves every shade of sourness and every tint of orange, from excess of salæratus. Our crust, in varying degrees of hardness and thickness, well illustrated the stratifications of the earth. Our loaves "did" in spots. Much prospecting was often necessary to develop pay-bread.

In the early portion of "51," just preceding the pie period, came an epoch of stewed dried apples. Even now, my stomachic soul shudders as I recall that trying time. After we had apple-sauced ourselves to satiety, with diabolical ingenuity we served it up to each other, hidden in thick, heavy ramparts of flour. It was a desperate struggle with duff and dumplings. Like Ney returning alone to Paris after the dreadful Russian campaign, I can now recall no living comrade of the dried apple era. But those who first ventured on pies were men possessed in some degree of taste and refinement. No coarser nature ever troubled itself with pie-making. The preparation and seasoning of the mince meat, the rolling out and manipulation of the crusts, their proper adjustment to the plate, the ornamental scallops around the edge (made with the thumb), and the regulation of the oven's heat to secure that rich shade of brown, required patience and artistic skill.

The early pie-makers of our State were men who as soon as possible slept in sheets instead of blankets, who were skilled in washing linen, who went in clean attire on Sundays, and who subscribed for magazines and newspapers. On remote bars and gulches such men have kept households of incredible neatness, their cabins sheltered under the evergreen oak, with clear rivulets from the mountain gorges running past the door, with clothes-lines precisely hung with shirts and sheets, with gauze-covered meat safe hoisted high in the branches of the overshadowing trees, protecting those pies from intruding and omnivorous ground squirrels and inquisitive yellow-jackets; while about their door-way the hard, clean-swept red earth resembled a well-worn brick pavement. There is morality in pies.

There was a canned provision era, fruitful in sardines and oysters. The canned oysters of those days were as destructive as cannister shot. They penetrated everywhere. In remote and seldom-visited valleys of the Sierras, I have grown solemn over the supposition that mine were the first footsteps which had ever indented the soil. And then I have turned but to behold the gaping, ripped, and jagged mouth of one of those inevitable tin cylinders scattered like dew over the land, and labeled "Cove Oysters." One of our prominent officials, giving evidence in a suit relative to the disputed possession of a mining claim in a remote district, when asked what, in the absence of a house or shaft, he would consider to be indications of the former presence of miners, answered: "Empty oyster cans and empty bottles."

Different mining partners have afforded me a rich and varied experience in cooks. I once lived near a slovenly, and, of course, literary cook. He was the literary anaconda of the Southern mines. Most of the older settlers leaving, to him by a sort of natural inheritance had fallen the library purchased in the palmy days of Hangville. And in this library, quite filling his cabin, did he eat, read, live, move, and have his being. He devoured together beef, bread, apple sauce, and Humboldt's Cosmos. His private mark was in every book and on every paper, the imprint of a greasy thumb or a dash of molasses. This simultaneous employment of brain and stomach resulted to him injuriously. He lost his memory. He forgot a book's contents a week after reading it. And so he revolved from year to year through the Hangville library in an endless circuit. He may be reading and eating yet. There are people who should reflect on this.

I spent one winter with a fickle and unmethodical cook. He oscillated from the extremes of method and neatness to those of neglect and slovenliness. There was a place for everything and everything in its place—about once a month. His coffee was too weak or too strong; his steaks of extreme rareness or burned to a crisp; his potatoes boiled to pieces or impervious to the fork; his bread subject to varying moods of heaviness. He had no patience for measuring quantities. In salting a dish for instance, he did but institute a wild guess as to the proper quantity. Hence came days of extreme saltiness. There were also days of extreme dish-washings. There were days of no dish-washing at all. There were periods of total culinary riot and demoralization, when old and new coffee were boiled together; when the tea-pot refused to pour a drop from the accumulation of tea-leaves; when no warm meals were prepared, and when old stews, trembling on the verge of sourness, were thrust upon our meek and suffering stomachs. Such things are outrages and insults unpardonable to the digestive organs.

I once prospected together an upper ledge and a mechanical and abstracted eater. This man's whole soul was at the time concentrated on a series of ledges that we had taken up. We were encamped well up the slope of Table Mountain, a wide expanse of country being spread out before us. Over this, while seated at breakfast under a tree, would the mechanical eater's eye wander. He was planning new mineral discoveries on those distant hills. Up and down silently oscillated his fork, conveying morsels of something from plate to mouth. The tines occasionally missed and fastened themselves in the table. Gastronomically considered, he was an unfeathered ostrich. He would swallow anything I placed before him. He confided his stomach to my care with the unthinking trustfulness of a child. There was merely a body brought by animal instinct to a table at certain regular intervals to be supplied with a few more hours' propelling force. As for the mechanical eater's soul, part of it was left behind at the bottom of our shaft fifty-two feet under ground, and the re-

"Pork and Beans in the Gold Diggins," 1849, by Robert H. Elton

mainder was skimming along the range of hills holding the line of claims we had taken up on the extension.

Fate then placed me with an experimental cook. He was always essaying new dishes, the result of his ponderings over a coverless old cook-book by some chance left in our cabin. And besides, he entertained culinary plans of his own invention which, when carried out, resulted in strange mixtures. The *debris* left over from several meals, on the score of economy, was tortured, simmered, stewed, and concentrated into hybrid conglomerates regardless of the assimilation of flavors. During the week the venerable cook-book's pudding recipes were intently studied. On Sundays these studies were practically carried out. So our Sabbath roast was slighted and cast in the shade through the excessive attention bestowed on that pudding, which generally turned out a wretched failure; a heavy, sodden, unassimilated, watery lump of flour, eggs, and suet, with a dejected mass meeting of plums on the "lower level." Where the experimental cook accomplished one success, he made ten failures. But he never flagged. Neither had he any hesitation during these investigations in risking his own stomach and that of his best friend. Science would be naught without experiment, yet it is often accompanied with danger. So it was here. I left him.

A solitary eight months' prospecting tour on the head waters of the Tuolumne and Walker rivers graduated me as a mountain cook. Indoors, we are ever

343

increasing the number of culinary conveniences. Out of doors, culinary science lies in diminishing them. A green willow stick is far better than a frying pan. Transfixed thereon, and held for a few moments over a bed of live coals, your steak acquires a flavor not to be lured inside of any kitchen. It incorporates in itself the freshness of the mountain air and the sublimated essence of wild green leaves. It is not deadened by the myriad stenches of the town. Locating mountain kitchens is an art. They must be where wood and water are in sight, and the soil free from dampness. Not under dead trees, or dead limbs, which have a strange propensity to fall in the calmest weather. Not in the midst of dry dead grass, which enkindled from your fire will burn you out of your migratory house and home. Devoid of wood ants, so prompt in five minutes after you are seated to institute exploring expeditions up your pantaloons. Your provisions and apparatus are carried in a series of bags. These, after picketing your horses, you arrange in a certain regular order on the windward side of the fire. Of the saddle and blankets is made a sort of couch. The fire burns five minutes. This brings the blaze into solidity; then on goes your coffee pot; *ad interim* you arrange on the cloth your plate, knife, fork, bread, sugar, and butter cans, cut your willow stick, and sharpen it; the water boiling, you pour in the "making" of coffee, and set it where it may only simmer; the fire is raked open, coals are disclosed, over these your steak is suspended, the stick being at one end set in the ground and the heat graduated by bending to or from the fire, two minutes and it is done; a dash of cold water settles the coffee. "Supper's ready." Time, twelve minutes.

And these were royal suppers and breakfasts, partaken high up on mountain sides, in little depressions, offering a bush for shelter, with a cool spring, and for the eye a grand drop curtain, covered with a confusion of mountains, valleys, lakes, plateaus, and snow-clad summits, each day changing the picture, and each hour painting its own tints and shades. True, there was regret that no sympathizing soul was by to enjoy with me the spectacle; still in loneliness there was compensation that, the meal past, I could linger long over the scene unmolested.... And while in the morning those great preparations went on, a saucy sneak of a coyote has often for me mingled a dash of comedy in the sublimity of the spectacle, by the inquisitive look with which at one moment he regarded me, as seated on a crag near by, he seemed to wonder what should tempt a man into his domain, and the next yelped impatiently for my departure, intent only on the remnants of food left by the amateur cook.

THE CELEBRATED JUMPING FROG
OF CALAVERAS COUNTY

MARK TWAIN

Mark Twain (1835–1910) was born in Missouri as Samuel Langhorne Clemens and came to California in 1861 with his brother Orion. After an unsuccessful stint as a silver prospector, Twain landed a job as editor of the Territorial Enterprise, *a newspaper in Virginia City, Nevada. It was here that his lively, self-aggrandizing style and penchant for bold exaggeration emerged. To bolster his rising popularity, he moved to San Francisco in 1864, joining the local literary scene—which included Bret Harte, Joaquin Miller, and Prentice Mulford—and writing for various newspapers and literary journals. He left California in 1866 for the New York lecture circuit. In the spring of 1867,* The Celebrated Jumping Frog of Calaveras County, and Other Sketches, *a collection of his Nevada and California tales, was published to wide acclaim. The title story first appeared as "Jim Smiley and his Jumping Frog" in the New York journal* Saturday Press *in 1865.*

IN COMPLIANCE WITH THE REQUEST of a friend of mine, who wrote me from the East, I called on good-natured, garrulous old Simon Wheeler, and inquired after my friend's friend, *Leonidas W.* Smiley, as requested to do, and I hereunto append the result. I have a lurking suspicion that *Leonidas W.* Smiley is a myth; that my friend never knew such a personage; and that he only conjectured that, if I asked old Wheeler about him, it would remind him of his infamous *Jim* Smiley, and he would go to work and bore me nearly to death with some infernal reminiscence of him as long and tedious as it should be useless to me. If that was the design, it certainly succeeded.

I found Simon Wheeler dozing comfortably by the bar-room stove of the old, dilapidated tavern in the ancient mining camp of Angel's, and I noticed that he was fat and bald-headed, and had an expression of winning gentleness and simplicity upon his tranquil countenance. He roused up and gave me good-day. I told him a friend of mine had commissioned me to make some inquiries about a cherished companion of his boyhood named *Leonidas W.* Smiley—Rev. *Leonidas W.* Smiley—a young minister of the Gospel, who he had heard was at one time a resident of Angels Camp. I added that, if Mr. Wheeler could tell me any thing about this Rev. Leonidas W. Smiley, I would feel under many obligations to him.

Simon Wheeler backed me into a corner and blockaded me there with his chair, and then sat me down and reeled off the monotonous narrative which follows this paragraph. He never smiled, he never frowned, he never changed his voice from the gentle-flowing key to which he tuned the initial sentence, he never betrayed the slightest suspicion of enthusiasm; but all through the interminable narrative there ran a vein of impressive earnestness and sincerity, which showed me plainly that, so far from his imagining that there was any thing ridiculous or funny about his story, he regarded it as a really important matter, and admired its two heroes as men of transcendent genius in *finesse*. To me, the spectacle of a man drifting serenely along through such a queer yarn without ever smiling, was exquisitely absurd. As I said before, I asked him to tell me what he knew of Rev. Leonidas W. Smiley, and he replied as follows. I let him go on in his own way, and never interrupted him once:

There was a feller here once by the name of *Jim* Smiley, in the winter of '49— or may be it was the spring of '50—I don't recollect exactly, somehow, though what makes me think it was one or the other is because I remember the big flume wasn't finished when he first came to the camp; but any way, he was the curiosest man about always betting on any thing that turned up you ever see, if he could get any body to bet on the other side; and if he couldn't, he'd change sides. Any way that suited the other man would suit him—any way just so's he got a bet, *he* was satisfied. But still he was lucky, uncommon lucky; he most always come out winner. He was always ready and laying for a chance; there couldn't be no solitry thing mentioned but that feller'd offer to bet on it, and take any side you please, as I was just telling you. If there was a horse-race, you'd find him flush, or you'd find him busted at the end of it; if there was a dog-fight, he'd bet on it; if there was a cat-fight, he'd bet on it; if there was a chicken-fight, he'd bet on it; why, if there was two birds setting on a fence, he would bet you which one would fly first; or if there was a camp-meeting, he would be there reg'lar, to bet on Parson Walker, which he judged to be the best exhorter about here, and so he was, too, and a good man. If he even seen a straddle-bug start to go anywheres, he would bet you how long it would take him to get wherever he was going to, and if you took him up, he would foller that straddle-bug to Mexico but what he would find out where he was bound for and how long he was on the road. Lots of the boys here has seen that Smiley, and can tell you about him. Why, it never made no difference to *him*—

he would bet on *any* thing—the dangdest feller. Parson Walker's wife laid very sick once, for a good while, and it seemed as if they warn't going to save her; but one morning he come in, and Smiley asked how she was, and he said she was considerable better—thank the Lord for his inf'nit mercy—and coming on so smart that, with the blessing of Prov'dence, she'd get well yet; and Smiley, before he thought, says, "Well, I'll risk two-and-a-half that she don't, any way."

Thish-yer Smiley had a mare—the boys called her the fifteen-minute nag, but that was only in fun, you know, because, of course, she was faster than that—and he used to win money on that horse, for all she was so slow and always had the asthma, or the distemper, or the consumption, or something of that kind. They used to give her two or three hundred yards start, and then pass her under way; but always at the fag-end of the race she'd get excited and desperate-like, and come cavorting and straddling up, and scattering her legs around limber, sometimes in the air, and sometimes out to one side amongst the fences, and kicking up m-o-r-e dust, and raising m-o-r-e racket with her coughing and sneezing and blowing her nose—and always fetch up at the stand just about a neck ahead, as near as you could cipher it down.

And he had a little small bull pup, that to look at him you'd think he wan't worth a cent, but to set around and look ornery, and lay for a chance to steal something. But as soon as money was up on him, he was a different dog; his under-jaw'd begin to stick out like the fo'castle of a steamboat, and his teeth would uncover, and shine savage like the furnaces. And a dog might tackle him, and bully-rag him, and bite him, and throw him over his shoulder two or three times, and Andrew Jackson—which was the name of the pup—Andrew Jackson would never let on but what *he* was satisfied, and hadn't expected nothing else—and the bets being doubled and doubled on the other side all the time, till the money was all up; and then all of a sudden he would grab that other dog jest by the j'int of his hind leg and freeze to it—not chaw, you understand, but only jest grip and hang on till they throwed up the sponge, if it was a year. Smiley always come out winner on that pup, till he harnessed a dog once that didn't have no hind legs, because they'd been sawed off by a circular saw, and when the thing had gone along far enough, and the money was all up, and he come to make a snatch for his pet holt, he saw in a minute how he'd been imposed on, and how the other dog had him in the door, so to speak, and he 'peared surprised, and then he looked sorter discouraged-like, and didn't try no more to win the fight, and so he got shucked out bad. He give Smiley a look, as much as to say his heart was broke, and it was *his* fault, for putting up a dog that hadn't no hind legs for him to take holt of, which was his main dependence in a fight, and then he limped off a piece and laid down and died. It was a good pup, was that Andrew Jackson, and would have made a name for hisself if he'd lived, for the stuff was in him, and he had genius—I know it, because he hadn't had no opportunities to speak of, and it don't stand to reason that a dog could make such a fight as he could under them circumstances, if he hadn't no talent. It always makes me feel sorry when I think of that last fight of his'n, and the way it turned out.

Well, thish-yer Smiley had rat-tarriers, and chicken cocks, and tom-cats, and all them kind of things, till you couldn't rest, and you couldn't fetch nothing for him to bet on but he'd match you. He ketched a frog one day, and took him home, and said he cal'klated to edercate him; and so he never done nothing for three months but set in his back yard and learn that frog to jump. And you bet you he *did* learn him, too. He'd give him a little punch behind, and the next minute you'd see that frog whirling in the air like a doughnut—see him turn one summerset, or maybe a couple, if he got a good start, and come down flat-footed and all right, like a cat. He got him up so in the matter of catching flies, and kept him in practice so constant, that he'd nail a fly every time as far as he could see him. Smiley said all a frog wanted was education, and he could do most any thing—and I believe him. Why, I've seen him set Dan'l Webster down here on this floor—Dan'l Webster was the name of the frog—and sing out, "Flies, Dan'l, flies!" and quicker'n you could wink, he'd spring straight up, and snake a fly off'n the counter there, and flop down on the floor again as solid as a gob of mud, and fall to scratching the side of his head with his hind foot as indifferent as if he hadn't no idea he'd been doin' any more'n any frog might do. You never see a frog so modest and straightfor'ard as he was, for all he was so gifted. And when it come to fair and square jumping on a dead level, he could get over more ground at one straddle than any animal of his breed you ever see. Jumping on a dead level was his strong suit, you understand; and when it come to that, Smiley would ante up money on him as long as he had a red. Smiley was monstrous proud of his frog, and well he might be, for fellers that had traveled and been everywheres, all said he laid over any frog that ever *they* see.

Well, Smiley kept the beast in a little lattice box, and he used to fetch him down town sometimes and lay for a bet. One day a feller—a stranger in the camp, he was—come across him with his box, and says:

"What might it be that you've got in the box?"

And Smiley says, sorter indifferent like, "It might be a parrot, or it might be a canary, may be, but it an't—it's only just a frog."

And the feller took it, and looked at it careful, and turned it round this way and that, and says, "H'm—so 'tis. Well, what's *he* good for?"

"Well," Smiley says, easy and careless, "He's good enough for *one* thing, I should judge—he can outjump ary frog in Calaveras county."

The feller took the box again, and took another long, particular look, and give it back to Smiley, and says, very deliberate, "Well, I don't see no p'ints about that frog that's any better'n any other frog."

"Maybe you don't," Smiley says. "Maybe you understand frogs, and maybe you don't understand 'em; maybe you've had experience, and maybe you an't only a amature, as it were. Anyways, I've got *my* opinion, and I'll risk forty dollars that he can outjump any frog in Calaveras county."

And the feller studied a minute, and then says, kinder sad like, "Well, I'm only a stranger here, and I an't got no frog; but if I had a frog, I'd bet you."

And then Smiley says, "That's all right—that's all right—if you'll hold my box a minute, I'll go and get you a frog." And so the feller took the box, and put up his forty dollars along with Smiley's, and set down to wait.

So he set there a good while thinking and thinking, to hisself, and then he got the frog out and prized his mouth open and took a teaspoon and filled him full of quail shot—filled him pretty near up to his chin—and set him on the floor. Smiley he went to the swamp and slopped around in the mud for a long time, and finally he ketched a frog, and fetched him in, and give him to this feller, and says:

"Now, if you're ready, set him alongside of Dan'l, with his fore-paws just even with Dan'l, and I'll give the word." Then he says, "One—two—three—jump!" and him and the feller touched up the frogs from behind, and the new frog hopped off, but Dan'l give a heave, and hysted up his shoulders—so—like a Frenchman, but it wan't no use—he couldn't budge; he was planted as solid as an anvil, and he couldn't no more stir than if he was anchored out. Smiley was a good deal surprised, and he was disgusted too, but he didn't have no idea what the matter was, of course.

The feller took the money and started away; and when he was going out at the door, he sorter jerked his thumb over his shoulders—this way—at Dan'l, and says again, very deliberate, "Well, *I* don't see no p'ints about that frog that's any better'n any other frog."

Smiley he stood scratching his head and looking down at Dan'l a long time, and at last he says, "I do wonder what in the nation that frog throw'd off for—I wonder if there an't something the matter with him—he 'pears to look mighty baggy, somehow." And he ketched Dan'l by the nap of the neck, and lifted him up and says, "Why, blame my cats, it he don't weigh five pound!" and turned him upside down, and he belched out a double handful of shot. And then he see how it was, and he was the maddest man—he set the frog down and took out after that feller, but he never ketched him. And—

(Here Simon Wheeler heard his name called from the front yard, and got up to see what was wanted.) And turning to me as he moved away, he said: "Just set where you are, stranger, and rest easy—I an't going to be gone a second."

But, by your leave, I did not think that a continuation of the history of the enterprising vagabond *Jim* Smiley would be likely to afford me much information concerning the Rev. *Leonidas W.* Smiley, and so I started away.

At the door I met the sociable Wheeler returning, and he buttonholed me and recommenced:

"Well, thish-yer Smiley had a yaller one-eyed cow that didn't have no tail, only jest a short stump like a bannanner, and—"

"Oh! hang Smiley and his afflicted cow!" I muttered, good-naturedly, and bidding the old gentleman good-day, I departed.

THE LUCK OF ROARING CAMP

BRET HARTE

Bret Harte (1836–1902) was born Francis Brett Harte in Albany, New York, and quit school at age thirteen to help support his widowed mother. In 1854 he sailed to California and found work as a druggist, teacher, stagecoach expressman, and news-paper writer. It wasn't until he was named editor of the Overland Monthly *in 1868 that his writing career skyrocketed—his sentimental tales of mining life, written well after the gold rush, made him the highest paid writer in the United States and an international star. Stories like "The Outcasts of Poker Flat" and "Tennessee's Partner" teemed with fallen women, steely gamblers, and grizzled miners with hearts of gold. Bret Harte provided the world a colorful, romantic picture of the gold rush that has dominated the memory of the event ever since. "The Luck of Roaring Camp" appeared in* Overland Monthly *in 1868.*

THERE WAS COMMOTION in Roaring Camp. It could not have been a fight, for in 1850 that was not novel enough to have called together the entire settlement. The ditches and claims were not only deserted, but "Tuttle's grocery" had contributed its gamblers, who, it will be remembered, calmly continued their game the day that French Pete and Kanaka Joe shot each other to death over the bar in the front room.

The whole camp was collected before a rude cabin on the outer edge of the clearing. Conversation was carried on in a low tone, but the name of a woman was frequently repeated. It was a name familiar enough in the camp— "Cherokee Sal." Perhaps the less said of her the better. She was a coarse and, it is to be feared, a very sinful woman. But at that time she was the only woman in Roaring Camp, and was just then lying in sore extremity, when she most needed the ministration of her own sex. Dissolute, abandoned, and irreclaimable, she was yet suffering a martyrdom hard enough to bear even when veiled by sympathizing womanhood, but·now terrible in her loneliness. The primal curse had come to her in that original isolation which must have made the punishment of the first transgression so dreadful.

It was, perhaps, part of the expiation of her sin that, at a moment when she most lacked her sex's intuitive tenderness and care, she met only the half-contemptuous faces of her masculine associates. Yet a few of the spectators were, I think, touched by her sufferings. Sandy Tipton thought it was rough on Sal, and, in the contemplation of her condition, for a moment rose superior to the fact that he had an ace and two bowers in his sleeve.

It will be seen also that the situation was novel. Deaths were by no means uncommon in Roaring Camp, but a birth was a new thing. People had been dismissed from the camp effectively, finally, and with no possibility of return; but this was the first time that anybody had been introduced *ab initio*. Hence the excitement.

"You go in there, Stumpy," said a prominent citizen known as "Kentuck," addressing one of the loungers. "Go in there, and see what you kin do. You've had experience in them things."

Perhaps there was a fitness in the selection. Stumpy, in other climes, had been the putative head of two families; in fact, it was owing to some legal informality in these proceedings that Roaring Camp—a city of refuge—was indebted to his company. The crowd approved the choice, and Stumpy was wise enough to bow to the majority. The door closed on the extempore surgeon and midwife, and Roaring Camp sat down outside, smoked its pipe, and awaited the issue.

The assemblage numbered about a hundred men. One or two of these were actual fugitives from justice, some were criminal, and all were reckless. Physically they exhibited no indication of their past lives and character. The greatest scamp had a Raphael face, with a profusion of blonde hair; Oakhurst, a gambler, had the melancholy air and intellectual abstraction of a Hamlet; the coolest and most courageous man was scarcely over five feet in height, with a soft voice and an embarrassed, timid manner.

The term "roughs" applied to them was a distinction rather than a definition. Perhaps in the minor details of fingers, toes, ears, etc., the camp may have been deficient, but these slight omissions did not detract from their aggregate force. The strongest man had but three fingers on his right hand; the best shot had but one eye.

Such was the physical aspect of the men that were dispersed around the cabin. The camp lay in a triangular valley between two hills and a river. The only outlet was a steep trail over the summit of a hill that faced the cabin, now illuminated by the rising moon. The suffering woman might have seen it from the rude bunk whereon she lay—seen it winding like a silver thread until it was lost in the stars above.

A fire of withered pine boughs added sociability to the gathering. By degrees the natural levity of Roaring Camp returned. Bets were freely offered

"Sunday Morning in the Mines," 1872, by Charles Nahl

and taken regarding the result. Three to five that "Sal would get through with it;" even that the child would survive; side bets as to the sex and complexion of the coming stranger.

In the midst of an excited discussion an exclamation came from those nearest the door, and the camp stopped to listen. Above the swaying and moaning of the pines, the swift rush of the river, and the crackling of the fire rose a sharp, querulous cry—a cry unlike anything heard before in the camp. The pines stopped moaning, the river ceased to rush, and the fire to crackle. It seemed as if Nature had stopped to listen too.

The camp rose to its feet as one man! It was proposed to explode a barrel of gunpowder; but in consideration of the situation of the mother, better counsels prevailed, and only a few revolvers were discharged; for whether owing to the rude surgery of the camp, or some other reason, Cherokee Sal was sinking fast. Within an hour she had climbed, as it were, that rugged road that led to the stars, and so passed out of Roaring Camp, its sin and shame, forever.

I do not think that the announcement disturbed them much, except in speculation as to the fate of the child. "Can he live now?" was asked of Stumpy. The answer was doubtful. The only other being of Cherokee Sal's sex and maternal condition in the settlement was an ass. There was some conjecture as to fitness, but the experiment was tried. It was less problematical than the ancient treatment of Romulus and Remus, and apparently as successful.

When these details were completed, which exhausted another hour, the door was opened, and the anxious crowd of men, who had already formed themselves into a queue, entered in single file. Beside the low bunk or shelf, on which the figure of the mother was starkly outlined below the blankets, stood a pine table. On this a candle-box was placed, and within it, swathed in staring red flannel, lay the last arrival at Roaring Camp.

Beside the candle-box was placed a hat. Its use was soon indicated. "Gentlemen," said Stumpy, with a singular mixture of authority and *ex officio* complacency—"gentlemen will please pass in at the front door, round the table, and out at the back door. Them as wishes to contribute anything toward the orphan will find a hat handy." The first man entered with his hat on; he uncovered, however, as he looked about him, and so unconsciously set an example to the next.

In such communities good and bad actions are catching. As the procession filed in comments were audible—criticisms addressed perhaps rather to Stumpy in the character of showman: "Is that him?" "Mighty small specimen;" "Hasn't more'n got the color;" "Ain't bigger nor a derringer."

The contributions were as characteristic: A silver tobacco box; a doubloon; a navy revolver, silver mounted; a gold specimen; a very beautifully embroidered lady's handkerchief, from Oakhurst the gambler; a diamond breastpin; a diamond ring, suggested by the pin, with the remark from the giver that he "saw that pin and went two diamonds better;" a slung-shot; a Bible, contributor not detected; a golden spur; a silver teaspoon, the initials, I regret to say, were not the giver's; a pair of surgeon's shears; a lancet; a Bank of England note for £5; and about $200 in loose gold and silver coin.

During these proceedings Stumpy maintained a silence as impassive as the dead on his left, a gravity as inscrutable as that of the newly born on his right. Only one incident occurred to break the monotony of the curious procession. As Kentuck bent over the candle-box half curiously, the child turned, and, in a spasm of pain, caught at his groping finger, and held it fast for a moment. Kentuck looked foolish and embarrassed. Something like a blush tried to assert itself in his weather-beaten cheek. "The d——d little cuss!" he said, as he extricated his finger, with perhaps more tenderness and care than he might have been deemed capable of showing.

He held that finger a little apart from its fellows as he went out, and examined it curiously. The examination provoked the same original remark in regard to the child. In fact, he seemed to enjoy repeating it. "He rastled with my finger," he remarked to Tipton, holding up the member, "the d——d little cuss!"

It was four o'clock before the camp sought repose. A light burnt in the cabin where the watchers sat, for Stumpy did not go to bed that night. Nor did Kentuck. He drank quite freely, and related with great gusto his experience, invariably ending with his characteristic condemnation of the newcomer. It seemed to relieve him of any unjust implication of sentiment, and Kentuck had the weaknesses of the nobler sex.

When everybody else had gone to bed, he walked down to the river and whistled reflectingly. Then he walked up the gulch past the cabin, still whistling with demonstrative unconcern. At a large redwood tree he paused and retraced his steps, and again passed the cabin. Halfway down to the river's bank he again paused, and then returned and knocked at the door. It was opened by Stumpy.

"How goes it?" said Kentuck, looking past Stumpy toward the candle-box.

"All serene!" replied Stumpy.

"Anything up?"

"Nothing."

There was a pause—an embarrassing one—Stumpy still holding the door. Then Kentuck had recourse to his finger, which he held up to Stumpy. "Rastled with it—the d——d little cuss," he said, and retired.

The next day Cherokee Sal had such rude sepulture as Roaring Camp afforded. After her body had been committed to the hillside, there was a formal meeting of the camp to discuss what should be done with her infant. A resolution to adopt it was unanimous and enthusiastic. But an animated discussion in regard to the manner and feasibility of providing for its wants at once sprang up. It was remarkable that the argument partook of none of those fierce personalities with which discussions were usually conducted at Roaring Camp.

Tipton proposed that they should send the child to Red Dog—a distance of forty miles—where female attention could be procured. But the unlucky suggestion met with fierce and unanimous opposition. It was evident that no plan which entailed parting from their new acquisition would for a moment be entertained. "Besides," said Tom Ryder, "them fellows at Red Dog would swap it, and ring in somebody else on us." A disbelief in the honesty of other camps prevailed at Roaring Camp, as in other places.

The introduction of a female nurse in the camp also met with objection. It was argued that no decent woman could be prevailed to accept Roaring Camp as her home, and the speaker urged that "they didn't want any more of the other kind." This unkind allusion to the defunct mother, harsh as it may seem, was the first spasm of propriety—the first symptom of the camp's regeneration. Stumpy advanced nothing. Perhaps he felt a certain delicacy in interfering with the selection of a possible successor in office. But when questioned, he averred stoutly that he and "Jinny"—the mammal before alluded to—could manage to rear the child.

There was something original, independent, and heroic about the plan that pleased the camp. Stumpy was retained. Certain articles were sent for to Sacramento. "Mind," said the treasurer, as he pressed a bag of gold dust into the expressman's hand, "the best that can be got—lace, you know, and filigreework and frills—d——n the cost!"

Strange to say, the child thrived. Perhaps the invigorating climate of the mountain camp was compensation for material deficiencies. Nature took the foundling to her broader breast. In that rare atmosphere of the Sierra foothills—that air pungent with balsamic odor, that ethereal cordial at once bracing and exhilarating—he may have found food and nourishment, or a subtle chemistry that transmuted ass's milk to lime and phosphorus. Stumpy inclined to the belief that it was the latter and good nursing. "Me and that ass," he would say, "has been father and mother to him! Don't you," he would add, apostrophizing the helpless bundle before him, "never go back on us."

By the time he was a month old the necessity of giving him a name became apparent. He had generally been known as "The Kid," "Stumpy's Boy," "The Coyote" (an allusion to his vocal powers), and even by Kentuck's endearing diminutive of "The d——d little cuss." But these were felt to be vague and unsatisfactory, and were at last dismissed under another influence. Gamblers and adventurers are generally superstitious, and Oakhurst one day declared that the baby had brought "the luck" to Roaring Camp. It was certain that of late they had been successful.

"Luck" was the name agreed upon, with the prefix of Tommy for greater convenience. No allusion was made to the mother, and the father was unknown. "It's better," said the philosophical Oakhurst, "to take a fresh deal all round. Call him Luck, and start him fair."

A day was accordingly set apart for the christening. What was meant by this ceremony the reader may imagine who has already gathered some idea of the reckless irreverence of Roaring Camp. The master of ceremonies was one "Boston," a noted wag, and the occasion seemed to promise the greatest facetiousness. This ingenious satirist had spent two days in preparing a burlesque of the Church service, with pointed local allusions. The choir was properly trained, and Sandy Tipton was to stand godfather.

But after the procession had marched to the grove with music and banners, and the child had been deposited before a mock altar, Stumpy stepped before the expectant crowd. "It ain't my style to spoil fun, boys," said the little man, stoutly eying the faces around him, "but it strikes me that this thing ain't exactly on the squar. It's playing it pretty low down on this yer baby to ring in fun on him that he ain't goin' to understand. And ef there's goin' to be any godfathers round, I'd like to see who's got any better rights than me."

A silence followed Stumpy's speech. To the credit of all humorists be it said that the first man to acknowledge its justice was the satirist thus stopped of his fun. "But," said Stumpy, quickly following up his advantage, "we're here for a christening, and we'll have it. I proclaim you Thomas Luck, according to the laws of the United States and the State of California, so help me God."

It was the first time that the name of the Deity had been otherwise uttered than profanely in the camp. The form of christening was perhaps even more ludicrous than the satirist had conceived; but strangely enough, nobody saw it and nobody laughed. "Tommy" was christened as seriously as he would have been under a Christian roof, and cried and was comforted in as orthodox fashion.

And so the work of regeneration began in Roaring Camp. Almost imperceptibly a change came over the settlement. The cabin assigned to "Tommy Luck"—or "The Luck," as he was more frequently called—first showed signs of improvement. It was kept scrupulously clean and whitewashed. Then it was boarded, clothed, and papered. The rosewood cradle, packed eighty miles by mule, had, in Stumpy's way of putting it, "sorter killed the rest of the furniture." So the rehabilitation of the cabin became a necessity.

The men who were in the habit of lounging in at Stumpy's to see "how 'The Luck' got on" seemed to appreciate the change, and in self-defense the rival establishment of "Tuttle's grocery" bestirred itself and imported a carpet and mirrors. The reflections of the latter on the appearance of Roaring Camp tended to produce stricter habits of personal cleanliness.

Again Stumpy imposed a kind of quarantine upon those who aspired to the honor and privilege of holding The Luck. It was a cruel mortification to Kentuck—who, in the carelessness of a large nature and the habits of frontier life, had begun to regard all garments as a second cuticle, which, like a snake's, only sloughed off through decay—to be debarred this privilege from certain prudential reasons. Yet such was the subtle influence of innovation that he thereafter appeared regularly every afternoon in a clean shirt and face still shining from his ablutions.

Nor were moral and social sanitary laws neglected. "Tommy," who was supposed to spend his whole existence in a persistent attempt to repose, must not be disturbed by noise. The shouting and yelling, which had gained the camp its infelicitous title, were not permitted within hearing distance of Stumpy's. The men conversed in whispers or smoked with Indian gravity. Profanity was tacitly given up in these sacred precincts, and throughout the camp a popular form of expletive, known as "D——n the luck!" and "Curse the luck!" was abandoned, as having a new personal bearing.

Vocal music was not interdicted, being supposed to have a soothing, tranquilizing quality; and one song, sung by "Man o'War Jack," an English sailor from her Majesty's Australian colonies, was quite popular as a lullaby. It was a lugubrious recital of the exploits of "the Arethusa, Seventy-four," in a muffled minor, ending with a prolonged dying fall at the burden of each verse, "On b-oo-o-ard of the Arethusa." It was a fine sight to see Jack holding The Luck, rocking from side to side as if with the motion of a ship, and crooning forth this naval ditty. Either through the peculiar rocking of Jack or the length of his song—it contained ninety stanzas, and was continued with conscientious deliberation to the bitter end—the lullaby generally had the desired effect.

At such times the men would lie at full length under the trees in the soft summer twilight, smoking their pipes and drinking in the melodious utterances. An indistinct idea that this was pastoral happiness pervaded the camp. "This 'ere kind o' think," said the Cockney Simmons, meditatively reclining on his elbow, "is 'evingly." It reminded him of Greenwich.

On the long summer days The Luck was usually carried to the gulch from whence the golden store of Roaring Camp was taken. There, on a blanket spread over pine boughs, he would lie while the men were working in the ditches below. Latterly there was a rude attempt to decorate this bower with flowers and sweet-smelling shrubs, and generally someone would bring him a cluster of wild honeysuckles, azaleas, or the painted blossoms of Las Mariposas.

The men had suddenly awakened to the fact that there were beauty and significance in these trifles, which they had so long trodden carelessly beneath their feet. A flake of glittering mica, a fragment of variegated quartz, a bright pebble from the bed of the creek, became beautiful to eyes thus cleared and strengthened, and were invariably put aside for The Luck. It was wonderful how many treasures the woods and hillsides yielded that "would do for Tommy." Surrounded by playthings such as never child out of fairyland had before, it is to be hoped that Tommy was content. He appeared to be serenely happy, albeit there was an infantine gravity about him, a contemplative light in his round gray eyes, that sometimes worried Stumpy.

He was always tractable and quiet, and it is recorded that once, having crept beyond his corral—a hedge of tessellated pine boughs, which surrounded his bed—he dropped over the bank on his head in the soft earth, and remained with his mottled legs in the air in that position for at least five minutes with unflinching gravity. He was extricated without a murmur. I hesitate to record the many other instances of his sagacity, which rest, unfortunately, upon the statements of prejudiced friends. Some of them were not without a tinge of superstition.

"I crep' up the bank just now," said Kentuck one day, in a breathless state of excitement, "and dern my skin if he wasn't a-talking to a jaybird as was a-sittin' on his lap. There they was, just as free and sociable as anything you please, a-jawin' at each other just like two cherrybums."

Howbeit, whether creeping over the pine boughs or lying lazily on his back blinking at the leaves above him, to him the birds sang, the squirrels chattered, and the flowers bloomed. Nature was his nurse and playfellow. For him she would let slip between the leaves golden shafts of sunlight that fell just within his grasp; she would send wandering breezes to visit him with the balm of bay and resinous gum; to him the tall redwoods nodded familiarly and sleepily, the bumblebees buzzed, and the rooks cawed a slumbrous accompaniment.

Such was the golden summer of Roaring Camp. They were "flush times," and the luck was with them. The claims had yielded enormously. The camp was jealous of its privileges and looked suspiciously on strangers. No encouragement was given to immigration, and, to make their seclusion more perfect, the land on either side of the mountain wall that surrounded the camp they duly pre-empted.

This, and a reputation for singular proficiency with the revolver, kept the reserve of Roaring Camp inviolate. The expressman—their only connecting link with the surrounding world—sometimes told wonderful stories of the camp. He would say, "They've a street up there in 'Roaring' that would lay over any street in Red Dog. They've got vines and flowers round their houses, and they wash themselves twice a day. But they're mighty rough on strangers, and they worship an Injin baby."

With the prosperity of the camp came a desire for further improvement. It was proposed to build a hotel in the following spring, and to invite one or two decent families to reside there for the sake of The Luck, who might perhaps profit by female companionship. The sacrifice that this concession to the sex cost these men, who were fiercely skeptical in regard to its general virtue and usefulness, can only be accounted for by their affection for Tommy. A few still held out. But the resolve could not be carried into effect for three months, and the minority meekly yielded in the hope that something might turn up to prevent it. And it did.

The winter of 1851 will long be remembered in the foothills. The snow lay deep on the Sierras, and every mountain creek became a river, and every river a lake. Each gorge and gulch was transformed into a tumultuous watercourse that descended the hillsides, tearing down giant trees and scattering its drift and débris along the plain. Red Dog had been twice under water, and Roaring Camp had been forewarned.

"Water put the gold into them gulches," said Stumpy. "It's been here once and will be here again!" And that night the North Fork suddenly leaped over its banks and swept up the triangular valley of Roaring Camp.

In the confusion of rushing water, crashing trees, and crackling timber, and the darkness which seemed to flow with the water and blot out the fair valley, but little could be done to collect the scattered camp.

When the morning broke, the cabin of Stumpy, nearest the river-bank, was gone. Higher up the gulch they found the body of its unlucky owner; but the pride, the hope, the joy, The Luck, of Roaring Camp had disappeared. They were returning with sad hearts when a shout from the bank recalled them.

It was a relief-boat from down the river. They had picked up, they said, a man and an infant, nearly exhausted, about two miles below. Did anybody know them, and did they belong here?

It needed but a glance to show them Kentuck lying there, cruelly crushed and bruised, but still holding The Luck of Roaring Camp in his arms. As they bent over the strangely assorted pair, they saw that the child was cold and pulseless. "He is dead," said one.

Kentuck opened his eyes. "Dead?" he repeated feebly.

"Yes, my man, and you are dying too."

A smile lit the eyes of the expiring Kentuck. "Dying!" he repeated; "he's a-taking me with him. Tell the boys I've got The Luck with me now;" and the strong man, clinging to the frail babe as a drowning man is said to cling to a straw, drifted away into the shadowy river that flows forever to the unknown sea.

from ROUGHING IT

MARK TWAIN

For his third book, Roughing It, *published in 1872, Mark Twain returned to his western experiences. Autobiographical but full of hyperbole, melodrama, and outright lies,* Roughing It *was admittedly designed to "top Bret Harte again or bust." It proved extremely popular, selling more than 90,000 copies in the first year. It was an early demonstration of Twain's infatuation with coarse, "unliterary" characters that would later lead to such American classics as* Adventures of Huckleberry Finn *and* Tom Sawyer.

IT WAS IN THE SACRAMENTO VALLEY ... that a deal of the most lucrative of the early gold mining was done, and you may still see, in places, its grassy slopes and levels torn and guttered and disfigured by the avaricious spoilers of fifteen and twenty years ago. You may see such disfigurements far and wide over California—and in some such places, where only meadows and forests are visible—not a living creature, not a house, no stick or stone or remnant of a ruin, and not a sound, not even a whisper to disturb the Sabbath stillness—you will find it hard to believe that there stood at one time a fiercely-flourishing little city, of two thousand or three thousand souls, with its newspaper, fire company, brass band, volunteer militia, bank, hotels, noisy Fourth of July processions and speeches, gambling hells crammed with tobacco smoke, profanity, and rough-bearded men of all nations and colors, with tables heaped with gold dust sufficient for the revenues of a German principality—streets crowded and rife with buisiness—town lots worth four hundred dollars a front foot—labor, laughter, music, dancing, swearing, fighting, shooting, stabbing—a bloody inquest and a man for breakfast every morning—*everything* that delights and adorns existence—all the appointments and appurtenances of a thriving and prosperous and promising young city,—and *now* nothing is left of it all but a lifeless, homeless solitude. The men are gone, the houses have vanished, even the *name* of the place is forgotten. In no other land, in modern times, have towns so absolutely died and disappeared, as in the old mining regions of California.

It was a driving, vigorous, restless population in those days. It was a *curious* population. It was the *only* population of the kind that the world has ever seen gathered together, and it is not likely that the world will ever see its like again. For, observe, it was an assemblage of two hundred thousand *young* men—not simpering, dainty, kid-gloved weaklings, but stalwart, muscular, dauntless young braves, brim full of push and energy, and royally endowed with every attribute that goes to make up a peerless and magnificent manhood—the very pick and choice of the world's glorious ones. No women, no children, no gray and stooping veterans,—none but erect, bright-eyed, quick-moving, strong-handed young giants—the strangest population, the finest population, the most gallant host that ever trooped down the startled solitudes of an unpeopled land. And where are they now? Scattered to the ends of the earth—or prematurely aged and decrepit—or shot or stabbed in street affrays—or dead of disappointed hopes and broken hearts—all gone, or nearly all—victims devoted upon the altar of the golden calf—the noblest holocaust that ever wafted its sacrificial incense heavenward. It is pitiful to think upon.

It was a splendid population—for all the slow, sleepy, sluggish-brained sloths staid at home—you never find that sort of people among pioneers—you cannot build pioneers out of that sort of material. It was that population that gave to California a name for getting up astounding enterprises and rushing them through with a magnificent dash and daring and a recklessness of cost or consequences, which she bears unto this day—and when she projects a new surprise, the grave world smiles as usual, and says "Well, that is California all over."

But they were rough in those times! They fairly reveled in gold, whisky, fights, and fandangoes, and were unspeakably happy. The honest miner raked from a hundred to a thousand dollars out of his claim a day, and what with the gambling dens and the other entertainments, he hadn't a cent the next morning, if he had any sort of luck. They cooked their own bacon and beans, sewed on their own buttons, washed their own shirts—blue woolen ones; and if a man wanted a fight on his hands without any annoying delay, all he had to do was to appear in public in a white shirt or a stove-pipe hat, and he would be accommodated. For those people hated aristocrats. They had a particular and malignant animosity toward what they called a "biled shirt."

It was a wild, free, disorderly, grotesque society. *Men*—only swarming hosts of stalwart *men*—nothing juvenile, nothing feminine visible anywhere!

In those days miners would flock in crowds to catch a glimpse of that rare and blessed spectacle, a woman! Old inhabitants tell how, in a certain camp, the news went abroad early in the morning that a woman was come! They had seen a calico dress hanging out of a wagon down at the camping-ground—sign of emigrants from over the great Plains. Everybody went down there, and a shout went up when an actual, bona fide dress was discovered fluttering in the wind! The male emigrant was visible. The miners said:

"*Fetch her out!*"

He said: "It is my wife, gentlemen—she is sick—we have been robbed of money, provisions, everything, by the Indians—we want to rest."

"Fetch her out! We've got to see her!"

"But, gentlemen, the poor thing, she—"

"*Fetch her out!*"

He "fetched her out," and they swung their hats and sent up three rousing cheers and a tiger; and they crowded around and gazed at her, and touched her dress, and listened to her voice with the look of men who listened to a *memory* rather than a present reality—and then they collected twenty-five hundred dollars in gold and gave it to the man, and swung their hats again and gave three more cheers, and went home satisfied.

Once I dined in San Francisco with the family of a pioneer, and talked with his daughter, a young lady whose first experience in San Francisco was an adventure, though she herself did not remember it, as she was only two or three years old at the time. Her father said that, after landing the ship, they were walking up the street, a servant leading the party with the little girl in her arms. And presently a huge miner, bearded, belted, spurred, and bristling with deadly weapons—just down from a long campaign in the mountains, evidently—barred the way, stopped the servant, and stood gazing, with a face all alive with gratification and astonishment. Then he said, reverently:

"Well, if it ain't a child!" And then he snatched a little leather sack out of his pocket and said to the servant:

"There a hundred and fifty dollars in dust, there, and I'll give it to you if you let me kiss the child!"

That anecdote is *true*.

But see how things change. Sitting at that dinner table, listening to that anecdote, if I had offered double the money for the privilege of kissing the same child, I would have been refused. Seventeen added years have far more than doubled the price.

DICKENS IN CAMP

BRET HARTE

After his melodramatic gold rush tales made him famous, Bret Harte left California in 1871, never to return. After an ill-fated stint with the Atlantic Monthly *in New York, he left his family in 1877 and moved to England. He continued to write stories set in the gold rush; ironically, the further from California he went, the more he was loved. His novels, plays, short stories, poetry, and literary criticism filled twenty volumes before his death in London in 1902. "Dickens in Camp" appeared in Harte's* Overland Monthly *in 1870.*

Above the pines the moon was slowly drifting,
    The river sang below;
The dim Sierras, far beyond, uplifting
    Their minarets of snow.

The roaring camp-fire, with rude humor, painted
    The ruddy tints of health
On haggard face and form that drooped and fainted
    In the fierce race for wealth;

Till one arose, and from his pack's scant treasure
    A hoarded volume drew,
And cards were dropped from hands of listless leisure
    To hear the tale anew.

And then, while round them shadows gathered faster,
    And as the firelight fell,
He read aloud the book wherein the Master
    Had writ of "Little Nell."

Perhaps 't was boyish fancy—for the reader
    Was youngest of them all—
But, as he read, from clustering pine and cedar
    A silence seemed to fall;

The fir-trees, gathering closer in the shadows,
    Listened in every spray,
While the whole camp with "Nell" on English meadows
    Wandered and lost their way.

And so in mountain solitudes—o'ertaken
    As by some spell divine—
Their cares dropped from them like the needles shaken
    From out the gusty pine.

Lost is that camp and wasted all its fire,
    And he who wrought that spell?
Ah! towering pine and stately Kentish spire,
    Ye have one tale to tell!

Lost is that camp, but let its fragrant story
    Blend with the breath that thrills
With hop-vine's incense all the pensive glory
    That fills the Kentish hills.

And on that grave where English oak and holly
    And laurel wreaths entwine,
Deem it not all a too presumptuous folly,
    This spray of Western pine!

from LIFE AMONGST THE MODOCS: UNWRITTEN HISTORY

JOAQUIN MILLER

The facts of Joaquin Miller's (c.1845–1913) life are hard to distinguish from the author's romantic embellishments, but it is almost certain he was born Cincinnatus Hiner Miller in Indiana and came to Oregon as a child. Adopting the nickname "Joaquin" as a nod to the famous Mexican bandit Joaquín Murieta, Miller's grandiose poetry and larger-than-life persona attracted attention in the San Francisco literary scene. A poet, playwright, and swaggering celebrity, he had also spent time as a horse thief, lawyer, newspaper editor, pony-express rider, Indian fighter, and Indian sympathizer. His Life Amongst the Modocs: Unwritten History (1873), which purportedly chronicled Miller's life with the Indians of the Mount Shasta region between 1856 and 1860, remains one of the liveliest autobiographical western tales ever written by a Californian. Its depiction of the treatment of Indians by the miners was, for its time, courageous and influential.

THERE WAS A TRIBE of Indians camped down on the rapid, rocky Klamat river—a sullen, ugly set were they, too: at least so said The Forks. Never social, hardly seeming to notice the whites, who were now thick about them, below them, above them, on the river, and all around them. Sometimes we would meet one on the narrow trail; he would gather his skins about him, hide his bow and arrows under their folds, and, without seeming to see any one, would move past us still as a shadow. I do not remember that I ever saw one of these Indians laugh, not even to smile. A hard-featured, half-starved set of savages, of whom the wise men of the camp prophesied no good.

The snow, unusually deep this winter, had driven them all down from the mountains, and they were compelled to camp on the river.

The game, too, had been driven down along with the Indians, but it was of but little use to them. Their bows and arrows did poor competition with the rifles of the whites in the killing of the game. The whites fairly filled the cabins with deer and elk, got all the lion's share, and left the Indians almost destitute.

Another thing that made it rather more hard on the Indians than anything else was the utter failure of the annual run of salmon the summer before, on account of the muddy water. The Klamat, which had poured from the mountain lakes to the sea as clear as glass, was now made muddy and turbid from the miners washing for gold on its banks and its tributaries. The trout turned on their sides and died; the salmon from the sea came in but rarely on account of this; and what few did come were pretty safe from the spears of the Indians, because of the coloured water; so that supply, which was more than all others their bread and their meat, was entirely cut off.

Mine? It was all a mystery to these Indians as long as they were permitted to live. Besides, there were some whites mining who made poor headway against hunger. I have seen them gather in groups on the bank above the mines and watch in silence for hours as if endeavouring to make it out; at last they would shrug their shoulders, draw their skins closer about them, and stalk away no wiser than before.

Why we should tear up the earth, toil like gnomes from sun-up to sun-down, rain or sun, destroy the forests, and pollute the rivers was to them more than a mystery—it was a terror. I believe they accepted it as a curse, the work of evil spirits, and so bowed to it in sublime silence.

This loss of salmon was a greater loss than you would suppose. These fish in the spring-time pour up these streams from the sea in incalculable swarms. They fairly darken the water. On the head of the Sacramento, before that once beautiful river was changed from a silver sheet to a dirty yellow stream, I have seen between the Devil's Castle and Mount Shasta the stream so filled with salmon that it was impossible to force a horse across the current. Of course, this is not usual, and now can only be met with hard up at the heads of mountain streams where mining is not carried on, and where the advance of the fish is checked by falls on the head of the stream. The amount of salmon which the Indians would spear and dry in the sun, and hoard away for winter, under such circumstances, can be imagined; and I can now better understand their utter discomfiture at the loss of their fisheries than I did then.

A sharp, fierce winter was upon them; for reasons above stated they had no store of provisions on hand, save, perhaps, a few dried roots and berries; and the whites had swept away and swallowed up the game before them as fast as it had been driven by the winter from the mountains.

What made matters worse, there was a bet of men, low men, loafers, and of the lowest type, who would hang around those lodges at night, give the Indians whiskey of the vilest sort, debauch their women, and cheat the men out of their skins and bows and arrows. There was not a saloon, not a gambling den in camp that did not have a sheaf of feathered, flint-headed arrows in an otter quiver, and a yew bow hanging behind the bar.

Perhaps there was a grim sort of philosophy in the red man so disposing of his bow and arrows now that the game was gone and they were of no further use. Sold them for bread for his starving babes, maybe. How many tragedies are hidden here? How many tales of devotion, self-denial, and sacrifice, as true as the white man lived, as pure, and brave, and beautiful as ever gave tongue to eloquence or pen to song, sleep here with the dust of these sad and silent people on the bank of the stormy river!

In this condition of things, about mid-winter, when the snow was deep and crusted stiff, and all nature seemed dead and buried in a ruffled shroud, there was a murder. The Indians had broken out! The prophesied massacre had begun! Killed by the Indians! It swept like a telegram through the camp. Confused and incoherent, it is true, but it gathered force and form as the tale flew on from tongue to tongue, until it assumed a frightful shape.

A man had been killed by the Indians down at the rancheria. Not much of a man, it is true. A "capper"; sort of tool and hanger-on about the lowest gambling dens. Killed, too, down in the Indian camp when he should have been in bed, or at home, or at least in company with his kind.

All this made the miners hesitate a bit as they hurriedly gathered in at The Forks, with their long Kentucky rifles, their pistols capped and primed, and bowie knives in their belts.

But as the gathering storm that was to sweep the Indians from the earth took shape and form, these honest men stood out in little knots, leaning on their rifles in the streets, and gravely questioned whether, all things considered, the death of the "Chicken," for that was the dead man's name, was sufficient cause for interference.

To their eternal credit these men mainly decided that it was not, and two by two they turned away, went back to their cabins, hung their rifles up on the rack, and turned their thoughts to their own affairs.

But the hangers-on about the town were terribly enraged. "A man has been killed!" they proclaimed aloud. "A man has been murdered by the savages!! We shall all be massacred! butchered! burnt!!"

In one of the saloons where men were wont to meet at night, have stag-dances, and drink lightning, a short, important man, with the print of a glass-tumbler cut above his eye, arose and made a speech.

"Fellow-miners (he had never touched a pick in his life), I am ready to die for me country! (He was an Irishman sent out to Sydney at the Crown's expense.) What have I to live for? (Nothing whatever, as far as anyone could tell.) Fellow-miners, a man has been kilt by the treacherous savages—kilt in cold blood! Fellow-miners, let us advance upon the inemy. Let us—let us— fellow-miners, let us take a drink and advance upon the inemy."

This man had borrowed a pistol, and held or flourished it in his hand as he talked to the crowd of idlers, rum-dealers, and desperadoes—to all of whom any diversion from the monotony of camp-life, or excitement, seemed a blessing.

"Range around me. Rally to the bar and take a drink, every man of you, at me own ixpense." The bar-keeper, who was also proprietor of the place, a man not much above the type of the speaker, ventured a mild remonstrance at this wholesale generosity; but the pistol, flourished in a very suggestive way, settled the matter, and, with something of a groan, he set his decanters to the crowd, and became a bankrupt.

This was the beginning; they passed from saloon to saloon, or, rather, from door to door; the short, stout Irishman making speeches and the mob gathering force and arms as it went, and then, wild with drink and excitement, moving down upon the Indians, some miles away on the bank of the river.

"Come," said the Prince to me, as they passed out of town, "let us see this through. Here will be blood. We will see from the hill overlooking the camp. I hope the Indians are 'on it'—hope to God they are 'heeled,' and that they will receive the wretches warmly as they deserve." The Prince was black with passion.

Maybe his own wretchedness had something to do with his wrath; but I think not. I should rather say that had he been in strength and spirits, and had his pistols, which had long since been disposed of for bread, he had met this mob face to face, and sent them back to town or to the place where they belonged.

We followed not far behind the crowd of fifty or sixty men armed with pistols, rifles, knives, and hatchets. The trail led to a little point overlooking the bar on which the Indian huts were huddled.

The river made a bend about there. It ground and boiled in a crescent blocked with running ice and snow. They were out in the extreme curve of a horse-shoe made by the river, and we advanced from without. They were in a net. They had only a choice of deaths; death by drowning, or death at the hands of their hereditary foe.

It was nearly night; cold and sharp the wind blew up the river and the snow flew around like feathers. Not an Indian to be seen. The thin blue smoke came slowly up, as if afraid to leave the wigwams, and the traditional, ever watchful and wakeful Indian dog was not to be seen or heard. The men hurried down upon the camp, spreading out upon the horse-shoe as they advanced in a run.

"Stop here," said the Prince; and we stood from the wind behind a boulder that stood, tall as a cabin, upon the bar. The crowd advanced to within half a pistol shot, and gave a shout as they drew and leveled their arms. Old squaws came out—bang! bang! bang! shot after shot, and they were pierced and fell, or turned to run.

Some men sprung up, wounded, but fell the instant; for the whites, yelling, howling, screaming, were among the lodges, shooting down at arm's length man, woman, or child. Some attempted the river, I should say, for I afterwards saw streams of blood upon the ice, but not one escaped; nor was a hand raised in defense. It was all done in a little time. Instantly as the shots and shouts began we two advanced, we rushed into the camp, and when we reached the spot only now and then a shot was heard within a lodge, dispatching a wounded man or woman. The few surviving children—for nearly all had been starved to death—had taken refuge under skins and under lodges overthrown, hidden away as little kittens will hide just old enough to spit and hiss, and hide when they first see the face of man. These were now dragged forth and shot. Not all these men who made this mob, bad as they were, did this—only a few; but enough to leave, as far as they could, no living thing. Christ! it was pitiful! The babies did not scream. Not a wail, not a sound. The murdered men and women, in the few minutes that the breath took leave, did not even groan.

As we came up a man named "Shon"—at least, that was all the name I knew for him—held up a baby by the leg, a naked, bony little thing, which he had dragged from under a lodge—held it up with one hand, and with the other blew its head to pieces with his pistol.

I must stop here to say that this man Shon soon left camp, and was afterwards hung by the Vigilance Committee at Lewiston, Idaho Territory; that he whined for his life like a puppy, and died like a coward as he was. I chronicle this fact with a feeling of perfect delight.

He was a tall, spare man, with small, grey eyes, a weak, wicked mouth, colourless and treacherous, that was for ever smiling and smirking in your face.

Shun a man like that. A man who always smiles is a treacherous-natured, contemptible coward.

This man threw down the body of the child among the dead, and rushed across to where a pair of ruffians had dragged up another, a little girl, naked, bony, thin as a shadow, starved into a ghost. He caught her by the hair with a howl of delight, placed the pistol to her head, and turned around as if to point the muzzle out of range of his companions who stood around on the other side. The child did not cry—she did not even flinch. Perhaps she did not know what it meant; but I should rather believe she had seen so much of death there, so much misery, the steady, silent work of the monster famine through the village day after day, that she did not care. I saw her face: it did not even wince.

Her lips were thin and fixed, and firm as iron.

The villain, having turned her around, now lifted his arm, cocked the pistol, and—

"Stop that, you infernal scoundrel! Stop that, or die! You damned assassin, let go that child, or I will pitch you neck and crop into the Klamat."

The Prince had him by the throat with one hand, and with the other he wrested the pistol from his grasp and threw it into the river. The Prince had not even so much as a knife. The man did not know this, nor did the Prince care, or he had not thrown away the weapon he wrung from his hand. The Prince pushed the child behind him, and advanced toward the short, fat Sydney convict, who had now turned, pistol in hand, in his direction.

"Keep your distance, you Sydney duck, keep your distance, or I will send you to hell across lots in a second."

There are some hard names given on the Pacific; but when you call a man a "Sydney duck" it is well understood that you mean blood. If you call a man a liar to his face you must prepare to knock him down on the spot, or he will perform that office for you. If he does not, or does not attempt it, he is counted a coward and is in disgrace. When you call a man a "Sydney duck," however, something more than blows are meant; that means blood. There is but one expression, a vile one, that cannot well be named, that means so much, or carries so much disgrace as this.

The man turned away cowed and baffled. He had looked in the Prince's face, and saw that he was born his master.

As for myself, I was not only helpless, but, as was always the case on similar occasions, stupid, awkward, speechless. I went up to the little girl, however, got a robe out of one of the lodges—for they had not yet set fire to the village—and put it around her naked little body. After that, as I moved about among the dead, or stepped aside to the river to see the streams of blood on the snow and ice, she followed close as a shadow behind me, but said nothing.

Suddenly there was a sharp yell, a volley of oaths, exclamations, a scuffle, and blows.

"Scalp him! Scalp him! the little savage! Scalp him and throw him in the river!"

From out the piles of dead somewhere, no one could tell exactly where or when, an apparition had sprung up—a naked little Indian boy, that might have been all the way from twelve to twenty, armed with a knotted war-club, and fallen upon his foes like a fury.

The poor little hero, starved into a shadow, stood little show there, though he had been a very Hercules in courage. He was felled almost instantly by kicks and blows; and the very number of his enemies saved his life, for they could neither shoot nor stab him with safety as they crowded and crushed around him.

How or why he was finally spared was always a marvel. Quite likely the example of the Prince had moved some of the men to more humanity. As for Shon and Sydney, they had sauntered off with some others toward town at this time, which also, maybe, contributed to the Indian boy's chance for life.

When the crowd that had formed a knot about him had broken up, and I first got sight of him, he was sitting on a stone with his hands between his naked legs, and blood dripping from his long hair, which fell down in strings over his drooping forehead. He had been stunned by a grazing shot, no doubt, and had fallen among the first. He came up to his work, though, like a man, when his senses returned, and without counting the chances, lifted his two hands to do with all his might the thing he had been taught.

Valour, such valour as that, is not a cheap or common thing. It is rare enough to be respected even by the worst of men. It is only the coward that affects to despise such courage. He is moved to this altogether by the lowest kind of jealousy. A coward knows how entirely contemptible he is, and can hardly bear to see another dignified with that noble attribute which he for ever feels is no part of his nature.

So this boy sat there on the stone as the village burned, the smoke from burning skins, the wild-rye straw, willow-baskets, and Indian robes ascended, and a smell of burning bodies went up to the Indians' God and the God of us all, and no one said nay, and no one approached him; the men looked at him from under their slouched hats as they moved around, but said nothing.

I pitied him. God knows I pitied him. I clasped my hands together in grief. I was a boy myself, alone, helpless, in an army of strong and unsympathetic men. I would have gone up and put my arms about the wild and splendid little savage, bloody and desperate as he was, so lonely now, so intimate with death, so pitiful! if I had dared, dared the reproach of men-brutes.

But besides that there was a sort of nobility about him; his recklessness, his desire to die, lifting his little arms against an army of strong and reckless men, his proud and defiant courage, that made me feel at once that he was above me, stronger, somehow better, than I. Still, he was a boy and I was a boy—the only boys in the camp; and my heart went out, strong and true, toward him. The work of destruction was now too complete.

The dead lay around us, piled up in places, limbs twisted with limbs in the wrestle with death; a mother embracing her boy here; an arm thrown around a neck there; as if these wild people could love as well as die.

from AN ENGLISH-CHINESE PHRASE BOOK

WONG SAM AND ASSISTANTS

In 1875, a slim volume entitled An English-Chinese Phrase Book *appeared in Wells Fargo banks in San Francisco and hundreds of other western towns. Written by Wong Sam and his assistants, the book offered phrases the writers thought Chinese workers would need to know. It offers a rare glimpse into the everyday concerns of post-gold rush California's Chinese laborers.*

你愛點樣價銀	What do you ask for them?
你舡減少些	Can you take less for them?
先生　不舡	I cannot, sir.
汝還有好過沒樣麼	Have you any other kind better than these?
價銀太高	The price is too high.
我唔舡俾淂咁多	I am not able to pay.
孩子我都不騙	I don't cheat, even a boy.
先驗明貨正買	Examine your goods before you buy.
因調稅飼太重	Because the duty is too heavy.
不防我騙汝	Don't fear I am cheating you.
我唔相信汝	I cannot trust you.

373

信道理授欺 — Christians bear great trials.

佢强搶我物 — He took it from me by violence.

我無意打佢 — I struck him accidentally.

我認唔該佢還想來打我 — I have made an apology, but still he wants to strike me.

佢無事打我 — He assaulted me without provocation.

我貫沒樓要沒包水 — I will rent the house if you include water.

裝滿箱蘋果 — The box contains apples.

女人暈倒在會堂 — The lady fainted in church.

佢想白認我行李 — He tried to obtain my baggage by false pretenses.

佢强搶我泥口 — He claimed my mine.

佢强霸我地 — He squatted on my lot.

佢逼勒我可銀 — He tries to extort money from me.

逼佢招出 — The confession was extorted from him by force.

佢受大頭人定佢罪 — He was convicted by a jury.

佢如今定罪 — He is now a convict.

佢騙了我之工艮 — He cheated me out of my wages.

我日出起身 — I arise at sunrise.

煩沒與我付此信 — Please send this letter for me.

from CALIFORNIA INTER POCULA

HUBERT HOWE BANCROFT

In the 1880s historians formally began to interpret the gold rush—none more eagerly than Hubert Howe Bancroft (1832–1918). More of a publisher than a scholar, Bancroft financed a "history factory" to compile voluminous histories of California and other regions of the United States as well as Mexico, Central America, and Britain. He worked with an enormous staff of writers and researchers, publishing their works under his own name. Not content to rest with his seven-volume History of California, *Bancroft published* California Inter Pocula *in 1888, a gold rush history that recast the rowdy forty-niners as industrious entrepeneurs.* Chronicles of the Builders, *a later multi-volume encyclopedia of pioneer biographies, offered more of the same.*

THE CALIFORNIA YEAR OF 1849; what was it? An exclamation point in the history of civilization; a dash in the annals of time. This twelve-month was not so much a year as an age, not so much an episode as an era. Heart throbs, they say, rather than time tell the age of man; here then was a century of heart throbs; we could as well drop out of history a hundred of other years, as this one most notable year. Other years have been repeated, and will be many times; this one, never. Throughout the records of the race, from first to last, there will never be reproduced on this planet the California flush-times drama. It stands out in the experiences of men unique and individual, each swift day of it equal to many another year.

How vain, then, the attempt to portray this fleeting hour! Dreaming will not achieve it, nor romancing; it is neither caricature, nor burlesque, nor extravaganza. These lead the mind further from the truth. Neither will the bald facts, though plainly and fairly stated, give a perfect idea of the time; there was present much besides plain facts; there were facts running riot, and the wildest fancy turned into facts—a pandemonium of romance and reality. There were here fifty thousand active and intelligent young workers, whose experiences fully written for that year would fill fifty thousand volumes, each as large as this. And then the subject would not be fully presented, unless into each of these fifty thousand volumes the breath of inspiration might place true and living soul; for the winds of California were redolent of soul, and every morning's sun kindled new fires of energy that went not out at night. The 1849 of California, of America, of the world! It was the pivot on which the framework of human progress turned a fresh side to the sun, a side breeding maggots hitherto, but now a new and nobler race of men.

Since the days of Adam, whose eyes were opened to behold himself by his maker, there never has been a mirror held up before man which so reflected him in his true light, stripped of all the shame and conventionalities of staid societies. Leaving in their old homes every restraint, every influence that bound them to ancient forms and traditions, the latter-day Argonauts entered the mines with name and identity sunk. They were no longer their former selves; they were born and baptized anew. Hence arose a social organism at once complex and peculiar, whose growth is at every turn a new development.

Digging in the dirt, selling rum, tobacco, flour, and bacon, hammering out mining machinery, assaying gold and the like seem dull and prosaic occupations enough when compared with the tilts and tournaments of knight-errantry, the pious enthusiasm of crusaders, and the thrilling deeds on the battle-fields; nevertheless the poetry and romance are here for all who prefer reality to fantasy. Here, weather-beaten and bearded diggers are unearthing primeval treasures which shall revolutionize commerce and society; they are bringing to light brilliant gold wherewith to buy happiness; and these ministering towns and cities which spring up on every side as if by magic are the marts of their servitors who feed and clothe their occupants. Gold-getting, however, is not an end but a means; it is only an incentive or impulse in the great plan of progress. The romance of it is found in the strange developments, the wonderful events, the grand display of that force which brings order out of chaos.

Until a late day we lacked home and the home feeling in California. We began by staying here a little while, and we have remained longer than we intended. We lack the associations running back for generations, the old homestead, the grandfather, and grandmother, and uncles, and aunts, and cousins. There is nothing around us hallowed by an indistinct past. There is nothing older than ourselves; all that we see has grown up under our eyes, and for these creatures of our own creation we have no reverence. We are not yet settled, we are constantly moving to and fro like restless spirits, living in hotels and boarding houses; or if we have a home we want to sell it and go into the country, or to Europe. It is so much trouble keeping house, with these Chinamen for chambermaids!

It is true that the people of California are very greatly absorbed in making money. And this is as it should be, for what is money-making but development and progress? Culture and refinement always follow material prosperity, they never precede it. We have here lands to be put under contribution, mines to be opened, railroads and cities to be built; would it be accounted to us as wise to sit down to play when we have made no provision for our dinner? First provide for the material man, else the mental will fare poorly enough. But, say your friends at the East, "You have made money enough; it is time you should turn your attention to something better than money, if ever you intend doing so." Very true, but railway trains are not stopped at full speed, cart horses do not usually make the best racers, and ships built for the water do not sail well in the air. Money-makers are simply machines, as are philosophers and scholars; take one to pieces and remodel it, and the working of it afterward is very doubtful. I see no other way but to give the country time. The next generation will beget new inventions, experiences thus brought together propagate. Hence it is that we are more fully up to the times in everything, much more, all things put together, than almost any other community.

It is easy to understand how men and women thus thrown together, strangers to each other, strangers in ideas, speech, and traditions, without the substratum, as a social foundation, which only can coalesce as society slowly develops, fail to have that interest in each other and that intense loyalty which characterizes older and more settled communities. Society here is a malformation, or rather it is yet not society, but only materials for society; yet nowhere will the people quicker or more heartily unite for the public good; nowhere are they more free and social than here; nowhere is there less clap-trap and ridiculous apings of things traditional than here.

Strangers coming together cannot immediately embrace and become brothers. They have too little in common, see too many faults in each other, and will not mellow on the instant asperities of character. The seeds of lasting friendship are usually planted in early life, and matured in a soil of warm and tender sympathy, in order to produce a plant which will endure the storms of selfishness that beat upon it in after life. Once the social heart of California lay so imbedded in gold that it could not throb. The passions were let loose, and a moral leprosy infected the people like an epidemic. But all this passed away, as every epidemic passes after having weeded society of some of its weaknesses, and left it in fair condition for permanent growth.

To the great majority of the pioneers the Sierra was a sphinx propounding a riddle, which they must answer. Thousands laid down their lives in the attempt, for there were the lion's claws to tear the unsuccessful venture in pieces. Of rare celestial beauty was the face and bosom of the goddess as she lured men to their destruction; of dark ferocity was she as she lapped them to their final doom.

from MOUNTAINEERING IN THE SIERRA NEVADAS

CLARENCE KING

Born in Rhode Island, Clarence King (1842–1901), rode to California on horseback with a friend in 1863, a year after graduating from Yale. Once there, King helped conduct the state's first geological survey and explored southern California's deserts. King went on to head the U.S. Geological Survey from 1878 to 1881, but eventually suffered a mental breakdown, perhaps due to the stress of a secret marriage to an African American woman. His precise, clever descriptions of post-gold rush California appeared in the Atlantic Monthly *in 1871 and the following year as the book* Mountaineering in the Sierra Nevadas.

WHY ALL SORTS AND CONDITIONS of men from every race upon the planet wanted gold, and twenty years ago came here to win it, I shall not concern myself to ask. Nor can I formulate very accurately the proportions of good, bad, and indifferent dramatic personae upon whom the golden curtain of '49 rolled up.

No venerated landmark or sacred restraint held those men in check. There were no precedents for the acting, no play-book, no prompter, no audience. "Anglo-Saxondom's idee" reigned supreme, developing a plot of riotous situation, and inconceivably sudden change. Wit and intellect wrought a condition the most ambitious savages might regard with baffled envy. History would not, if she could, parallel the state of society here from '49 to '55, nor can we imagine to what height of horror it might have reached had the Sierra drainage held unlimited gold. Those were lively days. The penniless '49er still looks back to them with bleared eyes as the one period of his life. "Dust" was plenty and to be had, if not for digging, at the modest price of a bullet.

For a few years the solemn pines looked down on a mad carnival of godless license, a pandemonium in whose picturesque delirium human character crumbled and vanished like dead leaves. It was stirring and gay, but Melpomene's pathetic face was always under that laughing mask of comedy.

This is the unpromising origin of our Sierra Civilization.

Early in the fifties, on a still, hot summer's afternoon, a certain man, in a camp of the northern mines which shall be nameless, having tracked his two donkeys and one horse a half-mile, and discovering that a man's track with spurmarks followed them, came back to town and told "the boys," who loitered about a popular saloon, that in his opinion "some Mexican had stole the animals."

Such news as this naturally demanded drinks all round. "Do you know, gentlemen," said one who assumed leadership, "that just naturally to shoot these Greasers ain't the best way. Give 'em a fair jury trial, and rope 'em up with all the majesty of law. That's the cure."

Such words of moderation were well received, and they drank again to "Here's hoping we ketch that Greaser."

As they loafed back to the veranda a Mexican walked over the hill brow, jingling his spurs pleasantly in accord with a whistled waltz. The advocate for law said in undertone, "That's the cuss." A rush, a struggle, and the Mexican, bound hand and foot, lay on his back in the bar-room. The camp turned out to a man.

Happily, such cries as "String him up!" "Burn the doggoned 'lubricator'!" and other equally pleasant phrases fell unheeded upon his Spanish ear.

A jury, upon which they forced my friend, was quickly gathered in the street, and despite refusals to serve, the crowd hurried them in behind the bar. A brief statement of the case was made by the *ci devant* advocate, and they shoved the jury into a commodious poker room, where were seats grouped about neat, green tables. The noise outside in the bar-room by-and-by died away into complete silence, but from afar down the cañon came confused sounds as of disorderly cheering.

They came nearer, and again the light-hearted noise of human laughter mingled with clinking glasses around the bar.

A low knock at the jury door; the lock burst in, and a dozen smiling fellows asked the verdict.

A foreman promptly answered, *"Not guilty."*

With volleyed oaths, and ominous laying of hands on pistol hilts, the boys slammed the door with, "You'll have to do better than that!"

In half an hour the advocate gently opened the door again.

"Your *opinion*, gentlemen?"

"Guilty!"

"Correct! You can come out. We hung him an hour ago."

The jury took theirs "neat"; and when, after a few minutes, the pleasant village returned to its former tranquillity, it was "allowed" at more than one saloon that "Mexicans'll know enough to let white men's stock alone after this." One and another exchanged the belief that this sort of thing was more sensible than " 'nipping' 'em on sight."

When, before sunset, the bar-keeper concluded to sweep some dust out of his poker-room back-door, he felt a momentary surprise at finding the missing horse dozing under the shadow of an oak, and the two lost donkeys serenely masticating playing-cards, of which many bushels lay in a dusty pile.

He was reminded then that the animals had been there all day.

During three or four years the battle between good and bad became more and more determined, until all positive characters arrayed themselves either for or against public order.

At length, on a sudden, the party for right organized those august mobs, the Vigilance Committees, and quickly began to festoon their more depraved fellow-men from tree to tree. Rogues of sufficient shrewdness got themselves enrolled in the vigilance ranks, and were soon unable to tell themselves from the most virtuous. Those quiet oaks, whose hundreds of sunny years had been spent in lengthening out glorious branches, now found themselves playing the part of public gibbet.

Let it be distinctly understood that I am not passing criticism on the San Francisco organization, which I have never investigated, but on "Committees" in the mountain towns, with whose performance I am familiar.

The Vigilants quickly put out of existence a majority of the worst desperadoes, and, by their swift, merciless action, struck such terror to the rest that ever after, the right has mainly controlled affairs.

This was, *perhaps*, well. With characteristic promptness they laid down their power, and gave California over to the constituted authorities. This was magnificent. They deserve the commendation due success. They have, however, such a frank, honest way of singing their praise, such eternal, undisguised, and virtuous self-laudation over the whole matter, that no one else need interrupt them with fainter notes.

Although this generation has written its endorsement in full upon the transaction, it may be doubted if history (how long is it before dispassionate candor speaks?) will trace an altogether favorable verdict upon her pages. Possibly, to fulfill the golden round of duty, it is needful to do right in the right way, and success may not be proven the eternal test of merit.

That the Vigilance Committees grasped the moral power is undeniable; that they used it for the public salvation is equally true; but the best advocates are far from showing that with skill and moderation they might not have thrown their weight into the scale *with* law, and conquered, by means of legislature, judge, and jury, a peace wholly free from the stain of lawless blood.

An impartial future may possibly grant the plenary inspiration of Vigilance Committees. Perhaps that better choice was in truth denied them; it may be the hour demanded a sudden blow of self-defense. Whether better or best, the act has not left unmixed blessing, although it now seems as if the lawlessness, which even till these later years has from time to time manifested itself, is gradually and surely dying out. Yet to-day, as I write, State troops are encamped at Amador, to suppress a spirit which has taken law in its own hand.

With the gradual decline of gold product, something like social equilibrium asserted itself. By 1860, California had made the vast inspiring stride from barbarism to vulgarity.

In failing gold-industry, and the gradual abandonment of placer-ground to Chinamen, there is abundant pathos. You see it in a hundred towns and camps where empty buildings in disrepair stand in rows; no nailing up of blinds or closing of doors hides the vacancy. The cheap squalor of Chinese streets adds misery to the scene, besides scenting a pure mountain air with odors of complete wretchedness. Pigs prowl the streets. Every deserted cabin knows a story of brave manly effort ended in bitter failure, and the lingering stranded men have a melancholy look as of faint fish the ebb has left to die.

I recall one town into which our party rode at evening. A single family alone remained, too desperately poor to leave their home; all the other buildings—church, post office, the half-dozen saloons, and many dwellings—standing with wide-open doors, their cloth walls and ceilings torn down to make squaw petticoats. If our horses in the great deserted livery stable were as comfortable as we, who each made his bed on a billiard table, they did well. With this slow decay the venturous, both good and bad, have drifted off to other mining countries, leaving most often small cause to regret them.

Pathos and comedy so tenderly blent can rarely be found as here. Enterprise has shrunken away from its old belongings; a feeble rill of trade trickles down the broad channel of former affluence. Those few '49ers who linger ought to be gently preserved for historic specimens, as we used to care for that cannon-ball in the Boston bricks, or whatever might remind this youthful country of a past. They are altogether harmless now, possessing the peculiar charm of lions with drawn teeth.

Behold this old-school relic, a type known as the real Virginia gentleman, as of a mild summer twilight he walks along the quiet street, clad in black broadcloth and spotless linen, a heavy cane hanging by its curved handle from his wrist. He pauses by the "s'loon," receiving respectful salutation from a mild company of bummers who hold him in awe, and call him nothing less than "Judge." They omit their habitual sugar-and-water, and are at pains to swallow as stiff a glass and as neat as their hero. The Judge is reminded of livelier days by certain unhealed bullet-holes in ceiling and wall, and recounts for the hundredth time, in chaste language, the whole affair; and in particular how three-fingered Jack blew the top of Alabam's head off, and that stopped it all.

"We buried the six," the Judge continues, "side and side, and it wasn't a week before two of us found old Jack and his partner on the same limb, and they made eight graves. The ball that made that hole went through my hat, and I traveled after that for a while, till the thing sort of blew over.

"Ah! boys," he winds up, in tones tremulous with tearful regret, "you fellows will never see such lively times as we of the early days."

His tall figure passes on with uncertain gait, stopping at garden fences here and there to execute one or two old school compliments for the ladies who are spending their evenings under vine-draped porches; and when he takes an easy-chair by invitation, and begins a story laid in the spring of '50, the Judge is conscious in his heart that the full saloon veranda is looking and saying, "The *wimmun* always did like him."

The '49 rough, too, still stays in almost every camp. He evaded rope by joining the "Vigilants," and has become a safe and fangless wolf in sheep's clothing. He found early that he could sponge and swindle a larger amount from any given community than could be plundered, to say nothing of the advantages of personal security. But now all these characters are, God be thanked! few and widely scattered.

We must admit the facts. California people are not living in a tranquil, healthy, social régime. They are provincial,—never, however, in a local way, but by reason of limited thought. Aspirations for wealth and ease rise conspicuously above any thirst for intellectual culture and moral peace. Energy and a glorious audacity are their leading traits.

To the charge of light-hearted gaiety, so freely trumpeted by graver home critics, I plead them guilty. There is nowhere that dull, weary expression, and rayless sedateness of face we of New England are fonder of ascribing to our tender conscience than to east winds. So, too, are wanting difficulties of bronchia and lungs, which might inferentially be symptoms of original sin.

Is Californian cheerfulness due to widespread moral levity, or because perpetual sunshine and green salads through the round year tempt weak human nature to smile?

I believe it climatic, and humbly offer my tribute to the thermometer-man, who among many ventures has this time probably stumbled upon truth.

Let us not grieve because the writers and lecturers have not found Californian society all their ideals demanded. Have they forgotten that these are less potent factors in development than the impulse, that what a man *is,* is of far less consequence than what he is *becoming?*

Show these gloomy critics a bare stretch of vulgar Sierra earth, and they will tell you how barren, how valueless it is, ignorant that the art of any Californian can banish every grain of sand into the Pacific's bottom, and gather a residuum of solid gold. Out of the race of men whom they have in the same shallow way called common, I believe Time shall separate a noble race.

Traveling to-day in foot-hill Sierras, one may see the old, rude scars of mining; trenches yawn, disordered heaps cumber the ground, yet they are no longer bare. Time, with friendly rain, and wind and flood, slowly, surely, levels all, and a compassionate cover of innocent verdure weaves fresh and cool from mile to mile. While Nature thus gently heals the humble Earth, God, who is also Nature, moulds and changes Man.

from CALIFORNIA FOR HEALTH, PLEASURE, AND RESIDENCE

CHARLES NORDHOFF

Charles Nordhoff (1830–1901), born in Prussia and raised in Ohio, worked as a newspaper journalist when he wasn't sailing with the U.S. Navy or exploring California, Oregon, and Hawaii. His travel writing made him famous, especially The Communistic Societies of the United States, *a complimentary account of life at various American communes. His grandson, also named Charles Nordhoff, co-authored* The Mutiny on the Bounty *in 1932.* California for Health, Pleasure, and Residence *(1872), one of Nordhoff's many travel books about the Golden State, addressed the environmental consequences of the gold rush.*

THE TOURIST IN CALIFORNIA naturally wishes to see something of mining, and fortunately he may do so without going much off the regular and beaten road of travel. Already, on the railroad, as he swept from the summit of the Sierra down to the Sacramento Plain, he saw along the road-side long flumes or wooden channels bearing water for the miners below. At Gold Run he may have seen the work of hydraulic-mining carried on in a deep valley below the railroad.

He will hardly see placer-mining, except by Chinese in some remote parts; but on his way to and from the Yosemite Valley, he may see preparations for turning a river, which is done that the miners may get at the gold which they have reason to believe is deposited on its bottom. And at many points on his journey to the famous sights of the State, he will meet with examples of mining work, either of what has been done in the past or what is now doing. For instance, as you journey from the Big Trees—the Calaveras Grove I mean—toward the Yosemite, after you leave Murphy's, every foot almost of the soil, for mile after mile, has been at some time turned over by the gold-seekers. River beds were laid bare, and the adjoining bottoms searched; the earth all the way to the foot-hills was removed; and as you near Columbia, you see immense fields made up of nothing but rocks and boulders sticking their barren water-worn heads into the landscape, with deep pits between, showing the water-eaten sides of the rocks, which the miners searched, scraped, and polished as a dentist does the teeth of his patient.

In this comparatively deserted mining tract, where now only small parties of Chinese or Mexicans earn a precarious living, or a lonely Digger Indian indolently pans out his bit's worth of gold squatted by the river bank, you see not only the beds where lay millions of gold, but you have laid bare a part of that ancient pre-Adamite river which, millions of years ago, washed down, from quartz veins now lost, the gold which remained till our Americans came to dig it up.

You see how the swift waters of this ancient river gnawed into the rocks until now they seem gnarled and twisted like the roots of trees—and in every corner and hole it deposited the precious gold. You can not realize how the country looked before our miners came to disturb it; for an old resident told me that where the rocks now lay bare and on a level with the road, which also had been mined out, from fifteen to thirty feet of soil, and often fifty feet, were removed before the gold was reached. They washed away hills, they shoveled away broad, elevated plains; dozens of square miles of soil disappeared and were driven off into lower valleys that they might exhume the gold. At intervals you find a small field, a vineyard, or a garden, planted in the midst of this desolation, surrounded on all sides by rocks. Your guide—if you are so fortunate as to meet with an old miner—will explain to you that here the "slum" (as they call it), the sediment of earth with which the water is charged which has been used in "placer-ruining," has been trapped and caused to deposit itself. Men have made acres and even dozens of acres of land by catching this slum. It is fine earth; all the flumes and water-courses still run red with it, for they are hydraulic-mining above; and when it dries out it makes the most fertile of gardens and vineyards.

If you visit Marysville, which lies on the tourist's way to Mount Shasta, drive out fifteen miles to Smartsville or Timbuctoo. You pass within sight of a classic locality—Yuba Dam; and you see and are made to understand what, until I saw it, I could not entirely comprehend—the whole practice of hydraulic-mining.

The ancient river bed from which, according to the miners, so much gold has been taken in this State, is in many places covered with earth to the depth of two or three hundred feet. Once, perhaps, they say here, it ran in a valley, but now a huge hill covers it. To dig down to it and to mine it out by ordinary processes would be too expensive; therefore hydraulic-mining has been invented. Water brought from a hundred or one hundred and fifty miles away, and from a considerable height, is led from reservoirs through eight, ten, or twelve-inch iron pipes, and through what a New York fireman would call a nozzle, five or six inches in diameter, is thus forced against the side of a hill one or two or three hundred feet high. The stream when it leaves the pipe has such force that it would cut a man in two if it should hit him. Two or three and sometimes even six such streams play against the bottom of a hill, and earth and stones, often of great size, are washed away, until at last an immense slice of the hill itself gives way and tumbles down.

At Smartsville, Timbuctoo, and Rose's Bar I suppose they wash away into the sluices half a dozen acres a day, from fifty to two hundred feet deep; and in the muddy torrent, which rushes down at railroad speed through the channels prepared for it, you may see large rocks helplessly rolling along.

Not all the earth contains gold. Often there is a superincumbent layer of fifty or more feet which is worthless before they reach the immense gravel deposit which marks the course of the ancient river; and from this gravel, waterworn, and showing all the marks of having formed once the bed of a rushing torrent, the gold is taken. Under great pressure this gravel—which contains, you must understand, rocks of large size, and is not gravel in our sense of the word at all—has been cemented together, so that even the powerful streams of water directed against it make but a feeble impression; and to hasten and cheapen the operation, a blast of from 1200 to 1500 kegs of powder is inserted in a hill-side, and exploded in such a way as to shatter and loosen a vast bulk of earth and stones, whereupon the water is brought into play against it.

If you want to know how a part of the surface of our planet looked some thousands of years ago, here is a good opportunity; for what two or three men with torrents of water wash away into the Yuba River in a few weeks must have taken many centuries to accumulate; and below, you see a mass of water-washed stone, rounded boulders, and large gravel, twenty or fifty or even a hundred feet deep, which was so plainly the bed of a torrent or rapidly rushing river once that even children recognize it.

Of course the acres washed away must go somewhere, and they are filling up the Yuba River. This was once, I am told by old residents, a swift and clear mountain torrent; it is now a turbid and not rapid stream, whose bed has been raised by the washings of the miners not less than fifty feet above its level in 1849. It once contained trout, but now I imagine a catfish would die in it.

The settlement of this country by Americans has produced many curious changes like this. General Bidwell, who lives at Chico, above Marysville, told me that fifteen years ago he had seen six grizzly bears lassoed and shot on his place by his men in one day—"and it was not a very good day for grizzlies either." So late as 1853 antelope and elk abounded on his pastures; the former, as well as deer, used to graze quietly with his cattle, and venison was a constant dish on his table. Before the gold discovery, trappers used to catch the beaver and otter on the Sacramento and Yuba rivers; but these creatures have, of course, disappeared with the elk.

All this change has taken place in little more than thirty years; and in a country which was for centuries occupied by men of another nation, who knew not either how to find out its mineral riches, to develop its agricultural wealth, or to subdue its native animals.

from THE MOUNTAINS OF CALIFORNIA

JOHN MUIR

John Muir (1838–1914), a profoundly influential naturalist and environmentalist, did not publish his first book until he was fifty-six. Born in Scotland, he grew up on a farm in Wisconsin. Most of his adult years were spent in the West studying glaciers, forests, and mountains. He helped establish his beloved Yosemite as a national park, founded the Sierra Club, and convinced Presidents Grover Cleveland and Theodore Roosevelt to protect thousands of acres of western lands. Published in 1894, The Mountains of California *was the first of his many books.*

MURPHY'S CAMP is a curious old mining-town in Calaveras County, at an elevation of 2400 feet above the sea, situated like a nest in the center of a rough, gravely region, rich in gold. Granites, slates, lavas, limestone, iron ores, quartz veins, auriferous gravels, remnants of dead fire-rivers and dead water-rivers are developed here side by side within a radius of a few miles, and placed invitingly open before the student like a book, while the people and the region beyond the camp furnish mines of study of never-failing interest and variety.

When I discovered this curious place, I was tracing the channels of the ancient pre-glacial rivers, instructive sections of which have been laid bare here and in the adjacent regions by the miners. Rivers, according to the poets, "go on forever"; but those of the Sierra are young as yet and have scarcely learned the way down to the sea; while at least one generation of them have died and vanished together with most of the basins they drained. All that remains of them to tell their history is a series of interrupted fragments of channels, mostly choked with gravel, and buried beneath broad, thick sheets of lava. These are known as the "Dead Rivers of California," and the gravel deposited in them is comprehensively called the "Blue Lead." In some places the channels of the present rivers trend in the same direction, or nearly so, as those of the ancient rivers; but, in general, there is little correspondence be-tween them, the entire drainage having been changed, or, rather, made new. Many of the hills of the ancient landscapes have become hollows, and the old hollows have become hills. Therefore the fragmentary channels, with their loads of auriferous gravel, occur in all kinds of unthought-of places, trending

Hydraulicking at the Malakoff Diggings, c. 1876, by Carleton E. Watkins

obliquely, or even at right angles to the present drainage, across the tops of
lofty ridges or far beneath them.

The importance of these ancient gravels as gold fountains is well known to
miners. Even the superficial placers of the present streams have derived much
of their gold from them. According to all accounts, the Murphy placers have
been very rich—"terrific rich," as they say here. The hills have been cut and
scalped, and every gorge and gulch and valley torn to pieces and disembow-
eled, expressing a fierce and desperate energy hard to understand. Still, any
kind of effort-making is better than inaction, and there is something sublime
in seeing men working in dead earnest at anything, pursuing an object with
glacier-like energy and persistence. Many a brave fellow has recorded a most
eventful chapter of life on these Calaveras rocks. But most of the pioneer
miners are sleeping now, their wild day done, while the few survivors linger
languidly in the washed-out gulches or sleepy village like harried bees around
the ruins of their hive. "We have no industry left *now*," they told me, "and no
men; everybody and everything hereabouts has gone to decay. We are only
bummers—out of the game, a thin scatterin' of poor, dilapidated cusses, compared with what we used to be in the grand old gold-days. We were giants
then, and you can look around here and see our tracks."

But although these lingering pioneers are perhaps more exhausted than the

389

mines, and about as dead as dead rivers, they are yet a rare and interesting set of men, with much gold mixed with the rough, rocky gravel of their characters; and they manifest a breeding and intelligence little looked for in such surroundings as theirs. As the heavy, long-continued grinding of the glaciers brought out the features of the Sierra, so the intense experiences of the gold period brought out the features of these old miners, forming a richness and variety of character little known as yet. The sketches of Harte, Hayes, and Miller have not exhausted this field by any means. It is interesting to note the extremes possible in one and the same character: harshness and gentleness, manliness and childishness, apathy and fierce endeavor. Men who, twenty years ago, would not cease their shoveling to saves their lives, now play in the streets with children. Their long, Micawber-like waiting after the exhaustion of the placers has brought on an exaggerated form of dotage. I heard a group of brawny pioneers in the street eagerly discussing the quantity of tail required for a boy's kite; and one graybeard undertook the sport of flying it, volunteering the information that he was a boy, "always was a boy, and d——n a man who was not a boy inside, however ancient outside!" Mines, morals, politics, the immorality of the soul, etc., were discussed beneath shade-trees and in saloons, the time for each being governed apparently by temperature.

Contact with Nature, and the habits of observation acquired in gold-seeking, had made them all, to some extent, collectors, and, like wood-rats, they had gathered all kinds of odd specimens into their cabins, and now required me to examine them. They were themselves the oddest and most interesting specimens. One of them offered to show me around the old diggings, giving me fair warning before setting out that I might not like him, "because," said he, "people say I'm eccentric. I notice everything, and gather beetles and snakes and anything that's queer; and so some don't like me, and call me eccentric. I'm always trying to find out things. Now, there's a weed; the Indians eat it for greens. What do you call those long-bodied flies with big heads?" "Dragon-flies," I suggested. "Well, their jaws work sideways, instead of up and down, and grasshoppers' jaws work the same way, and therefore I think they are the same species. I always notice everything like that, and just because I do, they say I'm eccentric," etc.

Anxious that I should miss none of the wonders of their old gold-field, the good people have much to say about the marvelous beauty of Cave City Cave, and advised me to explore it. This I was very glad to do, and finding a guide who knew the way to the mouth of it, I set out from Murphy the next morning.

The most beautiful and extensive of the mountain caves of California occur in a belt of metamorphic limestone that is pretty generally developed along

Riverbed mining operations at Grizzly Flats, c. 1852

the western flank of the Sierra from the McCloud River on the north to the Kaweah on the south, a distance of over 400 miles, at an elevation of from 2000 to 7000 feet above the sea. Besides this regular belt of caves, the California landscapes are diversified by long imposing ranks of sea caves, rugged and variable in architecture, carved in the coast headlands and precipices by centuries of wave-dashing; and innumerable lava-caves, great and small, originating in the unequal flowing and hardening of lava sheets in which they occur, fine illustrations of which are presented in the famous Modoc Lava Beds, and around the base of icy Shasta. In this comprehensive glance we may also notice the shallow wind-worn caves in stratified sandstones along the margins of the plains; and the cave-like recesses in the Sierra slates and granites, where bears and other mountaineers find shelter during the fall of sudden storms. In general, however, the grand massive uplift of the Sierra, as far as it has been laid bare to observation, is about as solid and caveless as a boulder.

Our way from Murphy's to the cave lay across a series of picturesque, moory ridges in the chaparral region between the brown foot-hills and the forests, a flowery stretch of rolling hill-waves breaking here and there into a kind of rocky foam on the higher summits, and sinking into delightful bosky hollows embowered with vines. The day was a fine specimen of California summer, pure sunshine, unshaded most of the time by a single cloud. As the sun rose higher, the heated air began to flow in tremulous waves from every southern slope. The sea-breeze that usually comes up the foot-hills at this season, with cooling on its wings, was scarcely perceptible. The birds were assembled beneath leafy shade, or made short, languid flights in search of food, all save the majestic buzzard; with broad wings out-spread he sailed the warm air unwarily from ridge to ridge, seeming to enjoy the fervid sunshine like a butterfly. Squirrels, too, whose spicy ardor no heat or cold may abate, were nutting among the pines, and the innumerable hosts of the insect kingdom were throbbing and wavering unwearied as sunbeams.

This brushy, berry-bearing region used to be a deer and bear pasture, but since the disturbances of the gold period these fine animals have almost wholly disappeared. Here, also, once roamed the mastodon and elephant, whose bones are found entombed in the river gravels and beneath thick folds of lava. Toward noon, as we were riding slowly over bank and brae, basking in the unfeverish sun-heat, we witnessed the upheaval of a new mountain-range, a Sierra of clouds abounding in landscapes as truly sublime and beautiful—if only we have a mind to think so and eyes to see—as the more ancient rocky Sierra beneath it, with its forests and waterfalls; reminding us that, as there is a lower world of caves, so, also, there is an upper world of clouds. Huge, bossy cumuli developed with astonishing rapidity from mere buds, swelling with visible motion into colossal mountains, and piling higher, higher, in long massive ranges, peak beyond peak, dome over dome, with many a picturesque valley and shadowy cave between; while the dark firs and pines of the upper benches of the Sierra were projected against their pearl bosses with exquisite clearness of outline. These cloud mountains vanished in the azure as quickly as they were developed, leaving no detritus; but they were not a whit less real or interesting on this account. The more enduring hills over which we rode were vanishing as surely as they, only not so fast, a difference which is great or small according to the standpoint from which it is contemplated.

At the bottom of every dell we found little homesteads embosomed in wild brush and vines wherever the recession of the hills left patches of arable ground. These secluded flats are settled mostly by Italians and Germans, who plant a few vegetables and grape-vines at odd times, while their main business is mining and prospecting. In spite of all the natural beauty of these dell cabins, they can hardly be called homes. They are only a better kind of camp, gladly abandoned whenever the hoped-for gold harvest has been gathered.

There is an air of profound unrest and melancholy about the best of them. Their beauty is thrust upon them by exuberant Nature, apart from which they are only a few logs and boards rudely jointed and without either ceiling or floor, a rough fireplace with corresponding cooking utensils, a shelf-bed, and stool. The ground about them is strewn with battered prospecting-pans, picks, sluice-boxes, and quartz specimens from many a ledge, indicating the trend of their owner's hard lives.

The ride from Murphy's to the cave is scarcely two hours long, but we lingered among quartz-ledges and banks of dead river gravel until long after noon. At length emerging from a narrow-throated gorge, a small house came in sight set in a thicket of fig-trees at the base of a limestone hill. "That," said my guide, pointing to the house, "is Cave City, and the cave is in that gray hill." Arriving at the one house of this one-house city, we were boisterously welcomed by three drunken men who had come to town to hold a spree. The mistress of the house tried to keep order, and in reply to our inquiries told us that the cave guide was then in the cave with a party of ladies. "And must we wait until he returns?" we asked. No, that was unnecessary; we might take candles and go into the cave alone, provided we shouted from time to time so as to be found by the guide, and were careful not to fall over the rocks or into the dark pools.

Accordingly taking a trail from the house, we were led around the base of the hill to the mouth of the cave, a small inconspicuous archway, mossy around the edges and shaped like the door of a water-ouzel's nest, with no appreciable hint or advertisement of the grandeur of the many crystal chambers within. Lighting our candles, which seemed to have no illuminating power in the thick darkness, we groped our way onward as best we could along narrow lanes and alleys, from chamber to chamber, around rustic columns and heaps of fallen rocks, stopping to rest now and then in particularly beautiful places— fairy alcoves furnished with admirable variety of shelves and tables, and round bossy stools covered with sparkling crystals. Some of the corridors were muddy, and in plodding along these we seemed to be in the streets of some prairie village in spring-time. Then we would come to handsome marble stairways conducting right and left into upper chambers ranged above one another three or four stories high, floors, ceilings, and walls lavishly decorated with innumerable crystalline forms.

After thus wandering exploringly, and alone for a mile or so, fairly enchanted, a murmur of voices and a gleam of light betrayed the approach of the guide and his party, from whom, when they came up, we received a most hearty and natural stare, as we stood half concealed in a side recess among stalagmites. I ventured to ask the dripping, crouching company how they had enjoyed their saunter, anxious to learn how the strange sunless scenery of the underworld had impressed them. "Ah, it's nice! It's splendid!" they all replied and echoed. "The Bridal Chamber back here is just glorious! This morning we came down from the Calaveras Big Tree Grove, and the trees are nothing to it." After making this curious comparison they hastened sunward, the guide promising to join us shortly on the bank of a deep pool, where we were to wait for him. This is a charming little lakelet of unknown depth, never yet stirred by a breeze, and its eternal calm excites the imagination even more profoundly than the silvery lakes of the glaciers rimmed with meadows and snow and reflecting sublime mountains.

Our guide, a jolly, rollicking Italian, led us into the heart of the hill, up and down, right and left, from chamber to chamber more and more magnificent, all a-glitter like a glacier cave with icicle-like stalactites and stalagmites combined in forms of indescribable beauty. We were shown one large room that was occasionally used as a dancing-hall; another that was used as a chapel, with natural pulpit and crosses and pews, sermons in every stone, where a priest had said mass. Mass-saying is not so generally developed in connection with natural wonders as dancing. One of the first conceits excited by the giant Sequoias was to cut one of them down and dance on its stump. We have also seen dancing in the spray of Niagara; dancing in the famous Bower Cave above Coulterville; and nowhere have I seen so much dancing as in Yosemite. A dance on the inaccessible South Dome would likely follow the making of an easy way to the top of it.

It was delightful to witness here the infinite deliberation of Nature, and the simplicity of her methods in the production of such mighty results, such perfect repose combined with restless enthusiastic energy. Though cold and bloodless as a landscape of polar ice, building was going on in the dark with incessant activity. The archways and ceilings were everywhere hung with down-growing crystals, like inverted groves of leafless saplings, some of them large, others delicately attenuated, each tipped with a single drop of water, like the terminal bud of a pine-tree. The only appreciable sounds were the dripping and tinkling of water falling into pools or faintly plashing on the crystal floors.

In some places the crystal decorations are arranged in graceful flowing folds deeply plicated like stiff silken drapery. In others straight lines of the ordinary stalactite forms are combined with reference to size and tone in a regularly graduated system like the strings of a harp with musical tones corresponding thereto; and on these stone harps we played by striking the crystal strings with a stick. The delicious liquid tones they gave forth seemed perfectly divine as they sweetly whispered and wavered through the majestic halls and died away in faintest cadence,—the music of fairy-land. Here we lingered and reveled, rejoicing to find so much music in stony silence, so much splendor in darkness, so many mansions in the depths of the mountains, buildings ever in process of construction, yet ever finished, developing from perfection to perfection, profusion without overabundance; every particle visible or invisible in glorious motion, marching to the music of the spheres in a region regarded as the abode of eternal stillness and death.

The outer chambers of mountain caves are frequently selected as homes by wild beasts. In the Sierra, however, they seem to prefer homes and hiding-places in chaparral and beneath shelving precipices, as I have never seen their tracks in any of the caves. This is the more remarkable because notwithstanding the darkness and oozing water there is nothing uncomfortably cellar-like or sepulchral about them.

When we emerged into the bright landscapes of the sun everything looked brighter, and we felt our faith in Nature's beauty strengthened, and saw more clearly that beauty is universal and immortal, above, beneath, on land and sea, mountain and plain, in heat and cold, light and darkness.

from MCTEAGUE

FRANK NORRIS

Frank Norris (1870–1902) was born in Chicago and came with his parents to San Francisco in 1884. He began writing short stories for the San Francisco literary journal The Wave *while a student at U.C. Berkeley and published three novels by the time he was thirty. In 1899 he moved to New York, but he continued to think of himself as a Californian and set his novels in the West. Published in 1899,* McTeague *presented a deliberately unromantic vision of San Francisco's middle and lower classes in the 1860s. Norris's budding career was cut short when he died suddenly following an appendectomy at the age of thirty-two.*

THE DAY WAS VERY HOT, and the silence of high noon lay close and thick between the steep slopes of the cañons like an invisible, muffling fluid. At intervals the drone of an insect bored the air and trailed slowly to silence again. Everywhere were pungent, aromatic smells. The vast, moveless heat seemed to distil countless odors from the brush—odors of warm sap, of pine needles, and of tar-weed, and above all the medicinal odor of witch hazel. As far as one could look, uncounted multitudes of trees and manzanita bushes were quietly and motionlessly growing, growing, growing. A tremendous, immeasurable Life pushed steadily heavenward without a sound, without a motion. At turns of the road, on the higher points, cañons disclosed themselves far away, gigantic grooves in the landscape, deep blue in the distance, opening one into another, ocean-deep, silent, huge, and suggestive of colossal primeval forces held in reserve. At their bottoms they were solid, massive; on their crests they broke delicately into fine serrated edges where the pines and redwoods outlined their million of tops against the high white horizon. Here and there the mountains lifted themselves out of the narrow river beds in groups like giant lions rearing their heads after drinking. The entire region was untamed. In some places east of the Mississippi nature is cosey, intimate, small, and home-like, like a good-natured housewife. In Placer County, California, she is a vast, unconquered brute of the Pliocene epoch, savage, sullen, and magnificently indifferent to man.

But there were men in these mountains, like lice on mammoths' hides, fighting them stubbornly, now with hydraulic "monitors," now with drill and dynamite, boring into the vitals of them, or tearing away great yellow gravelly scars in the flanks of them, sucking their blood, extracting gold.

Here and there at long distances upon the cañon sides rose the headgear of a mine, surrounded with its few unpainted houses, and topped by its never-failing feather of black smoke. On near approach one heard the prolonged thunder of the stamp-mill, the crusher, the insatiable monster, gnashing the rocks to powder with its long iron teeth, vomiting them out again in a thin stream of wet gray mud. Its enormous maw, fed night and day with the car-boys' loads, gorged itself with gravel, and spat out the gold, grinding the rocks between its jaws, glutted, as it were, with the very entrails of the earth, and growling over its endless meal, like some savage animal, some legendary dragon, some fabulous beast, symbol of inordinate and monstrous gluttony.

McTeague had left the Overland train at Colfax, and the same afternoon had ridden some eight miles across the mountains in the stage that connects Colfax with Iowa Hill. Iowa Hill was a small one street town, the headquarters of the mines of the district. Originally it had been built upon the summit of a mountain, but the sides of this mountain have long since been "hydraulicked" away, so that the town now clings to a mere back bone, and the rear windows of the houses on both sides of the street look down over sheer precipices, into vast pits hundreds of feet deep.

The dentist stayed over night at the Hill, and the next morning started off on foot farther into the mountains. He still wore his blue overalls and jumper; his woollen cap was pulled down over his eyes; on his feet were hob-nailed boots he had bought at the store in Colfax; his blanket roll was over his back; in his left hand swung the bird cage wrapped in sacks.

Just outside the town he paused, as if suddenly remembering something.

"There ought to be a trail just off the road here," he muttered. "There used to be a trail—a short cut."

The next instant, without moving from his position, he saw where it opened just before him. His instinct had halted him at the exact spot. The trail zig-zagged down the abrupt descent of the cañon, debauching into a gravelly river bed.

"Indian River," muttered the dentist. "I remember—I remember. I ought to hear the Morning Star's stamps from here." He cocked his head. A low, sustained roar, like a distant cataract, came to his ears from across the river. "That's right," he said, contentedly. He crossed the river and regained the road beyond. The slope rose under his feet; a little farther on he passed the Morning Star mine, smoking and thundering. McTeague pushed steadily on. The road

Erosion from hydraulic mining, Malakoff Diggings, 1954, by Alma Lavenson

rose with the rise of the mountain, turned at a sharp angle where a great
live-oak grew, held level for nearly a quarter of a mile. Twice again the dentist
left the road and took to the trail that cut through deserted hydraulic pits. He
knew exactly where to look for these trails; not once did his instinct deceive
him. He recognized familiar points at once. Here was Cold Cañon, where
invariably, winter and summer, a chilly wind was blowing; here was where the
road to Spencer's branched off; here was Bussy's old place, where at one time
there were so many dogs; here was Delmue's cabin, where unlicensed whiskey
used to be sold; here was the plank bridge with its one rotten board; and here
the flat overgrown with manzanita, where he once had shot three quail.

At noon, after he had been tramping for some two hours, he halted at a
point where the road dipped suddenly. A little to the right of him, and flank-
ing the road, an enormous yellow gravel-pit like an emptied lake gaped to
heaven. Farther on, in the distance, a cañon zigzagged toward the horizon,
rugged with pine-clad mountain crests. Nearer at hand, and directly in the
line of the road, was an irregular cluster of unpainted cabins. A dull, prolonged
roar vibrated in the air. McTeague nodded his head as if satisfied.

"That's the place," he muttered.

Mine in downtown Grass Valley, 1946, by Alma Lavenson

He reshouldered his blanket roll and descended the road. At last he halted again. He stood before a low one-story building, differing from the others in that it was painted. A veranda, shut in with mosquito netting, surrounded it. McTeague dropped his blanket roll on a lumber pile outside, and came up and knocked at the open door. Someone called to him to come in.

McTeague entered, rolling his eyes about him, noting the changes that had been made since he had last seen this place. A partition had been knocked down, making one big room out of the two former small ones. A counter and railing stood inside the door. There was a telephone on the wall. In one corner he also observed a stack of surveyor's instruments; a big drawing-board straddled on spindle legs across one end of the room, a mechanical drawing of some kind, no doubt the plan of the mine, unrolled upon it; a chromo representing a couple of peasants in a ploughed field (Millet's "Angelus") was nailed un-framed upon the wall, and hanging from the same wire nail that secured one of its corners in place was a bullion bag and a cartridge belt with a loaded revolver in the pouch.

The dentist approached the counter and leaned his elbows upon it. Three men were in the room—a tall, lean young man, with a thick head of hair surprisingly gray, who was playing with a half-grown great Dane puppy; another fellow about as young, but with a jaw almost as salient as McTeague's, stood at the letter-press taking a copy of a letter; a third man, a little older than the other two, was pottering over a transit. This latter was massively built, and wore overalls and low boots streaked and stained and spotted in every direction with gray mud. The dentist looked slowly from one to the other; then at length, "Is the foreman about?" he asked.

The man in the muddy overalls came forward. "What you want?" He spoke with a strong German accent.

The old invariable formula came back to McTeague on the instant. "What's the show for a job?"

At once the German foreman became preoccupied, looking aimlessly out of the window. There was a silence. "You hev been miner alretty?"

"Yes, yes."

"Know how to hendle pick'n shov'le?"

"Yes, I know."

The other seemed unsatisfied, "Are you a 'cousin Jack'?"

The dentist grinned. This prejudice against Cornishmen he remembered too. "No. American."

"How long since you mine?"

"Oh, year or two."

"Show your hands." McTeague exhibited his hard, calloused palms.

"When ken you go to work? I want a chuck-tender on der night shift."

"I can tend a chuck. I'll go on to-night."

"What's your name?"

The dentist started. He had forgotten to be prepared for this. "Huh? What?"

"What's the name?"

McTeague's eye was caught by a railroad calendar hanging over the desk. There was no time to think. "Burlington," he said, loudly.

The German took a card from a file and wrote it down. "Give dis card to der boarding-boss, down at der boarding-haus, den gome find me bei der mill at sex o'clock, und I set you to work."

Straight as a homing pigeon, and following a blind and unreasoned instinct, McTeague had returned to the Big Dipper mine. Within a week's time it seemed to him as though he had never been away. He picked up his life again exactly where he had left it the day when his mother had sent him away with the travelling dentist, the charlatan who had set up his tent by the bunk house. The house McTeague had once lived in was still

California miners on the Fourth of July, c. 1890

there, occupied by one of the shift bosses and his family. The dentist passed it on his way to and from the mine.

He himself slept in the bunk house with some thirty others of his shift. At half-past five in the evening the cook at the boarding-house sounded a prolonged alarm upon a crowbar bent in the form of a triangle that hung upon the porch of the boardinghouse. McTeague rose and dressed, and with his shift had supper. Their lunch-pails were distributed to them. Then he made his way to the tunnel mouth, climbed into a car in the waiting ore train, and was hauled into the mine.

Once inside, the hot evening air turned to a cool dampness, and the forest odors gave place to the smell of stale dynamite smoke, suggestive of burning rubber. A cloud of steam came from McTeague's mouth; underneath, the water swashed and rippled around the car-wheels, while the light from the miner's candlesticks threw wavering blurs of pale yellow over the gray rotting quartz of the roof and walls. Occasionally McTeague bent down his head to avoid the lagging of the roof or the projections of an overhanging shute. From car to car all along the line the miners called

401

to one another as the train trundled along, joshing and laughing.

A mile from the entrance the train reached the breast where McTeague's gang worked. The men clambered from the cars and took up the labor where the day shift had left it, burrowing their way steadily through a primeval river bed.

The candlesticks thrust into the crevices of the gravel strata lit up faintly the half dozen moving figures befouled with sweat and with wet gray mould. The picks struck into the loose gravel with a yielding shock. The long-handled shovels clinked amidst the piles of boulders and scraped dully in the heaps of rotten quartz. The Burly drill boring for blasts broke out from time to time in an irregular chug-chug, chug-chug, while the engine that pumped the water from the mine coughed and strangled at short intervals.

McTeague tended the chuck. In a way he was the assistant of the man who worked the Burly. It was his duty to replace the drills in the Burly, putting in longer ones as the hole got deeper and deeper. From time to time he rapped the drill with a pole-pick when it stuck fast or fitchered.

Once it even occurred to him that there was a resemblance between his present work and the profession he had been forced to abandon. In the Burly drill he saw a queer counterpart of his old-time dental engine; and what were the drills and chucks but enormous hoe excavators, hard bits, and burrs? It was the same work he had so often performed in his "Parlors," only magnified, made monstrous, distorted, and grotesqued, the caricature of dentistry.

He passed his nights thus in the midst of the play of crude and simple forces—the powerful attacks of the Burly drills; the great exertions of bared, bent backs overlaid with muscle; the brusque, resistless expansion of dynamite; and the silent, vast, Titanic force, mysterious and slow, that cracked the timbers supporting the roof of the tunnel and that gradually flattened the lagging till it was thin as paper.

The life pleased the dentist beyond words. The still, colossal mountains took him back again like a returning prodigal, and vaguely, without knowing why, he yielded to their influence—their immensity, their enormous power, crude and blind, reflecting themselves in his own nature, huge, strong, brutal in its simplicity. And this, though he only saw the mountains at night. They appeared far different then than in the daytime. At twelve o'clock he came out of the mine and lunched on the contents of his dinner-pail, sitting upon the embankment of the track, eating with both hands, and looking around him with a steady ox-like gaze.

The mountains rose sheer from every side, heaving their gigantic crests far up into the night, the black peaks crowding together, and looking now less like beasts than like a company of cowled giants. In the daytime they were silent; but at night they seemed to stir and rouse themselves. Occasionally the stamp-mill stopped, its thunder ceasing abruptly. Then one could hear the noises that the mountains made in their living. From the cañon, from the crowding crests, from the whole immense landscape, there rose a steady and prolonged sound, coming from all sides at once. It was that incessant and muffled roar which disengages itself from all vast bodies, from oceans, from cities, from forests, from sleeping armies, and which is like the breathing of an infinitely great monster, alive, palpitating.

McTeague returned to his work. At six in the morning his shift was taken off, and he went out of the mine and back to the bunk house. All day long he slept, flung at length upon the strong-smelling blankets—slept the dreamless sleep of exhaustion, crusted and overpowered with the work, flat and prone upon his belly, till again in the evening the cook sounded the alarm upon the crowbar bent into a triangle.

from THE LAND OF LITTLE RAIN

MARY AUSTIN

A naturalist, essayist, feminist, and passionate opponent of commercial development, Mary Austin (1868–1934) moved from her native Illinois to southern California in 1888. The desert with its arid beauty and ethnic mix of Mexicans, Native Americans, and Anglos inspired her and became the setting for many of her thirty-two books. The Land of Little Rain (1903), her best-known work, was a lyrical tribute to the rainshadow deserts of the eastern Sierra. She later helped found a bohemian artists' colony at Carmel. In 1925 she moved to Santa Fe, where she lived out the last years of her life in an adobe home.

I REMEMBER VERY WELL when I first met him. Walking in the evening glow to spy the marriages of the white gilias, I sniffed the unmistakable odor of burning sage. It is a smell that carries far and indicates usually the nearness of a campoodie, but on the level mesa nothing taller showed than Diana's sage. Over the tops of it, beginning to dusk under a young white moon, trailed a wavering ghost of smoke, and at the end of it I came upon the Pocket Hunter making a dry camp in the friendly scrub. He sat tailorwise in the sand, with his coffee-pot on the coals, his supper ready to hand in the frying pan, and himself in a mood for talk. His pack burros in hobbles strayed off to hunt for a wetter mouthful than the sage afforded, and gave him no concern.

We came upon him often after that, threading the windy passes, or by waterholes in the desert hills, and got to know much of his way of life. He was a small, bowed man, with a face and manner and speech of no character at all, as if he had that faculty of small hunted things of taking on the protective color of his surroundings. His clothes were of no fashion that I could remember, except that they bore liberal markings of pot black, and he had a curious fashion of going about with his mouth open, which gave him a vacant look until you came near enough to perceive him busy about an endless hummed, wordless tune. He traveled far and took a long time to it, but the simplicity of his kitchen arrangements was elemental. A pot for beans, a coffee-pot, a frying-pan, a tin to mix bread in—he fed the burros in this when there was need—with these he had been half round our western world and back. He

404

explained to me very early in our acquaintance what was good to take to the hills for food: nothing sticky, for that "dirtied the pots"; nothing with "juice" to it, for that would not pack to advantage; and nothing likely to ferment. He used no gun, but he would set snares by the water-holes for quail and doves, and in the trout country he carried a line. Burros he kept, one or two according to his pack, for the chief excellence that they would eat potato parings and firewood. He had owned a horse in the foothill country, but when he came to the desert with no forage but mesquite, he found himself under the necessity of picking the beans from the briers, a labor that drove him to the use of pack animals to whom thorns were a relish.

I suppose no man becomes a pocket hunter by first intention. He must be born with the faculty, and along comes the occasion, like the tap on the test tube that induces crystallization. My friend had been several things of no moment until he struck a thousand-dollar pocket in the Lee District and came into his vocation. A pocket, you must know, is a small body of rich ore occurring by itself, or in a vein of poorer stuff. Nearly every mineral ledge contains such, if only one has the luck to hit upon them without too much labor. The sensible thing for a man to do who has found a good pocket is to buy himself into business and keep away from the hills. The logical thing is to set out looking for another one. My friend the Pocket Hunter had been looking twenty years. His working outfit was a shovel, a pick, a gold pan which he kept cleaner than his plate, and a pocket magnifier. When he came to a water-course he would pan out the gravel of its bed for "colors," and under the glass determine if they had come from far or near, and so spying he would work up the stream until he found where the drift of the gold-bearing outcrop fanned out into the creek; then up the side of the cañon till he came to the proper vein. I think he said the best indication of small pockets was an iron stain, but I could never get the run of miner's talk enough to feel instructed for pocket hunting.

His itinerary began with the east slope of the Sierras of the Snows, where that range swings across to meet the coast hills, and all up that slope to the Truckee River country, where the long cold forbade his progress north. Then he worked back down one or another of the nearly parallel ranges that lie out desertward, and so down to the sink of the Mojave River, burrowing to oblivion in the sand,—a big mysterious land, a lonely, inhospitable land, beautiful, terrible. But he came to no harm in it; the land tolerated him as it might a gopher or a badger. Of all its inhabitants it has the least concern for man.

There are many strange sorts of humans bred in a mining country, each sort despising the queernesses of the other, but of them all I found the Pocket

Hunter most acceptable for his clean, companionable talk.... [He] had gotten to that point where he knew no bad weather, and all places were equally happy so long as they were out of doors. I do not know just how long it takes to become saturated with the elements so that one takes no account of them. Myself can never get past the glow and exhilaration of a storm, the wrestle of long dust-heavy winds, the play of live thunder on the rocks, nor past the keen fret of fatigue when the stone outlasts physical endurance. But prospectors and Indians get a kind of a weather shell that remains on the body until death.

The journeyings of the Pocket Hunter led him often into that mysterious country beyond Hot Creek where a hidden force works mischief, mole-like, under the crust of the earth. Whatever agency is at work in that neighborhood, and it is popularly supposed to be the devil, it changes means and direction without time or season. It creeps up whole hillsides with insidious heat, unguessed until one notes the pine woods dying at the top, and having scorched out a good block of timber returns to steam and spout in caked, forgotten crevices of years before. It will break up sometimes blue-hot and bubbling, in the midst of a clear creek, or make a sucking, scalding quicksand at the ford. These outbreaks had the kind of morbid interest for the Pocket Hunter that a house of unsavory reputation has in a respectable neighborhood, but I always found the accounts he brought me more interesting than his explanations, which were compounded of fag ends of miner's talk and superstition. He was a perfect gossip of the woods, this Pocket Hunter, and when I could get him away from "leads" and "strikes" and "contacts," full of fascinating small talk about the ebb and flood of creeks, the piñon crop on Black Mountain, and the wolves of Mesquite Valley. I suppose he never knew how much he depended for the necessary sense of home and companionship on the beasts and trees, meeting and finding them in their wonted places,— the bear that used to come down Pine Creek in the spring, pawing out trout from the shelters of sod banks, the juniper at Lone Tree Spring, and the quail at Paddy Jack's.

There is a place on Waban, south of White Mountain, where flat, wind-tilted cedars make low tents and coves of shade and shelter, where the wild sheep winter in the snow. Woodcutters and prospectors had brought me word of that, but the Pocket Hunter was accessory to the fact. About the opening of winter, when one looks for sudden big storms, he had attempted a crossing, by the nearest path, beginning the ascent at noon. It grew cold, the snow came on thick and blinding, and wiped out the trail in a white smudge; the storm drift blew in and cut off landmarks, the early dark obscured the rising drifts. According to the Pocket Hunter's account, he knew where he was, but

California prospector, c. 1908, by Charles C. Pierce

couldn't exactly say. Three days before he had been in the west arm of Death Valley on a short water allowance, ankle-deep in shifty sand; now he was on the rise of Waban, knee-deep in sodden snow, and in both cases he did the only allowable thing—he walked on. That is the only thing to do in a snow-storm in any case.

It might have been the creature instinct, which in his way of life had room to grow, that led him to the cedar shelter; at any rate he found it about four hours after dark, and heard the heavy breathing of the flock. He said that if he thought at all at this juncture he must have thought that he had stumbled on a storm-belated shepherd with his silly sheep; but in fact he took no note of anything but the warmth of packed fleeces, and snuggled in between them dead with sleep. If the flock stirred in the night he stirred drowsily to keep close and let the storm go by. That was all until morning woke him shining on a white world. Then the very soul of him shook to see the wild sheep of God stand up about him, nodding their great horns beneath the cedar roof, look-ing out on the wonder of the snow. They had moved a little away from him with the coming of the light, but paid him no more heed. The light broadened

407

and the white pavilions of the snow swam in the heavenly blueness of the sea from which they rose. The cloud drift scattered and broke billowing in the cañons. The leader stamped lightly on the litter to put the flock in motion, suddenly they took the drifts in those long light leaps that are nearest to flight, down and away on the slopes of Waban. Think of that to happen to a Pocket Hunter!

It was once in roving weather, when we found him shifting pack on a steep trail, that I observed certain of his belongings done up in green canvas bags, the veritable "green bag" of English novels. It seemed so incongruous a reminder in this untenanted West that I dropped down beside the trail overlooking the vast dim valley to hear about the green canvas. He had gotten it, he said, in London years before, and that was the first I had known of his having been abroad. It was after one of his "big strikes" that he had made the Grand Tour, and had brought nothing away from it but the green canvas bags, which he conceived would fit his needs, and an ambition. This last was nothing less than to strike it rich and set himself up among the eminently bourgeois of London. It seemed that the situation of the wealthy English middle class, with just enough gentility above to aspire to, and sufficient smaller fry to bully and patronize, appealed to his imagination, though of course he did not put it so crudely as that.

It was no news to me then, two or three years after, to learn that he had taken ten thousand dollars from an abandoned claim, just the sort of luck to have pleased him, and gone to London to spend it. The land seemed not to miss him any more than it had minded him, but I missed him and could not forget the trick of expecting him in least likely situations. Therefore it was with a pricking sense of the familiar that I followed a twilight trail of smoke, a year or two later, to the swale of a dripping spring, and came upon a man by the fire with a coffee-pot and frying-pan. I was not surprised to find it was the Pocket Hunter. No man can be stronger than his destiny.

A Peck of Gold

ROBERT FROST

Robert Frost (1874–1963) was born in San Francisco and moved to New England after his father's death in 1885. After many years as a schoolteacher and part-time farmer, Frost turned to poetry at age thirty-eight and quickly rose to wide popularity and transatlantic fame. He received the Pulitzer Prize four times for his innovative, pastoral poetry. West-running Brook, *published in 1928, featured this poem about his native California, playfully dated "as of about 1880."*

Dust always blowing about the town,
Except when sea fog laid it down,
And I was one of the children told
Some of the blowing dust was gold.

All the dust the wind blew high
Appeared like gold in the sunset sky,
But I was one of the children told
Some of the dust was really gold.

Such was life in the Golden Gate:
Gold dusted all we drank and ate,
And I was one of the children told,
"We all must eat our peck of gold."

from Songs from Gold Mountain

MARLON K. HOM, EDITOR

The Chinese nickname for the United States was "Gold Mountain," a name that reflected both the promise of wealth and hardship in store for Chinese immigrants. Semi-autonomous Chinatowns emerged in San Francisco, Los Angeles, Sacramento, and Stockton during the gold rush. Marginalized in their new home, Chinese Californians found work in a variety of occupations—they labored as miners, shopkeepers, domestics, and eventually railroad crewmen—usually at low wages with racist bosses and unsympathetic coworkers. Gamsaan go (or "gold mountain songs") were a new form of Cantonese poetry that emerged in the late nineteenth century to express the experiences of Chinese immigrants in the United States. The following Gamsaan go were written in San Francisco's Chinatown in the early 1910s.

At home I was in poverty,
    constantly worried about firewood and rice.
I borrowed money
    to come to Gold Mountain.
Immigration officers cross-examined me;
    no way could I get through.
Deported to this island,
    like a convicted criminal.
Here—
Mournful sighs fill the gloomy room;
A nation weak; her people often humiliated
Like animals, tortured and destroyed at others'
    whim.

American laws, more ferocious than tigers:
Many are the people jailed inside wooden walls,
Detained, interrogated, tortured,
Like birds plunged into an open trap—
    What suffering!

To whom can I complain of the tragedy?
I shout to Heaven, but there is no way out!
Had I only known such difficulty in passing
     the Golden Gate...
Fed up with this treatment, I regret my journey here.

Since my departure in Hong Kong,
She and I are each in different places.
A long separation makes a person even more miserable.
How can one ever forget home, sweet home?
Stranded in a foreign country,
In dreams my soul encircles my village home.
Words to wife and children: don't worry, you won't
     have to wait too long.
Once I amass the gold, I will be on my way.

It's a summerlike first month of the new year.
Ten thousand houses are decorated with New
     Year scrolls.
In a foreign country, we celebrate the joyous
     festival in springtime clothes;
We greet each other by the door, with auspicious
     sayings:
May you claim a mine full of gold.
May wealth soothe your soul.
Hosts and guests, so gaily, raise the jade winecups,
Sipping the spring wine, toasting merrily the
     swift, rosy clouds.

from GOLD

BLAISE CENDRARS

Blaise Cendrars (1887–1961) was the pseudonym of Frederick Sauser-Hall, a Swiss poet, novelist, actor, film director, Bohemian, and world traveler. He seriously took up writing after losing an arm while serving in the French Foreign Legion during World War I. His poetry, novels, and prose filled more than fifty books during his life. Published in 1925, Gold: Being the Marvelous History of General John Augustus Sutter *offered a fictional account of the tulmultuous life of John Sutter. It was Cendrars's first and most successful novel.*

YEARS PASS. ALL WASHINGTON gets to know the general. His big clumsy figure, his feet, which drag along the ground in down-at-heel shoes, his frock-coat, spotted with grease and covered with dandruff, his big bald head, nodding convulsively under its battered felt hat, are among the sights of the Capital City.

At first, thanks to the intrigues set on foot by his adversaries, he is harshly received. But, as years go by, many of his enemies die and functionaries are transferred or retire. A day comes when no one knows exactly what this senile madman wants. Who is this old general who has been in the Mexican War and who babbles about gold mines. There must be a tile loose—and a big one at that! A favorite sport among the attendants is to send him from one office to another. The General knows all the ins and outs of the Law Department by heart, and the corridors that lead to every ministry in Washington. He comes and goes, he climbs and descends staircases, he knocks at doors, he waits patiently in passages, he walks thousands of miles, he returns upon his traces thousands of times. He is for all the world like a man lost in a maze.

But he never despairs.

During these years Johann August Sutter subsists on his pension as general. "Subsists" is rather a figure of speech. In reality his pension is swallowed up every year by shady lawyers, unscrupulous go-betweens, and minor officials who periodically pretend to interest themselves in his case.

In 1863 a young Danish swindler from New York, whose acquaintance he has made at a religious revival, takes his papers, presents him next day to a confederate whom he passes off as a secretary at the Ministry of Justice. The precious pair take complete possession of the general. Sutter writes to Judge Thompson that his case is in the hands of God, and that the Minister is about to plead his case in person. He asks for ten thousand dollars—for the Minister! Mina, to whom he also writes, sends him one thousand dollars. He manages to have the meager marriage portion of his dead wife released and sent to him from Switzerland. All the money he can scrape together goes into the hands of the two crooks, who disappear one fine morning when their victim is squeezed dry.

Time and time again lawyers, real and sham, call upon him, listen attentively to his case, and make him sign a mass of documents by which Sutter assigns to them a quarter, a half, or even the whole of what he hopes to gain. For what are money, gold, real estate to him by now? It is justice for which he is fighting—a judgment—a sentence!

He falls into destitution and misery. To support life he takes to all kinds of casual jobs. He polishes shoes, runs messages, washes dishes in a soldiers' eating-house, where his title of general and his horror of whisky make him a popular figure. Mina sends him one hundred dollars a month, which goes with the rest, into the hands of a knot of crimps and rogues who leech on the poor old man. "The Case" takes everything—to his last dollar.

In 1866 Sutter presents himself before Congress and claims a million dollars in cash and the restitution of his plantations. To this step he has been persuaded by a certain Polish Jew.

In 1868 Sutter presents a petition to the Senate, in which the affair is detailed at great length. He will compromise for five hundred thousand dollars and the return of his land. The idea comes from the brain of an infantry sergeant of his acquaintance.

In 1870—a new petition to the Senate. It is drawn up by a certain Bujard, a photographer from the canton of Vaud. Sutter now claims no more than one hundred thousand dollars. He surrenders his land, promises to leave the territory of the United States and return to Switzerland. He cannot, he says, "after having been the richest man in the United States, return to his own canton destitute and become a public charge in the commune of his origin."

In 1873 he joins the Herrenhutter sect, confides his entire case to the Council of the Seven Johannite Ancients, and signs an instrument by which he bequeaths his eventual fortune and his Californian possessions to the fraternity, "so that in those beautiful valleys the stain of gold may be effaced by the purity of our first parents." The famous case is reopened, conducted this time by a member of the bar who is the founder and spiritual director of this German-American communist sect.

Sutter leaves Washington and goes to Lititz, in Pennsylvania, to be baptized and purified according to the great Babylonian rite. He is now a soul washed white as wool, an intimate of the Most High.

The Herrenhutter of Lititz have their headquarters on a big estate which they own in common and where they cultivate immense fields of wheat. They also own an oil-well. The sacks of flour and barrels of petroleum which they send to the seacoast are all stamped with their registered trademark, a paschal lamb holding a banner between its feet. On the banner are stamped the initials, J. C. They stand, not for Jesus Christ, but for Johannes Christitsch, founder and grand master of the sect. Christitsch is a lawyer of Servian origin, a tricky and formidable pleader, an unscrupulous and enterprising businessman, who is building up one of the largest industrial fortunes in the country on the backs of four hundred enthusiasts and visionaries, nearly all of German descent.

The principal articles of faith of the sect are: community of wives and goods, regeneration by work, certain "Adamist" rules of life, ecstasies, and possession by the Spirit. Their only gospel is the Book of Revelations. Sutter becomes rapidly famous through the profound knowledge which he has of this book and the personal commentaries which he gives upon its prophecies.

The Great Harlot who has given birth upon the Sea is Christopher Columbus, discovering America.

The Angels and the Stars of St. John are in the American flag. With California, a new star, the Star of Absinthe, has been added.

Anti-Christ is Gold.

The Beasts and Satans are the cannibal Indians, the Caribs and Kanakas. There are also black and yellow ones—the Negroes and Chinese.

The Three Riders are the three great tribes of Redskins.

Already a third of the peoples of Europe have been decimated in this land.

"I am one of the twenty-four Ancients, and it is because I have heard the Voice that I have descended among you.... I was the richest man in the world. Gold has ruined me...."

A Russian woman falls down in ecstasy at Sutter's feet while he is expounding the visions of St. John the Evangelist and recounting the episodes of his own life.

But Sutter is not permitted to give himself up to his rapturous madness.

Johannes Christitsch is his evil genius. It is Johannes Christitsch who reopens the historic case, who conducts it personally, and is determined to win, cost what it may. Christitsch goes to Washington every week. There he solicits, intrigues, fills up reams of stamped paper, flourishes briefs, rummages archives, brings new facts to light, and by his feverish energy galvanizes the ancient process into new and spasmodic life. Often he brings Sutter with him, or sends him in alone. He exhibits him, makes him speak—becomes his manager, in a word. Somewhere or another he has unearthed a general's uniform. He insists that the old man shall put it on, and even pins decorations on his breast.

So the martyrdom of the general commences afresh. He is dragged from office to office, from department to department. High officials deplore the case of this aged victim, take voluminous notes, promise to intervene and obtain him full satisfaction. When he is alone, groups of idlers form around him and make him tell them the story of the Discovery of Gold. Sutter is quite willing. He mixes his beloved Apocalypse and the doctrines of the Herrenhutters into the story of his life. His wits are gone. All the urchins of Washington can tell you he is crazy, and their amusement knows no bounds.

The old fool.

"The richest man in the world."

What a scream!

One day, upon the streets, he meets three orderlies who are taking a lunatic to the asylum. The man in their clutches is a ragged and filthy creature, an old man, who gesticulates, who fights with his guardians, and who shouts incoherently. Breaking for a moment from their hands, he flings himself in the gutter, filling his mouth, his eyes, and ears with garbage and grasping handfuls of mud and manure between his skinny, yellow fingers. His pockets bulge with ordure and he has a sack filled with stones.

While the orderlies are binding their patient the general looks at him closely. It is Marshall—Marshall the carpenter of Fort Sutter and Coloma. Marshall recognizes his old employer. "Master, master, didn't I tell you? There is gold everywhere—everywhere!"

One warm afternoon in June the general is sitting on the bottom step of the great flight that leads to the Capitol. Like many aged men, his head is quite empty of thought. He is simply enjoying a rare moment of physical well-being as he warms his old carcass in the sun.

"I am the general, general, general.

"I am the gen-e-ral!"

A ragged street urchin of seven is running down the great steps, taking four at a stride. It is Dick Price, the little match-seller, the old man's favorite.

"General! General!" he cries, flinging his arm round the drowsy old man's neck, "you've won! Congress has just settled it. A hundred million dollars—all for you, General!"

"You're sure...? Sure...?" cries Sutter, holding the wriggling boy tightly.

"Sure, General! It's in all the papers. Jim and Bob has gone to get them. I'm going to sell papers to-night! You watch 'em go!"

Sutter does not see seven little rascals behind his back who are wriggling with laughter like so many malicious sprites under the lofty portico, and gesticulating delightedly at their confederate. He jumps to his feet, draws himself to his full height, says but one word:

"Thanks!"

Then he thrashes the air with his arms and falls like a log.

General Johann August Sutter is dead.

It is three o'clock in the afternoon—the 17th of June, 1880.

It is Sunday, and Congress is not even in session.

The terrified urchins take to their heels.

The hours pass upon the vast deserted square and as the sun sinks the giant shadow of the Capitol covers the body of the general as with a pall.

from GHOST TOWN

G. EZRA DANE

In the 1940s, nostalgia ran high in honor of the centennial annniversary of Marshall's gold discovery. G. Ezra Dane, whose grandfather crossed the plains to California in 1849, led the wave of gold rush commemoration by editing a series of reprintings of California authors such as Alonzo Delano and Mark Twain. He had earlier helped revive the Ancient Order of E Clampus Vitus, a prankster fraternal organization that began in the gold rush. For Ghost Town, *published in 1941 and reprinted in 1948, Dane interviewed several "old-timers" and set all their sentimental anecdotes in the mining town of Columbia.*

NO SIR, NOBODY HAS A BETTER RIGHT than me to set on this stump. I planted the old poplar myself on the corner here, near sixty years ago. It got to be three foot through at the ground, as you can see, and it must of been eighty feet high. But the roots begun to upheave the sidewalk bricks, and when the limbs would blow they'd brush the shakes off the awning of Mike Rehm's Pioneer Saloon, so the old tree had to come down.

Well, they must come an end to all things, no matter how great or how good. With men, and trees, and towns, it's all the same. And so it is with me. I grew up with this old town and I've come down with it.

Here I set like an old owl or fox amongst the boulders and think of the days and times that used to be. Them days and these! Them days and these! It's like day and night, day and night. Oh, them was the days, I can tell you. Yes, sir, them was the days of great depravation and plenty of whisky.

A fellow didn't have to travel, in them days, to see the world. The whole world come here then with samples of all kinds of humanity. The gold, that was what they all come for, of course. They followed the track of it, in '48 and '49 and '50, like you'll see chickens follow a trail of corn, pecking and scratching away after it, up the Stanislaus River and the Tuolumne into these Sierra foothills, then along Wood's Creek, and acrost Shaw's Flat and up the main gulch here, that we called Miners' Avenue.

March 1850, that's when the first miners reached this flat—Dr. Thaddeus Hildreth and his party—and the five of them averaged fifteen pounds of gold

Cemetary at Sutter Creek, 1938, by Alma Lavenson

a day for three days. Why, even a lazy man could do pretty well in diggins as rich as that. You take, for instance, one of these first comers, he was even too lazy to wash his drawers. To save himself the work of scrubbing them, he just tied them to a limb that overhung a little stream and let them dangle in the water. He figured, you see, that the current would wash them for him over-night. And the next morning when he come to fish them out, lo and b'God! he found his drawers gold-plated.

Well, with stories like that a–spreading, it's no wonder that Columbia's population grew from five men to six thousand in six weeks. A good many of them, of course, went out like they had come in—with the next rush to another new discovery. But others come that built, and made the camp a town, and the town a city. Yes sir, the greatest on the Mother Lode it was in its day, and they called it the Gem of the Southern Mines.

Well, that's the way it was. Columbia was born of gold; yes, and died of it. It practically ate itself up, the old town did. When the miners had scraped the land down to bedrock all around, then they begun to close in on the town itself. One house after another come down for the sake of the rich ground underneath. These few old buildings that still straggle along Main Street here,

North San Juan, 1934, by Alma Lavenson.

you see, either they've been mined under without falling down or they happened to be built in places where the bedrock come near the surface and the gold was scarce.

So that's the way the miners come in, like a swarm of locusts. They stripped the country bare, right down to its poor old limestone bones, and then they left.

To look at the old place now, you wouldn't believe that it used to be as I remember it. I can set here and look down this street and see it as it was.

Toward the end of the afternoon the men would come in from the diggins in Matelot Gulch and from Miners' Avenue, and off Gold Hill and from Gold Springs and Murphy's Defeat and Texas Flat and the diggins out Springfield way, and down from French Camp and Italian Bar and Pine Log on the South Fork of the Stanislaus, and from Yankee Hill and from Martinez and Sawmill Flat. Say, that was a sight you ought to see! The street was so packed with people that a fellow could hardly cross. He'd just be carried along with the stream of humanity. The crowd would surge back and forth, and it was made up of all sorts and conditions of people from everywhere.

You'd see all kinds of dress, from frock coats and ruffled shirts and fancy vests down to red or blue flannel shirts with no coats or vests at all and old

Ruins of gold rush-era store at Mt. Ophir, 1950, by Alma Lavenson

pants tucked into heavy boots. These pants would be held up, along with a pistol and knife and other hardware, by a good stout belt; and they'd be held together by patches. Usually the patches would be made from flour sacks, each man advertising his favorite brand. Now you take, for instance, they was a fellow one time showed up with the label "Self-Rising Flour" right across the seat of his pants, and he was "Self-Rising Bill" from that day on.

Yes, and patches wasn't all they used the flour sacks for. A man didn't ever have to go without socks if he had a couple of flour sacks. He'd put his foot on the sack near one end and he'd fold the corners and the front end over the top of his foot, and then he'd bring the other end up in back over the heel and wrap it around his ankle and leg and pull his boot on over it; and that was called the "California socks."

Yes sir, and when the women begun to come in, they found the flour sack mighty useful, too. Old Mr. Bell that had the flouring mill down on Wood's Creek below Sonora—you can see his stone dam yet where the old mill stood— he used to tell how, time of the big flood at Sonora, when the creek over-flowed and the women came squealing and splashing out of the houses with their skirts lifted up to their waists, of course they showed considerable of their home-made underwear, and under each lifted skirt the crowd could read: BELL'S FLOURING MILLS. Yes sir, old Mr. Bell always said that was the best advertising he ever got, and it didn't cost him a cent.

from THE LAST DAYS OF THE LATE, GREAT STATE OF CALIFORNIA

CURT GENTRY

Curt Gentry (1931–) was born in Colorado and lived for many years in San Francisco. He is the author of more than fifteen books, including The Madams of San Francisco: An Irreverent History of the City by the Golden Gate *(1964) and coauthor of* Helter Skelter *(1974). Published in 1968,* The Last Days of the Late, Great State of California *was a mock history of California's final days.*

THEY CAME TO NORTHERN CALIFORNIA by horseback, wagon, foot, and ship, from every state and territory and every foreign land.

They came because there was gold.

By the hundreds, then the thousands, they panned the rivers, dug the gullies, sluiced the streams.

And every place they stopped at they named, as if to bestow permanence and identity.

Some places were named after the nationalities of their residents—Chinese Camp, Chili Gulch, Dutch Flat.

Others denoted qualities essential to survival in the miner's West—Rough and Ready, Fairplay.

Some, such as Hangtown and Cut Throat Bar, commemorated incidents in their early history.

Some dealt with their amusements—Ladies' Creek, Brandy City, Poker Flat, Whiskeytown—or with their aftereffects—Delirium Tremens and Puke Ravine.

Some, such as Rich Bar, were measurements of their success. But this was not always true of their opposites. Poverty Hill, for example, was so designated to keep other miners away.

Some were named in jest—Drytown had twenty-six saloons.

And other names were impolite terms to which they gave polite spellings, once the wives, ministers, and other "respectables" arrived—Asel, Putah Creek, and Guano Hill.

In time, as the color grew fainter, the strikes farther and farther apart, the miners deserted Northern California, leaving behind as their heritage abandoned mine shafts, a few thriving towns, a hundred more already dead, and the names. Often the names survived when the places did not.

This was the first great migration. It began in 1848 and lasted slightly more than a decade.

The last great migration began during World War II and lasted a quarter of a century.

This time they came by automobile, over Donner Pass, on Interstate 80, down the slopes of the Sierra Nevadas. ("Honey, do you have to go so fast? The sign says the speed limit is sixty-five." "Baby," he replied, "in California you can get a ticket for observing the speed limit if the rest of the traffic's going faster.")

They came across the desert from Needles on Route #66, the children watching for the first orange juice stand. ("Of course it doesn't taste like fresh orange juice, lady," the vendor explained with tolerant exasperation. "It's concentrate. We ship all the fresh oranges out of state.")

They came from out of the sky, dropping into the smog, then suddenly seeing the mammoth spread of Los Angeles for the first time. ("God, it's big!" There were no other words to describe it.)

They came from almost every place.

For almost every reason.

They came out of loneliness and love and desire and hate.

They came because the company had diversified or Hughes was hiring or Litton expanding or UC had a cyclotron or there were crops to pick.

They came because it was a new beginning or a last chance or because there was nowhere else left to go.

They came because they could never forget the look of the city as the troop ship sailed under the Golden Gate.

They came because the children were here or because the schools were better or because the old neighborhood frightened them or because the wife nagged.

They came because they believed that south of the Tehachapis they could find God, or a part in a movie.

They came because they'd heard that in San Francisco there were three single men for every single girl.

They came to sin or to soak old arthritic bones in the perpetual sun.

They came because it was as far away as you could get from the South or because the niggers were taking over Chicago.

They came because of a movie or a song or an advertisement or a book or a letter or a photograph.

They came because in Frisco they paid you good money to bare your boobs.

They came because people enjoyed themselves more here, because there was so much to do and see, because it was the New Frontier, because it was the Old West, because it was a swinging place, because it offered opportunity.

They came for a visit and never went back.

They came because there was more space or because they dug the scene.

They came because they didn't like the person they had been and hoped to achieve some marvelous alchemy merely by crossing the state line.

They came because the law was after them or because there were doctors here who might be able to cure their diseases or because it was as good a place as any to die or because they'd seen teenyboppers with their mini-skirts and cute waggy bottoms on TV.

They came because of a good deal or because it was easier to declare bankruptcy and save a little.

They came because it was more stimulating intellectually or because Robert Welch praised it so much.

They came because the climate was mild.

They came because the swami told them to.

They came because people were friendlier or more tolerant.

They came because all their lives they had been moving West.

They came because of surfing or skiing or sky diving or gay bars.

They came because they hoped it would be better than what they left behind.

They came because it was where things were happening.

They came because it was California.

From the end of World War II through the end of that final year, 1969, they came at a rate of 1000 a day. Or so the statistics say. But statistics can be deceptive. Actually some 1200 came, but only 1000 stayed.

For one-sixth of those who came, the reality did not measure up to the dream.

The Chicagoan found there were niggers here, too, and the Negro found the same discrimination and lack of opportunities.

The young secretary found that while there were more bachelors than bachelorettes in San Francisco, many of the former were less interested in the latter than in each other.

The homosexual found there was a premium on youth.

The farmer found there was no room for the small farm in agribusiness.

The farm laborer found that wages promised bore no relations to wages paid.

The buxom beauty found that the topless clubs didn't pay all that well.

The old-age pensioner found that mild climate meant one day was just like another.

The job hunter found there were more jobs—for the highly specialized.

Some found that people became friendlier faster—a minute after meeting someone you were on a first-name basis—but that deep, lasting friendships were rare.

Others found that they couldn't escape from themselves.

And all found that although wages were higher, so was the cost of living.

But most stayed. For them the prospects outweighed the disappointments.

Unlike their predecessors, the new immigrants for the most part ignored Northern California, passing through it quickly, if at all. Instead of seeking out solitary places, where there was the possibility of making a fresh strike, they headed straight for the most crowded metropolitan areas, many settling in the San Francisco Bay Area but even more heading for Southern California. And although time had wrought a thousand metamorphoses, large sections of Northern California, from the Sierra Nevadas to the Pacific, remained sparsely settled, the communities small and isolated, inbred, while the land stayed ruggedly beautiful, California as it once was. The natives were suspicious of "foreigners," i.e., anyone from Sacramento south. And they hated with a collective passion that greedy land- and water-grabbing monster south of the Tehachapis known as "L.A." Periodically they threatened to secede from California—to join Oregon or Nevada, or to form another state entirely.

Yet although most of the new immigrants did not choose to live here, their needs extended this far and farther.

from CALIFORNIA RICH

STEPHEN BIRMINGHAM

Stephen Birmingham (1932–) was born in Hartford, Connecticut, and has taught writing at the University of Cincinnati. He is the author of seven novels and fourteen works of nonfiction, many centering on America's upper class. California Rich *was published in 1980.*

CALIFORNIA, IT HAS BEEN POINTED OUT, has never, for all its riches, produced a fortune to equal the riches amassed in the East by such men as John D. Rockefeller, Jay Gould, and E. H. Harriman. Perhaps this is because in the 1850s and 1860s, when Rockefeller was putting together the Standard Oil Company, California was still too new and inexperienced a place to contain more than one get-rich enthusiasm at a time, and the enthusiasm of the moment, of course, was gold. The California gold fortunes had a way of being lost rather quickly, though the men who followed the prospectors—the speculators and con men, the supply merchants, the gamblers, the saloonkeepers, and madams—did somewhat better. In the 1850s some quarter of a million Americans thronged across the valleys and mountains of California in search of gold-rush wealth, ignoring the black viscous substance that squished beneath their feet, the substance that was making Rockefeller rich.

It lay all about, in pools and open pits and puddles. It oozed from canyonsides. The coastal Indians had been making use of the sticky stuff for generations. They used it to waterproof their woven baskets, to caulk the bottoms of their canoes, and as a sealant to make containers of food both air- and watertight. They had also learned that when swallowed, it made an excellent if not very tasty purgative, that rubbed on the skin it made a soothing balm for cuts and burns, and that it could itself be burned for heat and light. The coastal tribes traded their *brea*, or tar, with tribes of the interior for spearheads and furs. The first Spanish settlers were puzzled by the tar pits. Arriving in Upper California from Mexico in 1769 with Don Gaspar de Portolá and Fra Junípero Serra— whose orders from Carlos III were to oust the Jesuits from the missions and replace them with Franciscans—the Spaniards concluded that the tar pits perhaps caused the earthquakes and were somehow connected with volcanoes in the distant mountains. Though the black substance was cool to the touch, it was assumed to be some form of molten rock.

In 1855, taking their cue from the Indians, the Mexican General Andrés Pico and his nephew, Rómulo, had begun in a modest way to market the crude oil they scooped up from pits in a canyon north of the San Fernando Mission. General Pico was the brother of Pio Pico, the last Mexican governor of California, and was a fallen hero of the Mexican War—he had defeated the American General Stephen Kearney in 1847, but had later been forced to surrender to General John C. Frémont. The Picos peddled their "coal oil" as a medicine, as a lubricant for squeaky oxcart axles, and as a cheaper—and much smokier and smellier—substitute for whale oil in lamps. (Whale oil could then only be afforded by the well-to-do; the very poor went to bed when the sun went down.) To the gold and silver prospectors, meanwhile, the oil was simply a nuisance. It seeped into streams and rivers and polluted their drinking water.

In 1857 a former New York sperm-oil dealer named George S. Gilbert built a primitive oil refinery near the Ventura Mission. In order to reduce his oil to axle grease, which he hoped to market, he boiled the oil, and, in the process, the vaporous fumes of what would one day fuel the automobile industry escaped into the blue California sky. One of Mr. Gilbert's first sales that year was a consignment of a hundred kegs of grease to one Mr. A. C. Ferris of Brooklyn, New York. Alas, the heavy burden of Gilbert's oil was too much for the mule teams assigned to carry it across the Isthmus of Panama. The hundred kegs were jettisoned somewhere in the jungle. If Mr. Gilbert's oil had reached its intended destination, the birthplace of the oil industry might have been southern California instead of Titusville, Pennsylvania, where, that same year, a blacksmith named Uncle Billy Smith dug a hole in the ground that became America's first oil well. Within two years the great Pennsylvania oil stampede had begun and the desolate little farm community of Titusville had become a boomtown. And down from Cleveland, less than a hundred and fifty miles away, young John D. Rockefeller was already on hand.

It was not until April 1892 that the California oil industry was ready for a man named Edward L. Doheny. Ed Doheny was a most unlikely character to signal such a momentous event. He had been born in 1856 in Fond du Lac, Wisconsin, the son of a poor Irish immigrant who had fled from the great potato famine of the 1840s and had headed westward lured by the siren song of riches. The senior Doheny, however, had never found them, and at age sixteen his son had run away from home. Ed Doheny had worked variously as a booking agent, a fruit packer, a mule driver, and as a singing waiter at the Occidental Hotel in Wichita, Kansas, where he also picked up bits of change acting as a procurer of young ladies for the traveling drummers who passed through town. At the age of eighteen he embarked on what was to be his lifelong occupation—searching for wealth underground—and become a gold prospector.

For the next few years Ed Doheny was a man without a permanent address, and the chronology of his wanderings is unclear. He is known to have spent time in Texas, Arizona, New Mexico, and Mexico, sometimes making a small strike, sometimes going broke. During these years he acquired a reputation in prospecting circles that was unsavory, not to say dangerous. The sheriff of Laredo in 1878 described the passage through that town of one "E. Dohenny [sic] a rough character." Doheny had early learned to use a gun and was quick to reach for his holster in tough situations. It was rumored he had once killed a man—or possibly several. He seems to have been a man able to adapt himself easily to one side of the law or the other as he moved through the one-street towns of the Southwest, and in New Mexico, Doheny was known as the man who had cleared the little town of Kingston of local cattle thieves and bad men. One of these was said to have fired sixteen bullets at Doheny before Doheny was able to overpower and disarm him. As a prospector, however, he employed more mystical methods, and for a long time his principal mining tool was a divining rod. When the rod quivered and dipped in his hand, Doheny stopped on the spot and began digging for gold, occasionally finding some but usually not.

He was thirty-six years old in 1892 when he arrived in the still-raw California town that had been dedicated to Nuestra Señora de Los Angeles, and his prospects for discovering a real bonanza had begun to look exceptionally dim. He was still rawboned and fast on the draw, but youth was slipping away. His mining adventures in Arizona and New Mexico had all been failures and he was virtually penniless. But then one of those queer strokes of incredible luck that have marked the beginnings of so many American fortunes came to Ed Doheny. Passing in the street one day he noticed a black man driving a horse and wagonload of black, steaming, tarry stuff. Doheny asked the man what the substance was, and was told that it was *brea*, and that it bubbled from a pit on the edge of town, and that the poorer families of Los Angeles collected it without charge and used it for fuel.

From his diggings around the West, Doheny knew even without his divining rod that the *brea* was crude oil, and set off to investigate the bubbling pit. He located it in Hancock Park, decided that it looked promising, and with a small amount of hastily borrowed cash, leased the land. Because he could not afford to buy or lease a drill, Doheny dug by hand with a pick and shovel, arduously extending a four-by-six-foot shaft into the ground. At a depth of

460 feet he was able to dip up four barrels a day. The deeper he went the more oil came up, and within a few months he had brought in the first real gusher in California.

All at once, as news of Doheny's hand-dug discovery spread, it was Titusville all over again. Anyone who could scrape a few hundred dollars together began leasing land west of downtown Los Angeles to dig or drill for oil. The wells were shallow and cheap to dig; the average cost was $1500, including tanks and pumps, and by 1899 there were more than three thousand wells pumping oil, all from a narrow tract of land varying from 800 to 1500 feet wide and about four and a half miles long. The silhouettes of oil rigs dominated the skyline, and the drilling became so frenzied that the city fathers of Los Angeles declared that oil wells were a civic nuisance, and a moratorium was pronounced on further drilling within city limits. The moratorium did no good whatever. Everyone in Los Angeles, it now seemed, needed to drill a well for water. The city council could not deny its citizens the right to do that, and so the drilling continued. If the water wells spouted oil instead—well, that could be dismissed as just a lucky accident.

Ironically, what none of the restless explorers in the Great California Oil Scramble yet realized was that beneath the Los Angeles basin, and stretching out under the ocean beyond, lay one of the widest and deepest oil lakes in the world. It was forty-six miles across and twenty-two miles long, and from it in time would come three and a half billion barrels of oil. In the 1890s a visiting professor of geology at Yale named Benjamin Silliman had speculated that there was more oil beneath the soil of California "than in all the whales in the Pacific Ocean." Professor Silliman's projection was considered a naïve easterner's wild-eyed exaggeration. His estimate would turn out to be very much on the conservative side.

The California oil rush, of course, would always be overshadowed by the gold rush. The gold rush, after all, had more glamour. Gold is mankind's most ancient symbol of wealth, the basis for his most valuable coins. And yet, for all practical purposes, gold is an almost useless metal. Unlike other precious substances, including diamonds, there is little industrial use for gold, unless one counts dental inlays. (Recently, computer technology has found a few new uses for gold.) Gold is pretty, yes, but the beauty of gold is a matter of opinion, its value a matter of faith. It serves no practical, but only an emotional need, a religious need, and has decorated history's greatest altars and temples. And yet, for all the impracticality of gold, explorers and conquistadors throughout history have set forth in search of gold, of King Solomon's Mines. The quest of the Argonauts has always been a bit like the search for the Fountain of Youth, because once one finds gold, it doesn't quite work. Perhaps the ephemeral, spiritual context of gold, and the fact that the use of gold is essentially ornamental, explains why all the gold that was mined in the California gold rush—some three billion dollars' worth—made no man permanently rich. It slipped like dross through its finders' fingers and made its way underground again, to Fort Knox, the temple of United States currency.

With oil, on the other hand, the explorers were seeking a product that would have many practical uses and would reign as the most potent source of energy until the splitting of the atom. In the single year of 1950, for example, the output of California oil wells surpassed in dollar value the entire output of all the state's gold mines since the discovery of gold at Mr. Sutter's mill in Sacramento, which set off the gold rush. And oil made a number of California men permanently rich.

Meanwhile, throughout both rushes—the gold and the oil—the explorers and pioneers displayed a spirit and a character that would become typically Californian. The California élan involved a special doughtiness, a certain daring, a refusal to be fazed or put off by bad luck or circumstances, an unwillingness to give up. To the California pioneer, after all, California was more than the end of the rainbow; it was the last stop for the Conestoga wagon. The California pioneer had reached the edge of the continent, the last frontier, the last horizon. He could go no farther, and he would not turn back. To have made it to California was to have made it *all the way,* and those who did not make it were by definition failures. To those who made it to California success was the only possibility. The place had to be made to work. In the winterbound Sierras the Donner party would turn to cannibalism in order to make it over the hills to California.

In the early days of the California pioneers the region was not particularly hospitable. Northern California was damp and foggy most of the year, while the south was hot and waterless. The state was cut off from the rest of the country by an implacable backbone of rugged mountains, and most of its wide central valley was barren desert. And yet the Californians would change all that. They would change the landscape and, in the process, the climate. They would make the desert bloom with everything from cotton to peaches, lettuce, tomatoes, strawberries, artichokes, and alligator pears. In the process they would become rich.

They would remain daunted by nothing and they would retain the gambler's heart. They would build houses on mountainsides that were slipping into the sea, on the rims of canyons where in dry weather a single match would ignite

429

a hillside and make it burn like kerosene and where when it rained the hills would be deluged by mud slides. They would confidently build houses with swimming pools along the notorious San Andreas Fault and facing beaches that were periodically swept away by high seas.

But there is still more to the California spirit than a willingness to gamble and accept dares. Having arrived at the rim of the continent, the California pioneers, with no farther to go, became almost obsessive about the need to fight for a share of whatever it was they had found. From their faraway perch, the Californians promptly acquired rather large chips on their shoulders, and, in addition to a certain hauteur, the California character became notably disputatious and competitive. And, besides the amount of skulduggery, larceny, and blackmail that might be considered routine in the making of all great American fortunes, California's money was made by men who were ready, literally, to shoot it out with one another and would stop at nothing—not even murder—to get what they wanted.

HISTORY LESSON

JANICE GOULD

*Janice Gould (1949–), a mixed-blood Native Californian (Koyangk'auwi Maidu),
grew up in Berkeley and currently teaches creative writing and Native American literature at the University of Northern Colorado. She is the author of two collections of
poetry*—Beneath My Heart *(1990) and* Earthquake Weather *(1996).*

A TERRIBLE PESTILENCE, an intermittent lever, was reported as having almost
depopulated the whole valley of Sacramento and San Joaquin.... The country
was strewn with the remains of the dead wherever a village had stood, and from
the headwaters of the Sacramento to King's River only five Indians were seen.
                                                                —Hubert Howe Bancroft

1832
All this fall we have watched our families sicken
with astonishing rapidity. In a fever they chill to the bone,
then break into a profuse sweat. The shuddering heat and cold
alternates till they are too weak to rise from where they lay
and simply die. In our village no adults are left,
just one woman so heartbroken she can do nothing
but wail and smear her shorn head with pitch.
The children not stricken with fever neither sleep nor eat,
they are frightened and grieving, for the dead
clamor about us, even in this silence,
and poison the air with their stench.
There are too many to bury. We must wander away.
We cannot stay here.

Wandering, I thought I would feel no more.
Then I came to a place that filled me with disgust and shame
though at first only confusion and fear.
The skinned carcasses of hundreds of elk
lay swelling in the rain
at the foot of the Buttes.

Two white men lived there in a canvas tent.
Up they panted when they saw me
and pointed their guns at my chest.
If I escaped it is only with a prayer,
for it seems they kill everything that goes about on legs,
and upon doing this, cut away and take the skin
and leave the meat to rot for black-winged birds of prey.

1849

General Bidwell has hired us to work at his gold diggings
on the Feather River. If we work well, we'll be paid
two red handkerchiefs a day.
Otherwise we'll be paid but one.

1851

Several headmen among us Maidu have signed a treaty
with the white government.
We are to stay on the land between Chico and Oroville,
clear up to Nimshew, and we are not to stray.

For this the men will receive a pair of jeans,
a red flannel shirt, and a plow.
Women will get a linsey gown,
a few yards of calico, scissors and thread.

1852

At first we could not understand how the whites could settle on the land
granted us by the Treaty. They came in droves. Then we learned the U.S.
Senate had secretly rejected all treaties with Maidu and other Indian tribes,
and we were to be removed to Nome Lackie reservation, several miles away.

1863

They told us, *Because of conflict between Indians and whites, you will be moved for
your own safety to Round Valley Reservation. It is in Mendocino County, some three
days' march away.*

The removal has taken two weeks,
and of the 461 Indians who began this miserable trek,
only 277 have come to Round Valley.

432

Many died as follows: Men were shot who tried to escape.
The sick, or old, or women with children
were speared if they could not keep up,
bayonets being used to conserve ammunition.
Babies were also killed, taken by the feet
and swung against trees or rocks to crack their skulls.

1984
There are some things I don't want to talk about.
That chapter, for example, on California Indians which read:
*California Indians were a naturally shiftless and lazy people. The Mission padres had
no trouble bringing them into the Mission for these Indians were more submissive than
the Plains warriors.*
California Indians were easily conquered.

When mama was brought to the city,
she heard a neighbor remark,
"Why did they ever adopt an Indian? Don't they know
Indians are too dumb to learn anything?"
Mama said, "I'll show her!" and went off to Julliard and Columbia.
But when she came back to marry my dad,
her future mother-in-law turned to him and said,
"Why, she speaks English as well as we do!"

Mama used to say, "Why can't you kids learn anything?
What's wrong with you? Are you too dumb?
Perhaps you're just lazy and stupid.
Why don't you do as well as your friends?
Why do you give up? Why do you want to fail?
Why don't you make the effort?"
But how could we answer?

Sometimes I wake up in the night, clenching my fists, crying.
This morning it was because when I had to report about
Christopher Columbus, the whole class turned away, bored,
and began to talk amongst themselves.
"Christopher Columbus," I began, "had two motives
behind his voyage. He was intrigued by the discovery
of hitherto unknown languages,

and by the discovery of skull shapes and sizes
unlike the European."
Here I held up a small discolored skull, then continued,
"Christopher Columbus meant to sail around the world
until he found a language
with a shape which matched its sounds."
I held up an alphabet in beautiful calligraphy.

I knew the class did not care
and I raged into a frenzy, beating desktops,
throwing chairs aside.
The professor got up to leave the room,
her eyes sad and frightened.
I glared at her.
"You can finish your talk," she said,
"when you pull yourself together."

I stood in a corner of the room
and cried in humiliation and grief.

from THOUSAND PIECES OF GOLD

RUTHANNE LUM McCUNN

Ruthanne Lum McCunn (1946–) was born in San Francisco's Chinatown and was taken as a child to China, where she grew up attending Chinese and English schools. She returned to San Francisco as an adult, where she still resides. Thousand Pieces of Gold, *published in 1983, told the story of Lalu (later Polly Beemis), a real Chinese woman who was sold into slavery by her father and shipped to California in the 1870s.*

LIKE THE HOLD OF THE SHIP, the San Francisco customs shed was dimly lit, but at least the lanterns did not pitch and sway; and the air, though stale and stinking from the press of unwashed bodies, did not reek of vomit or human waste. If anything, the din from hundreds of voices, mostly male, had grown louder. But there was life and excitement in the shouting, joyful expectation in the rush for luggage, relatives, and friends.

Lalu, waiting for her turn to come before the customs officer, caught the contagion of nervous excitement, and she felt the same thrill, bright and sharp as lightning, that had shot through her when the Madam had told her she was going to America, the Gold Mountains at the other end of the Great Ocean of Peace.

"I have never been there, but Li Ma, the woman for whom I bought you, says there is gold everywhere. On the streets, in the hills, mountains, rivers, and valleys. Gold just waiting to be picked up...."

"Gold that will make me rich. So rich, no one, not even Old Man Yang, will dare speak against me if I go home," Lalu had whispered, ignoring the rest of the Madam's words.

Hugging herself inwardly, she had pictured her parents' and brothers' faces when she gave her father the gold that would make him the richest man in the village. The pride they would have in her, their *qianjin*. And she had held fast to this picture, as to a talisman. First, when the Madam had turned her over to Li Ma, the crotchety, foul-mouthed woman who would take her to the Gold Mountains. Then, during the long voyage, when only the men's talk of gold had kept alive her dream of going home. And now, as she folded and refolded the forged papers Li Ma had given her. For the demons who ruled the Gold Mountains wished to keep their gold for themselves, and in order to gain the right to land, Lalu must successfully pretend to be the wife of a San Francisco merchant.

Over and over, during the long weeks crammed in the hold of the ship, Li Ma had forced Lalu and the other five women and girls in her charge to rehearse the stories that matched their papers, sternly warning, "Pass the examination by customs, and you will soon return to China a rich woman, the envy of all in your village. Fail, and you will find yourself in a demon jail, tortured as only the demons know how."

Could the torture be worse than the journey she had just endured? Lalu thought of the sweltering, airless heat and thirst that had strangled the words in her throat, making her stumble when she recited for Li Ma, earning her cruel pinchings and monotonous harangues. The aching loneliness that came from homesickness and Li Ma's refusal to permit the girls to talk among themselves. The bruising falls and the tearing at her innards each time the ship rocked, tossing her off the narrow shelf that served as bed, knocking her against the hard wood sides of the hull. The long, black periods of waiting for the hatch to bang open as it did twice each day, bringing a shaft of sunlight, gusts of life-giving salt air, the smell of the sea. The struggle to chew the hard, sour bread and swallow the slop lowered down as though they were pigs in a pen.

Lalu tossed her head, straightened her jacket, and smoothed her hair. That was all over. Behind her. No more than a bad dream. She was in America, the Gold Mountains. And soon, just as soon as she gathered enough gold, she would go home.

"Next."

Lalu felt herself shoved in front of the customs officer. She had never been close to a white man before and she stared amazed at the one that towered above her. His skin was chalk white, like the face of an actor painted to play a villain, only it was not smooth but covered with wiry golden hair, and when his mouth opened and closed, there were no words to make an audience shake with anger or fear, only a senseless roaring. Beside him, a Chinese man spoke.

"Your papers. Give him your papers," Li Ma hissed.

"My papers?" Lalu said in her native Northern dialect. "I've ..."

She stopped, horrified. How could she have been so stupid? True, Southern speech was still strange to her, but during the long voyage, Li Ma had taught her the dialect, for the majority of Chinese immigrants on board came from the Southern province of Guongdong, and her papers claimed her as such. Now she had betrayed herself, proven her papers false. There would be no gold on the streets for her and no homecoming, only jail and torture.

Li Ma snatched the papers from Lalu. "Don't mind the girl's foolish rambling. You'll see everything's in order. Here's the certificate of departure and the slip with her husband's address here in the Great City."

Gold flashed as she passed the papers up to the Chinese man beside the demon officer. "A respected tradesman he is. Could have his pick of beauties. Why he wants this simpleton back is anyone's guess. Should have let her stay on in China when she went back to nurse his old mother. But you know how men are. So long as the woman satisfies that muscle below their belt, they don't care about anything else."

The Chinese man laughed. He passed the papers to the customs officer. Again gold flashed. They talked between them in the foreign tongue, their eyes stripping Lalu, making her feel unclean. Finally, the demon officer stamped the papers. Smirking, he thrust them down at Lalu. Her face burning with embarrassment, she hugged the precious papers against her chest and followed Li Ma past the wooden barricade. She was safe.

"Look," Li Ma barked, pointing to the huddle of waiting women and girls. "Some of them are only ten, eleven years old. Children. Yet they showed more intelligence and good sense than you. Now you mark my words. That's the first and the last time I put out good gold to save your neck, so watch yourself, do you hear?" Cuffing Lalu's ears for emphasis, she herded her charges together and out onto the wharf.

Lalu, weak from lack of nourishing food and exercise, felt as if the boat were still pitching and rolling beneath her feet. But she walked briskly, not wanting to provoke another storm of abuse from Li Ma who was speeding past heaps of crated produce, sacks of flour and beans, and stacks of barrels. Above her, she heard the screech of seagulls, and beyond the wharf, the clip–clop of horses' hooves, the creak and rattle of wagons, voices deep and shrill. But she could see no further than Li Ma's back, for the same thick fog which had shrouded the Gold Mountains when they disembarked enveloped them, its cold dampness penetrating, leaving the salty taste of tears. Lalu swallowed her disappointment. She would see the mountains soon enough. Meanwhile, she would look for the nuggets the men said lay in the street.

Beneath the sickly glow of street lamps, she saw horse droppings, rats feasting on piles of garbage, rags, broken bottles. Metal glittered. A discarded can or gold? Stooping to grab it, Lalu did not see the rock until it stung her cheek. Startled, she looked up just as a mud ball splashed against Li Ma's back.

Li Ma whirled around. "You dead girl," she screamed at Lalu. "How dare you!"

She broke off as high-pitched squeals and cries burst from the girls around her. Through the heavy mist, Lalu made out white shadows, demon boys, hurling stones and mud, yelling, words she did not understand but could feel.

"You dead ghosts," Li Ma cried, shaking her fist at them.

Giggling, the boys concentrated their missiles on the short square woman. Without thinking, Lalu picked up the stones that landed nearest her, flinging them back at the boys as fast as they could throw them. Years of playing with her brothers had made her aim excellent and the boys soon fled.

Li Ma fell on Lalu. "Stop that you dead foolish girl or you'll have the authorities after us."

"But they started it."

"Are you so dim-witted that you don't know you're in a demon land? The laws are made by demons to protect demons, not us. Let's just hope we can get to Chinatown before they come back with officers or we'll find ourselves rotting in a demon jail."

Shouting, pushing, and shoving, she hurried them up steep cobbled streets with foul-smelling gutters, past wagons pulled by huge draft horses and un-washed demon men loafing on upturned barrels until they reached narrow streets crowded with Chinese men. Chinatown. Even then, she did not per-mit the women and girls to rest. But the warm familiar smells and sounds soothed Lalu's confusion, and she barely felt Li Ma's parting cuff as she herded them down a flight of stairs into a large basement room with more young women and girls like herself.

"Those with contracts come over to this side, those without go stand on the platform," an old woman in black lacquer pants and jacket directed.

Lalu held out her papers. The old woman took them. She pushed Lalu in the direction of the women without contracts.

"No, I belong over there," Lalu said, trying to take back the papers.

The old woman snorted. "What a bumpkin you are! Those papers were just to get you into the country. They have to be used again."

"But Li Ma said ..."

"Don't argue girl, you're one of the lucky ones," the old woman said. She pointed to the group of women with contracts. "Their fates have been de-cided, it's prostitution for them, but if you play your cards right, you may still get the bridal chair."

A shocked murmur rippled through the group of women. One of them took a paper from an inner pocket. "I have a marriage contract," she said. "Not what you suggest."

"And I! And I!" the women around her echoed.

The old woman took the contract from the young woman. The paper crackled as she spread it open. "Read it!" she ordered.

The young woman's lips quivered. "I can't."

The old woman jangled the ring of keys at her waist. "Does anyone here read?"

The women looked hopefully at each other. Some shook their heads. Others were simply silent. None could read.

"Then I'll tell you what your contracts say." Without looking at any of the papers, the old woman continued, "For the sum of your passage money, you have promised the use of your bodies for prostitution."

"But the marriage broker gave my parents the passage money," the young woman persisted.

"You fool, that was a procurer, not a marriage broker!" She pointed to the thumb print at the bottom of the paper. "Is that your mark?"

Sobbing quietly, the young woman nodded.

"Well then, there's nothing more to be said, is there?"

"Yes there is," a girl said boldly. "I put my mark on one of those contracts, and I knew what it was for." Her face reddened. "I had to," she added.

"So?" the old woman, hands on hips, prompted.

"The contract specifies the number of years, five in my case, so take heart sisters, our shame will not last forever."

"What about your sick days?"

"What do you mean?" the girl asked.

"The contract states your monthly sick days will be counted against your time: two weeks for one sick day, another month for each additional sick day."

"But that means I'll never be free!"

"Exactly."

Like a stone dropped in a pond, the word started wave after wave of talk and tears.

"Keep crying like that," the old woman shouted, "and by the time your owners come to get you, your eyes will be swollen like toads."

"What difference does it make?" a voice challenged.

"Depending on your looks, you can be placed in an elegant house and dressed in silks and jewels or in a bagnio."

"Bagnio?"

"On your way here you must have seen the doors with the barred windows facing the alleys, but perhaps you did not hear the chickens inside, tapping and scratching the screens, trying to attract a man without bringing a cop. Cry, make yourself ugly, and you'll be one of those chickens, charging twenty-five cents for a look, fifty cents for a feel, and seventy-five cents for action."

Slowly the sobs became muted sniffles and whimpers as stronger women hushed the weaker. The old woman turned to Lalu's group. "Now get up on that platform like I told you."

Silently Lalu and the other women and girls obeyed. When they were all on the platform, the old woman began to speak.

"This is where you'll stand tomorrow when the men come. There'll be merchants, miners, well-to-do peddlers, brothel owners, and those who just want to look. They'll examine you for soundness and beauty. Do yourself up right, smile sweetly, and the bids will come in thick and fast from those looking for wives as well as those looking to fill a house.

"When the price is agreed on, the buyer will place the money in your hands. That will make the sale binding, but you will turn the money over to me. Do you understand?"

The women and girls nodded. A few murmured defeat.

The old woman pointed to some buckets against the wall. "There's soap and water. Wash thoroughly. You will be stripped for auction."

"Stripped?"

"Women in the Gold Mountains are scarcer than hen's teeth and even a plain or ugly girl has value. But when a man has to pay several thousand dollars for a woman, he likes to see exactly what he is buying," the old woman said.

She grabbed a tight-lipped, thin, dark girl from the back of the group. The girl stared defiant as the old woman ripped off her jacket and pointed out scars from a deep hatchet wound, puckered flesh the shape of a hot iron. "Look carefully and be warned against any thought of disobedience or escape." She threw the girl's jacket onto the floor. "It will be the bagnio for you. If you're lucky."

She pulled the women closest to her down from the platform and herded them toward the buckets of water. "Now get going, we've wasted time enough."

All around her, Lalu could hear the sounds of women and girls preparing themselves for auction, but she made no move to join them. It had taken all her concentration to make out the words that had been spoken in the strange Southern dialect, and she was only just beginning to feel their impact.

She had been duped, she realized. By the soft-voiced, gentle Madam, a cormorant who had nothing to give except to its master. By Li Ma, the foul-mouthed procuress charged with Lalu's delivery to the auction room. By the talk of freemen whose dreams could never be hers. For the Gold Mountains they had described was not the America she would know. This: the dingy basement room, the blank faces of women and girls stripped of hope, the splintered boards beneath her feet, the auction block. This was her America.

Through a haze as chilling as the fog that had surrounded her at the wharf,

Lalu became aware of warm breath, an anxious nudging. It was the thin, dark girl the old woman had exposed as warning.

"Didn't you hear what the old woman said? You're one of the lucky ones."

"The Madam in Shanghai said that too."

"But it's true. There are women far worse off than you. Like those smuggled into the Gold Mountains hidden in padded crates labeled dishware or inside coal bunkers. Many of them don't survive the journey or arrive so bruised and broken they cannot be sold." The girl leaned closer and lowered her voice still further. "Those women are taken straight to the same 'hospitals' as slave girls who have ceased to be attractive or who have become diseased. There, alone in tiny, windowless cells, they're laid on wooden shelves to wait for death from starvation or their own hand." She brightened. "But you made the journey with papers and a woman to look out for you. You're thin, but beautiful and sound."

"What does that change except my price?"

The girl took Lalu's hands in hers, holding them tight, quieting their trembling. "You must learn as I have to let your mind take flight. Then you won't feel, and if you don't feel, nothing anyone does can hurt you."

QUESTIONS FOR A MIWOK UNCLE:
AHWAHNEECHEE MAN

WENDY ROSE

Wendy Rose (1948–) was born in Oakland and is of Hopi and Miwok descent. She is the author of ten books of poetry, including Going to War with All My Relations, *published in 1993. She lives in Coarsegold, in the Sierra foothills, and teaches at Fresno City College.*

It was before they came with their ranches,
cattle upturning and chewing our flesh.
It was before they ripped the memory from our tongues
and riddled the hills with their hungry machines.
They came from their cities, they came
from the east, they came on the water
to measure our bones
against a string of shell beads
and stolen gold, O so long ago.
Spreadeagled, uncle, preserved
against some book
you have but the ashes
of clapstick and bone flute
to color your hands as you would have them.

Is it too late to record
the monument of your movement
down and away from where you once were
parting the bear grass with a song
so quietly you came upon
the deer drinking
and put down the bow
to feel the rhythm
of her throat?

Ahwahneechee: the indigenous people of Yosemite, a band of the Miwok Nation

On the Western

CZESLAW MILOSZ

Czeslaw Milosz (1911–) was born in Lithuania, raised in Poland, and emigrated to the United States in 1960. He is the author of more than forty books of poems, essays, and prose and was awarded the Nobel Prize for Literature in 1980. He has been a professor emeritus of Slavic languages and literature at U.C. Berkeley since 1978. "On the Western" appeared in his Visions from San Francisco Bay *(1982), an exploration of Bay Area history and culture.*

SO MANY WORDS, so much talk about spirit, but hasn't that cinematic myth accepted by all Europe, the Western, built around who is fastest on the draw, reduced some confidence in spirit? The Western is a product of California, and not only because Hollywood is located there. In the outdoor scenes it is easy to recognize the familiar grassy hills with their rocks and their black smudges of thorny oaks and juniper as either the Mohave Desert or the forests of the Sierra Nevada.

That aside, the annals in the old California newspapers can furnish all the plot lines your heart desires, for the art of humorous reportage was highly developed back then; in that regard, Mark Twain was not an exception. In the European city of my youth, one of my friends lost his job on the local newspaper because he wrote a verse account of the trial of a spurned rival who had murdered the bride at a peasant wedding. I still remember these words of the poet:

> In her grave she lay, cold as a slice of herring.

This approach offended the editor, who saw it as a trifling with human emotions. No one set any such limits on the American reporters in the era of the lasso, pistol, and stagecoach, and so it is still enjoyable to read their brief, compact stories aloud over a glass of California wine on foggy evenings, thick logs burning in the fireplace. For example, the story about the feud between two little towns, and the pharmacist who was weighing powders when he spotted someone from the enemy town; tossing his powders aside, he grabbed his pistol and emptied it into the hated intruder, while the rest of the town did the same through their windows.

If, however, the journalist's pen filtered and reworked actual events in accordance with the requirements of humor and punch line, the Western itself passed entirely into fable, formalizing its own motifs, arranging them in nearly algebraic equations to divide the characters into the good and the bad, with the inevitable triumph of justice. Not having bypassed California in his cosmopolitan travels, Blaise Cendrars, the French poet, wrote a documentary story, *Gold, or the Marvelous History of General Johann August Sutter*, which is sufficient indication of the distance between the facts and the Western fable drawn from them. Johann August Sutter was apparently neither particularly good nor evil, and his unusual adventures lack a happy ending. The bankrupt scion of an old paper manufacturing firm in Basel, he fled to Paris, leaving his wife and children behind, then continued on to New York, where by means none too savory he acquired a little money and then traveled west. Reaching Oregon, he went on to Hawaii to organize a business dealing in slaves taken in the Polynesian islands.

Later, after Sutter had prepared a consignment of natives who were to serve him as a work crew, a Russian sailing ship dropped him off alone (the transport of natives was to arrive separately) on a deserted shore, the spot where San Francisco now stands. This occurred when there were no white men in California except a few families of Spanish cattle-breeders, a few dozen Mexican soldiers, and a Russian fort with a garrison that outnumbered them. Sutter acquired lands extending thousands of square miles from the foot of the Sierras to the ocean, and he established his own sovereign state, which, in memory of his native land, he called New Helvetia, and of which he was sole master. His will caused aqueducts to be constructed, transformed deserts into cultivated fields and vineyards, and his fortune grew yearly. A king surrounded by a bodyguard of Yankee sailors who had jumped ship, he protected the Indians who worked for him, he waged war with recalcitrant tribes, he had mule trains haul Europe's costly goods, including a Pleyel grand piano, across the continent for him. After some time, his wealth fully established, he sent for his family, the children already grown up; they came by ship through the Straits of Magellan, for this was before the Panama Canal.

The French poet's imagination was struck less by Sutter's scaling of the heights than by his sudden downfall, resembling that, as he puts it, of Shakespeare's kings. By chance, during the building of a mill, gold was found on Sutter's lands, and it could not be kept secret. New Helvetia was invaded by hordes that respected no boundaries, hanged Sutter's Indians, plundered and pillaged. Soon Sutter had lost everything, and to crown his misfortunes, his sons died tragically. What does it matter that at one point he was paid the highest honors as the founder of San Francisco, that he was given the honorary title of general, that today streets bear his name and Sutter's Fort in Sacramento has been preserved as a historical monument? In his old age, Johann August Sutter was only a bankrupt man with a mania for litigation, appealing in Washington for the property rights legally granted him by Mexico, imploring congressmen for help, but to no avail.

The moral of the story is unclear, as is every line of fate. Though the French poet avoided the naïveté of the Western, he did construct his plot as the considerations of literary composition dictated. That biography could certainly have been presented ten different ways, and each with equal right to claim verisimilitude. Sutter was a cutthroat, a slave trader, an example of the highest courage and the energy able to realize dreams, an exploiter of Polynesians and Indians, their patriarchal protector, a farmer, a civilizer, a frivolous deserter who left his family in poverty, a sensitive husband and father, a braggart, a madman—whatever you like.

The truth of that bygone California, of all America, is elusive, ambiguous, and it would be pointless to seek it in myths devised to keep us from being overly troubled by the disorder of the world. Besides the skillful shot, the hand barely leaving the hip, there is also the wound which might fester for weeks on end, the fever, the stink of the sweat-drenched body, the bed of filthy rags, the urine, the excrement, but this the Western never shows. One is not supposed to think past the colorful costumes to tormenting lice itch, feet rubbed bloody, all the misery of men's and women's bodies thrown together, trying to survive when the rules they had learned no longer counted for very much. The tangle of motivations behind fair play in someone or the lack of it must not be overly scrutinized. Since the white man acquired what he wanted in constant battle with other men, red and white, a fable idealizing ascendancy, praising the righteous and damning the unrighteous, had to adorn the victors. I have often felt inclined to predict that someday a completely different sort of Western will appear in America, a Western able to extract from the documents and annals the unrelieved terror and strangeness of those days. But I cannot be that sure, because the truth would still be opposed by the age-old tastes of the listeners, readers, viewers, who long to identify with heroes. Besides, let's be fair, those annals are full of heroism, for the most part the heroism of nameless people.

Donner Pass seems ominous to me no matter how often I pass through it on the way from California to Nevada, despite the fact that the written testimonies are contradictory and I don't know how much truth there is in the lurid saga forever associated with that place. In 1846 Donner was leading a caravan of a dozen families from the East and when he at last reached the pass it was too late, the snow in the High Sierras prevented their descent into the valley. After the supplies were exhausted and everything fit to be eaten had been consumed, even pieces of leather, their camp became the scene of events which we prefer not to think about, because we lack the ultimate certainty that we would not ever succumb to the temptation of cannibalism. The highest heroism of the few people who chose death in an impossible attempt to cross the mountains and bring help from the valley remains the irreducible secret of their personal fate, just as it would later on for some behind the barbed wire of European prisons.

from BIG DREAMS

BILL BARICH

Bill Barich's (1943–) autobiographical travel writing and short stories have filled four books, including Laughing in the Hills *(1980),* Traveling Light *(1984), and* Hard to Be Good *(1987). He criss-crossed California in a rented car while writing his travel narrative* Big Dreams, *published in 1994. He lives in the San Francisco Bay Area.*

MY CAMP ON THE SOUTH FORK of the American River was in a grove of oaks. In the warm evening air, observed by squawking scrub jays, the yentas of the forest, I set up my tent. The river was swift and riffly, but I took two small, hatchery-reared trout in minutes and made them my dinner. With a heel of bread, I mopped up some pan juices from the skillet, buried the trout bones so no birds would choke, and finished the last of the Buena Vista Chardonnay, my back against a log and my thoughts in the big sky above.

It felt good to be out in the country again, real country, after the bustle and the congestion of Wine Country. This piece of Placer County, toward its western edge, was in the Mother Lode, where the gold rush had burst forth and changed the course of history in California.

In Coloma, at Marshall Gold Discovery State Historic Park, people were still looking for gold, or for its shadow. At nine the next morning, a lanky man in a bowling-team Windbreaker could be seen rushing from monument to monument and sprinting ahead of his wife, who shouldered a videocam and fell into step with me. Together we examined the replica of a Chinese store, where tinned herbal medicines crowded a shelf, and she was careful to point out to me the stuffed turkey that dangled from the ceiling by a cord.

"It must have been almost Thanksgiving," she said, confusing the celestials with the Puritans.

We paused at a miner's log cabin, and she pressed her nose to a dusty window. "Look!" she shouted. "There's a little man inside!"

The little man was a dummy miner. He resembled Gabby Hayes stretched out for an autopsy, asleep for the duration beneath a cotton sheet. The woman's husband came along and interrupted us, fidgety because he hadn't yet found what he called "the actual site" of Marshall's discovery.

"Look at the little man, honey," his wife instructed him, filming his response. "How'd you like to live in there?"

"Better than a tent," he said.

The little man didn't have it so bad, really. He had no mortgage payments and owed nothing to a bank.... Gold mining was much easier for him in Coloma than it would have been in Alaska or South Africa. The snow fell infrequently in the foothills, and there were fruit and nut trees. There were trout in the river and deer for venison steaks. The little man had a can of tobacco on a bench and doubtless some whiskey under his cot. He had his paradise.

Another song leaped into my mind, one that the artists and the bohos used to sing when they could still live cheaply around Monterey, in a time before the coming of the realtors:

> Oh! some folks boast of quail on toast.
> Because they think it's tony
> But I'm content to owe my rent
> And live on abalone.

The woman's husband had found *the actual site.* "Yo, Judy!" he yelled. "The gold's over here!" They filmed a sequence of him standing by another monument, after which he held up some pebbles from the stream and pretended that they were nuggets. He did some digging with an invisible shovel and mopped his brow with a handkerchief, overacting like a star of the silent cinema. Then they got into their car and left, ready for the Gold Country's next attraction.

I drove Highway 49 through the Gold Country for a week or so and made a few notes.

Some towns and mining camps of the Mother Lode: Gold Hill, Fair Play, Shingle Springs, Enterprise, Volcano, Fiddletown, Sutter Creek, San Andreas, Drytown, Felix, Tiger Lily, Calaveras, Pleasant Valley, Jackass Hill, Mokelumne Hill, Frogtown, Indian Diggins, Negro Hill, Coyoteville, Jesus Maria, Angels Camp, Bummerville, and El Dorado.

What you see in Mother Lode towns: retired people; new subdivisions and trailer parks; old frame houses with clapboards and gable roofs; porches where old dogs snore; quilts and rocking chairs; picket fences; taverns with card rooms; museums; gold samples sold in bottles, as jewelry, and in tiny, plush-lined caskets; ruins; mini-malls; renovated hotels with flocked wallpaper and an

Recreational gold panning on Angels Creek, 1994, by Dick James

upright piano; chiropractors and acupuncturists; vineyards; biker girls in oil-stained jeans; and many images of miners on signs and on billboards kneeling, panning, or having a general hoot.

A thing to be avoided in the Mother Lode: the Mark Twain Center, a mini-mall in Angels Camp.

Copperopolis, a foothill town in Calaveras County, was trying to revive itself from the dead. It had a population of one hundred and fifty, but that could change at any minute if the mining operation at Royal Mountain King Mine were to strike some serious paydirt.

Royal Mountain King was a high-tech, $62 million attempt to recover all the gold that the forty-niners had missed. The 2100-acre property included the famous Madame Felix mining district—the Madame had once owned a stagecoach depot at the south end of Salt Spring Valley—and there were three open-pit mines in it that were being scoured and probed with the finest machinery available.

At its peak, Copperopolis had about two thousand residents. Its copper mines were among the most generous in the country. There were four hotels, three schools, two churches, and dozens of stores. Mark Twain had spent a reluctant night in town in 1865, waiting for a stage that would take him to Stockton. He'd been staying at a friend's cabin on Jackass Hill, doing some desultory surface mining, writing in notebooks, and studying French, but he had tired of the rustic scene and was eager to lodge again at the Occidental Hotel in San Francisco, which he called his "heaven on the entire shell."

I had an appointment with John Gruen, the president of Royal Mountain King, and he met me at his office promptly at one-thirty on a scorching afternoon. Punctuality was probably second nature to him. He was a scion of the famous watch family from Ohio. His teen-age son, Jonathan, accompanied him, and they were dressed alike in Izod shirts and khakis.

John Gruen reminded me of those amiable, principled eastern gents in the movies, who come to California unassumingly on a stagecoach and soon get the other half of their education. He was a former stockbroker and investment banker and had the happy buzz of somebody who had thrown off the shackles of the predictable to grab for the brass ring.

Gruen introduced me to Kim Witt, his director of safety and human resources, a title that baffled me. I guessed that Witt must hire miners and then do his best to keep them from being hurt. He was from Utah and had learned his mining around Park City.

Witt had a twenty-minute spiel that he gave to the mine's neighbors and opponents that demystified large-scale gold mining by framing it in homely analogies. The furnace where gold was baked into bars was like a microwave, he explained. He showed me some chalky lumps of cyanide in a Mason jar. The cyanide was used to extract gold from ore, he said, but people were afraid of it. They didn't understand its place in everyday life. Caterpillars gave off cyanide, and so did lima beans as they cooked. Anybody who smoked cigarettes inhaled massive amounts of it.

"I'd rather sleep with this jar than next to a propane tank," Witt revealed, and I pictured the two of them in bed.

After the instructional talk, we piled into a Blazer to look over the mine. The three open pits were very deep and wide, and bulldozers were gnawing at them. In the north pit, there were thousands of numbered blast holes with ash and debris around them. The subsoil had been sent to a lab for analysis. The forty-niners had prospected by eye, Witt said, and they'd been pretty damn good at it. The gold that remained was buried deep.

To get at it, Royal King had to move the earth. That robbed it of all vegeta-

Calaveras County Fair and Jumping Frog Jubilee, Angels Camp, 1994, by Dick James

tion, and the mildest breeze raised dust clouds. Dust turned up in your pockets and in your shoes. Water trucks circled and sprayed about five hundred gallons of water a day.

A loader and a hauler were working the pit. Gruen let it drop that the machines were not cheap. The loader was made by Hitachi and had cost about $1.3 million. That was a lot of money to sink into a speculative venture, Gruen implied.

It took four scoops of a big, toothy shovel for the loader to fill the hauler with dirt, sand, pebbles, and stones. Some loads were delivered right to the primary crusher at a fully automated gold mill. Although the mill was huge, it could be operated by as few as three men. One of them sat in a dark, cool computer room before TV monitors and a computer screen that informed him about everything that was going on at Royal King, from the blasting schedule to the crushing of ore.

We stood on a catwalk to watch a conveyor belt ferry some ore into the mill, where a series of progressively smaller grinding balls pulverized it. The residue would be sifted through, in one way or another, for gold. A good, rich, mineral smell accompanied the grinding. At times, a pungent, acidy smell of cyanide cut through it, and you could feel a scratchiness in your throat and your nose. Up to four thousand tons of earth cycled through the mill every day.

The doré bars from the furnace were stored in a vault. Each bar was about the size of a large loaf of bread and contained unrefined material—seventy percent of it gold, twenty percent silver, and ten other minerals. Behind the vault's many locks, a fortune of untold proportions might be slumbering.

According to John Gruen, miners in the Mother Lode had left about two-thirds of the gold in the ground—scientific studies had determined as much. But since the mill had started grinding and sifting about four months ago, Royal Mountain King had not recovered as much gold as projected. There were layers of copper blanketing the better deposits.

In spite of the chanciness of mining, Gruen seemed to be weathering his gamble well. Sometimes his face had the hopeful energy of somebody working a slot machine that might still pay off with three cherries. As we left his office, we ran into a solid wall of Mother Lode heat, and he offered to treat us to cold sodas. A vending machine nearby foiled him, though, and Jonathan had to take over and align George Washington's head with the secret motors scanning dollar bills.

We walked to our cars, sodas in hand, and Gruen remembered something. "Hey, Jonathan? Did you get the change?" he asked.

Jonathan stared at his old man as if to say that fifty cents, plus or minus, was a meager sum to worry about when you'd already invested a share of the family's fortune in a gold mine. So Gruen himself went back to the vending machine, dipped two fingers into the coin-return slot, and came up with two quarters.

"Look," he said, smiling and displaying the coins on the palm of a hand. "Silver."

from CALIFORNIA FAULT

THURSTON CLARKE

Thurston Clarke (1946–) was born in New York and graduated from Yale in 1968. His diverse works include By Blood and Fire: The Attack on the King David Hotel *(1981),* Lost Hero: The Mystery of Raoul Wallenberg *(1982), and* Equator: A Journey *(1988). In his 1996 travel book,* California Fault, *he explored California in search of information about his forty-niner relative J. Goldsborough Bruff.*

MY ANCESTOR J. GOLDSBOROUGH BRUFF left Washington, D.C. (then Washington City) for the California goldfields on April 2, 1849, in command of sixty-six men ranging in age from fifty-nine to fifteen who called themselves the Washington City and California Gold Mining Association. A Washington newspaper described "truly a well-chosen band, handsomely uniformed and well-equipped for the dangers they might have to encounter." Bruff praised them as "energetic gentlemen," joining the gold rush to enrich themselves "by every honorable means."

Their departure was an event. Bruff had drilled them to the standard of light infantry and dressed them in gray frock coats with gilt eagle buttons, black-striped pantaloons, and forage caps. Each man carried a rifle, two pistols, a bowie knife, and belt hatchet. Led by a military band, they marched across Lafayette Square to the White House. President Zachary Taylor shook Bruff's hand and praised his men's "courage and enterprise." Bruff assured him they were all men of "strength and character," adding, "As we are on the eve of an extraordinary journey, of great extent, and which must be fraught with arduous trials, most probably many of us will never again have the pleasure of greeting you."

Bruff's only qualifications for guiding this band of civil servants through deserts, mountains, and hostile Indian territory were a West Point education cut short when he wounded a classmate in a duel, followed by seven years as a merchant seaman that his wife claimed had provided him with "many wonderful adventures, full of thrilling escapes," and left his brain "stored with anecdotes of his travels." For the previous twenty years he had worked as a draftsman at the Bureau of Topographical Engineers, sometimes reproducing maps

of the American West drawn by pioneers and explorers. The year before joining the gold rush he had copied Captain Frémont's maps of California, his
hand tracing, although he did not know it at the time, the tangle of mountains
where he would soon prospect for gold, the squiggly rivers whose headwaters
he would discover, and possibly, the remote ridge a plaque still identifies as
Bruff's Camp, where six months after leaving the White House, with winter
approaching, his well-chosen band of honorable gentlemen would leave him
to starve within sight of the Sacramento Valley.

This betrayal has remained a family mystery ever since. Had it happened in
the goldfields, or had he been a cruel or incompetent leader, it might be
understandable. But according to historians of the California Trail, he was "a
man of strength and courage" who possessed "natural ability as a leader," commanded "with skill and authority," and was "one of the very best Captains of
the whole year ... [an] officer of the type who keeps his men together because
he takes good care of them." He combined "the military man's dedication to
duty with a reflexive kindness," "demanded that the strong help the weak,
particularly women and children on the trail," and was "a soft touch for anyone in need." He distributed food to starving Pawnees, denounced a squaw's
rape as "villainous conduct," and condemned emigrants who defaced rocks
with graffiti and whipped their oxen. Their beasts' eyes spoke "eloquently," he
said, and "if any four-footed animal has soul, it is an ox."

Most paramilitary companies squabbled on the trail, dividing assets and
dissolving constitutions before reaching California. But Bruff kept his men
together, and for six months and two thousand miles they passed the smashed
wagons, discarded supplies, and crude headstones of less well-commanded
outfits. Because he insisted on nightly guard duty, the only scalp injuries to his
men occurred when they rolled over upon waking on cold mornings, yanking
out patches of their hair frozen to the ground.

Certainly the Washington Miners' Fourth of July celebration on the banks
of the Platte River did not foreshadow what was to come when they reached
California. The men covered wagons with tent cloths to make a banquet hall,
raised Old Glory through a roof, donned uniforms, and dined on "luxuries of
the season," Bruff reported. After toasting "California—El Dorado and Pacific
Emporium," he delivered a grandiloquent speech praising their "spirit of daring adventure and indomitable enterprise," promising "the trials of this travel
will serve as amusing tales for our children and friends," and extolling their
"bravery, judgment, patience, and perseverance." They were, he said, "the
right kind of people for California."

Six weeks later they halted near the Idaho-Wyoming border for a formal reelection of officers as mandated by the company constitution. Every man was voted out except Bruff, who was reelected unanimously. Soon afterward Bruff, like many emigrant leaders that summer, made the mistake of taking the Lassen Trail, a cutoff from the California Trail that meandered north through Nevada's Black Rock Desert before looping back into California near the Oregon border. The Danish settler Peter Lassen had promoted it as having a lower altitude and milder weather than the route across the Sierras, which had claimed so many members of the Donner Party in 1846. But it had the disadvantages of adding hundreds of miles to the journey and traversing a terrain so forbidding that emigrant graffiti and wagon ruts remain untouched to this day.

When the veteran guide Captain Milton McGee chose the Lassen Trail in mid-August of 1849, every large emigrant party behind him followed suit. The earliest found barely enough grass and water for their oxen, while later parties like Bruff's, who traveled it in mid-September, found less. Some Lassen Trail stragglers abandoned their possessions along the way, others burned the grass to reduce competition in the goldfields, and still others, displaying the fusion of materialism and optimism that would become characteristic of their new state, buried them in "graves" marked by bogus headboards, convinced they would soon be returning to collect them.

The forty-niners on the Lassen Trail became true Californians when they reached the Fandango Pass that crosses the Warner Mountains just inside the state line. Its last two hundred yards rise steeply and diaries of the time describe emigrants wrapped in blankets and shivering with fevers, clinging to the necks of skeletal donkeys. At the top, they could simultaneously see where they had been—a wasteland of black rock and barren hills—and where they were going—dramatic waves of thickly wooded mountains. "What a scene from here!" Bruff wrote in his diary, marveling at "the Snow Butte [probably Mount Shasta], and his blue neighbors, deep vales, silver thread-like streams, near mountains, dense forests, bright deep valleys," and stunned by a landscape created by one hundred million years of earthquakes.

His men crossed the Fandango with famished oxen and reduced supplies, but not in extremis. His first wagon planted the Stars and Stripes at the crest where a sign indicated Peter Lassen's ranch and fresh provisions were another 228 miles. "At least 150 miles longer than we all thought it would be," Bruff wrote. "Well, here are the facts, and they *are* stubborn things!"

Three weeks later, the Wolverine Rangers of Michigan became the last organized company to cross. Unlike Bruff's men, they disbanded and divided their stores when they saw California, then fed their constitution to a bonfire and danced a fandango around it with the daughters of a straggler, giving the pass its name. Other emigrants reported wild figures throwing huge shadows against the rocks and mistook them for Indians celebrating a massacre. Later, it was said the Michigan men danced because the daughters were beautiful, because they were striking out for the goldfields on their own, or because with winter approaching, they expected to die; they danced naked, to keep warm, or to celebrate California.

While they danced, Bruff's company was making camp several hundred miles west on a ridge only two days' walk from the Sacramento Valley and Peter Lassen's ranch. Although their rations were low and many animals near death, they had fared better than other emigrant groups, losing only one man, the least of any organized party that year. Bruff volunteered to guard the company property while the others descended into the valley with the surviving mules, six wagons with bare necessities, and his horse. His men, Bruff reported, "were delighted, and they immediately set about the task, selecting indispensable articles to pack in, etc.—They promised most faithfully to come out with my team and my horse." The Western historian George Stewart has called Bruff's decision "a final demonstration of his responsibility as a captain," adding, "However ... [his company] may even be said to have deserted him."

As his men departed, Bruff was astonished that the man riding his horse, already packed with the remaining food, "entirely forgot to offer me either flour or bread as he rode by."

A week later, six Washington Miners sneaked back into his camp at dusk. "My own comrades, for whom I had done so much, did not ask me how I had subsisted," he noted. They cooked themselves a hearty meal. When he inquired after his horse he was told "in a tone of indifference" that it was "in the valley." As his comrades well knew, Bruff was incapacitated by rheumatoid arthritis, barely able to walk. Finally he saw the truth. "You came for me!" he snapped. "No sir! You came for these wagons, and their contents, that's what you came for!—take the plunder and roll on. I'll not disgrace myself by further companionship with you!"

The next morning they demanded his tent, arguing it was company property. He watched them "avariciously" pile their wagons and wrote, "Thus ends my connections with the Washington City Company, as an organized body, and with some of them, all future acquaintance."

Bruff was stranded in the mountains six months. His sufferings almost equaled those of the Donner Party, and had he eaten a companion he might be a household word, too. He hunted deer and assisted stragglers who found in him "a kind friend." He sent desperate notes to the settlements, begging his comrades for "provisions and tea, or at least a riding animal." He suffered "infirmity, cold, dampness, starvation, and yelping of my cur, and howling of wolves." He slept in an open wagon, waking up buried under drifting snow, and was "in a snap truly, without food, helpless, and subject to spells of prostration," with "apprehensions of insanity." He hallucinated he was sitting at home, his son "parting my long matted hair with his little hands." He shared a diet of candles, coffee grounds, and woodpeckers with a four-year-old boy abandoned by his father, until the boy died. He refused to butcher his dog—"my faithful watch ... who has shared my sufferings." When he stumbled on the footprints of an Indian—"pigeon-toed and I judge small," his mouth "watered," and he imagined "a good broil." He tracked him for miles, but in the end, "could not shoot the poor wretch in the back."

During an early April thaw he gathered his strength, buried his diaries, and staggered into the valley, collapsing a hundred yards from the first homestead. He stayed a year in California. His diaries are largely silent about prospecting, but filled with ecstatic descriptions of a "wild," "beautiful," and "remarkable" country. He discovered Indian hieroglyphics, drew panoramas of mountains never visited by whites, named a lake after a friend, was assaulted by bears and wolves, drew plans for a small city, watched Sacramento burn to the ground, stumbled on a lynched corpse, and was shocked by a small earthquake, the only adventure I could duplicate.

At other times, and in other places, such experiences would have guaranteed several biographies, perhaps a county named in your honor, but they were so commonplace in 1849 California that after returning east, Bruff failed to find a publisher for his diaries and sketches. Columbia University Press finally published them in 1944 and I read them when I was twelve. The story seemed obvious: a noble man betrayed by scoundrels. It did not occur to me to wonder why Bruff had been unanimously reelected along the trail in August, and unanimously abandoned in California in October. The editors of his diaries offered no explanation. They had not researched the lives and motivations of his comrades because, as they delicately put it, "Their descendants, if any, might not welcome the attention."

I took the Washington City roster with me to California so I could check it against telephone books and historical-society membership lists. If I found a Capron, Coumbs, Fowble, or Moxley, or any of the more unusual names, I planned calling to ask if Goldsborough Bruff had led their relations across the Fandango Pass, if they had any diaries or letters, and if they cared to meet; but not asking them, at least over the telephone, to speculate why their ancestors had left mine to starve, and why California appeared to have worked on them such different magic.

During [a] trip into Northern California I finally visited Bruff's camp. I called from Red Bluff to the Lassen National Forest office in Chester and was told a firefighting pilot named John Little was the "resident Bruff expert." When I met him the next day and he saw my flimsy rental car and confusion at directions beginning "follow Ponderosa Way to Lassen Trail and look for a blank wooden sign hanging half off a tree," he volunteered to drive me. He said the camp looked close on a map, but the road was so bad the drive took two hours even in a four-wheel-drive vehicle. Besides, Bruff was one of his heroes and his camp lay at the edge of the newly declared Ishi Wilderness, one of the prettiest and most unspoiled places in Northern California.

Little was a forty-niner out of a Bruff sketch—short, round-faced, and gray-whiskered. He was certainly the calmest Californian I met, a quality useful in a job he compared to piloting a spotter plane in wartime. He flew above fires, selecting targets, coordinating the attack of planes, helicopters, and trucks, and reporting on the battle's progress. During the summer he spent seven days a week over northeastern California and northwestern Nevada, a landscape so empty he could see ruts left by emigrant wagons. He, too, had been bewitched by the story of the Wolverine Rangers, and when he drove through the Fandango Pass he imagined them dancing around that campfire. He had become a Bruff fan when he noticed how perfectly his topographical descriptions matched what he saw from the air. This convinced him everything else in the diary was probably true. He also admired how Bruff had cared for the Lambkin boy, "and the way he tried to create a community even after he was abandoned, turning his camp into a kind of village, and helping the stragglers."

As we drove to Bruff's camp, we followed Ponderosa Way, a rutted track laid out in the 1930s by the Civilian Conservation Corps. Little pointed to where the Lassen Trail ran along a steep ridge that looked scarcely wide enough for a man to walk down, much less a team of oxen. Forest Service employees and archaeologists from the Oregon-California Trails Association [OCTA] still recovered emigrant wagons that had tumbled into the canyons.

The same harsh geographic features causing the emigrants such hardship now attracted marijuana growers. Road crews saw the headlights of cars winking as they bumped along logging roads to remote patches where federal agents found even the hammocks and whiskey bottles covered in camouflage cloth. The only vehicle we passed in an hour was a clunker driven by a pasty-faced couple Little believed were growers for sure. He said the logging roads had transformed the back country by making it accessible to dopers and recreational vehicles. From his plane he sometimes saw circles of Winnebagos on land that the year before was trackless wilderness.

Without Little I never would have found Bruff's camp, and even he missed the path at first, forcing us to double back.... Recently a fire had burned twenty thousand acres nearby. Lumberjacks salvaged the surviving trees, and the camp attracted scavengers who, having read descriptions of emigrants burying household goods, swept the ground with metal detectors, thereby becoming modern versions of Lassen's shingle men.

Despite all the digging and logging, it remained a delightful spot—breezy, fragrant, and the only ground for some distance suited for pitching tents and building fires. In 1967, OCTA had erected an imposing cenotaph of boulders set in concrete. A plaque said *Bruff's Camp, Lassen's Trail. J. G. Bruff, leader of the Washington City Mining Company, camped on this site from October 21, 1849, to December 31, 1849. While here guarding company goods at what he called "his mountain lodge in prosperity," he aided, fed, and cheered many weary, hungry, and sick emigrants, struggling to the goldfields.*

A smaller marker commemorating the Alford family began, *In a common grave at this site or in close proximity to it there are buried four emigrants who were killed by a falling tree.... Thanks to the detailed account by J. Goldsborough Bruff, the man for whom this campsite is named, we know the full story of this tragic event.... This is part of your American heritage—honor it, protect it, preserve it for your children.*

On December 31, Bruff moved a mile south down the Lassen Trail to winter at Obie Fields, where an emigrant named Roberts had built a log cabin. Bruff raised his tent nearby and developed an instant dislike for Roberts, who seemed willing to be a spectator to Bruff's starvation, and kept busy digging up caches of valuables buried by emigrants, filling his cabin with what Bruff called "plunder." Obie Fields now lies just inside the newly declared Ishi wilderness, so it will probably remain undisturbed for centuries. It is on the edge of an open ridge and surrounded by groves of oak, so perfectly proportioned and landscaped it resembles a park. Little called it "one of the most beautiful small-scale places in California."

The view of the Sacramento Valley was so spectacular he often brought his son camping here. When he looked down on the twinkling lights only a long day's hike away, he wondered if Bruff had seen the distant campfires of his former companions.

We walked a mile down the Lassen Trail so Little could check on a trail crew that was breaking a new loop for recreational hikers. An earlier crew had become hopelessly lost in the tangle of gullies. A rescue party found them the next day, exhausted and scared.

The land had never been logged, so the ruts under our feet had been carved by emigrant wagons. Little said it was about as pure Lassen Trail as you could find. It was the same path the Washington Miners had followed into the settlements in October, and that Bruff stumbled down six months later.

We turned around when we came to a fresh bear print. On the way back I caught my boot in a wagon rut, twisting my ankle and tripping forward. "Don't break a leg," Little joked, grabbing my arm. "I might leave you. Remember, you're a Bruff."

Back at Obie Fields we rested under the pines where Bruff had made his winter camp. There was a marker here, too, noting it had been his home between January 1 and April 4, 1850. While I picnicked on smoked turkey on pumpernickel and drank a bottle of diet raspberry iced tea over the ground where he had almost starved, Little argued the Fandango Pass showed Bruff "just didn't get it," and had not understood that when you arrived in California the rules changed, and you burned your constitution and danced a fandango. Instead, he had remained an Easterner, trying to hold his men together in an organized community. He had been more interested in his notebooks than gold, in helping stragglers than striking it rich, in his journey than its destination. He was, if I had to summarize Little, the wrong man for California.

Gesturing to the valley, he said, "After they arrived here, and after the ordeal of the trail, they finally said screw him. Why not, since they'd arrived in the Promised Land?"

I could never hope to know what had gone through the minds of the Washington Miners without finding their letters, or a more forthcoming diary. Some, no doubt, nursed grudges fostered by the military discipline Bruff imposed on them. Some perhaps resented his slow, deliberate pace across the continent, his insistence on burying the dead left by others, and his frequent stops to sketch the landscape and take notes. Some must have been in poor health themselves and convinced a two-day journey back to rescue him would finish them. Some must have reasoned that if he only abandoned his notebooks, surveying equipment, and other possessions, he could, despite his infirmities, stumble into the valley on his own (conveniently ignoring that his offer to remain and lend them his horse had made it possible for them to salvage their own possessions). And some surely assumed they would never be called to account for what they did in California.

This was speculation. But what I knew for sure after seeing Bruff's camp and Obie Fields was that the disciplined community he brought across the continent had shared this spectacular panorama of California's fault-created landscape, stretching unoccupied and unexploited, and then shattered, its members scattering to pursue their individual dreams.

Bruff's men were by no means the most despicable emigrants to travel the Lassen Trail that autumn. Some set grass fires after their livestock had grazed, hoping to starve the parties behind them and reduce the competition for California's riches. Bruff described an old man nearly dead with scurvy whose "friends" had ejected him from their wagon and "abandoned him to his fate," and he encountered a Dutchman breaking up tools he could no longer carry so others could not use them.

Yet even in 1849, and even on the Lassen Trail, you could find evidence of the contradictory California Dream of community and sacrifice. It was there in the food and shelter Bruff supplied to stragglers passing through his camp, and there in Major Rucker's relief column, organized by California residents to ride back along the trail with food and prevent a repetition of the Donner Party disaster. If this contradictory dream ever becomes the principal California one, as may happen in the aftermath of a great earthquake, then Bruff may someday be seen as the right man for California, but one who simply had the misfortune to arrive 150 years too soon.

from THE KLAMATH KNOT

DAVID RAINS WALLACE

David Rains Wallace (1945–) is an acclaimed naturalist, novelist, and critic who has written twelve books. His works include Idle Weeds *(1980),* The Untamed Garden and Other Personal Essays *(1986),* The Vermilion Parrot: A Novel *(1991), and* The Quetzal and the Macaw: The Story of Costa Rica's National Parks *(1992). The* Klamath Knot *(1983) explored the mysteries of evolution as they are exemplified in the Klamath Mountains of northern California. He lives in Berkeley.*

THE KLAMATH MOUNTAINS have felt the force of civilization's obsession with exalting on rockpiles in the past century. Precious metals from their creek beds helped raise the towers around San Francisco Bay and the Los Angeles Basin. Miners ransacked the Klamaths as violently as they did the Mother Lode in the Sierra. I'm in awe of miners' work, more than that of glaciers and volcanoes; it's harder to conceive of human hands leveling hills or scouring out stream beds. There's something titanic about the way miners fasten on a piece of earth and chew it up. I remember a little, swarthy gold miner I met in British Columbia. With his little, blonde wife and his mushroom white hardhat, he might have been one of the dwarfs from *Das Reingold,* though he lived in a trailer, not a cave. His life was epic. He showed me a black bear track and told me it was a lynx's—the lynxes of his mind were bigger than he was, and he never stepped outside without a 30.06 and a bowie knife. The next claim over was run by a group of Texans so expensively equipped, with uniformly white and baby blue hardhats, overalls, and placer machinery, that they might have been an interplanetary exploration team.

Miners I've met in the Klamaths have been less colorful, but equally determined. A middle-aged couple who were staking a claim halfway up Virgin Creek in the Trinitys carried enough rifles and pistols to repel every bear in the county. (They complained of not seeing any wildlife.) A young couple had been living four years in a cabin on the New River that was reachable in winter only by sliding across the river on a cable. This present activity is only a faint echo of the mining that went on once. Many river beds are now undulating heaps of cobbles left by big companies that washed away entire bluffs with giant hoses and extracted millions of dollars' worth of gold.

I'm amazed how far into the wilderness the old miners got. After hiking

462

five days into the Trinity Alps, the largest wilderness in the Klamaths, I came upon a stone dam built by a mining company to supply water for hydraulic mining several dozen miles south on the Trinity River. Some of these old mining sites are eerie, like Taggart's Bar in the Kalmiopsis. Taggart's Bar is on the Chetko River, which runs between steep cliffs of volcanic stone and is only accessible from above in a few places. I camped several days on the cliffs and have rarely felt such wildness and loneliness in a place. Overhung with mossy oaks, the gorge has an enchanted quality, as though there might be dragons' dens under the cliff. A small bear almost walked into me on the path, so little did he expect to find people there.

But there once was a town on the cramped, shadowed flat beside the river; I stumbled one evening on stone foundations so covered with fern and alder that, unseeing, I'd walked past them many times. Historians think many of the early miners who worked the Chetko were Chinese, but the stones told nothing about the people who'd lived there. Considering its remoteness even today, at least a long day's fast walk from a trailhead, it must have been a strange community, perhaps like the ones Ambrose Bierce described in his gruesome tales about the Mother Lode. There is an old legend in the Klamaths that a mining town on the Chetko was attacked and destroyed by shaggy giants that swarmed out of the hills, enraged because a miner had killed one of them.

The early miners were so ubiquitous that a weekend prospector I met on the Trinity River said he found most of his gold attached to relics of old mines. Gold dust coats clots of mercury and rusty nails that have been lying on the river bottom since escaping from some turn-of-the-century placer rig. The relics are not all so old. The Kalmiopsis contains fully equipped chromium mines left over from World War II that look as though they could be started right up again with a little grease and rust remover. One of the prettiest little marsh-meadows I found in the Kalmiopsis—a botanical jewelbox of leopard lilies, cobra plants, azaleas, white bog laurels, sneezeweeds, and coneflowers—was perched between an old bulldozer scar and a rusty but intact steam shovel of a kind I hadn't seen since I was a child in the 1940s.

An iron behemoth overrun by wildflowers shows the vanity of human attempts to attain what we've fancied to be the strength and stability of the mineral world. The flowers will be there long after the steam shovel has rusted into thin air. At the same time the steam shovel demonstrates the weakness of rock when confronted with soft human brains. Nobody has yet devised a way of grinding up entire mountain ranges for mining purposes, but with gold nearing a thousand dollars an ounce as I write this, who knows? We are leveling Appalachian hills to get the coal under them.

WHAT HAPPENED HERE BEFORE

GARY SNYDER

Gary Snyder (1930–) was born in San Francisco and grew up in the Pacific North-west. He worked as a trail crew laborer and became involved in the flowering of West Coast poetry in the mid-1950s. After studying Zen Buddhism for a decade in Japan, he returned to establish residence in California. He has published sixteen books of poetry and prose, winning the Pulitzer Prize for Poetry in 1975. He lives with his family in the watershed of the South Yuba River outside Nevada City.

—300,000,000—

First a sea: soft sands, muds, and marls
  —loading, compressing, heating, crumpling,
  crushing, recrystallizing, infiltrating,
several times lifted and submerged.
intruding molten granite magma
  deep-cooled and speckling,
    gold quartz fills the cracks—

—80,000,000—

sea-bed strata raised and folded,
  granite far below.
warm quiet centuries of rains
  (make dark red tropic soils)
  wear down two miles of surface,
lay bare the veins and tumble heavy gold
  in streambeds
    slate and schist rock-riffles catch it—
volcanic ash floats down and dams the streams,
  piles up the gold and gravel—

—3,000,000—

flowing north, two rivers joined,
  to make a wide long lake.

and then it tilted and the rivers fell apart
   all running west
   to cut the gorges of the Feather,
      Bear, and Yuba.

Ponderosa pine, manzanita, black oak, mountain yew.
   deer, coyote, bluejay, gray squirrel,
ground squirrel, fox, blacktail hare,
   ringtail, bobcat, bear,
      all came to live here.

—40,000—

And human people came with basket hats and nets
   winter-houses underground
   yew bows painted green,
   feasts and dances for the boys and girls
      songs and stories in the smoky dark.

—150—

Then came the white man: tossed up trees and
   boulders with big hoses,
   going after that old gravel and the gold.
horses, apple-orchards, card-games,
   pistol-shooting, churches, county jail.

We asked, who the land belonged to.
   and where one pays tax.
(two gents who never used it twenty years,
and before them the widow
   of the son of the man
   who got him a patented deed
   on a worked-out mining claim,)
laid hasty on land that was deer and acorn
   grounds of the Nisenan?
   branch of the Maidu?

(they never had a chance to speak, even,
   their name.)
(and who remembers the Treaty of Guadalupe Hidalgo.)

   the land belongs to itself.
   "no self in self; no self in things"

Turtle Island swims
in the ocean-sky swirl-void
biting its tail while the worlds go
    on-and-off
      winking

& Mr. Tobiassen, a Cousin Jack,
    assesses the county tax.
(the tax is our body-mind, guest at the banquet
    Memorial and Annual, in honor
    of sunlight grown heavy and tasty
    while moving up food-chains
in search of a body with eyes and a fairly large
      brain—
    to look back at itself
      on high.)

        now,

we sit here near the diggings
in the forest, by our fire, and watch
the moon and planets and the shooting stars—

my sons ask, who are we?
drying apples picked from homestead trees
drying berries, curing meat,
shooting arrows at a bale of straw.

military jets head northeast, roaring, every dawn.
my sons ask, who are they?

WE SHALL SEE
WHO KNOWS
HOW TO BE

Bluejay screeches from a pine.

PERMISSIONS

The editor thanks the following authors and publishers for their permission to reprint the selections included in this anthology. Selections in the public domain have been listed with their original date of publication for purposes of reference.

Austin, Mary. From *The Land of Little Rain*. Boston: Houghton, Mifflin and Company, 1903.

Bancroft, Hubert Howe. From *California Inter Pocula*. San Francisco: The History Company, 1888.

Ballou, Mary. From *I Hear the Hogs in My Kitchen*. New Haven, CT: Frederick W. Beinecke, 1962.

Barich, Bill. From *Big Dreams*. Copyright © 1994 by Bill Barich. Reprinted by permission of Pantheon Books, a division of Random House, Inc., New York.

Beckwourth, James P. From *The Life and Adventures of James P. Beckwourth*. Edited by T. D. Bonner. New York: Harper & Brothers, 1856.

Bidwell, John. *Echoes of the Past*. Chico, CA: *The Chico Advertiser*, 1914. Originally published in *Century Magazine*, Nov. 1890 to Feb. 1891.

Birmingham, Stephen. From *California Rich*. Copyright © 1980 by Stephen Birmingham. Reprinted by permission of Brandt and Brandt Literary Agents, New York.

Borthwick, J. D. From *Three Years in California*. Edinburgh and London: W. Blackwood and Sons, 1857.

Brown, Rachel Ann. "A Dream that Almost Came True: Afro-American Voices during the California Gold Rush." Edited by Annegret Ogden. *The Californians*. (Jan./Feb. 1991) p.12-13.

Browne, J. Ross. From *Crusoe's Island*. New York: Harper & Brothers, 1864.

Browning, Peter, ed. From *To the Golden Shore*. Lafayette, CA: Great West Books, 1995.

Bruff, J. Goldsborough. From *Gold Rush*. Edited by Georgia Willis Reed and Ruth Gaines. Copyright © 1944 by Columbia University Press, New York. Reprinted by permission of Columbia University Press.

Bryant, Edwin. From *What I Saw in California*. New York: D. Appleton, 1848.

Canfield, Chauncey L., ed. From *The Diary of a Forty-Niner*. San Francisco and New York: Morgan Shepard Company, 1906.

Carr, John. From *Pioneer Days in California*, Eureka, CA: Times Publishing Company, 1891.

Carson, James H. From *Early Recollections of the California Mines*. Stockton: *San Joaquin Republican*, 1852.

Cendrars, Blaise. From *Gold*. Translated by Henry Congan Stuart. New York: Harpers and Brothers, 1926.

"Chong-Chee, Tse." From "A Chinese De Tocqueville: The Letters of Tse Chong-Chee" by Chris Burchfield. *The Californians* 8, no. 2, (Jul./Aug. 1990) p. 53-55. Originally published in *The San Jose Republican*, (Mar./Apr. 1953).

Clappe, Louise Amelia Knapp Smith. From *The Shirley Letters from the California Mines, 1851-52*. San Francisco: Thomas C. Russell, 1922. Originally published in *The Pioneer*, (Jan. 1854 to Dec. 1855)

Clarke, James. From *An Emigrant of the Fifties: The Letters of James Clarke*. Edited by

David Davies. Los Angeles: Historical Society of Southern California, 1937. Originally published by Ballantine Books, New York.

Clarke, Thurston. From *California Fault*. Copyright © 1996 by Thurston Clarke. New York: Ballantine Books, 1996. Reprinted by permission of the author.

Coit, Daniel Wadsworth. From *Digging for Gold Without a Shovel*. Edited by George P. Hammond. Denver: Old West Publishing Co., 1967.

Coleman, William T. "San Francisco Vigilance Committees." *Century Magazine* 43, no. 1 (Nov. 1891) p. 133-150.

Colton, Walter. From *Three Years in California*. New York: A. S. Barnes & Co., 1852.

Dana Jr., Richard Henry. From *Two Years Before the Mast*. Boston: Fields, Osgood & Co., 1869.

Dane, G. Ezra. From *Ghost Town*. New York: Alfred A. Knopf, 1941.

Delano, Alonzo. From *Alonzo Delano's California Correspondence*. Sacramento: Sacramento Book Collectors Club, 1952.

Delano, Alonzo. From *Life on the Plains and Among the Diggins*. Auburn and Buffalo: Miller, Orton & Mulligan, 1854.

Derby, George Horatio. From *Phoenixiana*. New York: D. Appleton and Co., 1855.

Dickens, Charles, ed. From *The Household Narrative of Current Events*. London: Bradbury and Evans, 1850-1853.

Dornin, George. From *Thirty Years Ago*. Berkeley: 1879.

Downie, William. From *Hunting for Gold*. San Francisco: The California Publishing Company, 1893.

Emerson, Ralph Waldo. From *The Conduct of Life*. Boston: Ticknor and Fields, 1860.

Farnham, Eliza. From *California In-Doors and Out*. New York: Dix, Edwards & Co., 1856.

Ferris, A. C. "To California in 1849 Through Mexico." *Century Magazine* 42, no. 5 (Sept. 1891) p. 666-679.

Freeman, Andrew. "Nomlaki Ethnography." *University of California Publications in American Archaeology and Ethnology* v. 42, no. 4 (1951), p. 311.

Frost, Robert. "A Peck of Gold." *From The Poetry of Robert Frost*. Edited by Edward Connery Lathem. Copyright 1956 by Robert Frost, copyright 1928, © 1969 by Henry Holt & Co., Inc., New York. Reprinted by permission of Henry Holt & Co., Inc.

Garnier, Dr. Pierre. From *A Medical Journey in California*. Translated by L. Jay Oliva. Los Angeles: Zeitlin & Ver Brugge, 1967. Originally published as *Voyage Médical en Californie*. Paris: Chez L'Auteur, 1854.

Gentry, Curt. From *The Last Days of the Late, Great State of California*. New York: G. P. Putnam's Sons, 1968.

Gerstäcker, Friedrich. *Narrative of a Journey Round the World*. New York: Harper & Brothers, 1853.

Gibbs, Mifflin Wistar. From *Shadow and Light*. Washington D.C.: 1902.

Gillespie, Charles B. "A Miner's Sunday in Coloma." From *Tales of California*. Edited by Frank Oppel. Secaucus, NJ: Castle Books, 1989. Originally published in *Century Magazine, 1891*.

The Gold Rush Song Book. Edited by Eleanora Black and Sidney Robertson. San Francisco: Colt Press, 1940. (Also from *The Heath Anthology of American Literature*. Edited by Paul Lauter, et al. Vol. 1. Lexington, Mass.: D. C. Heath and Co., 1994.)

Gould, Janice. "History Lesson." From *Beneath My Heart* by Janice Gould. Copyright © 1990 by Janice Gould. Reprinted by permission of Firebrand Books, Ithaca, New York.

Harte, Bret. "Dickens in Camp." *Overland Monthly*, 1870.

Harte, Bret. "The Luck of Roaring Camp." *Overland Monthly*, 1868.

Hastings, Lansford W. From *The Emigrant's Guide to Oregon and California*. Cincinnati: George Conclin, 1845.

Heco, Joseph. From *The Narrative of a Japanese*. Edited by James Murdoch. San Francisco: American-Japanese Publishing Association, 1950.

Helper, Hinton. From *The Land of Gold: Reality Versus Fiction*. Baltimore: Hinton Helper, 1855.

Hirschfelder, Hannchen. Unpublished letter. Translated by Ruth Eis and Ruth Steiner. Printed with the permission of the Western Jewish History Center, Magnes Museum, Berkeley.

Holliday, J. S. Adapted from *The World Rushed In* with the permission of Simon & Schuster, New York. Copyright © 1981 by J. S. Holliday.

Hom, Marlon K., ed. *Songs of Gold Mountain: Cantonese Rhymes from San Francisco Chinatown*. Berkeley: Copyright © 1987 by the University of California Press, Berkeley. Reprinted by permission of the University of California Press.

Hutchings, James M. *The Miners' Ten Commandments*. San Francisco: 1853.

Joseph, William. "Indian Boy Hanged for Stealing Gold." Edited by Hans Uldall and William Shipley. *University of California Publications in Linguistics* 46 (1966), p. 177-179.

King, Clarence. From *Mountaineering in the Sierra Nevada*. Boston: J. R. Osgood and Co., 1872.

Kirby, Georgiana Bruce. From *Georgiana, Feminist Reformer of the West: The Journal of Georgiana Bruce Kirby, 1852-1860*. Copyright © 1983 by the Santa Cruz Historical Trust. Reprinted with the permission of the Museum of Art and History, Santa Cruz.

Larkin, Thomas O. From *Documents for the History of California: Papers of Thomas O. Larkin*. Bancroft Library.

Letts, John M. From *California Illustrated*. New York: William Holdredge, 1852.

Manly, William L. From *Death Valley in '49*. San Jose, CA: Pacific Tree and Vine Company, 1894.

Marks, Bernhard. From *A California Pioneer: The Letters of Bernhard Marks to Jacob Solis-Cohen (1853-1857)*. Edited by J. Solis-Cohen, Jr. Baltimore: American Jewish Historical Society, 1954.

Marryat, Frank. From *Mountains and Molehills*. London: Longman, Brown, Green, and Longmans, 1855.

Marshall, James W. "Marshall's Own Account of the Gold Discovery." *Century Magazine* 41, no. 4 (Feb. 1891), p. 537-538.

Massey, Ernest de. From *A Frenchman in the Gold Rush*. Translated by Marguerite Eyer Wilbur. San Francisco: California Historical Society, 1927. Reprinted with the permission of the Los Angeles Public Library, Rare Books Department.

McCunn, Ruthanne Lum. From *Thousand Pieces of Gold*. Copyright © 1981 by Ruth Lum McCunn. Used by permission of Beacon Press, Boston.

Merrill, Jerusha. Reprinted from *So Much to Be Done: Women Settlers on the Mining and Ranching Frontier*. Edited by Ruth B. Moynihan, Susan Armitage, and Christiane Fischer Dichamp, by permission of the University of Nebraska Press. Copyright © 1990 by the University of Nebraska Press.

Miller, Joaquin. From *Life Amongst the Modocs: Unwritten History*. London: R. Bentley, 1873.

Milosz, Czeslaw. " On that Century" and "On the Western." From *Visions from San Francisco Bay*. Translated by Richard Lourie. Translation Copyright © 1982 by Farrar, Straus, & Giroux. Reprinted by permission of Farrar, Straus, & Giroux.

Muir, John. From *The Mountains of California*. New York: The Century Company, 1894.

Mulford, Prentice. "California Culinary Experiences." From *Prentice Mulford's California Sketches*. Edited by Franklin Walker. San Francisco: Book Club of California, 1935.

Newell, Rev. William W. From *The Glories of a Dawning Age*. Syracuse, NY: Thomas S. Truair & Co., 1853.

Nordhoff, Charles. *California for Health, Pleasure, and Residence*. New York: Harper & Brothers, 1872.

Norris, Frank. From *McTeague*. New York: Doubleday, Page and Co., 1899.

Pérez Rosales, Vicente. From *We Were '49ers!: Chilean Accounts of the California Gold Rush*. Edited by Edwin A. Beilharz and Carlos U. Lopez. Pasadena, CA: Ward Ritchie Press, 1976.

Perkins, William. From *Three Years in California: William Perkins' Journal of Life at Sonora, 1849-1852.* Edited by Dale L. Morgan and James R. Scobie. Copyright © 1964 by University of California Press, Berkeley. Reprinted by permission of the University of California Press.

Pfeiffer, Ida. From *A Lady's Second Journey Round the World.* London: Longman, Brown, Green, and Longmans, 1855.

Potts, Marie. From *The Northern Maidu.* Copyright © 1977 by Naturegraph, Happy Camp. Reprinted with the permission of Naturegraph.

Revere, Joseph Warren. From *A Tour of Duty in California.* New York: C. S. Francis & Co., 1849.

Ridge, John Rollin. From *The Life and Adventures of Joaquín Murieta.* San Francisco: W. B. Cooke and Company, 1854.

Rodríguez Ordoñez de Montalvo, Garci. From *Las sergas de Esplandián. c. 1510.*

Rose, Wendy. "Questions for a Miwok Uncle: Ahwahneechee Man." From *Going to War with All My Relations.* Flagstaff, AZ: Northland Publishing Co. Copyright © 1993 by Wendy Rose. Reprinted by permission of the author.

Royce, Sarah. From *A Frontier Lady.* Copyright © 1932 by Yale University Press, New Haven CT. Reprinted by permission of Yale University Press.

Sherman, William Tecumseh. From *Memoirs of General William T. Sherman.* New York: D. Appleton and Co., 1875.

Snyder, Gary. "What Happened Here Before." From *Turtle Island.* Copyright © 1974 by Gary Snyder. Reprinted by permission of New Directions Publication Corporation, New York.

Starkey, James R. "Letter from James R. Starkey." From *Frederick Douglass' Paper.* 27 May 1852.

Steele, John. From *In Camp and Cabin.* Lodi, WI: J. Steele, 1901.

Sutter, John. "The Discovery of Gold in California." *Hutchings' California Magazine* v. 2, no. 5 (Nov. 1857), p. 194-198.

Taylor, Bayard. From *El Dorado.* New York: G. P. Putnam, 1850.

Taylor, William. From *Story of My Life.* New York: Hunt & Eaton, 1896.

Thomes, William H. From *On Land and Sea or California in the Years 1843, '44, and '45.* Boston: DeWolfe, Fiske & Co., 1884.

Thoreau, Henry David. From *The Journal of Henry D. Thoreau.* Vol. 1. New York: Dover Publications, Inc., 1962.

Twain, Mark. From *Roughing It.* Hartford, CT: American Publishing Company, 1872.

Twain, Mark. "The Celebrated Jumping Frog of Calaveras County." From *The Celebrated Jumping Frog of Calaveras County and other Sketches.* New York: C. H. Webb, 1867.

Tyson, James L. *From Diary of a Physician in California.* New York: D. Appleton & Company, 1850.

Vallejo, Mariano Guadalupe. From *Recuerdos históricos y personales tocante a la alta California.* Translations from *The Course of Empire.* Edited by Valeska Bari. New York: Coward-McCann, Inc., 1931 and *The Heath Anthology of American Literature.* Edited by Paul Lauter, et al. Vol. 1. Lexington, MA: D. C. Heath and Co., 1994.

Villegas, Ygnacio. From *Boyhood Days.* San Francisco: California Historical Society, 1983. Reprinted by permission of the San Francisco Historical Society.

Wallace, David Rains. *The Klamath Knot.* Copyright © 1983 by David Rains Wallace. Reprinted by permission of Sierra Club Books.

Wierzbicki, Felix. From *California As It Is, and As It May Be.* San Francisco: Washington Bartlett, 1849.

Wong Sam and Assistants. *An English-Chinese Phrase Book.* San Francisco: Cubery & Co., 1875.

Woods, Daniel B. From *Sixteen Months at the Gold Diggings.* New York: Harper & Brothers, 1851.

Young, Brigham. From *Discourses of Brigham Young.* Edited by John A. Widtsoe. Salt Lake City: Deseret Book Company, 1925.

ILLUSTRATIONS

Page 326. Courtesy of the Bancroft Library. 1905.16242.65

Page 328. Courtesy of the Oakland Museum of California.

Page 329. Courtesy of the California Society of Pioneers. #C002950

Page 335. Courtesy of the Bancroft Library. #1987.021:285

Page 336. Courtesy of Dugan Aguilar.

Page 343. © Collection of the New-York Historical Society. #16261

Page 353. Courtesy of the Crocker Art Museum, E. B. Crocker Collection. #1872.38

Page 389. Courtesy of the California State Library. #3899a

Page 391. Courtesy of the Bancroft Library. #1905.16242.95

Page 398. Courtesy of the Bancroft Library. #1987.021:285

Page 399. Courtesy of the Bancroft Library. #1987.021:179

Page 401. Courtesy of the California Department of Parks and Recreation. #080-23-41

Page 407. Courtesy of the Bancroft Library. #1964.056

Page 418. Courtesy of the Bancroft Library. #1987.021:338

Page 419. Courtesy of the Bancroft Library. #1987.021:289

Page 420. Courtesy of the Bancroft Library. #1987.021:246

Page 449. Courtesy of Dick James Stock Photography. #EVCAGP005-3

Page 451. Courtesy of Dick James Stock Photography. #EVFJ94011-3

Page 478. Courtesy of the Star Tribune/Minneapolis-St. Paul, © 1994.

AUTHOR INDEX

FOR FURTHER READING

The following works have been essential resources in the compiling of this anthology. Readers interested in the California gold rush would do well to begin with these books.

Dillion, Richard. *Captain John Sutter: Sacramento Valley's Sainted Sinner.* Santa Cruz: Western Tanager Press, 1987.

Fender, Stephen. *Plotting the Golden West: American Literature and the Rhetoric of the California Trail.* Cambridge: Cambridge University Press, 1981.

Goodman, David. *Victoria and California in the 1850s.* Stanford: Stanford University Press, 1994.

Hart, James D. *A Companion to California.* Berkeley and Los Angeles: University of California Press, 1987.

Holliday, J. S. *The World Rushed In.* New York: Simon and Schuster, 1981.

Hurtado, Albert L. *Indian Survival on the California Frontier.* New Haven, CT: Yale University Press, 1988.

Jackson, Donald Dale. *Gold Dust.* New York: Alfred A. Knopf, 1980.

Jackson, Joseph Henry. *Gold Rush Album.* New York: C. Scibner's Sons, 1949.

Kurutz, Gary F. *The California Gold Rush: A Descriptive Bibliography.* San Francisco: The Book Club of California, 1997.

Lapp, Rudolph. *Blacks in Gold Rush California.* New Haven, CT: Yale University Press, 1977.

Levinson, Robert E. *The Jews in the California Gold Rush.* Berkeley: Commission for the Preservation of Pioneer Jewish Cemeteries and Landmarks of the Judah L. Magnes Museum, 1994.

Levy, Jo Ann. *They Saw the Elephant: Women in the California Gold Rush.* Norman, OK: University of Oklahoma Press, 1992.

Lewis, Oscar. *Sea Routes to the Gold Fields.* New York: Alfred A. Knopf, 1949.

Margolin, Malcolm, ed. *The Way We Lived: California Indian Stories, Songs and Reminiscences.* Berkeley: Heyday Books, 1993.

Owens, Kenneth N., ed. *John Sutter and a Wider West.* Lincoln, NE: University of Nebraska Press, 1994.

Paul, Rodman W., ed. *The California Gold Discovery.* Georgetown, CA: Talisman Press, 1966.

Pitt, Leonard M. *The Decline of the Californios.* Berkeley: University of California Press, 1970.

Rohrbough, Malcolm. *Days of Gold.* Berkeley: University of California Press, 1997.

Starr, Kevin. *Americans and the California Dream, 1850-1915.* New York: Oxford University Press, 1973.

Walker, Franklin. *San Francisco's Literary Frontier.* New York: Alfred A. Knopf, 1939.

ABOUT THE EDITOR

Michael Kowalewski is an associate professor of English and American Studies at Carleton College in Minnesota. He has a special interest in literary regionalism and the cross-disciplinary notion of "place" in American art and writing. A native Californian who grew up in Redding, he has been teaching and writing about California for the past decade, both at Carleton and at Princeton University. His essays and reviews have appeared in more than a dozen periodicals. He is the author, among other works, of Deadly Musings: Violence and Verbal Form in American Fiction *(1993) and the editor of* Reading the West: New Essays on the Literature of the American West *(1996). He is presently finishing a book-length study of California writers, artists, and filmmakers.*